THE AUTHOR   Harry Adès is an author family has a long connection with Egypt, whi country from childhood. Since leaving Camb ̣ ̣ ̣ ̣ ̣ ̣ ̣ ̣ ̣ ̣ ̣ ̣ ̣ ̣ has concentrated on writing, editing and research. His books include *The Rough Guide to Ecuador, The History of Ireland, The Famine* and *Malcolm X.*

SERIES EDITOR   Professor Denis Judd is a graduate of Oxford, a Fellow of the Royal Historical Society and Professor of History at the London Metropolitan University. He has published over 20 books including the biographies of Joseph Chamberlain, Prince Philip, George VI, historical and military subjects, stories for children and two novels. He has reviewed and written extensively in the national press and in journals and is an advisor to the *BBC History* Magazine.

THE TRAVELLER'S HISTORY SERIES

'Ideal before-you-go reading' *The Daily Telegraph*

'An excellent series of brief histories' *The New York Times*

'I want to compliment you. . . on the brilliantly concise contents of your books.' *Shirley Conran*

Reviews of Individual Titles

A Traveller's History of France

'Undoubtedly the best way to prepare for a trip to France is to bone up on some history. *A Traveller's History of France* by Robert Cole is concise and gives the essential facts in a very readable form.' *The Independent*

A Traveller's History of China

'The author manages to get 2 million years into 300 pages. An excellent addition to a series which is already invaluable, whether you're travelling or not.' *The Guardian*

A Traveller's History of India

'For anyone. . . planning a trip to India, the latest in the excellent Traveller's History series. . . provides a useful grounding for those whose curiosity exceeds the time available for research.' *The London Evening Standard*

A Traveller's History of Japan

'It succeeds admirably in its goal of making the present country comprehensible through a narrative of its past, with asides on everything from bonsai to *zazen*, in a brisk, highly readable style ... you could easily read it on the flight over, if you skip the movie.' *The Washington Post*

A Traveller's History of Ireland

'For independent, inquisitive travellers traversing the green roads of Ireland, there is no better guide than *A Traveller's History of Ireland*.' *Small Press*

A Traveller's History of Egypt

This book is dedicated to Sally Ades
and the memory of Remy Ades

A Traveller's History of Egypt

HARRY ADÈS

Series Editor DENIS JUDD
Foreword by PENELOPE LIVELY
Line Drawings PETER GEISSLER

Interlink Books

An imprint of Interlink Publishing Group, Inc.
Northampton, Massachusetts

First published in 2007 by
INTERLINK BOOKS
An imprint of Interlink Publishing Group, Inc
46 Crosby Street, Northampton, Massachusetts 01060
www.interlinkbooks.com

Library of Congress Cataloging-in-Publication Data

Adès, Harry.
 A traveller's history of Egypt / Harry Adès.
   p. cm. -- (Traveller's histories)
  ISBN 1-56656-654-1 (pbk.) ISBN 13: 978-1-56656-654-4
 1. Egypt--Description and travel. 2. Egypt--History. I. Title. II.
Title: Egypt. III. Series: Traveller's history.
  DT56.2.A337 2006
  962--dc22

                                          2006011522

Printed and bound in Canada

To order or request our complete catalog,
please call us at 1-800-238-LINK or write to:
INTERLINK PUBLISHING
46 Crosby Street, Northampton, MA 01060-1804
email: info@interlinkbooks.com
www.interlinkbooks.com

Table of Contents

MAPS

DIAGRAM

Note on transliteration
The Arabic transliterations in this book omit diacritical marks and, for the most part, favour familiar English spellings at the expense of consistency.

Preface

Egypt has been both the beneficiary and the victim of its geographical condition. It is situated at the conjunctions of three continents – Africa, Asia, and Europe. It has been blessed by the self-renewing fertility of the Nile valley, and by a profound sense of its ancient civilisation as well as its modern identity. Less enabling has been the desire of other powers to conquer and control it. Even today Egypt, though independent, is balanced – not without difficulty – between the strident demands of fundamentalist Islam and the ambitions of the West to keep it on side as a quasi-ally, and an essential aid in 'the war on terror'.

Although the first stirrings of the Egyptian civilisation began 6000 years ago, the country's long history has been marked by several crucial, seismic shifts in its development. One was the unification of the 'Two Lands', Lower and Upper Egypt during the third millennium BC. Thus began the glories of the age of the Pharaohs, which are best recalled in enduring monuments like the pyramids, the rock tombs in the Valley of the Kings, the temples at Luxor and much else.

Simultaneously the ancient Egyptians were among the first people to believe in life after death. They also built in stone and brick, used the plough, developed a system of writing, charted the heavens, performed surgical operations, sailed far from their shores, and decorated tombs with vivid naturalistic murals.

The second great defining event in Egypt's history was the Arab conquest of 641 AD. This resulted in the Islamisation of the country and its placing in the Arab world. Despite this, a substantial minority of Coptic Christians survives to this day, and cities like Cairo and Alexandria bear witness to an ancient and enduring cultural diversity.

At the beginning of the sixteenth century, in a third great shift in development, Egypt was incorporated into the Ottoman Empire. Although Ottoman rule was mostly adapted to Egyptian sensibilities and requirements, it lasted until the fourth powerful change – the forcible intervention of France and Britain as expanding commercial and imperial powers. From the opening of the Suez Canal in 1869, it was only a matter of time before Egypt was once more conquered. After the British invasion of 1882, Egypt was, in effect, a colony of the British Empire. It took the Suez crisis of 1956, however, finally to achieve a genuine national independence.

Since then Egypt has successfully negotiated the conflicting pressures of the Cold War, and has even, and courageously, signed a separate peace agreement with Israel. Though still clearly identifiable as an Arab country, Egypt currently plays an invaluable diplomatic role as a potential peacemaker in a chronically volatile Middle East.

The foreign visitors who annually visit the country in such numbers, however are overwhelmingly focussed on Egypt's cultural and architectural splendours rather than on the small print of the Camp David Accords. This excellent, comprehensive and very accessible book can only enhance their enjoyment of a unique set of traveller's experiences.

Denis Judd, London

Foreword

Egypt's landscape is a perfect instance of the presence of the past. Its history has high visibility: the Sphinx and the Pyramids are iconic symbols for those who have never been anywhere near the country, but the visitor soon realises that there is a great deal more on offer than those familiar images, and that much of it is both challenging and confusing. Everything co-exists, here – ancient, old and new in teasing juxtaposition. I was born in Cairo, and spent my childhood just outside the city, amid the canals and the fields of sugarcane. Cairo, Alexandria, the Delta were the familiar backdrop to my life – pharaonic tombs, Roman catacombs, the great mosques. I was aware that these things were old, that they were signals from other times, but had no way to interpret or relate. The entire landscape told a story, it seemed, but one that had to be unravelled.

Harry Adès's history, covering the entire sweep of Egypt's past, will allow the discerning traveller to get things into perspective. He has provided a crisp, dispassionate and judiciously informative account, from the first appearance of man in the Nile Valley to the tensions of present day Egyptian society. Each section illuminates a particular period; the reader can pick out the relevant explanation and set it against the visible evidence, whether the puzzle is the great temple of Karnak, the Roman period coffin images in the Egyptian Museum, or one of Cairo's surviving Mamluk buildings. Chronology is the essential scaffolding; to make some sense of what we see, we have to understand the sequence. Only then does the whole complex process of time and change become intelligible, and Egypt's eloquent land can bear witness to what happened here, century by century.

Those who visit Egypt are themselves taking part in an old tradition. The Nile Valley has drawn travellers and commentators from Herodotus to Flaubert and Laurence Durrell. We know it through those who recorded its different incarnations. For centuries, visitors climbed the Great Pyramid; you may no longer do that – I must be amongst the last to remember that strange sight of striving figures who hauled themselves up the huge blocks, in the 1940s when every soldier on leave from the Libyan front had to have a go. The Great Pyramid is out of bounds now, but the voyage up the Nile is still very much on offer, not quite as it was for Thomas Cook's first clients in the late nineteenth century, when you while away a tedious afternoon with a spot of crocodile shooting, and have the catch slung from the bowsprit of your dahabiya, but still an unparalleled experience, as you slide through that fascinating landscape – the busy fields, the villages and the people, the ancient technologies still in use, the flights of ducks, egrets and ibis that echo the scenes on pharaonic tomb walls. To visit Egypt is to indulge in time-travel: you will see the fellahin irrigating their fields with the shaduf, just as their forebears did in antiquity, you will hear the call of the muezzin from the minarets of Cairo, a sound unchanged since the mosques were built.

Earlier travellers did it the hard way, and were perhaps more inclined to be curious and enquiring in consequence. Travel today is cushioned, for the most part, and too many travellers are content to exclaim, point a camera, and leave it at that. This book is for those who want to go further, who want to know the story of the sights that they see, to discover what came before and after, to learn what is meant by the New Kingdom, or how Cleopatra manipulated Rome, or what happened when the tide turned against the British presence a few decades ago. History supplies the context to everything. If you are ignorant of history, all that you see is just scenery; history supplies the narrative, unlocks the codes, turn scenery into vivid testimony.

Penelope Lively

CHAPTER ONE

Land, Origins and Prehistory

33,000,000–3000 BC

The Land

Egypt is a phenomenon of its geography. Its land and location have steered the development of its people, culture and history from the earliest times. In the northeast corner of Africa, joined to Asia by the Sinai peninsula and facing Europe across the Mediterranean Sea, Egypt stands at the nexus of three continents, a vantage-point that has allowed it both to draw on diverse influences and influence diversely since antiquity. It is the hub of land routes between Africa and Asia and, at the neck of the Sinai peninsula, is the shortest link between the Mediterranean and the Indian Ocean via the Red Sea, a passage greatly enhanced by the completion of the Suez Canal in 1869. Yet Egypt is also bounded by a ring of natural barriers – vast deserts on either side, seas to north and east, and river cataracts to the south – that have helped protect and insulate it from the fitfulness of the outside world.

Within Egypt, no single geographic feature is more important than the Nile, the vital artery that pumps its fertile course across the length of the country, painting a streak of green on a parched landscape that scarcely gets a drop of rain all year. This thin strip of life – where most Egyptians have lived and died – accounts for barely 3 per cent of the total surface area of the modern state. The rest, except for a few remote oases, consists of vast and unpeopled deserts, covering an area twice the size of Spain.

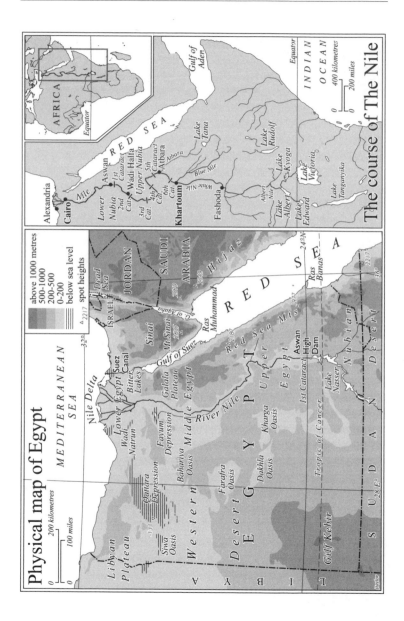

Physical map of Egypt

The course of The Nile

THE NILE

Without the Nile the Egyptian civilisation would not have come into being. In a rainless land, the rise and fall of the Nile waters dictated the rhythm of life. In June, under ferocious heat, the Nile began to rise, reaching its peak between August and September. In October it receded, depositing a layer of fertile silt over the watered floodplain, creating exceptionally productive soil that was the envy of the Ancient World. The dark silt gave ancient Egyptians the name for their country, *Kemet* meaning 'black land', the all-important life-giving earth that was enveloped by *Deshret*, the sterile 'red land' of the desert.

The annual flood, or inundation, was Egypt's heartbeat until the early nineteenth century when the construction of a series of dams, barrages and sluices began to regulate its flow, culminating in the completion of the Aswan High Dam in 1970, which stopped the yearly deluge altogether. Throughout its Egyptian course, the Nile has no tributaries and very little drainage, and yet it rises in the hottest months, the cause of which was a mystery until relatively recently. The secret of the inundation lay in the river's great length – and the Nile is the longest river in the world, unfurling for 4160 miles (6695km) to the centre of the continent, where the summer rains of Central Africa and the thawing snows in the Ethiopian mountains send a surge of water and alluvial silt coursing towards the sere northern deserts.

The Nile's source at Lake Victoria was not discovered until 1860 by John Speke, who followed a river northwards and eventually found himself face to face with Nile explorers in Sudan heading southwards. He announced his discovery to the world in the celebrated telegram message: 'The Nile is settled.'

Three rivers in the south come together in the Nile: the White Nile, the Blue Nile and the Atbara. The White Nile leaves the Great Lakes of Central Africa (other sources are at Lakes Albert and Edward), and winds its way into Sudan where it is swollen by the Bahr el-Ghazal, Bahr el-Zaraf (Gazelle and Giraffe Rivers, respectively) and Sobat tributaries. The Blue Nile flows from Lake Tana in the Ethiopian highlands, from where the river's richest deposits are derived, and meets the White Nile at Khartoum, while the Atbara, the last great tributary of the Nile, joins a few hundred miles further north.

Six cataracts, rocky areas of rapids created by abrupt geological changes in the riverbed, interrupt the Nile's course between Khartoum and Aswan, the area that corresponds to ancient Nubia. The border between Egypt and Nubia lay at the First Cataract, just south of Aswan, where the roiling water was thought to be evidence of a deep and sacred underground spring that fed the Nile. Today the Egypt–Sudan frontier lies south of the Second, and the region between the two cataracts, which ancient historians call Lower Nubia, has been engulfed by Lake Nasser, the huge man-made reservoir that backs up over 300 miles (500km) from the Aswan High Dam. When work began on the dam in 1960, UNESCO co-ordinated a massive operation to record and rescue the monuments before they were swallowed by the lake. Some, including Philae and Abu Simbel were dismantled and reassembled, others were given as gifts to museums around the world.

North of Aswan the Nile Valley is released from the granite and sandstone cliffs so typical of Nubia, and eventually broadens into floodplains over 14 miles (22km) in places. Upstream of Luxor, the river loops markedly to the east at the Qena bend, the closest the river gets to the Red Sea (about 90 miles or 150km away), and the departure point for ancient caravan routes to the coast.

Just beyond Cairo, the river splits into two branches that embrace the Delta, an 8500 square-mile (22,000 square-kilometre) triangular silt-plain formed through centuries of inundations, constituting more than 60 per cent of Egypt's habitable land. The westerly arm of the Nile debouches into the Mediterranean at Rosetta (el-Rashid) and the easterly at Damietta (Dumyat), forming a broad chevron from which a plexus of canals, drains and irrigation channels are derived. Only its northernmost region, the Bareri, is sterile, a wasteland of salty coastal marshes peppered with lagoons. In the time of the pharaohs (the 'pharaonic period', also called the 'Dynastic period' spanning 31 dynasties between 3000 BC and the conquest of Alexander the Great in 332 BC), there were five tributaries forming the Delta, but the Canopic, Sebennytic and Pelusiac branches dried up in the Islamic period.

The contrast between the open Delta and the narrow Nile Valley is believed to be the basis of the ancient Egyptian concept of the 'Two Lands' of Upper and Lower Egypt that were united into a single state by the first pharaoh. Upper Egypt corresponds to the upstream section of the Nile in the south, while Lower Egypt refers to the 'lower', downstream, but northern area of the Delta.

NILE AGRICULTURE

Agriculture in one form or another has existed in the Nile floodplain since prehistory and continued to underpin Egyptian society until the twentieth century. For most of this time, the process of cultivation followed an essentially unchanging pattern. Canals and irrigation channels were built to extend the reach of the Nile during the inundation. As the flood subsided at the end of summer, farmers sealed up the channels to hold the water until October or November, the land was tilled by hoe or ox-drawn plough and the seed was scattered by hand and trampled into the land by sheep and goats. The natural softening and fertilisation of the soil by the inundation made farming in Egypt relatively easy; as the ancient historian Diodorus Siculus remarked: 'Every kind of agricultural labour among other peoples involves them in great expense and toil, and only among the Egyptians is the harvest gathered in with an insignificant outlay of time and money.'

The principal crops of barley and emmer wheat could be grown on freshly deposited silt with little prior preparation to the ground, though other produce such as vegetables, pulses, flax and fruits (cotton was not cultivated in large quantities until the 1820s), or a second yearly crop, required more intensive work and watering. Irrigation was done by hand using buckets attached to a yoke worn across the shoulders, until the *shaduf* was introduced during the New Kingdom (*c.*1550–1069 BC). This was a suspended wooden pole with a bucket at one end and a counterweight at the other end which allowed farmers to raise water out of the river or channel with much greater ease. The *shaduf* can still be spotted in use around modern-day Egypt, though it was superseded long ago, first by the Archimedes screw (*tanbur*) of the fifth century BC, and then by the waterwheel (*saqiya*) two centuries

The ancient *shaduf* system of irrigation which was first introduced over 3500 years ago in Egypt and is still in occasional use today

later. The *saqiya* was a major advancement that opened up large new areas of land to agriculture, as it provided a greater quantity of water for irrigation in a constant stream and allowed the farmer to attend to other tasks while animals drove the wheel.

In the pharaonic period, the grain was harvested in spring with stone or metal sickles, threshed using cattle to tread the grain out, and winnowed by tossing the grain and chaff into the air with small wooden scoops. Once sieved, the grain was ready for making bread and beer, the staples of the Egyptian diet, or recorded for storage. Regular and meticulous surveys of the land and productivity were undertaken for the purpose of taxation, which was paid in produce and rigorously enforced. Nilometers, as found at Dendera, Esna, Edfu, Kom Ombo, Elephantine and Philae, were used to measure the height of the inundation in order to predict crop yields and also perhaps to determine tax. An inundation of seven or eight yards was deemed ideal, but too much or too little could devastate the economy. In the agricultural year there was a 'slow' period during the inundation when there was little farming work to do; this allowed the pharaoh to call on peasants to perform corvée tasks (labour tribute) for the state, such as monumental building projects, mining expeditions or even military campaigns.

WESTERN DESERT

Occupying more than two-thirds of the country, the Western Desert extends from the Nile Valley's west edge to the die-straight frontiers of Libya and Sudan – from where the wastes continue for hundreds of miles as part of the immense North African desert belt. Despite an almost total absence of rain, the Western Desert's water table is remarkably high, allowing artesian springs and wells to be tapped across a string of depressions. These form five major oases – Siwa, Bahariya, Farafra, Dakhla and Kharga – running from northwest to southeast, and a number of smaller wells and springs, that have unlocked the region to humans from prehistoric times, and allowed migration between the Nile and desert interiors.

The desert itself is a huge limestone plateau tilting gently upwards to the south at a height of 1500ft (450m) where it collides with another plateau of Nubian sandstone. In the southwest the surface erupts at the Gilf Kebir plateau in a rash of peaks topping 3000ft (900m), which are overlooked by an even higher massif, the Gebel Uweinat, extending into Sudan and Libya. Amid the desolation are several unusual geological features, most notably the rippling oceans of golden dunes that wash south of the salty Qattara Depression and swell into 300ft (90m) waves in the Great Sand Sea along the Libyan border. Another is the so-called White Desert just north of Farafra Oasis, an unearthly collection of calcite crystal deposits that jut out of the sand like wind-sculpted icebergs.

EASTERN DESERT

On the other side of the Nile, the Eastern Desert is a rugged and mountainous region, notched by deep wadis that remain dry for much of the year, only discharging water into the Nile or Red Sea after rare cloudbursts. A chain of lofty peaks runs along the Red Sea coast, many of which soar above 4000ft with the highest, Gebel Shaayib el-Banat, reaching 7175ft (2187m). The massif consists of igneous and metamorphic rocks, the source of raw materials and valuable minerals since prehistory, such as schist, gneiss, granite, diorite, quartzite, sandstone and porphyry. Ancient trade routes striate the inhospitable interior, following deeply incised passages such as the Wadi Hammamat, the most important link between the Nile and the Red Sea.

SINAI

The Sinai peninsula, a triangular landmass lying between the Gulf of Suez and the Suez Canal in the west and the Gulf of Aqaba and the Negev Desert in the east, is part of the same geological system as the Eastern Desert. The southern region is dominated by a knot of knife-edged peaks, including Egypt's highest, Mt Catherine (8668ft; 2642m), and Mt Sinai (7497ft; 2285m), the Biblical mountain where Moses received the Ten Commandments. The northern portion of the peninsula is less rugged but just as severe, a windswept wilderness of sand and gravel pans marbled with boulder-strewn wadi channels, interrupted only by occasional clusters of lonely hills and outcrops. Along the coast, pale dunes and salt marshes take over, punctuated by a chain of freshwater wells linking Egypt to the Near East. More than a mere trading corridor, Sinai has long been infused with history, myth and war. It is the route by which the Israelites left for the Promised Land and by which Christianity and Islam arrived; many times its deserts have been the battlefields for Egypt's defence.

CLIMATE

Egypt has a climate to match its predominantly desert geography. In the broadest terms, the weather is hot and dry in summer (May to September), cool and mild in winter (November to March), and sunny throughout the year. In the north, the heat and aridity are soothed to a degree by the Mediterranean, and it is Alexandria that receives the most rainfall, around seven inches (180mm) per year delivered almost entirely in the winter and transitional months. In the summer, the mixture of stifling heat and high humidity there can be overpowering, but the winter can be cold, wet and windy.

Moving southwards, precipitation falls off markedly, with Cairo getting a very modest sprinkling of rain, an inch (25mm) on average each year; Aswan barely an eighth of an inch (3mm); and the deserts even less still. Summer average maximum temperatures also increase sharply from north to south, rising from 86°F (30°C) in Alexandria, to 97°F (36°C) in Cairo, to 105°F (41°C) in Aswan (range 30°F or 17°C), though these are only averages and in hot years the mercury can climb above 120°F (50°C). In fact, extremes in weather are not infrequent, with the country being plunged into summer heat waves and winter cold snaps for unpredictable periods.

The Sinai mountains tend to take the brunt of the country's most inclement conditions, suffering snowstorms on higher ground in winter and flash floods at any month, while between March and May the Western Desert blows up savage winds called *khamsin*, because they traditionally rage in the fifty (*khamsin*) days between Easter and Pentecost. These hot, dry sand gales that blot out the sun with thick sand, can scour the paint from a wall, and deposit a grainy film of dust on everything they pass.

Human Prehistory

When Herodotus, the Greek historian, wrote in the fifth century BC that Egyptians thought they had existed 'ever since mankind appeared on the earth', he was voicing an opinion already commonly held in the Ancient World – that the story of humanity in Egypt was unimaginably old, reaching back to the beginnings of human consciousness itself. Indeed, it is not too fanciful to say that modern palaeontology is close to confirming the hyperbole, for it was in Egypt, at the Fayum Depression, that a 33-million-year-old skeleton was found of a small and agile mammal, *Aegyptopithecus zeuxis*, resembling a present-day lemur. Some claim that this antique primate is the earliest known

direct ancestor of humans and apes, a contention that is strangely grat-
ifying for a region that went on to cradle one of the earliest civilisations in the world.

With this is mind, it is frustrating that no other discoveries have
come to light about our prehistoric human ancestry in Egypt, and we
must jump in time and space to pick up the thread again. The earliest
humans – or, more accurately, hominids – can be traced back to East
Africa up to five million years ago. It is thought these 'australop-
ithecines' eventually migrated from there, reaching the Middle East
less than two million years ago and most of Europe about 700,000
years ago. Although no fossil remains have yet been found to prove it,
there is every cause to suspect that the Nile Valley served as the
corridor for their journey northwards. The disappointing lack of
evidence can at least in part be blamed on the floodwaters and movements of the Nile, which over the millennia have washed away countless sites, skeletons and artefacts, or slathered them in a thick layer of
silt deposits that have so far kept them hidden from archaeologists.

THE FIRST TOOLS AND EARLIEST REMAINS

The earliest indications of human activity in Egypt have been inferred
from tool objects rather than the skeletal remains. Stone pieces resembling early handheld tools recovered from gravel beds along the desert
margins of the Nile Valley have been tentatively dated at between
700,000 and 500,000 years old. Swept away and scattered by the river's
floodwaters long ago, however, none was discovered in its original site,
making them unreliable witnesses at best; indeed, a proportion of these
much-weathered pieces may not have been of human manufacture at all.

From about 400,000 years ago onwards Egypt's prehistory stands on
somewhat surer footing. Numerous hand-axes, the favourite tools of
Homo erectus, have been unearthed at sites along the Nile from Cairo
to Khartoum and are hard evidence of an early human presence in
Egypt. The axes are of the 'Acheulean industry', the first tradition of
standardised tool-making. At other Acheulean sites near the Second
Cataract and the Dungul Oasis southwest of Aswan, are the remnants
of the earliest Egyptian shelters, among the oldest in the world, stone

circles and oval pits probably covered by animal skins or brushwood attached to a frame and tied down to the ground with large stones.

A major change in the climate around 120,000 years ago (known as the Abbassia Pluvial) transformed Egypt's arid wastes into extensive swathes of savannah. Bountiful rainfall turned depressions in the land into springs and lakes, where wild horses, buffalo, rhino, antelope, giraffe and elephants found succour. Bands of hunter-gatherers were also present, ranging the grasslands to the rhythms of migration of the great herds. In the dry seasons they took refuge at the year-round watering holes, where plant food was rich and could be supplemented by gazelle and other game. One such site was Bir Sahara deep in the Western Desert, described now by its excavator as 'one of the most isolated and desolate places on earth'. Here the bones of a wild ass were found, the first animal remains known in Egypt associated with human settlement, and ostrich eggshells, possibly used to carry and store water. The gentler climate extended to the Red Sea mountains and coast, where excavations northwest of Quseir have revealed a seasonal camp littered with the remains of antelope, elephant, buffalo and crocodile.

This time of plenty, however, came to an end after about 30,000 years. The rains died out and the deserts once again crept over the land, forcing the people, by now somewhere on the evolutionary seam between *Homo erectus* and *Homo sapiens*, to join others in the Nile Valley. Save for a few desert oases, the river's floodplain was practically the only source of food in the region, and it has been suggested that the intensification of the population here stimulated intense competition between rival groups, spurring a leap forward in tool-making technology. The new 'Levallois' technique enabled the creation of many sharp and regular flakes from a single tortoise-shaped core of stone. The tools were of greater variety and better quality and could be produced using less raw material. One of the greatest revolutions was the development of the fine stone point that could be attached to wooden shafts to make spears and javelins – an immeasurable improvement in armoury over the old hand-axes and sharpened sticks. Tool-making production continued to evolve, and by about 50,000 BC, extensive quarries were being used to extract chert (a flint-like stone) to make increasingly sophisticated blades, points and serrated edges. A site near Qena reveals open trenches and pits covering many square miles, a reflection not only of a good understanding of geology, but also a new level of social organisation. In nearby Dendera across the river, the earliest known Egyptian, a damaged skeleton of a physiologically 'modern' child, was disinterred from the oldest known grave on the Nile.

At around 30,000 BC, a quarry at Nazlet Khater near Tahta in Middle Egypt shows evidence of underground galleries as well as trenches and pits, making the site one of the world's earliest subterranean mines. Not far from this quarry, two grave sites of about the same age were also found, one of them holding an ancient quarryman buried with his axe, the other a badly crushed corpse laid to rest alongside the bones of a foetus and some ostrich eggshells. Interred beneath large slabs of stone, these skeletons are Egypt's oldest testaments to the observance of funerary rites, particularly the burial of objects alongside a body – a practice that would take on enormous cultural significance thousands of years later in a civilisation renowned for the treatment of its dead.

THE LATE PALAEOLITHIC (*c*.20,000–10,000 BC)

The number and quality of archaeological sites along the Upper Nile Valley from the Late Palaeolithic age, are far greater than for any earlier time, reflecting a surge of human activity between 20,000 and 10,000 BC. Sadly, little has been recovered from Lower Egypt during this period, where – as so often in the archaeology of the Delta – it is supposed the treasures of the past are lost or lie many yards beneath the floodplain.

The Late Palaeolithic saw the emergence of a new technological age, first developed by the Halfan culture, named after the Wadi Halfa in Lower Nubia where their sites were first found, which inhabited the Nile as far north as the Kom Ombo plain between about 18,000 and 15,000 BC. They were hunter-gatherers keen on big game such as wild cattle as well as fish from the river, who began to use ever smaller and refined pieces of flint in their tool-making. The miniaturised stone

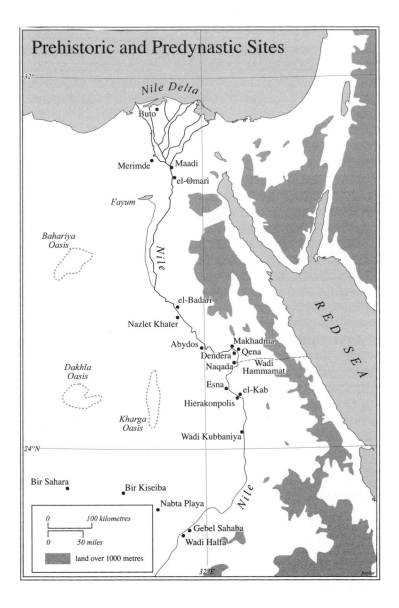

Prehistoric and Predynastic Sites

32°

Nile Delta

Buto

Merimde • Maadi
• el-Omari

Fayum

Bahariya Oasis

Nile

el-Badari

Nazlet Khater

Abydos • Makhadma
Dendera • Qena
Naqada • Wadi Hammamat

Dakhla Oasis

Esna • el-Kab
Hierakonpolis

Kharga Oasis

Wadi Kubbaniya

RED SEA

24°N

Bir Sahara

Bir Kiseiba

Nabta Playa

Nile

| 0 | 100 kilometres |
| 0 | 50 miles |

Gebel Sahaba
Wadi Halfa

land over 1000 metres

32°E

pieces and blades, known as microliths, could be combined with bone or wood to make a number of new tools such as arrows, darts, sickles and harpoons. The use of microliths by the Halfan culture was extremely precocious, pre-dating their counterparts in the Near East and Europe by at least 6000 years.

Another important development came at Wadi Kubbaniya near Aswan, where small semi-sedentary groups stored food, gutting and smoking fish for consumption during lean times of year, and moved between a number of sites on the dunes and floodplain depending on the season. They picked off mammals such as hartebeest, aurochs and gazelle when the heat drove the animals out of the desert to the river. During the flood season they occupied higher ground and caught fish trapped in a temporary lake formed by a sand bar across the mouth of the wadi. Up in the dunes, they snared birds in the winter, while on the plain, they gathered edible plants and tubers, grinding them in pestles and mortars to aid digestion of tough fibres.

At Makhadma, north of Qena, the Afian group also showed a knowledge of storage. The people here used nets, bone hooks and baskets to catch the huge numbers of fish languishing in the dwindling pools as the flood waters retreated. The glut of fish was far too much for a small community to eat in one go, and it seems they preserved their catch through drying and smoking the meat using charcoal pits nearby. Storing food required a fundamental shift in the social dynamics of a community, as it worked out how best to guard and distribute its produce. Moreover, the group would have preferred to stay in one place as long as possible to maximise storage potential, a stark rupture with the way humans had lived for hundreds of thousands of years, drifting across the land with the passing of the seasons.

EXPERIMENTS WITH AGRICULTURE

The Qadan group based around northern Sudan and southern Egypt, and the Isnan of the Esna region, of around 13,000 to 10,500 BC, were also food-storing cultures with a near-sedentary lifestyle. What distinguishes them, however, is an even more exciting advance – humanity's first ever flirtations with agriculture. A high proportion of grinding tools and sickle blades have been recovered, slick with a gloss that attests they were used for grains and grasses. Pollen samples suggest that the harvests were of wild *Gramineae* (wheat-like grasses) and possibly barley, and at the Isnan sites, a conspicuous lack of fish and small mammal remains implies a reliance on a new food source. It was a plentiful one at that, because the size of the sites had almost quadrupled by around 10,500 BC. Compelling circumstantial evidence suggests that there was at least a primitive knowledge of how to tend, harvest and store certain grasses in the Nile Valley thousands of years before agriculture had taken off in the Near East, traditionally regarded as the birthplace of farming.

Unfortunately, it was an experiment that was destined to fail. A dramatic wet period in sub-Saharan Africa between about 12,000 and 10,500 BC, brought deluges in the valley up to ten yards above today's floodplain. After this so-called 'Wild Nile' phase, when the Qadan, Isnan and Makhadma cultures were flourishing, there was a sudden return to aridity and a catastrophic turn for the worse in living conditions. It is telling that after 10,500 BC there is a total absence of sickles and grinding tools associated with agriculture, but a proliferation of more conventional hunting tools, suggesting these people were forced to change their strategies for survival.

An extraordinary Qadan cemetery at Gebel Sahaba dating from about this time also points to a period of calamitous upheaval. It contained fifty-nine skeletons, almost half of which had flint tips embedded in their bones or deep cut marks on them, suggesting they had been killed in a ferocious attack. Perhaps the change in climate triggered a period of conflict between communities that had overextended themselves during the fertile Wild Nile years. Their relationship with the environment was fatally disrupted and consequently these cultures seemed to have vanished from the Nile Valley altogether. At any rate, there is no evidence for a human presence on the Egyptian Nile between around 9000 and 5500 BC, save for a few sites of the seventh millennium at Elkab in Upper Egypt and around the Fayum Depression in Lower Egypt. Of course, this does not necessarily mean that the valley had been completely abandoned, but it is probable that its population did fall significantly. Nevertheless this relatively fallow period in the history of the Nile was balanced by a burgeoning human presence in the Western Desert.

CERAMIC CULTURES OF THE WESTERN DESERT

From around 10,000 BC, the climate in the Sahara became far wetter, rejuvenating the ancient desert lakes and springs of previous epochs. Monsoon rains fanned out from tropical Africa northwards into the Western Desert, bringing new life to the region. Humans followed too, probably from the Nubian Nile, at first only during or after the summer rains, possibly in search of pasture for small herds of cattle that they had begun to keep (a very early form of domestication, though it is still in dispute), but also to hunt hare and gazelle, and gather fruits and wild grasses. Even the earliest settlements from around 8800 BC reveal the presence of simple pottery, among the first known examples in the world, decorated with pinpricks and parallel lines to mimic baskets. The ceramics are unique to the region, indicating that they were an independent invention of these cultures.

During the next four millennia, their settlements at Nabta Playa and Bir Kiseiba, about 90 and 100 miles (145-160 km) west of Abu Simbel respectively, flourished and expanded until some became true permanent villages with streets, wells, wattle-and-daub houses, and large pits for the storage of grain. This is not to say that these were isolated communities; there must have been communication with distant places, as shells from the Red Sea and the Mediterranean found at these desert sites indicate. Furthermore, around 5600 BC, sheep and goat herds make their first appearance, having been introduced from the Levant.

These cultures also demonstrated a new level of sophistication and knowledge. At Nabta Playa, there is a megalithic complex consisting of a carefully aligned arrangement of large stone blocks, two slab-covered tumuli, and a small stone circle resembling a miniature Stonehenge, the world's first known astronomical calendar, used to identify the summer solstice, perhaps to help predict the arrival of the monsoon rains.

By the beginning of the fifth millennium, pottery was made with a smooth, burnished finish and a blackened top – an early appearance of a radically different style that predominated in the Nile Valley during Predynastic times. Around 4500 BC, the desert climate underwent another reversal; the rains diminished, the lakes and water holes dried up, returning grasslands to the scorched landscape so familiar today. As the conditions worsened, it is highly likely that these peoples migrated from the Western Desert back to the Nile Valley.

Early Predynastic Egypt

The bridge between prehistory and history was made in Egypt during the Predynastic period, which began around 5500 BC with disparate and sedentary Neolithic communities eking a subsistence from the banks of the Nile, and culminated in about 3000 BC with the creation of a unified Egyptian state, ruled by one very wealthy king sitting at the head of a deeply stratified society and the centre of a complex belief system. Along the way, the various components of the pharaonic civilisation appeared in embryonic form at different places and different times, taking shape slowly at first, but then with almost precipitous speed in the last two centuries, aggregating and consolidating in a unique formula that defined Egypt for the next three millennia.

NEOLITHIC LOWER EGYPT

In Lower Egypt, the Fayumian culture (*c.*5450–4400 BC), based along the shores of Lake Qarun in the Fayum Depression, and the Merimde (*c.*5000–4100 BC), on the western edge of the Nile Delta, were Egypt's first successful agriculturalists. They cultivated crops of barley and emmer wheat, harvested them with sickles and stored their produce in large mat-lined pits. They kept cattle, sheep, goats and pigs, but still obtained much of their meat from hunting and fishing. The Fayumian culture's rich and varied menu also included crocodiles, elephants, gazelles, and hippos that then inhabited the lakeside areas. The Merimde supplemented their diet by fishing with hooks, nets and harpoons, and lived in oval houses of mud and straw, topped off with matted reeds or branches. A step made from a hippo's tibia at the doorway led down to a sunken floor, dotted with dug-out spaces to keep water jars, pottery and grain. Among the artefacts unearthed belonging to the later Mermide culture, are a number of small clay figurines and a cylindrical head, Egypt's earliest known representations of humans.

While the Predynastic Lower Egyptians crafted fine arrowheads and harpoons from flint and bone, and wove beautiful baskets, their skill as potters was comparatively unrefined, favouring highly utilitarian and undecorated vessels using a rough, straw-tempered clay. This is in stark contrast to contemporary groups in Upper Egypt, whose elegant ceramics exhibit a greater degree of both technological know-how and aesthetic appreciation. Another major difference between the regions was in their treatment of the dead. The cemeteries and burial pits of the Fayumian, Merimde and the later el-Omari (*c*.4600–4350 BC) culture of the Helwan area, showed little or no social stratification, while in Upper Egypt the opposite trend was emerging. Distinct cultural traditions were developing between the Nile's northern and southern peoples, a division that neatly predates the long-standing separation between the Two Lands of Upper and Lower Egypt.

NEOLITHIC UPPER EGYPT: THE BADARIAN CULTURE

There is little evidence for much contact between Upper and Lower Egypt during the early centuries of the Predynastic period, and indeed the two regions nurtured communities that had developed cultures consistent with their ecologies, cultures that as yet had no need, nor perhaps desire, to journey the Nile for the sake of trade or communication. The Badarian culture (conventionally *c*.4400–4000 BC, but possibly beginning *c*.5500 BC), named after the archaeological site at el-Badari near Asyut, was the first Predynastic culture of Upper Egypt and the first to practise agriculture and animal husbandry there. At its height, it extended from el-Badari in the north as far south as Hierakonpolis near Edfu in the south.

As for most of the southern Predynastic cultures, much of our knowledge of the Badarian culture comes from cemeteries and graves, many hundreds of which have been discovered away from the cultivable land on the fringes of the desert. Their contents describe the beginnings of a complex and stratified society that took root in later cultures and unquestionably influenced the later traditions of Dynastic Egypt. The corpses, sometimes dressed in short loincloths, were interred in oval pits on a mat and pillow of straw, and wrapped in animal skins. With them were buried 'grave goods' – the votive offerings that accompanied the departed into the hereafter – which included the choicest artefacts known to the culture.

First among these luxury objects were the rippled, black-topped ceramics – exceptionally fine, thin-walled vessels, sublimely delicate but supremely strong, of a quality that has astounded archaeologists and was never again matched in Ancient Egypt. Their handiwork also extended to bone and ivory, which they crafted into figurines, bracelets, hairpins, rings and combs as well as needles and awls for sewing. Cosmetic palettes, items that figured greatly in later cultures, were made from siltstone and used for grinding malachite and ochre pigments for application to the skin. Hammered copper, the first metal to be smelted and worked in Egypt, also appeared in small quantities. The richest people, bedecked in necklaces and bracelets of shells from the Red Sea, and dozens of shiny blue and green steatite beads (a soft stone that hardens with an attractive glaze after heating), commanded a separate portion of Badarian cemeteries. Clearly, high social status was revered in death as much as in life, a custom that evolved to extreme levels in pharaonic Egypt.

Naqada Period

NAQADA I

Archaeologists divide the Naqada period (*c.*4000–3000 BC), named from the Naqada site between Luxor and Dendera in Upper Egypt where an enormous cemetery holding more than 3000 graves was discovered, into three cultural phases. The first, Naqada I (*c.*4000–3500 BC), also known as Amratian, initially presented no obvious break with the Badarian, but gradually became more prosperous and developed, and eventually extended across all of Upper Egypt. Technological advances included the creation of faience, a ceramic made from quartz sand and coated in a dazzling blue or green glaze in imitation of semi-precious gems, but the most striking development was the appearance of new decoration on pottery, palettes and ivory figurines, that would eventually form the iconography at the centre of the ancient Egyptian civilisation. White-painted geometric, animal and floral designs grace Amratian ceramics, as well as human figures often portrayed as heroic hunters or warriors in scenes pre-empting a later age and suggesting that culture's hunter-warriors were coming to the fore in terms of status and power. Macho imagery is also in evidence on male figurines, which sport new triangular beards, power symbols that eventually mutated into the false beards worn only by Egyptian gods and kings. Meanwhile, the wealthy were buried in larger, richer graves, some interred with ceremonial maces, a weapon that would become a symbol of kingly power until the Roman period.

NAQADA II: TRADE, EXPANSION AND THE FIRST CITIES

Evidently, the germ of the pharaonic civilisation was already present, but it spread quickly during the Naqada II, or Gerzean, phase (*c.*3500–3200 BC) and rapidly accelerated during the Naqada III phase (*c.*3200–3000 BC), at the end of which Egypt had become a unified state.

During Naqada II, an elite class emerged in three main Upper Egyptian power centres, Naqada (Nubt), Hierakonpolis (Nekhen) and Abydos (Abdju), which became, in effect, chiefdoms controlling nearby farmland and natural resources. The rulers of each came to amass considerable surplus grain stores and also controlled access along wadis to the mineral riches and gold deposits of the Eastern Desert. Indeed, Naqada, located at the mouth of Wadi Hammamat, had the Egyptian name 'Nubt' – 'gold town' – which could hardly be more expressive of the new wealth focused there. The elite had grain and mineral riches at their disposal, and sought to trade them for 'foreign' prestige goods. In the process, the Naqada culture expanded from its

Upper Egyptian heartland in both directions along the Nile. To the north, a highly fruitful relationship with Lower Egypt was initiated, an area which had already made extensive contact with communities in the Levant. Commercial links were established with the culture at Maadi (*c.*3800–3200 BC), situated in what are now the suburbs of Cairo, where large quantities of imported copper ore were processed, worked and traded alongside products from Palestine, Sinai and the Near East. The Delta seaport of Buto had contact with Mesopotamia, and traded Sumerian goods as well as producing its own Sumerian-style pieces such as clay 'cones' for wall mosaics.

Eventually, Upper Egypt was at the centre of a far-reaching trade network, drawing luxury items and raw materials into the valley to satiate the desire of a ruling class that was constantly growing in power and wealth. Oils, wines, resins, stone, seashells and timber were imported from the Levant; gold, ivory, ebony, incense, animal skins and obsidian were transported from Nubia and other parts of Africa; turquoise, schist, porphyry and copper were brought from Sinai; while lapis lazuli came from as far away as Afghanistan. After thousands of years of being a simple provider of food and water, the Nile took on a new and important role as a channel of communication and wealth. Precious raw materials and luxury goods were ferried down the Nile on boats, which themselves, as carriers of fabulous riches, became status symbols and objects of awe. In art, the boat consequently starred as the principal decorative motif, while the Nile assumed a cosmic dimension as the mythical thoroughfare of the gods, merging the divine and human worlds in a way that underpinned later religious belief.

That the elite stood at the top of an increasingly stratified society is revealed by the development of ever more elaborate and spacious tombs containing a greater number of sumptuous objects. No grave of this period was grander than the Painted Tomb (Tomb 100) of Hierakonpolis, its exact location now lost beneath farmland since its excavation at the end of the nineteenth century. It was the only deco-rated tomb of its kind recovered from Predynastic Egypt, and the first Egyptian tomb to be decorated with wall-paintings – depicting a procession of laden boats, and heroic individuals in hunting scenes and hand-to-hand combat.

The demand for funerary art and artefacts of the highest quality encouraged the development of a class of specialised craftsmen to fulfil the requirements of the elite. The outstanding luxury objects of the time were ornamental flint knives, exquisitely knapped with delicately curving, ultra-fine serrated edges, and sometimes carved ivory handles – the pinnacle of flint craftsmanship in Egypt if not the world. Functional flint tools, however, were being phased out by advances in metallurgy, and copper was replacing stone as medium of choice for blades, axes, spear tips, hooks and needles. Even so, stoneworkers were rising in accomplishment and experimenting with a wide range of new materials such as limestone, alabaster, marble, basalt, gneiss and diorite to name but a few, laying the foundations for the artistic and architectural triumphs of the Old Kingdom.

Craftsmen were not only on hand for the whims of the wealthy; workshops also opened to mass-produce pottery, aided it seems by the

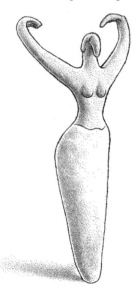

An elegant figurine of the Naqada II period *c.* 3500–3200 BC

introduction of the hand-turned wheel, for export along the length of the Egyptian Nile. Over time, Naqada ceramics were prevalent across Egypt, part of the growing cultural domination by Upper Egypt. Having said that, Naqada culture itself began to display the influence of foreign styles in art, architecture and imagery, most notably from Mesopotamia and the Kingdom of Elam in what is now southwest Iran.

The existence of a class of full-time artisans implied that urban centres were developing where workshops, craftsmen, apprentices and their clientele lived in close proximity, supported by a much larger number of agricultural labourers who produced food for them. Small cities emerged of densely-packed rectangular mud-brick houses with walled courtyards; evidence suggests Hierakonpolis was home to between five and ten thousand people, while at Naqada, the remains of an enormous mud-brick structure have been excavated, all that is left of an early royal palace perhaps, and near it, clusters of houses guarded by a thick defensive wall that betrays the need for protection from attack, a testament to the growing rivalry between urban centres.

NAQADA III: TOWARDS THE UNIFICATION OF THE TWO LANDS

The very end of the Predynastic period, towards the point at which the Two Lands of Upper and Lower Egypt were unified in a single state, is one of the most tantalising episodes in Egypt's long narrative. The appearance of embryonic hieroglyphic writing, in the form of dozens of tiny inscribed labels found in a large Naqada III tomb at Abydos, marks a culture on the threshold of literacy – and, therefore, recorded history. Nevertheless, much of this crucial phase is shrouded in obscurity and uncertainty.

It is clear, however, that the trends established during Naqada II accelerated in the two centuries before unification. By about 3200 BC, the local material culture of Lower Egypt had been completely replaced by that of Upper Egypt, but this is not to imply that the Two Lands were already politically united. On the contrary, it appears that Upper Egypt was still dominated by the three key power centres at

Naqada, Hierakonpolis and Abydos, whose rulers began to jockey for ultimate control. Struggles and skirmishes seem attested by a number of ceremonial palettes and mace-heads depicting battles, heroes overpowering beasts (a Mesopotamian motif), animals emblematic of localities trampling enemies and demolishing town walls, the subjugation of entire peoples under a ruler, and many other scenes of turmoil and conquering authority. The richness of burials during this period suggests a possible outcome to the upheaval: Naqada's glory was eclipsed, while the leaders of Hierakonpolis ('falcon city' in Greek, the cult centre of the hawk-headed god Horus) remained influential, but not nearly as powerful as the rulers buried at Abydos, which went on to be the royal cemetery of the First Dynasty kings of Egypt.

Excavations have revealed the existence of several kings during Naqada III, the so-called 'Dynasty 0' kings pre-dating those of the First Dynasty, who were more than likely to have had some part to play in the unification process, or may even have presided over a fully united Egyptian kingdom. From labels and primitive hieroglyphic inscriptions (for more on the development of writing see p.30), we know of kings such as Iry-Hor and Ka, whose tombs have been unearthed at Abydos, and the mysterious 'King Scorpion' who is shown inaugurating an irrigation channel (the first evidence of the use of irrigation in the Nile Valley) on a ceremonial mace-head found at Hierakonpolis.

Around 3000 BC, the rulers of Upper Egypt took political control of Lower Egypt, though exactly how this was done is unknown. Nineteenth-century Egyptologists believed that the 'sudden' appearance of the Egyptian state was the result of an invasion from the east, but it is now thought far more plausible that the union came slowly, in the wake of the steady rise and expansion of Upper Egyptian culture. The Lower Egyptian site at Buto in the northwest Delta, for example, gradually assimilated the culture of the south over many decades without any sign of the death and destruction associated with a full-blooded conquest. It seems that the people of the north and south lived peacefully together here long before 3000 BC. The battle scenes portrayed on contemporary ceremonial objects, therefore, probably represented the frequent clashes against outsiders from the west – semi-nomadic pastoralists usually referred to by historians as 'Libyans' – who tried to settle in the Delta, having been attracted to the region by its natural wealth, which helps to explain why prisoners and the slain are often depicted with a non-Egyptian appearance.

Whatever the exact processes for the unification of the Two Lands were, the Egyptian state, and all its attendant customs, art and beliefs, did not simply materialise from desert wastes and Nile plains in around 3000 BC, but came as the final stage in a lengthy process of development and expansion over many centuries. The civilisation that emerged became the most powerful in the Ancient World, a civilisation whose influence is still felt across the world today.

CHAPTER TWO

The Rise and Fall of Early Egypt

The Early Dynastic Period and the Old Kingdom (*c.*3000–2160 BC)

The Chronology of Dynastic Egypt

Prehistory, the time before recorded history, ended with the beginning of the Dynastic period. From this point onwards, there are records of varying quality and reliability about kings and their reigns, made by ancient Egyptians. They used a dating system which allocated dates to important events according to the number of years that had passed since the accession of the current king, called 'regnal years'. For this reason we know the dates of the reigns of many ancient Egyptian kings, which we give where possible with the first mention of their names, but not the dates of their lives. With each new ruler, the date returned to zero. As the Dynastic period progressed, long sequences of rulers, known as 'king lists', developed which were recorded by scribes in inscriptions on the walls of tombs and temples, as well as on papyrus scrolls kept in temple libraries. Using such a list, a priest or scribe could determine how long ago an event took place.

The challenge for Egyptologists has been to incorporate this 'free-floating' and frequently patchy sequential history of Egyptian rulers into our own dating system, that is, relative to a fixed point in history, typically the birth of Christ. Several methods have been used to devise a chronology, the framework by which events in antiquity can be assigned dates. There are scientific dating techniques, such as radiocarbon dating, thermoluminescence and dendrochronology; there are 'relative' dating techniques, such as 'seriation' or 'sequence dating', whereby artefacts are put in order relative to each other, depending on their style, material and the location of their excavation; there are also techniques that rely on textual references, not least the accounts of astronomical events, especially the rising of the dog star Sirius (see below), which can be given 'absolute' dates.

The broadly accepted chronology of Ancient Egypt depends on all of these approaches, but it is not without its problems. For example, we do not know for sure if the ancient scribes always used the 365-day Egyptian year in their records, or perhaps referred to the solar year which was slightly longer. There is also confusion about the practice of the 'co-regency' in which kings and their heirs may have reigned together for a short period to ensure the smooth passage of power. It is not clear how co-regencies are accounted for on king lists, nor even if they took place at all. Even the dates of astronomical events, which would seem to be incontrovertible, may vary depending on the place from where they were observed, a detail that is unknown and also contested.

The result of this is an imperfect, but largely accurate chronology that is supported by the majority of Egyptologists. At its worst, it is unlikely to be more than 150 years adrift at the beginning of the First Dynasty, a margin of error that steadily drops over time, decreasing to around fifty years during the Old Kingdom, and falling to a decade or so in the New Kingdom. It is not until 664 BC and the Assyrian invasion of Egypt which is attested in many Classical sources that we have our earliest absolute fixed date.

KINGDOMS AND INTERMEDIATE PERIODS

While the chronology improves in accuracy as the years progress, there are certain moments in Egypt's ancient history which suffer from a dearth of records, artefacts and archaeological discoveries. Often these times coincide with confused entries on king lists that posit a rash of little-known and short-ruling royals. These times have come to be known as 'Intermediate Periods', supposed 'dark ages' of internal discord and disunion that separate the more stable and better documented periods of centralised rule described as the Old, Middle and New Kingdoms.

However, it is unlikely that ancient Egyptians saw themselves as belonging to any such kingdom or period. Rather, these are the constructs of modern historians, useful divisions that apportion large chunks of time into periods that share certain key characteristics. In reality, social and cultural change was a slow process, and these great divisions blur into one another with more fluidity than such artifices reveal.

DYNASTIES

One of the most important historical annals is the *Aegyptiaca* written by Manetho, an Egyptian priest of the third century BC. He was the first to divide the history of Ancient Egypt into thirty 'dynasties' (a thirty-first was added later), spanning the entire pharaonic period from the unification of Egypt in around 3000 BC to the conquest of Alexander the Great in 332 BC. Even today, Manetho's dynasties form the building blocks of Egyptian chronology, historical units which, broadly speaking, coincide with the country's major political and cultural developments. Each dynasty contains a succession of kings usually grouped together on the basis of kinship or the location of the capital, but sometimes for reasons that appear more arbitrary.

Unfortunately, the surviving fragments of the *Aegyptiaca* are sometimes at odds with each other, and come to us preserved in the works of later historians. Some gaps and confused periods can be clarified by other important sources, such as the Palermo Stone from the Fifth Dynasty, a basalt slab inscribed with royal annals stretching back to mythical rulers, and the Turin Canon, a papyrus dating from the thirteenth century BC recording the reigns of kings from the First Dynasty right up to the beginning of the New Kingdom.

While Manetho's dynasties have proved to be an extremely robust and convenient means of ordering a chronology of Egypt, it is a system with some limitations. The rich social and cultural fabric of ancient Egyptian life is not well conveyed by monochrome dynastic divisions. On another level, recent archaeological discoveries have revealed the existence of Predynastic kings that predate Manetho's dynasties, as we have seen in the first chapter. These kings, who ruled an Egypt that was of much the same political and social makeup of the

Early Dynastic period, have consequently been assigned to a 'Dynasty 0'. The Egyptians themselves believed that demigods ruled before the first human pharaohs.

THE EGYPTIAN CALENDAR

The Egyptian year was divided into three seasons, based on the agricultural year: the inundation (*akhet*), the growing period (*peret*) and harvest time (*shemu*). The seasons had four months apiece, each of them containing three weeks of ten days. To this were added five extra days, to bring the total number of days to 365.

The beginning of the year was associated with the 'heliacal' rising of the star Sirius (known as Sopdet or Sothis by the Egyptians), that is, when it first becomes visible at dawn on the eastern horizon. This was because the star's appearance in mid-July coincided with the onset of the Nile inundation. However, the discrepancy between the 365-day Egyptian year and the real solar year, which was a quarter of a day longer, meant that they gradually slipped out of synchrony over time and only came together again once every 1460 years, a period known as the 'Sothic cycle'.

The Alexandrian astronomer and mathematician of the first century BC, Sosigenes, was employed by Julius Caesar to sort out the muddled Roman calendar. He came up with the 'leap year', which added a day to the 365-day year every four years. Caesar adopted the idea in 45 BC for the entire Roman Empire, which was soon to include Egypt. With only minor modifications Sosigenes' system became the modern Gregorian calendar used by the Western world today.

The Development of Writing

The origins of writing in Egypt are lodged in the haze of the prehistoric past, pre-dating the first Dynastic kings by as much as five hundred years. The earliest examples of writing are on labels, which would have been tagged to goods for accounting and administrative purposes, noting any of a combination of data, such as contents, quantity, owner and origin; antique symbols which essentially meant 'produce of Lower Egypt', are eerily resonant for the modern reader. The embryonic symbols in use began to grow in number and become standardised as 'hieroglyphs' (from the Greek *hieroglyphika grammata*, 'sacred carved letters'), probably even before the political union of the country. The development of hieroglyphs parallels the formation of cuneiform script in Mesopotamia; traditionally it was thought that the idea of writing was Mesopotamian in origin, but the Egyptian and Mesopotamian systems are so different that it is now believed they were invented independently.

Writing did not stay confined to the mundane demands of administration for long, but began to serve the elite as a tool of propaganda and power. Hieroglyphs began appearing in royal art, usually to trumpet kingly power and reinforce the notion of his divinity in temple reliefs, commemorative inscriptions and funerary monuments. By its association with people, buildings and occasions of high prestige, the script itself came to represent power as much as the message it was conveying. In a society in which less than one per cent of the population knew how to read, writing was also a means to restrict the transmission of knowledge and power, and keep the literate elite in control of the state and religion. Writing quickly became a crucial part of the Egyptian state, tying together the bureaucracy with an artistic form that sanctified supreme royal authority.

Early on, the symbolic potency of writing was exploited to great effect, but it was not until the beginning of the Old Kingdom that continuous speech could effectively be encoded into writing. Hieroglyphic script is not an alphabetic system; hieroglyphs were either phonograms (representing sounds, as in speech), logograms (representing a complete word or idea) or determinatives (picture signs to clarify the sense of preceding phonograms). During the pharaonic period, there were around a thousand hieroglyphs in the script's repertoire, but the number rose to more than five thousand in the Ptolemaic period when the script was only used by the priestly class.

A more convenient form of writing called 'hieratic' developed in parallel with hieroglyphic script as a kind of shorthand for administration and other secular communication, usually written in ink on papyrus or potsherds. By the seventh century BC, hieratic developed into an even more cursive form, known as 'demotic' which survived into the middle of the fifth century AD, less than sixty years after the latest known hieroglyphic inscription, which dates to 394 AD.

SCRIBES

As writing emerged as a means of organising power, the scribe became crucial to the administration of the country. Scribes not only knew how to read and write, but formed an elite class of bureaucrats, clerks, record-keepers, surveyors, taxmen and managers, on whom the entire administration depended. Only a tiny portion of the population was literate, and scribes were prestigious men (it seems to have been an exclusively male preserve), who passed on their knowledge to their sons, keeping the professions within certain families for generations. Scribal training was given in special institutions known as 'Houses of Life', which were attached to temples or, for the uppermost classes, the royal household itself. A young scribe's education was broad with mathematics, medicine, law, geography and astronomy being taught alongside reading and writing. The school regime was hard; young boys, distinguished from their elders by the 'sidelock of youth' (a long plaited curl of hair which was worn until puberty), were regularly acquainted with the rod: 'A boy's ear is on his backside – he listens best when he is beaten'.

Ancient Egyptian Religion

The ancient Egyptians had no comparable word for what we call 'religion', perhaps because for them it was not a separate entity from a secular world, but infused in every part of life – from art, science and history to society, economy and government. Religion also operated on several levels: state religion, which was bound up with the king and the most important state gods and temples; local religion based around worship at provincial temples and cult centres; and popular religion concerning 'household' deities, which were more associated with everyday concerns. Within these three interconnected spheres jostled more than two thousand gods, in animal or human form, or combining an animal's head with a human body. There were deities for natural phenomena like the stars, the wind or the Nile inundation or abstract concepts like magic and justice, or personifications of seemingly mundane things like the king's beard or the royal food table.

Deities were linked to each other and to the physical world in a complex web of relations described by innumerable myths and stories, which often intertwined and sometimes even contradicted themselves. The relationship of gods to each other, to cult centres and to the earthly realm also changed as centuries passed. Gods fused with each other, such as Atum-Ra in the Old Kingdom and Amun-Ra in the New Kingdom, or borrowed characteristics or developed new associations. Over the years ideas accrued one on the next, like layers of Nile silt, without any being discarded. For instance, Egyptian religion accommodated several creation myths centred around at least five creator gods (Atum, Ptah, Ra, Khnum and the goddess Neith) and a variety of beliefs about the afterlife. The deceased could dwell in the underworld with Osiris, lord of the dead, or tow the sun barque (boat) of Ra, or be in the night sky as a star, or inhabit a statue as a spirit, or

The ancient gods of Isis, Osiris and Horus

till the land in the 'Field of Reeds'. And despite the flux and complexity of religion, its iconography was virtually unchanged during the course of the pharaonic period.

One other concept also remained unchanged at the core of religious, social and political life. This was *maat* (personified by the goddess Maat), divine order and harmony that had pervaded the universe since creation. It was everyone's duty to preserve *maat*, maintain the established balance of things and prevent the spread of chaos through just and truthful deeds. The king's role in this respect was paramount as he was both god and man, identified with Horus while living, and his father Osiris when dead (see p.46). Set apart from the rest of humanity, he was the sole link between the divine and earthly worlds; he represented the gods to his people, and his people to the gods. The unique position made the king the linchpin of the nation, indispensable for its survival, and by the same token, any harm to the king and the system that held him at its centre threatened to disrupt *maat*. In this way, *maat* guaranteed the reproduction of the status quo and the long endurance of the supremacy of kingship; *maat* therefore underpinned the deep conservatism in Egyptian civilisation.

State religion was focused around major gods at the main temples and consisted of cult practice and festivals. In cult worship, the king (usually represented by priests) made offerings and sacrifices for the gods, and cared for the cult images; in return the gods would bless the king and by extension humanity. The temple was not a place of public worship, but the 'house' of the deity, represented by a cult image held in its innermost chamber, where the celebration of the cult was enacted by priests alone. The temple did, however, have a large associated workforce and endowments of land to produce food for daily offerings to the deity, which was eventually redistributed to staff. Temples, their estates, and their employees came to comprise a large share of the national economy. During festivals, the deity would be paraded outside the temple when the public had an opportunity to offer prayers or ask oracular questions, but even at these times the cult images were often kept hidden from view in covered shrines carried on processional barques.

Apart from festivals, the official cults and main temples were effectively closed to the public. Ordinary Egyptians found other ways to express their piety by visiting local shrines of lesser deities (or of important deities in another form) or going on pilgrimages to holy sites. They also used religion – and what we might now call magic – to keep harm, illness and the evil eye at bay. Some of the most popular household gods, such as Taweret and Bes, were those associated with protection during pregnancy and childbirth, especially dangerous times of life in the Ancient World. Medicine and magic, science and religion, spells and prayers were all used without clear distinction to ward off evil and chaos, and uphold the harmony of the universe in life as in death.

FUNERARY RITUAL AND MUMMIFICATION

Since Predynastic times, the Egyptians buried their dead in the fringes of the Western Desert, the forsaken wasteland where the ground was barren, where the sun died every evening, where the god Osiris, long associated with the departed, was in his element. Precious objects and provisions were buried too, and the dryness of the early pit-graves desiccated the body, preserving it for eternity in the afterlife. In the pharaonic period, the fundamentals of religious belief were the same, even if the rituals, architecture and expression of those beliefs had become far more complicated.

The moment of death, it was believed, was just a brief hiatus in an individual's existence, and eternal life could be gained by behaving devoutly in the earthly world, preserving the body through mummification, and being buried with the right funerary equipment. A happy existence in the afterlife also depended on passing the Judgement of Osiris (see p.72) and the protection and sustenance of the five elements of each individual – the body, the *ka*, the *ba*, the *akh*, the name and the shadow (see Glossary on p.419). This might be achieved by private individuals in simple graves with a few select artefacts. For a dead king, on the other hand, there might be a royal cult, a sprawling mortuary complex including temples staffed with priests, and farmland used exclusively to provide plentiful offerings.

As a god, the king's place in the heavenly realm alongside the other gods was assured. As a human, however, he had to ensure that his physical being was preserved after his death to achieve immortality. On his death, a series of rituals were enacted to this end usually taking seventy days to complete, before the body was transported by boat to the king's necropolis and laid to rest.

Much of this time was spent mummifying the body, preserving it for eternity so that the *ka* spirit could recognise its earthly form and regularly return to find succour. The process involved pulling the brains of the deceased out through the nostrils with a hook, cutting a slit into the trunk and extracting the internal organs, which were treated and stored in 'canopic jars'. The body would then be sprinkled with natron (a salty mineral) and left to desiccate for several weeks, before being coated in a dark sticky resin, which the Arabs mistook for bitumen (*mummiya*), from where we get the word 'mummy'. Those of modest means could expect less elaborate procedures, typically being pumped full of cedar oil and being eviscerated via the anus, and the poor were simply interred straight into the dry desert sand, a practice which often desiccated and preserved their bodies naturally. After embalming, a royal corpse was wrapped in hundreds of yards of bandages interspersed with protective amulets. Before its transferral to a coffin and sarcophagus, the 'opening of the mouth ceremony' was performed which restored the deceased's senses, bringing the mummy to life.

The rituals did not end once the tomb was sealed and the entrance hidden. Daily rites had to be carried out by a collection of priests and assistants to sustain the various aspects of the king's identity. During the rites, the *ka* (life-force) and *ba* (individual soul), interacted with the preserved body to release the *akh*, the glorified spirit of the deceased in the afterlife. The *ka* of the dead king needed five meals a day, three of which he would partake with the gods, perhaps sitting with Ra in the celestial barque as it traversed the sky. The other two were provided by the priests, offered to royal statues or presented on offering tables, some of which were carved with images of food as magical substitutes for the real thing, or at the foot of a 'false door', from which the *ka* would emerge from the netherworld in the west to take its sustenance.

Early Dynastic Egypt (c. 3000–2686 BC)

MEMPHIS

At the beginning of the third millennium BC, the first king of the First Dynasty held sway over a territory that stretched from Elephantine by the First Cataract in the south to the mouth of the Nile at the Mediterranean Sea in the north. According to Herodotus (c.484–420 BC) and the Egyptian historian Manetho, this first king of Egypt was Menes, the great ruler who united Upper and Lower Egypt and founded the capital city of Memphis where the two territories met. It was a sensible political decision to build the administrative centre in a location between the Delta and the Nile Valley, from where the new kingdom could be most effectively governed.

At Memphis the young kingdom was consolidated. The country was governed from the royal palace, the *per-aa* ('great house'), which by the time of the New Kingdom (1550–1069 BC) was equated with the king himself and is the origin of our word 'pharaoh'. The palace was probably fortified with dazzling limestone walls which gave the city its ancient name Ineb-hedj, 'White Walls'; 'Memphis' is probably a much later Greek corruption of Men-nefer, the name of a nearby pyramid complex at Saqqara associated with King Pepy I (c. 2321–2287 BC) of the Sixth Dynasty. The great house was the apex of a centralised administrative system that relied on the written word and a class of scribes to bring every aspect of Egyptian life under the king's authority. With his team of bureaucrats and officials, the king could oversee the exploitation of the best agricultural land in the known world. He could collect taxes to fund monumental works and organise labour to build them. He could send expeditions to gather minerals and raw materials from the deserts and faraway lands, and launch military campaigns to secure his borders and control lucrative trade routes.

For much of the pharaonic period Memphis was the capital, and even when it was not – as during the New Kingdom when it moved to Thebes – it remained a national administrative centre. It was also the cult centre for one of the earliest Egyptian deities, the creator-god Ptah, patron of craftsmen, whose temple was called *Hut-ka-Ptah*, ('house of the spirit of Ptah'), corrupted much later by Greeks into the word '*Aiguptos*', from where we get the modern name Egypt. The city's terminal decline began with the foundation of Alexandria in 331 BC and swiftly accelerated with the appearance in 643 AD of the Arab capital Fustat (later swallowed by Cairo) some 15 miles (24 km) to the north. Although the remains of the city could clearly be seen as late as the thirteenth century, sustained plunder of its buildings and the movements of the Nile which has buried their ruins under metres of silt, means that little of Memphis today survives.

THE TRUE IDENTITY OF MENES, FIRST KING OF EGYPT

By tradition, King Menes was the founder of Memphis and first king of Egypt, but it is not known which king in the archaeological record this legendary Menes might be. He appears to be a semi-mythical figure, perhaps concocted by later generations who wished to venerate one great king at the head of a long line of pharaohs, the sole founder of a civilisation. Equally, he could have been a composite of several rulers, whose achievements were conveniently packaged together into a single figure.

Yet, there are links between Menes and a couple of the earliest Egyptian kings, which suggest that the former was not a mere fiction. One possible candidate is King Narmer, whose name has been linked to Menes on ancient jar labels. Narmer is primarily known to us by a carved limestone mace-head and a mudstone ceremonial palette, both of which were discovered in Hierakonpolis. The Narmer Palette, the most celebrated artefact of the period (held in the Egyptian Museum, Cairo), depicts Narmer smiting his foe with a mace (a pose still used in royal art three thousand years later), wearing the conical white crown of Upper Egypt (*hedjet*). On the other side, he parades with his courtiers in the chair-shaped red crown of Lower Egypt (*deshret*) as he inspects the decapitated corpses of his enemy. Many think the palette commemorates the unification of Egypt itself, though this is increasingly thought by experts to be too narrow an interpretation of its significance. To complicate matters, there are also compelling links between Menes and Narmer's probable son, Aha 'the fighter', in an inscription which appears to call him 'Men'. Aha also has a strong presence in the Memphis area, which suggests he may have ruled from the new city, while Narmer's connections to the capital are weaker. Either way, Egyptologists conventionally identify Menes with Narmer or Aha, and begin the First Dynasty with one of these two kings.

KINGSHIP AND ROYAL NAMES

During the First Dynasty (*c.*3000–2890 BC) the mechanisms, institutions and ideologies that cemented the union of the Two Lands and enshrined royal power were forged. One of the most important was the notion of kingship itself, which had emerged from Predynastic times imbued with divine qualities. This is clear from the royal titles that the kings, who even before the First Dynasty times took a 'Horus name' written in a *serekh* frame topped off with a falcon, to go with their birth name or 'nomen'. By the end of the First Dynasty, the monarch was given five names, known as the 'royal fivefold titulary', which consisted of the Horus name, the Two Ladies name (*nebty*), the Golden Horus name, the throne name or 'prenomen' (*nesu-bit*), and the birth name or 'nomen', which was the only one given as soon as the pharaoh was born and the one most commonly used to identify him – this book being no exception.

Some of these names emphasised royal divinity, others also stressed the king's role as ruler of the Two Lands. For instance, the prenomen referred to the king as 'He of the sedge and bee', the sedge plant standing for Upper Egypt and the bee identified with Lower Egypt. Similarly, the 'Two Ladies' of the *nebty* name were the vulture goddess Nekhbet and the cobra goddess Wadjet, representing Upper and Lower Egypt respectively. The vulture and cobra (*uraeus*) also appeared on royal headgear, while the crown itself was actually a 'double crown' (*pschent*), a combination of the crowns of Upper and Lower Egypt. Although they were not used in the fivefold titulary, the lotus and papyrus were also commonly used in iconography to represent the Two Lands.

As we have seen, the king was the nexus between heavenly and mortal realms and was responsible for upholding *maat*, the divine order of the universe. In a way therefore, the wealth and strength of a king

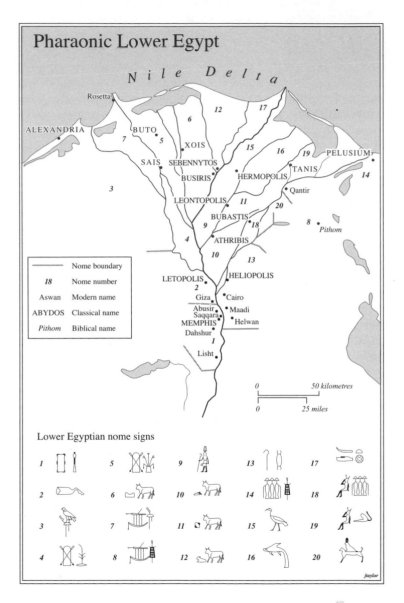

Pharaonic Lower Egypt

N i l e   D e l t a

Rosetta

ALEXANDRIA

BUTO

7   5

XOIS

6

12   17

15   16   19   PELUSIUM

SAIS   SEBENNYTOS

BUSIRIS   HERMOPOLIS   TANIS

3   14

LEONTOPOLIS   11   Qantir

20

BUBASTIS

9   18   8   Pithom

4   ATHRIBIS

10   13

LETOPOLIS   HELIOPOLIS

2

Giza   Cairo

Abusir   Maadi
Saqqara
MEMPHIS   Helwan
Dahshur

1

Lisht

——	Nome boundary
18	Nome number
Aswan	Modern name
ABYDOS	Classical name
Pithom	Biblical name

0   50 kilometres

0   25 miles

Lower Egyptian nome signs

1   5   9   13   17

2   6   10   14   18

3   7   11   15   19

4   8   12   16   20

jtaylor

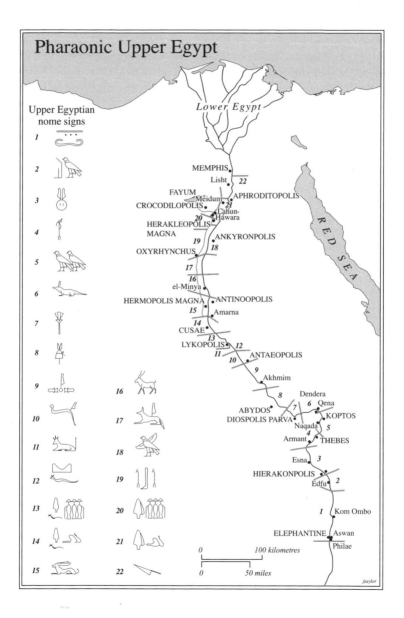

Pharaonic Upper Egypt

Upper Egyptian
nome signs

Lower Egypt

MEMPHIS
Lisht *22*
FAYUM
Mēidum APHRODITOPOLIS
CROCODILOPOLIS
Lahun-
Hawara
21
HERAKLEOPOLIS
MAGNA
20
19 ANKYRONPOLIS
OXYRHYNCHUS *18*

17
16
el-Minya
HERMOPOLIS MAGNA ANTINOOPOLIS
15 Amarna
14
CUSAE
13
LYKOPOLIS *12*
11 ANTAEOPOLIS
10
9
Akhmim
8 Dendera
7 *6* Qena
ABYDOS KOPTOS
DIOSPOLIS PARVA Naqada *5*
Armant THEBES
4
3
Esna
HIERAKONPOLIS
Edfu *2*

1 Kom Ombo

ELEPHANTINE Aswan
Philae

RED SEA

1			
2		*16*	
3		*17*	
4		*18*	
5		*19*	
6		*20*	
7		*21*	
8		*22*	
9			
10			
11			
12			
13			
14			
15			

0   100 kilometres

0   50 miles

jtaylor

reflected the health and happiness of his kingdom and subjects, encouraging the concentration of authority in his hands and the lavish expression of his power in the construction of grand temples, tombs and monuments. In a long reign, a king was able to reaffirm his unique royal and divine qualities during the *sed* festival, traditionally held in the thirtieth jubilee year. As part of the ceremony, the king would run between markers representing the borders of his realm, demonstrating his fitness to rule and symbolically renewing his physical and spiritual energy. The festival dates at least to the First-Dynasty king, Den, who was also the earliest king to be depicted wearing the double crown of Upper and Lower Egypt.

ABYDOS: THE TOMBS OF THE FIRST KINGS

All the First Dynasty monarchs were buried at Abydos, 31 miles (50 km) south of modern Sohag, in the low desert in the shadow of an imposing cliff-face. Abydos was, even at this early moment in Egyptian history, regarded as a sacred cemetery of great antiquity. Later generations made pilgrimages to the site as one of the great centres of the cult of Osiris and from the Middle Kingdom onwards, the tomb of Djer, Aha's successor, was thought to be the burial place of the god himself. The Early Dynastic section of Abydos is now known as Umm el-Qaab, 'mother of pots', because of the huge number of pottery fragments littering the site, the shattered remains of countless votive offerings made by pilgrims.

In broad terms, the tombs consisted of a subterranean pit lined with bricks and roofed or covered by a mound of sand, and identified by a pair of carved stone stelae. The main tomb was surrounded by a series of chambers that served as store-rooms for provisions and luxury items such as wine and aromatic oils, or subsidiary graves for the court retainers who, it seems, were either killed or committed suicide for the privilege of waiting on the king in the afterlife. Aha's tomb complex, for example, includes thirty-three subsidiary graves containing the remains of young men, all under twenty-five years old, and seven lions. The practice reached its excesses under Djer, who had 338 subsidiary burials, and continued on an increasingly modest scale till the end of the dynasty when sacrificial victims were replaced by funerary statuettes and later *shabtis* (see p.419) – a far less bloody and costly way of doing the king's bidding in the divine realm.

In addition to their tombs, the kings (except Aha) built 'funerary enclosures' closer to the Nile, large walled-off areas where the cult of the dead king was perpetuated. Early archaeologists interpreted the structures as fortresses, and it may have been that the body of the king was guarded here while tombs were constructed and preparations made. Indeed, it was not until the reign of Den, the fourth of the First Dynasty, that a staircase had been introduced into the architecture of the tomb, which meant that the whole complex, including roof or mound on top, could be built before the king's death.

EARLY TOMBS OF SAQQARA

Saqqara was the principal necropolis of Memphis and its northern area is the location of a number of Early Dynastic mastaba tombs, so called by modern Arabic-speakers, because of the resemblance of the rectangular shape to a bench (*mastaba*) commonly found outside an Egyptian house.

The discovery of a number of imposing and relatively well-preserved mastaba tombs dating from the First Dynasty in North Saqqara, complete with intricate 'palace-façade' mud-brick walls (an elaborate architectural design derived from Mesopotamia of rippling buttresses and recesses to give a panelled effect), traces of painted exteriors and even wooden floors, led early excavators to speculate that these were the true burial places of the first kings, and that the less spectacular monuments at Abydos were only cenotaphs. Treasures discovered within the mastabas, notably a stunning inlaid gaming disc and the earliest sample of papyrus ever found, did much to bolster this view, sparking off a debate that has yet to be settled conclusively. Current opinion maintains that these mastaba tombs belonged not to the kings, but to high officials and members of the royal family, the most rich and powerful people serving beneath the king.

The tombs of the early Second Dynasty kings, however, were certainly constructed at Saqqara, immense underground galleries hewn out of the limestone escarpment. Exactly why these kings forsook the royal necropolis at Abydos is lost to obscurity, but it is hard not to infer some significant cultural and political break with the First Dynasty.

SECOND DYNASTY UNREST

The shift of the royal necropolis to the Memphis region during the Second Dynasty (*c.*2890–2686 BC) probably reflected a broader movement in power northwards. There are signs the move may have been premature and temporarily injured the union by weakening the king's authority in the south, triggering internal unrest. During the middle of the dynasty in particular, a number of poorly-attested and short-reigning figures based in the north seemed to have commanded only limited, if any, authority in Upper Egypt. On the other hand, the penultimate king of the dynasty, Peribsen, was buried in Abydos next to the First Dynasty kings, and has no contemporary inscriptions outside southern Egypt. Wherever his name occurs in a *serekh* (a rectangular frame, surmounted by the Horus falcon, in which the king's Horus name is usually written), the usual Horus motif has been replaced by Seth's image, his arch-rival (see p.46). This provocative switch has been interpreted as a symbol of rebellion against some aspect of the existing order, and it is telling that Peribsen's successor, who began his reign with a Horus *serekh*, later added a Seth-animal to it. He also lengthened his name from Khasekhem ('the power has appeared') to Khasekhemwy ('the two powers have appeared') and added the sobriquet 'the Two Lords are at peace in him', possibly implying that he was able to quash the rebellion and rule a newly united Egypt.

KHASEKHEMWY

Khasekhemwy was the last and most successful of the Early Dynastic kings. Having stamped out an insurrection that might have killed Egyptian civilisation before it had really begun, he consolidated national interests in Lower Nubia and the north, and made his presence felt as far away as Byblos in modern-day Lebanon, earning another designation, 'overseer of foreign lands'. He was also the most ambitious builder of the period, and his elaborate tomb, the last at the hallowed royal cemetery at Umm el-Qaab in Abydos, was lined with blocks of quarried limestone – the earliest known large-scale stone construction – and included fifty-eight store-rooms that would have been space enough for all the First Dynasty grave goods put together. The colossal walls of his vast funerary enclosure nearby still stand over 30ft (9m) high in places, representing a huge commitment of labour and resources – and yet they are mirrored by a structure of similarly imposing size at Hierakonpolis. There may well have been others besides, as the fractured pieces of granite at Elkab bearing his *serekh* suggest. The achievements of Khasekhemwy's reign, the return of political stability and economic prosperity, the reassertion of a grand vision of kingship, and the architecture and conception of his funerary monuments, seemed to have laid the foundations for the triumphs of the Old Kingdom and the pyramid age.

The Old Kingdom and the Pyramid Age (c.2686–2125 BC)

The Old Kingdom encompasses the Third to the Sixth Dynasties, a long period of stable and centralised rule from Memphis by kings with extraordinary power and unequalled riches at their fingertips. State religion, economic success and administrative advances made it possible for these rulers to divert substantial portions of the nation's wealth into building projects, most notably their burial tombs and mortuary temples, through which they hoped to secure their regal status in the afterlife for eternity. The result was an architectural and artistic revolution that saw the construction of monuments of unprecedented scale and quality, among them the most celebrated edifices of all time – the pyramids.

By the Fourth Dynasty, a standard form of the funerary complex had emerged, the dominant element of which was the pyramid. This was far more than just a reliquary for the dead king, it was also the vehicle by which the king was resurrected to the afterlife, taking his blessed place alongside Ra in the celestial sun barque. The other components included a mortuary temple, the king's palace of eternity where his cult was observed; the valley temple by the water's edge, at the entrance of the complex where funeral rites were performed; the causeway, a covered walkway leading from the valley temple to the pyramid and mortuary temple; satellite pyramid, associated with the king's *ka*; queens' pyramids, subsidiary tombs for the wives and daughters of the king; and boat pits, where royal funeral barques were disassembled and buried. Some even had extensive cemeteries for courtiers and relatives, street upon street of mastaba tombs either side of the main pyramid, so that the king could enjoy the company of his favoured ones in death as in life.

HELIOPOLIS

At the beginning of the Third Dynasty (*c.*2686–2613 BC), the sun god Ra emerged as a leading state deity, and his cult centre was Heliopolis (Iunu or On), 'city of the sun'. Ra had been supplanted onto an earlier cult of the creator god, Atum, and was deemed to have been progenitor of the major cosmic deities, having himself appeared out of the primeval water (personified by the god Nun), on a sacred primeval mound. From this mound he 'single-handedly' begat Shu (god of the air) and his sister Tefnut, and they Geb (god of the earth) and sister Nut (goddess of the sky), who in turn parented Osiris, Isis, Seth and Nephthys. These nine gods comprised the 'Great Ennead of Heliopolis', one of the earliest and most important Egyptian cosmogonies. They became connected to a number of myths which drew on local gods and legends from across the country, probably as a way of uniting the land behind a generally acceptable set of state beliefs.

The most famous of these myths concerned the conflict between the brothers Osiris and Seth. As the story goes, Osiris was murdered and dismembered by his brother, who scattered his body-parts across the country. Isis, the wife and sister of Osiris, gathered the pieces, embalmed and resurrected him so that he could take his place as king of the underworld. They had a child, Horus, who, during the course of many trials and after the loss of an eye, eventually succeeded in avenging his father's death by slaying Seth and taking back the throne of Egypt. So it was that Osiris came to be identified with the dead king, and Horus with the living king.

In Heliopolis, the holiest object was a conical stone known as the *benben*, a symbol of the primordial mound where the rays of the rising sun were thought to fall first, which was probably located in the sacred precinct in the city. It is thought that the eventual development of the pyramid, originally encased in shining white limestone and topped by a gleaming gilded pyramidion (the crowning uppermost piece), and the obelisk, the top of which was also originally gilded, was both an emulation of the *benben* and representation of the rays of the reborn sun rising at dawn as they cascaded through the clouds from the celestial realm. The king's tomb mound which grew and reached its magnificent peak with the Great Pyramids, was probably an image of the sacred primordial mound, the origin of life in the heavens and on the earth, as well as the architectural expression of the reborn morning sun and the ascension of the resurrected king.

THE FIRST PYRAMIDS

A short distance from the Early Dynastic mastaba tombs of Saqqara stands the Step Pyramid of Djoser, believed to be the first large-scale building in the world to be constructed entirely of stone. Although little is now known of Djoser (*c.*2667–2648 BC), he was a king revered even into the Ptolemaic period as a sage and virtuous ruler. His architect Imhotep, however, credited with the invention of building in dressed stone, was even more venerated and eventually became deified, quite a rarity for commoners in Ancient Egypt. Architecture was not considered his only talent, and he was greatly respected for his skills as astronomer, medic and learned scribe. The deified Imhotep was patron of wisdom, writing and medicine and became associated with Ptah and Thoth, while the Greeks identified him with Asklepios, their god of medicine. Despite these honours, it seems Imhotep stumbled on the design for the world's first pyramid rather than conceiving

Djoser's Step Pyramid at Saqqara, thought to be the first large-scale
building in the world constructed entirely of stone

it from the outset. Excavations reveal that Djoser's tomb began in the
manner of his forebears as a mastaba covering an underground burial
chamber, before it underwent a series of enlargements eventually to
rise to 204ft (62m) as a six-stepped pyramid cased in fine dressed limestone from the quarries at Tura.

As impressive as the pyramid was, it was just an element of a larger
funerary complex that included a grand entrance colonnade, and a
number of other shrines and buildings that hitherto had been built of
wood, reeds, straw and matting. Faced with the problem of how to
construct traditionally lightweight structures in stone, the new material of eternity, they set about copying the old style, carving planks,
ropes and poles out of the limestone, replicating 'reed mats' with
faience tiles and erecting stone pillars like magnified papyrus stems. A
courtyard area was built for the celebration of the *sed* festival, a kind
of jubilee ceremony typically celebrated after a reign of thirty years, in
which the king's powers were symbolically rejuvenated. By building in
stone, Djoser would be able to renew his powers for perpetuity in the
hereafter.

Djoser's Step Pyramid set a new standard in royal tomb building,
both in form and grandeur. His Third-Dynasty successors,
Sekhemkhet (*c.*2648–2640 BC) and Khaba (*c.*2640–2637 BC), began
similar step pyramids at Saqqara, but neither was completed before

they died. No comparable structure has yet been found for Huni (*c*.2637–2613 BC), the last king of the dynasty but the first king to have a cartouche inscribed around his name, though a minority of scholars attribute the foundations of the Meidum pyramid to him. Most believe, however, this was all the work of his successor Sneferu (*c*.2613–2589 BC), the first king of the Fourth Dynasty and the most prolific pyramid builder of them all.

SNEFERU'S QUEST FOR THE TRUE PYRAMID

Like Djoser before him, Sneferu was a popular king honoured by later generations as the paradigm of the good and glorious ruler. He led successful military expeditions into Nubia and the Sinai peninsula to protect trade routes and establish turquoise mines. His campaigns also secured for his increasingly ambitious building projects valuable raw materials, and doubtless much of the manpower too – according to (probably exaggerating) inscriptions, as many as seven thousand Nubians were taken prisoner in one raid, and eleven thousand Libyans in another.

Sneferu's first undertaking was a step pyramid at Meidum, a new royal necropolis over thirty miles south of Saqqara. Although most of his family and high officials were buried in mastabas around this pyramid, the king himself seems to have had a change of heart and shifted his attentions back north to a high desert plateau at Dahshur, where he began to build the first true pyramid, having a square base and straight rather than stepped sides. Unfortunately he had not reckoned on the softness of the clay foundations, and when the pyramid was a little over half built, cracks appeared in the masonry. Widening the base was not enough to avert a disaster, so his engineers greatly lessened the angle of the top section, resulting in the so-called Bent Pyramid. As a precaution, Sneferu simultaneously began filling in the steps of his Meidum pyramid, converting it into the 'true' form, but neither this nor his Bent Pyramid satisfied him, and he set to work at Dahshur on constructing a third pyramid, now known as the North or Red Pyramid. It is estimated that in his efforts to build a perfect true pyramid, Sneferu's labourers quarried, hauled and placed nine

million tons of stone, a greater amount than for any other Old
Kingdom ruler.

KHUFU AND THE GREAT PYRAMID

Sneferu may have shifted the most stone, but it is his son, Khufu
(*c.*2589–2566 BC), better known by his Greek name Cheops, who has
been immortalised for constructing the acme of the canon – the
largest, most accomplished stone pyramid ever built. He chose a new
and dramatic location for his necropolis at Giza, a large elevated
plateau clearly visible from the capital and close to quality limestone
quarries. Dominating Khufu's funerary complex, most of which is
now lost, was the Great Pyramid itself, composed of some 2.3 million
stone blocks, more stone than was used in all English churches since
the time of St Augustine. The gargantuan project, angled at 51° to

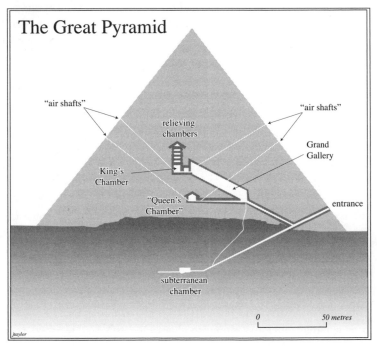

The Great Pyramid

"air shafts"

"air shafts"

relieving
chambers

Grand
Gallery

King's
Chamber

"Queen's
Chamber"

entrance

subterranean
chamber

0   50 metres

jtaylor

reach a height of 481ft (146m), took at least thirty years to complete – provided that each standard block of stone, weighing about 2.5 tons, was put into position every two to three minutes for ten hours a day. Even using a combination of ramps, levers and small swinging cranes, it is hard for modern minds to imagine how this was achieved. Beyond its sheer bulk and size, the pyramid is a marvel of ancient engineering: for example, its almost perfectly square sides are aligned with the cardinal compass points to within a fraction of a degree; its thirteen-acre base is level to within less than an inch; its 756ft (230m) sides differ by under two inches at most; the ratio of its perimeter to twice its height approximates pi to two decimal places; its internal 'air shafts' pointed to the northern polar stars at one end and Sirius and Orion at the other. It is also the last survivor of the Seven Wonders of the World, despite being the first to be built.

Unlike any other pyramid, the Great Pyramid also boasts three internal chambers. The largest of them, known as the King's Chamber, was built unusually high inside the pyramid and was completely lined with Aswan granite, including nine enormous ceiling slabs thought to weigh in excess of four hundred tons. Above them, five narrow 'relieving' chambers deflect the great burden of the overlying masonry to the sides of the edifice, an ingenious innovation with few ancient parallels. The most breathtaking element of the internal design, however, is the Grand Gallery leading up to the King's Chamber, a 26-ft (8m) high corridor made by an awe-inspiring arrangement of tapering corbelled walls.

Although the Great Pyramid is probably the most measured, surveyed and discussed building in existence, its mystery never seems to diminish. The latest surprises include the discovery in 1993 of a miniature stone 'door' with copper 'handles' at the end of a shaft beginning at the so-called Queen's Chamber (almost certainly not built for a queen). In 2002 a robot equipped with a drill and fibre-optic camera was able to see beyond this obstacle only to come up against another door, which as yet remains to be penetrated. In 2004, a French team using geo-radar claimed to have evidence of a corridor leading to a fourth chamber at the very heart of the pyramid. They believe it may be Khufu's true burial chamber, which, if they are right, may still even contain the king's remains; the grand sarcophagi inside this and other pyramids are empty, leading some to speculate the kings may have been buried elsewhere. Such developments seem to underline the capacity of the Great Pyramid to generate new enigmas ensuring its mystery will never diminish; despite the technology thrown at it, it will probably guard its secrets for eternity.

Little either is known of Khufu the man. Herodotus, writing two millennia after events, tells us he was supremely wicked and went to despotic ends to finish his pyramid, even forcing his daughter to work in brothels to raise extra funds. As Herodotus has it, she, in turn, persuaded each of her suitors to donate a stone for her own monument – the middle of the three subsidiary pyramids to the east of the Great Pyramid was reputed to be the product of her labours, but there is no shred of evidence to confirm any details of this salacious story. In fact, it seems pyramid building did not depend on the toil of hundred of thousands of brutalised slaves as is commonly perceived (indigenous slaves did not really exist in Egypt at this time), but on a few small teams of highly skilled craftsmen, engineers and builders working in tandem with larger numbers of corvée labourers who were farmers and peasants for the rest of the year. Archaeological finds suggest they were fed, clothed and lodged by the state, and were probably dedicated to the task in hand by the belief that it would help their passage to the afterlife.

Ironically, the only known likeness of Khufu (held in the Egyptian Museum, Cairo), fearsome author of the largest of Ancient Egypt's monuments, is a tiny ivory figurine barely three inches high.

KHAFRA AND THE SPHINX

The other two pyramids making up the famous Giza trinity were built by Khufu's son, Khafra (Chephren in Greek, *c.*2558–2532 BC) and grandson, Menkaura (Mycerinus, *c.*2532–2503 BC). Khafra's pile, commanding the central position on the plateau, was originally 10ft (3m) shorter than his father's, but its clever placement on elevated ground gives it the appearance of being equal or even higher than its neighbour. In quality it does not compete: its interior is less complex and grandiose, and its masonry work less accurate. The rest of Khafra's funerary complex, however, includes a valley temple, one of the best-preserved to survive from the Fourth Dynasty, and a colossal statue 236ft (72m) long and 65ft (20m) high, long thought to be the largest in the world.

The Great Sphinx tirelessly guards the causeway leading up from the valley temple to Khafra's pyramid, its unblinking sentinel gaze the inspiration for tales of dread for centuries. The Greeks imagined that the Sphinx put riddles to passing travellers, and murdered them if the answer was wrong. In Arabic it is called *Abu al-Hol* 'the father of terror', and the Greek term *sphinx* means 'strangler'. However, this is probably a corruption of the Egyptian phrase *shesep-ankh*, 'living image', and originally the Sphinx was not a murderous and malicious spirit but a protective one identified with kingly power and the sun god. The Sphinx's human head is thought to be in the image of Khafra wearing the royal *nemes* head-scarf and once also the other parapher-nalia of kingship, the false beard, shards of which were found in the sand by Napoleon's expedition, and a *uraeus*, the sacred cobra worn on the headdress. A statue of the king may have once stood between the lion's paws too. The nose was said to have been smashed off in the fifteenth century by Muslim soldiers opposed to the idolatry that the great statue represented.

The Sphinx was carved from a knoll of limestone left behind after material was quarried for two of Khafra's nearby temples. The lion's body is composed of softer bedrock, and has apparently been elon-gated to compensate for a large fissure running through its length, accounting for its unusual proportions. The poor quality of the rock and its location in a depression have made the statue the subject of rescue work even during pharaonic times, most famously its clearance from sand by Thutmose IV (*c.*1400–1390 BC) recorded on the stela between its legs (see also p.100). Its stone cladding was also added in this period and enhanced many times since; conservation work is currently ongoing. The unhappy condition of the upper part of the body has sparked speculation that the Sphinx is much older than once thought, with the more outlandish commentators claiming it was built over ten thousand years ago. Archaeological and historical evidence suggests otherwise, and nearly all Egyptologists credit the Sphinx to Khafra.

MENKAURA AND THE END OF THE FOURTH DYNASTY

Menkaura was responsible for the last and smallest of the principal Giza pyramids, a reduction in circumstances that heralds the decline of the Fourth Dynasty. Indeed it was Menkaura's antecedents, Sneferu, Khufu and Khafra, whose monuments signal the golden age of pyramid building – three generations of kings whose combined pyramid construction projects used over twice the mass of material than those of all their successors put together. While Menkaura's pyramid is the runt of the Giza three, barely a tenth the volume of the Great Pyramid, it does make use of a great quantity of granite, a material far more expensive to quarry, transport and finish than limestone. Unfortunately, one of the great treasures of his tomb, a beautifully carved basalt sarcophagus, went down in the Mediterranean when its transport was shipwrecked on its way to England in 1838.

Menkaura died before his monument was complete, and it was left to his son, Shepseskaf (*c.*2503–2498 BC), last king of the Fourth Dynasty, to finish it off. He did so in some haste, using mud-brick where he could and leaving much of the pyramid's granite casing undressed. Whether it was because of lack of space or resources at Giza, or because of a religious schism or dynastic crisis, Shepseskaf selected an isolated site at South Saqqara for his tomb, which he chose to build as a huge mastaba, the Mastabat al-Faraun ('Pharaoh's Bench'). There is speculation that he rejected the pyramid form because it was linked too closely with the sun cult and its priesthood, which was steadily gaining in power. But it may well be that this relatively impoverished monument was merely the first phase of some more ambitious scheme that was cut short by his death.

FIFTH DYNASTY: RISE OF THE SOLAR CULT

If Shepseskaf was attempting to quash the influence of the solar priests, he certainly failed in his goal. The Fifth Dynasty (*c.*2494–2345

BC) saw only the increase in their power, while the kings' authority waned. According to a story in the Papyrus Westcar (a collection of stories written in the Second Intermediate Period) Khufu was warned that the children of another would replace his own as the rulers of Egypt. Despite his murderous attempts, triplets were born to the wife of the priest of Ra, sired by Ra himself, and became the first three kings of the Fifth Dynasty. The fable seems to reflect a radical shift in Egyptian religion which is borne out by the monuments of the period. The first in the new line, Userkaf (*c.*2494–2487 BC) started the trend of building temples dedicated to the sun god, which was followed by five of his six dynastic successors at the expense of their own pyramid complexes, which suffered a decline in size and quality. Ra had become the most important god in the Egyptian pantheon and his cult was effectively the state religion. The new sun temples, like the pyramid complexes, were each endowed with land in perpetuity, granted royal donations, and staffed by new personnel, marking a noticeable expansion in the wealth, power and size of Ra's priesthood.

THE EROSION OF ROYAL POWER

Userkaf had inadvertently loosened the king's stranglehold on heavenly power by encouraging the cult of Ra. Soon the king's central position at the centre of the kingdom's administration was also disturbed when it was decided to appoint commoners rather than princes to the highest positions of responsibility. The vizier (*tjaty*) was the highest ranking official, in charge of managing the judiciary, architecture, state records and many other executive roles. Beneath the vizier were a number of 'overseers' and high officials who controlled expeditions, the treasuries, the granaries, the armouries and public works. All departments were based in Memphis in a single administrative compound, which also included the residential rooms of the royal household.

This changed during the Fifth Dynasty, when it evidently became difficult to run the country from Memphis and officials were sent from the capital to work in the administrative districts in their charge, known as nomes (*sepat*). Traditionally there were forty-two nomes, twenty in Lower Egypt and twenty-two in Upper Egypt, many of which were derived from Predynastic chiefdoms. The governors of the nomes, called nomarchs, were paid in land and kind, payments which were initially inseparable from the duty of the office and remained property of the king. Over time, the best administrative jobs came to be inherited and the payments became private property. The result was the seeping away of power and resources from the crown to numerous provincial centres, which began to rival the influence of Memphis. Djedkara (*c.*2414–2375 BC), the penultimate king of the dynasty, even instituted a vizier of Upper Egypt in recognition of the growing autonomy of the south of the country. Meanwhile, the king's family, bloated by polygamy and intermarriage into a tangled and extended web of dependents, were kept happy by being given parallel titles for each high office, for which they performed only ceremonial duties.

As the years went by, the tremendous wealth of the king leached into the hands of a new and burgeoning decentralised priestly and official class. Royal monuments diminished in scale and distinction, while private individuals began erecting increasingly impressive tombs, built from the best materials by the most proficient craftsmen. Neither were these 'nobles' concerned to be buried near their kings. Where once they had made their mastabas deferentially around the pyramids, hoping for the bounty and favour of the king in the after-life as they had in the royal court, they now built their tombs in the provinces or at sites of their choosing even in the royal necropolis. For example, just north of Saqqara at Abusir, the tombs of Ptahshepses, vizier to Djedkara, and the roughly contemporary Ty, the 'royal hair-dresser' and overseer of several important temples, boast some of the richest mastaba decorations in the Old Kingdom, celebrating – in beautifully executed, painted raised relief – the comfortable lives of two affluent court officials. Ptahshepses is even depicted enjoying a manicure and a pedicure in a faded mural above the entrance to his tomb.

PYRAMID TEXTS

By the end of the dynasty, it seems that the kings were undergoing a crisis of confidence in the early grand, monumental pyramids and the theology associated with them. They had probably by now seen that some of the most ingenious designs of their forefathers had not kept tomb robbers at bay, and perhaps wondered if the divinity of kingship guaranteed eternal life after all. As a result, magic formulae, spells and incantations came into use to protect the royal burial place and secure the passage of the deceased to a glorious existence in the afterlife. King Unas (c.2375–2345 BC), the last ruler of the Fifth Dynasty and owner of the smallest of the Old Kingdom pyramids, was the first to inscribe the formulae, known collectively as the 'Pyramid Texts', on the interior of his tomb at Saqqara. It was a practice that was copied by most of the Sixth Dynasty kings, who modified the texts and added their own spells according to their needs. The texts form the earliest substantial body of Egyptian religious literature, and much of the material was in oral circulation long before the reign of Unas, perhaps originating as far back as the Predynastic period.

Although the spells or 'utterances' were probably composed by Ra's priesthood at Heliopolis, they are the first to identify the dead king with Osiris, originally a Delta fertility god associated with vegetation and agriculture. Linked to the natural cycle of death and rebirth in the agricultural year, Osiris was an obvious deity to assume the role of god of the dead, lord of the underworld, who could resurrect the dead as he himself had been resurrected by his sister-wife Isis. The priests of Heliopolis incorporated him as a key deity in the sun Heliopolitan cult (see p.46), making Osiris the son of the sky goddess Nut, whose arching body, often seen decorating royal tombs and temple walls, symbolised the firmament. Every evening she would swallow the sun god Ra, and every morning give birth to him, renewing the day as Osiris yearly renewed the crops on the Nile. Nut became associated with coffin lids and was later commonly depicted on the underside of coffins and sarcophagi, swallowing the deceased inside her enveloping body like she did the sun, ready for rebirth in the hereafter. One Pyramid Text utterance says, 'O my mother, Nut, spread yourself over me, so that I may be placed among the imperishable stars and never die.'

Ironically, the extra assurances that the Pyramid Texts represent effectively debased the divine powers of the king, undermining his once innate right for a blessed existence in the beyond. Further changes in funerary belief were to come in later periods on the back of this development, as private individuals sought to identify themselves with Osiris as if they were kings (see p.70).

SIXTH DYNASTY DECLINE (*c.*2345–2181 BC)

At the beginning of the Sixth Dynasty, the king was still the most powerful man in the country, but his wealth and influence were crumbling away. There were still successes in external affairs, such as exploitation of minerals in the Sinai and the deserts, and expeditions to Byblos for cedar wood and Punt (an East African country thought to be somewhere around eastern Sudan and Eritrea) for prestige goods such as myrrh, incense, electrum, gold, ebony, ivory, resins, gums and exotic animals. Punitive military actions were conducted in the Palestine region, and beyond the First Cataract into Nubia to secure caravan routes. But domestic conditions were steadily deteriorating.

Teti (*c.*2345–2323 BC), the first king of the Sixth Dynasty, was reported by Manetho to have been assassinated, perhaps by his successor Userkara (*c.*2323–2321 BC). Pepy I (*c.*2321–2287 BC) strove to bolster royal influence in Upper Egypt by building monuments in the main religious centres (Abydos, Dendera, Hierakonpolis and Elephantine); donations and tax exemptions doled out to temples and villages in such cases bought influence but drained the royal treasury and diminished the crown's power. Pepy also married two daughters of a powerful official of Abydos, probably for political and financial necessity, a significant development because the king would normally have taken wives from within the royal circle. Incest was a royal prerogative that set the sovereign family apart from its subjects, a custom regularly practised by gods in myth and emulated by the king to ensure the divinity of his line. Common marriages made it ever harder to differentiate the king from the increasingly influential high officials and priests that served him. As it turned out, one of these queens plotted unsuccessfully to topple him from the throne.

Matters only worsened during the ninety-four-year reign of Pepy II (*c.*2278–2184 BC), the longest in the history of Ancient Egypt. As his reign dragged on decade by decade, the country's administration ossified and the underlying strains in the system came to the surface. The centralised economy and administration collapsed, and the state fell to pieces with the provinces slipping under the control of a number of local rulers. It was a situation that could not be reversed by his two short-reigning successors, Merenra II (*c.*2184 BC) and Queen Nitiqret (*c.*2184–2181 BC).

THE FALL OF THE OLD KINGDOM

The descent into confusion at the close of the Sixth Dynasty continued into the Seventh and Eighth Dynasties (*c.*2181–2160 BC), when a flurry of ephemeral kings came and fell from the throne in quick succession. The historian Africanus (*c.*180–250 AD) said that the Seventh Dynasty had 'seventy kings in seventy days' – no doubt an exaggeration, but the political chaos of the period is clear. The heavily centralised rule of the Old Kingdom had effectively ceased at the close of the Sixth Dynasty as power diffused outwards to local magnates in the provinces. The little-known kings of the Seventh and Eighth Dynasty struggled to rule the splintering country from the capital and in around 2160 BC this hallowed seat of authority fell when the Memphis royals were ousted by a new dynastic line ruling from Herakleopolis, near the entrance to the Fayum Depression. So the country descended into one of its darker periods, a time of obscure competing kings, rival territories and few monuments, an era traditionally characterised by civil war, famine and social disarray. Egypt's first great epoch was over – but there would be many others to follow.

CHAPTER THREE

Renaissance and Upheaval

The First Intermediate Period, the Middle Kingdom and the Second Intermediate Period (c.2160–1550 BC)

First Intermediate Period (c.2160–2055 BC): Egypt Divided

The eighteen or more kings of the Ninth and Tenth Dynasties could not hold dominion over the whole country as their Old Kingdom forebears had done. From Herakleopolis near the entrance to the Fayum Depression they ruled Lower Egypt and much of Middle Egypt (though often only through alliances with local magnates), but the southernmost nomes of Upper Egypt had fallen to local rulers who vied and tussled with each other for supremacy. This era of division and war between the two shining epochs of the Old and Middle Kingdom is known as the 'First Intermediate Period' (c.2160–2055 BC).

However, the period was not quite the 'dark age' that the histories have tended to portray, a misconception that can be blamed in large part on the so-called 'pessimistic texts' of the Middle Kingdom, such as the *Prophecy of Neferty* and the *Admonitions of an Egyptian Sage*, which talk of the desperation, upheaval, invasion, collapse and profanity of the period – propaganda and justification for the absolute authority of the Middle Kingdom pharaohs and the highly centralised system they employed.

Sources from the First Intermediate Period itself do mention famine, low inundations and economic crisis, but usually as dramatic backdrop to adulatory stories of local leaders serving society and protecting the vulnerable – part of their moral duty which was also integrally bound up in their right to rule. These rulers bragged of saving their towns from devastation and their people from starvation, as in the inscription of Ankhtifi, who ruled two nomes in Upper Egypt: 'I gave bread to the starving and clothing to the naked; I anointed those without oil and gave sandals to the barefooted. All of Upper Egypt was dying of hunger and people were eating their children, but I did not allow anyone to starve in this nome.'

The changing social make-up of a decentralised Egypt had also served to level out some of the more extreme inequalities of the past. Wealth was more evenly distributed as attested by the sudden and prolific appearance of funerary stelae for ordinary Egyptians, tombstones carved with immodestly self-important autobiographical inscriptions that reveal a new creativity in literature. Meanwhile, the better-off classes chose to be buried with the kind of funerary equipment once reserved for pharaohs, adopting regalia such as mummy masks, sceptres and crowns.

THEBAN ASCENDANCY

Nevertheless, the period certainly did have its crises, not least the protracted conflict between neighbouring provinces in Upper Egypt. After decades of attack and counterattack, Intef the Great (Eleventh Dynasty, *c.*2125–2112 BC), the nomarch of Thebes, prevailed and brought the six southernmost nomes under his command, declaring himself 'Great Overlord of Upper Egypt', writing his name in a royal cartouche and proclaimed himself king. He also built himself a huge *saff* tomb – a long sunken court decorated by a row (Arabic *saff*) of rock-hewn pillars around its sides leading to a chapel and burial shaft – that broke with the funerary traditions of the Old Kingdom and asserted a new and distinct Theban culture.

His brother, Intef II (*c.*2112–2063 BC) sparked off a war against the Herakleopolitan Tenth Dynasty kings when he captured Abydos, the key centre of Upper Egyptian administration, and pushed on towards Asyut in Middle Egypt. The war raged in fits and starts between Abydos and Asyut for several decades but there's little material to describe its highs and lows. The eventual Theban victory at Asyut was the beginning of the end for the Herakleopolitan rulers, whose authority quickly evaporated as their neighbouring local allies switched sides.

Middle Kingdom (c.2055–1650 BC)

It fell to Mentuhotep II (*c.*2055–2004 BC), probably the son of Intef III (*c.*2063–2055 BC) to win the final glory by seizing Herakleopolis itself, a task made easier by the untimely death of the Herakleopolitan king, Merykara, a few months before the attack. The city's smashed funerary monuments suggest that Mentuhotep showed his rivals little mercy, but his actions allowed him to reunite Egypt, providing the platform for another long period of prosperity, artistic accomplishments and political unity known as the Middle Kingdom.

In a reign that lasted fifty-one years, Mentuhotep II had time to consolidate his power, transforming Thebes from a provincial backwater to the capital of a resurgent Egypt. Under his leadership, mines were re-opened in Sinai for the extraction of gold and turquoise, quarries were again exploited for stone and building materials, and international trading links were re-established to obtain foreign goods; campaigns into Nubia regained control over goldfields; monument building picked up pace; and impetus was created for a renaissance in art, writing and architecture. It was a huge turnaround and Mentuhotep's successes were celebrated by ancient Egyptians almost a thousand years after his death.

He rooted out the nomarchs who had supported the Herakleopolitans, and employed his own officials to keep other governors in check, returning the country to strong central government. Mentuhotep asserted himself as a true royal, mixing his iconography with the divine, taking on godly names such as 'son of Hathor', and initiating a slew of building works. First among them was the lavish terraced mortuary complex at Deir el-Bahri on the Theban west bank, which blended the typically Theban *saff* tomb and the Old Kingdom mastaba, and signalled his clear intention to be worshipped as a god, anticipating the desires of New Kingdom pharaohs by almost five centuries. Mentuhotep's design for Deir el-Bahri was imitated and expanded by Queen Hatshepsut (*c.*1473–1458 BC) for her own temple lying just to the north, for which the site is now famous.

It was an auspicious beginning to the Middle Kingdom, but the longevity of his dynasty was destined to be short-lived, coming to an end less than twenty years after he died. Of his two successors, Mentuhotep III (*c*.2004–1992 BC), was a prolific builder and also the first of several kings of the period to oversee an expedition to Punt to procure exotic goods, and Mentuhotep IV (*c*.1992–1985 BC) sent quarrying teams into the Wadi Hammamat under his vizier Amenemhat. It's possible that there was a succession crisis at Mentuhotep III's death and Mentuhotep IV may have usurped the throne. At any rate, he seems of non-royal lineage and has been omitted from king lists. Little is known about him, whether he died naturally or had a legitimate heir, but his vizier, Amenemhat, appears to have taken the throne and founded the Twelfth Dynasty (*c*.1985–1773 BC).

AMENEMHAT I AND ITJTAWY, THE NEW CAPITAL

Amenemhat I (*c*.1985–1956 BC) tried to compensate for his common background with stories of miraculous omens, even during his trip to the Wadi Hammamat under Mentuhotep IV, that suggested he had been chosen for kingship by divine forces. Another piece of propaganda was the *Prophecy of Neferty*, likely to have been written around the time of his reign, and not so much a prophecy as a celebration of his sovereignty:

> But a king will come from the south,
> Ameny, the true of voice…
> He will take up the white crown,
> He will raise the red crown
> He will join the two [crowns]…
> Rejoice, people of his time!
> Asiatics will fall to his sword,
> Libyans will fall at his fire…
> Order is returned,
> And evil is cast out.
> Rejoice, whoever will see,
> Whoever will follow the king.

The desire for a symbolic break with the recent past and for a new beginning under his kingship may have been behind his decision to transfer the capital away from Thebes to Amenemhat–itj-tawy ('Amenemhat, possessor of the two lands'), often shortened to Itjtawy, thought to have been near the new royal necropolis at Lisht, some 30 miles (48km) south of modern Cairo. Its exact location is still unknown. The move may also have helped Amenemhat protect the country from attack by Libyans and 'Asiatics' (how Egyptologists translate the Egyptian word '*Aamu*', meaning people from the Near East), mentioned in the *Prophecy*.

Amenemhat I may also have introduced the 'co-regency', a mechanism to ensure the easy passage of power between kings, whereby the pharaoh and his chosen heir ruled simultaneously for part of the reign. His efforts may have helped legitimise his rule and consolidate the Egyptian state, but they were not enough to save him from assassination. We know of the crime from the *Instruction of Amenemhat I*, a literary text which presents the murdered king's story as if he were speaking to his son and successor, Senusret I (*c.*1956–1911 BC), from the afterlife. Senusret was leading a campaign in Libya at the time and the *Instruction*, apparently written on his behalf, upholds his claim to the crown. 'I awoke to fighting,' the dead king relates, 'but no one is strong in the night, no one can fight alone. My injury happened when you were not with me, when the court did not yet know that I would hand the throne to you.'

FOREIGN RELATIONS

Although Mentuhotep II had flexed his muscles in Lower Nubia and stationed soldiers in Elephantine for raids, foreign policy became far more aggressive during the Twelfth Dynasty. As heralded by the *Prophecy of Neferty*, Amenemhat I was not afraid of military action and was the first Middle Kingdom ruler known to have overseen campaigns against Near Eastern foes. He also constructed the 'Walls-of-the-Ruler', a celebrated fortress of the time, yet to be located, which guarded routes into north-eastern Egypt, as well as other strongholds in Lower Nubia. His son Senusret I was no less bellicose, describing himself as the 'throat-slitter of Asia' and he and his heir, Amenemhat II (*c.*1911–1877 BC), led campaigns into the Near East and Sinai, slaughtering or enslaving many hundreds of people. According to one inscription, the latter ruler came home from one sortie with 1554 Asiatic slaves.

Senusret I and Senusret III (*c.*1870–1831 BC) were the two most militaristic of the Middle Kingdom pharaohs, and jumbled oral histories of their exploits are likely to have given rise to the legendary figure of King Sesostris (the Greek form of the name), lionised in the writings of Herodotus and Manetho. Both kings waged a series of ferocious wars in Lower Nubia and Senusret I built a fortress at Buhen near the Second Cataract, effectively annexing it as an Egyptian province, while Senusret III was able to impose his will at least as far as the Third Cataract thanks to a chain of impressive brick fortresses constructed or strengthened during his reign, and later expanded by his son, Amenemhat III (*c.*1831–1786 BC). The forts and garrisons in Nubia gave the Egyptians control of a mineral-rich region famous for its gold, but also a source of turquoise, gneiss, copper and amethyst.

Senusret III, one of the most militaristic of the Middle Kingdom pharaohs

The Middle Kingdom relationship with the Near East was more complex. Several Twelfth Dynasty kings led campaigns into the Levant, but they appeared to have little desire to occupy and colonise the region, preferring to augment existing trade channels with important cities such as Byblos. There is no question that Asiatic leaders were strongly influenced by Egypt, adopting pharaonic titles and being buried with Egyptian objects. Rather it seems the main aims of these military forays were to capture slaves and discourage Asiatic nomads from drifting into the Delta. When Senusret III was on the throne, xenophobic feeling about Asiatics was running high judging by the large number of Near Eastern names on 'execration texts', lists of evil or enemy peoples and places written on jars or figurines which were smashed and buried in a symbolic ritual aimed to bring about their destruction. Egyptian anxiety about their neighbours was not entirely misplaced – by the end of the Thirteenth Dynasty (*c.*1773–1650 BC), it was the burgeoning Asiatic population in the Delta that contributed to the downfall of the Middle Kingdom.

Trading routes were well established with the Levant and Syria, but further indirect links seem to have been in place with Babylon, Cyprus and Anatolia. Expeditions were also sent to the African states of Kush (Upper Nubia) and Punt for luxury items. Contact with Crete is suggested by the appearance of Minoan pottery fragments in Egypt from this period as well as homemade imitations of Cretan styles; some Egyptian objects have also been found in Crete.

ART AND ARCHITECTURE

The Middle Kingdom was regarded by later Egyptians as a golden age for art and architecture. The cultural renaissance borrowed heavily from the Old Kingdom, and during the reign of Mentuhotep II, provincial Theban styles in relief carving were subsumed into those used by the Fifth Dynasty stoneworkers of Memphis, reflecting the desire to recapture the modes of Egypt's glorious past. The pyramid was also revived for royal burials and Twelfth Dynasty rulers built complexes at the royal necropolises of Lisht, Hawara, Lahun and Dahshur around the capital. The most famous and elaborate of these was at Hawara and belonged to Amenemhat III (*c.*1831–1786 BC). The vast complex included a mortuary temple with dozens of interconnecting colonnaded courtyards and hundreds of chambers linked by winding corridors, and became known as 'the Labyrinth' by classical authors, who considered it to be the model that the mythical Daedalus had used for the labyrinth of the Minotaur. They also thought it more impressive than the Pyramids of Giza and Herodotus called it a 'work beyond words'. Pliny noted that it had sections for each of twenty-one nomes, as well as temples for all of Egypt's many gods graced with ramps and stairways, columns of imperial porphyry, subterranean chambers, statues of kings and carvings of deities and monsters, while Diodorus Siculus warned it was 'impossible to find one's way out again without difficulty, unless one lights upon a guide who is perfectly acquainted with it'. He also claimed it was 'absolutely perfect in construction' when he was writing in the first century BC, but very little of it remains to be seen today.

The Middle Kingdom pharaohs built dozens of temples across Egypt. Senusret I alone erected monuments from Lower Nubia to Tanis in the northern Delta, his most important being a temple to the local Theban god Amun at Karnak, which during the New Kingdom would become the most important sanctuary in Egypt and Amun the principal deity. His 'White Chapel' there, a barque shrine carved from alabaster and decorated with exquisite raised reliefs, is deemed to be one of the most accomplished buildings at Karnak.

The largest architectural project of the Middle Kingdom was the Fayum irrigation system, a huge scheme probably completed during the reign of Senusret II (*c.*1877–1870 BC) that transformed the region's unworkable marshes into productive agricultural land. A network of irrigation canals and dykes were dug from the Bahr Yussef, the waterway linking the Nile to Lake Moeris (modern Lake Qarun) at the centre of the Fayum Depression which drew water away from the lake and surrounding swamps to irrigate land reclaimed from its receding shores. Senusret II favoured the Fayum and built a number of monuments in the area, as well as a pyramid at Lahun. Close to the remains of his pyramid, a large workman's village was discovered, complete with building tools, agricultural implements, household furniture, leather bags, cooking utensils, medical equipment, jewellery, cosmetics and children's toys. While most of our information from Ancient Egypt comes to us from the burial sites of royals and high officials, the Lahun village provides a glimpse into the lives of ordinary people. Among the finds were papyrus fragments discussing everyday matters, from records of grain production and tips on caring for livestock, to mathematical formulae, wills and tracts on women's health. The village was divided into walled-off districts, with workers housed in small mud-brick dwellings neatly set out in parallel rows, while the local priests and officials enjoyed more spacious lodgings.

The Middle Kingdom was a time of architectural innovation and it is a pity that so few buildings from the period have survived. Many were built of mud-brick which has not endured the centuries, while those of stone were routinely dismantled and reused by the New Kingdom pharaohs. As a result, what little is left of Middle Kingdom monuments compares unfavourably to the pyramids of the Old Kingdom and fabulous decorated tombs and temples of the New. Instead, the artistic legacy of the Middle Kingdom is less grandiose but no less impressive, boasting some of the best relief carvings of Ancient Egypt, some of the finest and most expressive statuary – the unmistakable world-weary eyes and drooping mouth of Senusret III, for example – and jewellery which scholars have lauded as unsurpassed throughout the entire ancient period. New techniques in gold working were introduced, such as granulation, and craftsmen had at their disposal a huge variety of additional skills, including repoussé and cloisonné work, most in evidence on the splendid pieces recovered from the shaft tomb of a princess in Senusret II's funerary complex at Lahun.

LITERATURE

The Middle Kingdom was also a fantastically rich period for literature, and its texts were regarded by later generations as paradigms of the form. A good selection of works has survived encompassing several genres including teachings, laments, hymns, insights and fiction. Among the best known are stories such as the *Shipwrecked Sailor*, whose narrative includes a tale within a tale within a tale, and the *Life of Sinuhe*, about the adventures of a palace official who flees Egypt after the murder of the pharaoh, a fictional reworking of the assassination of Amenemhat I. Of the laments, one of the most extraordinary is the *Dialogue between the Man Tired of Life and his Soul*, in which a man contemplating suicide is persuaded by his *ba* (see p.419) to cherish life.

While the hymns and teachings often revolve around the courts and kings, it is striking that many of the writings deal with people of lower social standing, ordinary people who frequently have extraordinary skills. The *Tale of Khuninpu*, often called *The Eloquent Peasant*, for instance, is about a simple man who is robbed on his way to market by a servant of a high official. Khuninpu finds the official and tells him what happened, but in such a compelling and eloquent manner that the official hurries to tell the king of the peasant's gift for oratory. The king determines to hear his masterful use of language by locking him up to extract ever more beautiful petitions, and the peasant complies, believing that his family is starving at home when they are being cared for by the king. Eventually the king sees justice done, punishes the official's servant and rewards the peasant for his talents. It is significant how the honesty of the simple peasant is set against the dishonesty of those more powerful, who cause his suffering. It can be read as an indictment of the corruption of power, but it also points to egalitarian trends emerging in Middle Kingdom society in which the virtues of individuals from the lower classes could be celebrated in ways that would have been impossible during the Old Kingdom.

'DEMOCRATISING' THE AFTERLIFE

The elevated position of the ordinary man was as evident in funerary practice as it was literature. In the Old Kingdom, individuals could only secure their place in the afterlife at the discretion of the king, who was himself reborn after death as Osiris, the lord of the underworld. During the Middle Kingdom, it became a common belief that anyone, not just the king, could be assimilated with Osiris in death, and be resurrected to win eternal life.

The change began with the collapse of the Old Kingdom and the dissipation of the king's power, when his subjects no longer looked to him for their safe passage into the afterlife. Wealthy Egyptians began to rely on their own resources, building their own tombs and appropriating elements of the Pyramid Texts, once reserved for the royal household, blending them with new formulae according to their circumstances. They decorated their coffins with these inscriptions, which are known as 'Coffin Texts', which were intended to guarantee their safe passage to and existence in the afterlife. In other words, the Coffin Texts gave everyone a chance to reach the hereafter regardless of their association with the king, a process that has been described as the 'democratisation of the afterlife'. During the Middle Kingdom, the democratisation had become so ingrained that even the lowliest citizens, who could not afford tombs and coffins, believed they could gain a place in the hereafter by leading a virtuous life.

Osiris was said to have the ultimate decision about who would be granted an eternal life, and his cult became increasingly important as a result. The god's original cult centre was probably at Busiris in the Delta, but during the Middle Kingdom, Osiris became associated with the tombs of the first Egyptian kings at Abydos, which consequently became the principal focus of the cult. Pilgrims flocked to the site, particularly when annual Mystery Plays were held celebrating his life, death and resurrection, and it became highly desirable to have some funerary connection with Abydos. Short of being buried there, the wealthy made arrangements to have their mummified corpses taken there for special rites before being interred in their local district. Others depicted boats on their coffins or tombs, or had model boats interred with them, which would symbolically carry them to Abydos after death. Thousands of funeral stelae were erected there in this period, a less expensive option for those not able to fund more elaborate shrines and memorial chapels.

Senusret III was the first Middle Kingdom ruler to build a cenotaph at Abydos, but royal interest in Osiris was strong from the beginning of the period. A statue of Mentuhotep II has the king's flesh painted black and his arms crossed on his chest, as Osiris is commonly portrayed. The rituals enacted in the Mystery Plays were also associated with the major ceremonies of a king's reign, his accession, coronation and jubilees as much as the natural cycles of life and death that Osiris represented. As such, the cult of Osiris was still closely connected to the divine elements of kingship, even if the god was now accessible to the population at large.

Immortality was not the guaranteed right of Osiris's worshippers, and acceptance into the afterlife hinged on the 'Judgement of the Dead', a trial before forty-two gods presided over by Osiris, that each Egyptian had to face on death. The defendant was required to profess innocence before each god in the form of a 'negative confession', an assertion of the wrongs that he had not committed in his lifetime. Then his heart was taken by Anubis, the jackal-headed god of embalming, and placed on a large set of scales to be weighed against a single feather of Maat, the goddess personification of truth and the universal order of things. To the ancient Egyptians, the heart – not the brain – was the seat of intelligence, memory and emotion, which would be heavily burdened by bad deeds. If the scales tipped towards the heart, then the heart was deemed false and thrown to a fearsome beast, part crocodile, part leopard, part hippopotamus, known as Ammut, which would gobble it up; the deceased would die a 'second death' and be condemned to oblivion. A heart that did not outweigh the feather was held to be 'true of voice', a verdict which Thoth, the ibis-headed god of writing and learning, duly recorded, and the deceased could enter the afterlife, known as the 'Field of Reeds', the domain of Osiris. There they would receive a verdant plot of fertile land that never suffered from drought or pestilence and produced bountiful harvests. For the poor, this was paradise indeed, but those who were already enjoying a privileged existence in the land of the living sought to avoid the labours of the afterlife by equipping their tombs with dozens of miniature *shabti* figurines, usually inscribed with instructions to work for their owners in the afterlife.

ORDINARY EGYPTIANS

Most Egyptians were simple farmers, who spent their lives in the fields dressed in a simple kilt or loincloth, toiling day after day to keep the country in food (see also 'Nile Agriculture' p.5-7). A lucky few had their own property and could barter their surplus produce at the market, but the majority were effectively serfs who worked on the vast royal and temple estates and had little chance of self-improvement. Even with 'the gift of the Nile', a peasant's life was hard (though the following extract from a scribal training text, the *Satire of the Trades* was a deliberate exaggeration of his travails):

> The farmer carries a yoke which over the years gives him a stoop and brings his neck up in blisters and festering sores… He works himself into an early grave…His fingers are bloated and stink to high heaven. He is exhausted from standing in the mud; his clothes are ragged and torn…

Once a harvest was in, farmers could expect a visit from the tax collectors. Penalties for non-payment could be severe:

> When he reaches the field… he does not see a green blade. He sows three times more with borrowed grain. His wife has gone to the merchants and found nothing to barter. Now the taxman turns up. He surveys the harvest. Attendants are behind him with sticks, Nubians with clubs. One says, 'Hand over the grain!' He replies, 'There is none.' He is beaten savagely. He is tied up, thrown in the well, dunked by the head. His wife is bound before his eyes. His children are put in chains. His neighbours abandon them and flee. When it is over, there is no grain.

Papyrus Lansing

Their principal crops were emmer wheat and barley, which were laboriously ground on millstones called saddle querns to make flour for bread and beer, the two foods that underpinned the Egyptian diet at all levels of society. A soldier's provisions, for example, included twenty rolls of bread per day, and traditional prayers for offerings inscribed in tombs included a plea for 'a thousand of bread, a thousand of beer'. The grit, sand and chips of millstone found in bread caused considerably damage to Egyptian teeth, judging from skeletal remains. Beer, widely believed to be an Egyptian invention, was made by crumbling partly baked barley loaves into water and adding malt; sometimes it was flavoured with spices, honey or dates. It was not necessarily very alcoholic, but was full of nutrients and safer to drink than river-water.

This cereal diet was supplemented by vegetables (especially onions and garlic, but also leeks, celery, radishes, lettuce, cucumbers and pulses), fish and wildfowl. Red meat was a luxury that only the wealthy could afford to eat regularly; although cattle farming (and animal husbandry) was widespread, a single cow was worth as much as a full year's income for a typical craftsmen – too much to blow on a meal. Wine, made from grapes grown in the Delta, was also mainly enjoyed by the upper classes.

A farmer's life was difficult, but few occupations were as hazardous and unpopular as mining and quarrying. Quarrymen picked and chiselled piece by piece in an open pit if they were lucky, or in cramped underground spaces if they were not. Worse still was the plight of the miners scratching away in the dark for gold and turquoise in deep and unsupported mine shafts. If they were not crushed to death by falling rocks, they probably died early of lung disease from dust inhalation. Little wonder that mining was usually reserved for convicts and prisoners of war.

The metals and semi-precious stones from the mines, as well as hardwoods from overseas, were royal monopolies, which meant that it was difficult for a craftsman to set up an independent business. Most worked for manufacturing estates and temples, and were not particularly highly regarded despite their evident skills and expertise. At least they themselves felt superior to the average Egyptian, if the tomb inscription of one sculptor is anything to go by: 'I am an artist who excels in my art, a man above the common herd in knowledge.' Herdsmen's lives, of course, did revolve around a common herd. They lived with their animals, leading them from pasture to pasture according to the season, defended them from the predations of crocodiles and hyenas, and carried sick animals on their backs.

In such a highly stratified society, few enjoyed such freedom as the marsh-dwellers of the Delta. They hunted and fished for their food, and gathered papyrus to trade at the market. Papyrus, the heraldic plant of Lower Egypt, was a sought-after commodity, used to make baskets, simple boats and writing material similar to paper, also called papyrus. The marsh-dwellers' food and produce was naturally occurring and abundant, allowing them to lead an unusually independent existence.

GOVERNMENT

The growing power of the Egyptian nomarchs (provincial governors) had been one of the forces that brought about the decline of the Old Kingdom, and the subsequent political instability of the First Intermediate Period. Mentuhotep II was swift to remove potentially dangerous nomarchs. As for those that remained, he scrutinised their activities closely with his own court officials, limiting their independence and influence. When he usurped the throne in about 1985 BC and established the Twelfth Dynasty, Amenemhat I found it necessary to reinstall some of the nomarchs' privileges if his initially precarious position as king was to be widely supported. At their strongest, nomarchs oversaw local courts, collected taxes and could raise armies, so any Egyptian king had to strike a careful balance between winning their allegiance and handing them too much power.

One of the most revered rulers of the Middle Kingdom, Senusret II, seems to have struck upon a solution to the problem by having the heirs of nomarchs educated at the royal palace from childhood. In this way, they not only became loyal to the king, but also learnt skills designed to be of use in other areas of the Egyptian state. They were well looked after, eventually accorded positions of high status and consequently had very little cause for complaint. Little by little, the post of nomarch began to disappear from administrative structure and town mayors, far less powerful officials, came to oversee the minutiae of provincial business. By the reign of Senusret III, only two nomarchs are reported to have been in office, apparently the last of the Middle Kingdom. The decline of the nomarchs is further attested by the fairly sudden demise of fine provincial tombs for nobles around this time, as wealth and power were diverted towards the capital.

A more serious structural change took place towards the end of the long and productive reign of Amenemhat III. The grand scale of the king's construction and mineral projects led him to import extra labour from the Near East. The large influx of Asiatic workers into Egypt began a process that would ultimately lead to the undermining of indigenous rule and the fall of the Middle Kingdom. This was a gradual development, however, that did not take full effect until decades after his death.

The obverse of a gold pectoral showing Amenemhat III smiting Egypt's
enemies – in this case the Asiatics

FALL OF THE MIDDLE KINGDOM

Amenemhat III enjoyed a prosperous reign, but in the last few years of
his forty-five-year rule, a series of low Nile inundations badly
disrupted agricultural production, triggering food shortages and
economic recession. It could not have helped matters that he died
shortly after, or maybe during, this crisis, and that his successor,
Amenemhat IV (*c.*1786–1777 BC), ruled for a relatively brief period.
He was probably married to his sister, Queen Sobeknefru
(*c.*1777–1773 BC), the last ruler of the Twelfth Dynasty. Little is known
about either monarch, but the 'Sobek' element of the queen's name
was regularly taken during the following dynasty, in reference to the
crocodile god, whose cult centre at Crocodilopolis in the Fayum had
become important. Queen Sobeknefru took masculine titles and
combined traditional male pharaonic forms of dress with more

feminine styles, an indication that she may have been attempting to placate those who objected to rule by a woman. In any case, she ruled for less than four years.

The two short reigns at the end of the Twelfth Dynasty seemed to set the standard for the Thirteenth (*c.*1773–1650), which saw a quick procession of kings, apparently from a number of different families as the elite tried in vain to provide a succeeding line. At times the speed of change at the top was so swift, with some kings lasting only weeks or even days, that it has been suggested a system of royal 'circulation' was in use, whereby rulers regularly swapped throne, but there is no hard evidence for this. Curiously, the Middle Kingdom state purred on during the first half of the Dynasty, seemingly unaffected by the rapid-fire change of monarch at its head. The capital remained Itjtawy, taxes were collected, the lands won in Nubia were held, the arts flourished, and royal building works continued across the country – though judging from what has been recovered from the period, these monuments were not of the same quality as the Twelfth Dynasty, perhaps indicating the diminished resources of the kings.

The lack of continuity and stability at the apex of government eventually took its toll about halfway through the Thirteenth Dynasty. Reduced royal circumstances damaged the integrity of the Egypt's borders, and by the later years of the eighteenth century BC, non-acculturated Asiatics were beginning to establish themselves in the north-eastern Delta, particularly at Avaris, the modern-day archaeological site of Tell el-Daba. The town already had a prominent Asiatic population, which had been brought to Egypt to serve in the households of the wealthy, or in royal or public building works. Avaris itself was a strategically important town on one of the main routes into Sinai and Syria–Palestine, and as such, a centre for trade and a base for mining expeditions. Gradually, Asiatics took control of influential positions in the local administration and eventually found themselves in charge of much of the state's import and export operations with the Near East. Before long, they effectively had control over the town, its environs, the local population and lucrative international trade. At first, they recognised the primacy of the Egyptian king, but not long after the reign of Sobekhotep IV Khanaferre (*c.*1720 BC), the last ruler of the Thirteenth Dynasty to wield real power, the ruler of Avaris, Nehesy, decided to establish his own royal house, so founding the obscure Fourteenth Dynasty. Shortly afterwards, indigenous agitation in the Nubian territories led to the establishment of a line of native kings at Kerma in Kush. As no single monarch could lay claim to the whole of the country, the Middle Kingdom, Egypt's second great flowering, drew to a close ushering in a second intermediate period of disunity when poorly documented kings ruled from various provincial power centres.

Second Intermediate Period (c. 1650–1550 BC)

THE HYKSOS

The Fourteenth Dynasty (*c.*1773–1650 BC) kings ruled from Avaris while the last kings of the Thirteenth Dynasty held sway from the traditional Middle Kingdom seat of Itjtawy. However, at some point around the middle of the seventeenth century BC, a group known as the 'Hyksos' took control of Avaris and Lower Egypt, establishing the Fifteenth Dynasty (*c.*1650–1550 BC) and triggered a collapse of native authority at Itjtawy; Egyptian power retreated southwards to Thebes and other Upper Egyptian centres, from where the kings of the Sixteenth (*c.*1650–1580 BC) and Seventeenth Dynasties (*c.*1580–1550 BC) ruled contemporaneously with the Hyksos.

The name 'Hyksos' comes from a Greek corruption of the Egyptian '*hekau khasut*', meaning 'rulers of foreign countries', generally held to be speakers of western Semitic languages from the Near East. Exactly how the transition was made between the early Avaris kings and the Hyksos, and what the relationship was between them is not known. Josephus, quoting Manetho, claims that the Hyksos launched an all-out invasion:

> …from the regions of the east, invaders of ignoble birth marched in confidence of victory against our land. By force they easily prevailed without striking a blow; and having overpowered the rulers of the land, they then burned our cities ruthlessly, razed to the ground the temples of the gods, and

treated all the natives with a cruel hostility, massacring some and leading into slavery the wives and children of others. Finally they appointed King Salitis. He had his seat at Memphis, levying tribute from Upper and Lower Egypt and always leaving garrisons in the most advantageous positions...

There is scant archaeological evidence to support the level of destruction that Josephus suggests, and it's more likely the Hyksos came up from the higher Asiatic echelons of Avaris society established after decades of immigration into the Delta, rather than from a rampaging foreign horde. On the other hand, it is true that Memphis fell well within their territory and would have made a more convenient base to administer Lower Egypt than Avaris, the location of the royal residence. The Hyksos had a border control at Cusae (near modern-day Mallawi), about 155 miles (250km) south of Memphis, where taxes were levied on anyone travelling into their lands.

In contrast to the native Egyptian kings of the time, the Hyksos seem to have enjoyed relatively stable governance: six kings whose combined reigns totalled 108 years. Much about their way of life at Avaris and system of government was Egyptian, which also suggests a more gradual handover of power than is typical of an invasion. They maintained the same administrative structure and official titles, but changes in the arrangement and makeup of houses, and the burial of the dead within residential areas is indicative of foreign influence. In religious terms, the Hyksos worshipped the god Seth, probably as an adaptation of a Syrian storm god – showing the importance of weather to a people that relied on international trade that included shipping routes across the Mediterranean. They introduced many new technologies into Egypt from the Near East, not least several military innovations such as the horse and chariot, the composite bow (made in layers of wood and horn for greater drawing power and range), and new alloys of bronze for sharper, harder weaponry – advances which would enable Egypt to become a militaristic empire during the New Kingdom. They also brought an improved potter's wheel, the vertical loom, new vegetables and fruits, new livestock, including woolly sheep and the hump-backed zebu cow, as well as new musical instruments such as the tambourine and harp.

The Hyksos also seem to have had immense respect for Egyptian culture, and during the reign of Apepi (*c.*1555 BC), the longest-lived and most powerful of their kings, orders were given to copy and preserve the great documents of Egyptian learning, which even at that time were regarded as ancient. Among them was an extraordinary medical treatise originally dating to Early Dynastic Egypt known now as the Edwin Smith Papyrus, which provides instructions on how to treat a range of conditions like fractures, sprains, wounds and tumours. The so-called Rhind Papyrus was also copied for posterity at this time, and is now one of the oldest mathematical documents in existence.

KUSH AND THEBES

The Hyksos maintained relations with the Nubian kings of Kush based at Kerma, south of the Third Cataract, by means of a trading route via the Western Desert oases that bypassed the Egyptian-controlled areas. The Theban kings also dealt with the Nubians for valuable minerals such as amethyst, diorite and gold. The chain of Nubian fortresses built during the Middle Kingdom had by now slipped into the hands of the Kushites and their fearsome bowmen, and Egyptians had to pay for the privilege of travel in Lower Nubia.

It was a difficult time for the native Egyptian kings: large portions of their country were being ruled by foreign kings; they had lost direct access to important trading partners in Asia and the Mediterranean; and with the resurgent powers at Kush, exotic goods from the south were harder to come by. Worse still, the sacred scriptures kept in the repositories of learning at Memphis were out of reach. This may have prompted Thebans to compose a new set of texts for funerary rituals, and one of the earliest collection of spells now known as the *Book of the Dead* was found on the coffin of a Sixteenth Dynasty queen. The Thebans had few resources to train new generations of scribes and craftsmen and the artistic standards of the Middle Kingdom could not be maintained. Material culture was similarly impoverished. Crude sycamore coffins appeared where immaculate caskets of cedar would once have been used, and tombs were either left undecorated or recycled from an earlier period.

'Let me understand what this strength of mine is for! One prince is in Avaris and another is in Kush, and here I sit associated with an Asiatic and a Nubian! Each man has his slice of Egypt, dividing up the land with me.' Such was the lament of King Kamose (*c.*1555–1550 BC), the last king of the Seventeenth Dynasty, who decided that this unfortunate state of affairs should not be allowed to continue: 'I will wrestle with him that I may slice open his belly! My wish is to save Egypt and smite the Asiatic!'

WAR ON AVARIS

The antagonism between Avaris and Thebes was already acute by the time Kamose made his vow to rid Egypt of the Asiatics. According to a story written 350 years later, the Hyksos king Apepi had sent an insulting message to Seqenenra Tao II (*c.*1560 BC), Kamose's predecessor, complaining that bellowing Theban hippopotami were keeping him awake at night. Seqenenra gathered his advisors, but the concluding part of the papyrus is lost and it is not known if he managed to concoct any scathing reply in return. However, it does appear that this was the narrative preamble to a war between the kingdoms, which in reality lasted for at least thirty years and ended with the reunification of Egypt. It seems that Seqenenra himself did not survive its early stages; his remains reveal a shattered cheekbone and a forehead marked by a blow from an Asiatic axe. Having fallen he was stabbed in the back of the neck to hasten his dispatch.

From the bombastic inscriptions on two commemorative stelae, we know that Kamose took up the Theban cause against Apepi with relish: 'As the mighty Amun endures, I will not leave you alone. I will not let you tread the fields without being upon you. O wicked of heart, vile Asiatic.' First he secured his southern front, pushing the Kushites out of Lower Nubia as far as Buhen, and then turned his attention northwards, laying waste with his army and war boats to the border control at Cusae. As he continued towards Avaris, he intercepted a messenger heading for Kush to request help, and immediately sent troops west to raze Bahariya Oasis, severing the Hyksos' inland communication channel. When he reached the capital, he encircled it, positioning his fleet in all the surrounding watercourses and his foot-soldiers along the river banks. The inscriptions trumpet his success: 'I shall drink the wine of your vineyard, which the Asiatics whom I captured press for me. I lay waste to your dwelling place, I cut down your trees. After I deposited your women in the ships' holds, I took away your chariots.' He and his army plundered the land, taking off 'gold, lapis-lazuli, silver, turquoise, and innumerable bronze battle-axes…oil, incense, fat, honey, and precious woods'. 'I carried them off completely,' Kamose taunts. 'I did not leave a scrap of Avaris without being empty.'

Kamose returned to Thebes a hero, and was worshipped as such by Egyptians for several centuries after his death, but his campaign was arguably of limited success, as he failed to reunify the land and banish the Hyksos. Perhaps the story would have been different had Kamose not died after only five years as king; Apepi, his Hyksos counterpart, also died around this time, and it seems both sides paused to regroup. The new Theban king, Ahmose (*c.*1550–1525 BC), was only a small child when he came to the throne, and his mother, Ahhotep took charge of the kingdom until his majority. As a result at least eleven years passed until the Thebans were ready to engage in war again.

THE EXPULSION OF THE HYKSOS

Ahmose launched the final attack against the Hyksos, sailing up the Nile during the summer inundation to capture Heliopolis. When the water level began to drop off in October, he deployed his chariotry, assaulting Tell el-Habua at the north-eastern edge of the Delta to prevent the Hyksos from escaping into Sinai. He then laid siege on Avaris. According to Josephus, the Hyksos 'gave up the siege in despair', and their king Khamudi 'concluded a treaty by which they should all depart from Egypt…On these terms the Hyksos, with all their possessions and households complete…left Egypt and journeyed over the desert into Syria.'

The archaeological record from Avaris and Memphis shows that at this time the kind of ceramics associated with the Asiatic influence completely disappear while there is no obvious sign of a massacre, suggesting that Josephus's history may be accurate on this point.

Ahmose made the largest possible territorial gains in the void left by the Hyksos, adding to his victory by capturing the town of Sharuhen in Palestine after a siege of three years. He also travelled to the south to shore up his Nubian border at Buhen, and quashed two internal uprisings before embarking on the restoration of some of Egypt's great religious centres: Heliopolis, Memphis, Abydos and Karnak. He tore down the Hyksos palace at Avaris, and built his own, curious for its Minoan-style frescos with labyrinthine patterning, bulls and leaping acrobats, imagery quite alien to the Egyptian canon but used perhaps because of his political marriage to a Cretan princess.

By the time Egypt was reunified and its borders secure, Ahmose's dynamic reign was almost at an end. Although of the same line as the late Seventeenth Dynasty kings, his achievements had such long-lasting effects that he was regarded as the first king of the Eighteenth Dynasty (*c.*1550–1295 BC), arguably the most famous dynasty in ancient Egyptian history. He had set the foundations for a new empire and a long period of unrivalled wealth and power known as the New Kingdom.

CHAPTER FOUR

The New Kingdom

c.1550–1069 BC

Thebes

The rise of Thebes from a dusty provincial village to the most glorious city on earth was completed during Egypt's greatest imperial age, now known as the New Kingdom. It was an era of unparalleled power and prosperity, in which a succession of Egypt's most famous pharaohs cultivated luxurious and extravagant styles in art and architecture, and commissioned some of the grandest buildings that the world had ever seen. Naturally enough, the focus of the activity was the metropolis and capital of the empire, Waset, better known to us by its Greek name Thebes, and now called Luxor from the Arabic *al-qasr*, meaning 'palace' after the palatial ruins of its gigantic temples. At its peak during the Eighteenth and Nineteenth Dynasties, the city was inhabited by a million people, over ten times its current population; no other city in the world could match it for size for centuries and in the modern era Beijing and London only reached this number in around 1800, more than three millennia later. Its opulence was a marvel to Egypt's neighbours; in Homer's *Iliad*, it is held up as the supreme example of a rich and powerful capital 'where the houses are crammed with treasures, a city of a hundred gates, through each of which two hundred warriors sally forth with their chariots and horses'.

Even though Thebes's influence quickly shrank after the collapse of the New Kingdom, its vast stone monuments and temples endured. When the city's great obelisks and pylons suddenly came into view before Napoleon's troops as they approached in 1799, an officer recalled that 'without an order being given, the men formed their ranks and presented arms, to the accompaniment of the drums and bands'. Ever since this moment of rediscovery, Thebes has been a major centre of archaeological research and its three principal sites – Karnak, the Temple of Luxor, and the Theban Necropolis – are always among the highlights of any tour of Egypt. The concentration of majestic temples and tombs, so many of them still beautifully preserved, is breathtaking and it is easy to imagine that the pharaohs, ever driven to impress their greatness on the world for eternity, would be pleased that their illustrious buildings still reduce people to awed and reverential silence.

KARNAK

As well as being the capital of the empire, Thebes also contained the spiritual heart of the nation, a suitably gargantuan religious complex – in fact, one of the largest ever built – called Ipet-isut, 'the most esteemed of places', now known by its Arabic name, Karnak. Thebans considered it the site of creation, the place of 'the majestic rising of the first time', where Amun-Ra had brought the world into being from the primordial ocean. Amun had been the local Theban god, but had assumed the qualities of the older sun god Ra, dominant during the Old Kingdom, to become Amun-Ra, the 'king of gods' and supreme deity of the New Kingdom.

Karnak was an immensely wealthy institution and during the zenith of its powers counted amongst its assets 81,000 workers, 422,000 cattle, 239,500 hectares (591,800 acres), 433 gardens, 83 ships and 65 villages. It comprised three vast precincts surrounded by trapezoidal enclosure walls dedicated to Montu (a falcon-headed god of war), Mut (a vulture goddess), and most importantly, Amun-Ra. Within these precincts were subsidiary temples to a number of other deified kings and gods, such as Khonsu, a moon god and son of Amun and Mut, who together comprised the holy family of Thebes, the 'Theban triad'.

The Temple of Amun-Ra dominates the complex. Built over a period of thirteen centuries, it is a bewildering agglomeration of courts, pylons, halls, obelisks, colossal statues and shrines, encompassing an area large enough to accommodate the world's largest cathedral, synagogue, Buddhist temple, church and mosque in one. Its extraordinary size and magnificence were derived from its central importance as both the earthly residence of the highest god and the site of royal coronations and jubilees, the source of kingly legitimacy for all the New Kingdom pharaohs.

An imposing processional way runs east-west through six pylons and the crowning glory of the entire complex, the Great Hypostyle Hall (see p.119), to the secluded shadows of the inner sanctuary where the sacred image of Amun, 'the hidden one', 'mysterious of form', resided. The precinct was out of bounds to ordinary people, but only the pharaoh or high priests could enter this most holy core. Halfway down, by a vast sacred lake, a second axis cuts away at right-angles through four more pylons and an avenue of sphinxes towards the Precinct of Mut, Amun's consort. The holy congress between Amun and Mut was celebrated each year during the Opet festival, one of the year's most important feasts lasting several weeks, when the average Egyptian had a chance to pay his respects to Amun as his likeness was carried from Karnak to the Temple of Luxor (see p.101) on a cedar-wood barque, which was lined with silver and adorned with gold.

Emerging Empire

Ahmose (*c.*1550–1525 BC), the first pharaoh of the Eighteenth Dynasty (*c.*1550–1295 BC), succeeded in driving the hated Hyksos out of Egypt and reunifying the country – marking the start of the New Kingdom. Soon taxes and tributes began pouring into the state's empty coffers, trade routes were re-established, and mines and quarries re-opened to supply the king's artisans with materials to build a resurgent nation. The world outside had changed during Egypt's occupation and Ahmose recognised his realm could not expect to be the isolated kingdom of the past, insulated from its neighbours by geography and culture. New powers were emerging in the Near East, and Ahmose determined that his army could no longer be composed of corvée labourers and mercenaries, and transformed it into a professional fighting machine of polished infantry and chariot units that would strike terror in the nation's enemies. He was soon able to secure the Nubian border and stamp his authority on Palestine, which became both a buffer zone for protection and a launching-pad for further expansion.

The king also began to repair the country's neglected temples, paying special attention to the local god of Thebes, Amun, who was credited with the recent change of Egyptian fortunes. He refurbished the temple for Amun at Karnak, reinvigorating a cult that would soon become the nation's richest and most important, and instituted a direct link between the royal family and Amun by making his queen Ahmose Nefertari 'god's wife of Amun', the deity's earthly consort for religious ceremonies, emphasising the idea that kings were the offspring of the supreme god. The 'god's wife of Amun' was granted an independent income and later came to wield considerable political and religious power through her association with Amun's influential priesthood. It is no coincidence that a series of prominent and powerful royal women came to the fore during the New Kingdom.

After Ahmose's death in about 1525 BC, his wife became regent on behalf of their young son and successor, Amenhotep I (*c.*1525–1504 BC), who had been thrust into the spotlight following the unexpected death of the crown prince. Amenhotep's was a relatively quiet reign, as free from calamity as from the military panache that glamorised the reigns immediately before and after. Nonetheless, between Ahmose's dynamic changes and Amenhotep's stabilising influence, a blueprint of a highly successful state had been drawn and the foundations laid for the remaining pharaohs of the Eighteenth Dynasty to build an empire and become the wealthiest, most powerful and famous kings of the Ancient World.

THUTMOSE I: WARRIOR KING

Amenhotep I had no heir, but his chosen successor seems to have taken the throne without a hint of trouble from possible rivals. A high-born general probably with links to the royal family, Thutmose I (*c.*1504–1492 BC) was an inspired choice, a man whose comparatively short reign was to leave a deep impression. He married Ahmose, thought to be the daughter of the venerated queen Ahmose Nefertari, to bolster his royal ties, and declared that he was the child of Osiris, establishing a standard of divine descent which became a strong feature of the dynasty.

In the second year of his reign, he launched an attack to 'repel the intruders from the desert region' of Nubia, but he surged far beyond the Fourth Cataract and made the whole region Egypt's colony. The stelae he left along the route described the bloody campaign: 'The Nubian bowmen fall by the sword and are thrown aside on their lands; their stench floods their valleys...The pieces cut from them are too much for the birds that carry off the prey to another place.' As a gruesome coda, he returned to the Temple of Amun at Karnak with the body of a Nubian, probably the king of Kush, dangling from the prow of his ship, a dreadful warning to those who dared to challenge Egypt's might.

Thutmose also had imperial ambitions for the Near East and was the first of the New Kingdom pharaohs to bring large parts of the Levant under his control. At this time the region was governed by a number of semi-independent city-states, some of which were allied to the powerful Mitanni kingdom, which itself roughly corresponded to modern Syria, southeastern Turkey and western Iraq. An astute soldier, Thutmose chose not to go up against the full force of the Mitanni army on his first expedition, preferring to skirmish with a few lesser Mitanni vassals. Even so, he went as far as Carchemish and erected a victory stela on the far bank of the Euphrates, before marching home in triumph, stopping only to hunt elephants on the way. In reality, his successes in Syria were fairly limited, but he had awakened interest in the possibilities of expansion into western Asia.

Like Ahmose, Thutmose made lavish offerings to Amun in grateful appreciation of his victories on the battlefield, and began a complete overhaul of the temple at Karnak, replacing mud-brick for sandstone, constructing two imposing ceremonial gateways (the Fourth and Fifth Pylons), and raising a pair of magnificent 75ft-high (23m) obelisks, one of which still stands. He also built a mortuary temple to himself on the west bank at Thebes, the fragments of which are scattered around Deir el-Bahri. Amenhotep I had been the first king to build his mortuary temple and tomb in separate locations, the former in a prominent place for worship and offerings, and the latter secreted away to thwart tomb robbers. Thutmose followed the example and was the first to build his tomb in the Valley of the Kings not far from his temple, beyond a crest of hills and away from rapacious eyes. This set the standard for the rest of the New Kingdom, starting a trend which eventually saw the construction of sixty-three royal tombs in this parched and crumbling valley, and a string of stunning mortuary temples on the west bank of the Nile at the fringes of the desert.

DEIR EL-MEDINA

The continuous construction at the Theban necropolis from the time of Amenhotep onwards demanded a dedicated team of craftsmen, builders, painters and sculptors, who set up residence on the west bank at Deir el-Medina, a village for the families of the royal workforce. Its compact houses were enclosed by high walls, the gateway to which was guarded by trusted court officials; the workers were searched to make sure no precious materials were stolen, and cut off from the outside world so that the secrets of the royal tombs would never leave the village. In return, the state paid them with regular supplies of wheat, barley, beer, salted fish, onions and beans, and on special occasions bonus supplies of sesame oil, salt and meat. Such privileges put them well above farmers and standard artisans. These were special craftsmen, who, unlike most of the population, knew how to read and write. They made notes on their work and business using stone flakes and pottery shards, which have become an invaluable source of information for archaeologists. Some villagers even kept small collections of books, one of which, the *Dream Book*, listed the interpretations of dreams:

> If a man sees himself in a dream looking out of a window, then good – his god will answer him.

> If a man sees himself in a dream drinking a warm beer, then bad – he will soon suffer.

> If a man sees himself in a dream with a bare backside, then bad – he will soon be an orphan.

As with most trades, expertise was passed on through the generations, father to son. The village flourished until the late Twentieth Dynasty (*c*.1186–1069 BC), when payments were reduced or failed to appear altogether, prompting the world's first strikes and sit-ins.

HATSHEPSUT, THE FEMALE KING

Thutmose I was already into his middle years when he became king, and his royal wife, Ahmose, had borne him a daughter – the formidable Hatshepsut (*c*.1473–1458 BC) – but no son. Fearing a crisis at his death, the pharaoh singled out another Thutmose, the child of one of his harem wives. In case his bloodline was not considered suitably royal, the young Thutmose was married to his half-sister, Hatshepsut, already an imposing figure at court and 'god's wife of Amun'. At the end of his father's glorious eleven-year reign, Thutmose II (*c*.1492–1479 BC) assumed the throne with Hatsheput, but before he was able to make much of a mark, he died unexpectedly. Contrary to the chronology, there is evidence that he may only have reigned for three years. His mummified corpse revealed a rash of scabs across his body, possibly an indication of a sudden fatal disease but perhaps just the result of mistakes made during the embalming process.

In their short time together, Hatshepsut had had a daughter by him, and once again the kingdom passed to the son of a concubine, Thutmose III (*c*.1479–1425 BC). The new king was little more than an infant, however, and his aunt and step-mother, Hatshepsut, following a precedent that dated back to the Old Kingdom, stepped in as regent. For the first couple of years, she was the model guardian, overseeing affairs of state dutifully on the young boy's behalf. But after six years as regent, Hatshepsut declared herself king.

Her claim to sovereignty could hardly have been harmed by her exceptional royal breeding. She was the daughter of Thutmose I and his principal queen (known as the 'great royal wife'), Ahmose, and a direct descendant of Ahhotep, the influential and revered mother of King Ahmose, the founder of the dynasty. Hatshepsut may have felt that she had a right to rule regardless of her marriage to Thutmose II, and she had reliefs carved at her mortuary temple that depicted

Thutmose I choosing her as heir, while other scenes have her as the divine child of the god Amun. Her unchallenged rise to the top is a measure of how powerful royal women had become, thanks to institutions such as the 'god's wife of Amun' and the gradual accumulation of influence and respect since the wars with the Hyksos, when a series of strong royal women were relied upon to look after the running of the country while the kings were away fighting. The practice of incest within the royal family also enhanced the exclusivity of royal women and their association with the divine realm. Kings of the Eighteenth Dynasty were encouraged to marry their sisters and occasionally even daughters, who were forbidden from wedding commoners no matter how highborn nor even foreign royals. These royal wives and daughters usually became the most important members of the king's harem, and the 'great royal wife' was second only to the king in status. Meanwhile, the royal gene pool was kept healthy by secondary commoner wives, who were relied on to provide the king with princes. Only one, however, the crown prince was part of the royal nuclear family, consisting of king, 'great royal wife' and her daughters. The closed-off nature of the family was naturally very effective at preventing challenges for the throne from outside, while thwarting the dissipation of royal wealth over the generations.

There seems to have been little resistance to Hatshepsut's assumption of kingship, and indeed she ruled Egypt for twenty years without trouble, except for the odd local disturbance in Nubia which she suppressed as competently as any man. The political stability allowed her to exploit fully the gold and turquoise mines and the quarries for fine stone, as well as to mount trade missions for special goods. The most celebrated of these was the expedition to Punt – colourfully recorded inside her temple at Deir el-Bahri – which returned laden with highly prized exotica including ebony, ivory, incense, resins and fragrant trees transported in specially designed baskets. A prolific builder, Hatshepsut started works across the country including several sites in Middle Egypt, a region which had been largely neglected since the arrival of the Hyksos. But she was no more active than at Thebes. At the Temple of Amun she added a new sandstone gateway (the Eighth Pylon), a barque shrine of red granite and two soaring obelisks plated in electrum (an alloy of gold and silver) to symbolise the shining rays of sunlight at the dawn of creation. Only one obelisk remains, but at 97ft (30m), it is the tallest left in Egypt. The mammoth unfinished obelisk at Aswan, also thought to have been one of her projects, would have stood at nearly 137ft (42m), making it the world's tallest had it not developed a flaw during quarrying.

HATSHEPSUT'S TEMPLE AT DEIR EL-BAHRI

Easily the most famous of Hatshepsut's monuments is her mortuary temple at Deir el-Bahri on the Theban west bank, deemed by many to be among the most beautiful ancient Egyptian monuments ever built. At the base of a sweeping arc of high cliffs, the elegant ramps and colonnaded limestone terraces of Hatshepsut's temple, named by her '*djeser djeseru*' ('holy of holies'), was the architectural centrepiece of her reign, incorporating in its decoration and inscriptions all the highlights of her life and rule. Cooled with trickling fountains and scented with aromatic myrrh trees imported from Punt, it was dedicated to Amun, but combined a variety of shrines and chapels on its three tiers as well

Queen Hatshepsut's temple at Deir el-Bahri on the Theban west bank, one of the most beautiful of ancient Egyptian monuments

as a large alabaster altar for the solar cult, and offering places for Hatshepsut herself and her father.

One of the curiosities of the building are the dozens of portraits of Senenmut, the royal architect, secreted around the temple in dark corners and alcoves hidden behind doors. The self-promotion of a commoner in such sacred precincts was unheard of, but Senenmut may have been Hatshepsut's lover, so it is likely that these images were accepted and approved. Senenmut even began to excavate his own tomb – some say in secret – beneath the temple, but he suddenly disappears from the historical record before it was completed. It is tempting to imagine that Hatshepsut made him pay the ultimate price for his violation of her holy temple; after all, the warning 'he who shall do her homage shall live, he who shall speak evil in blasphemy of her Majesty shall die,' was incised on her temple walls. The more prosaic truth is likely to be that he died from natural causes.

REWRITING HISTORY

About twenty years after Thutmose III nominally became pharaoh, his step-mother, Hatshepsut, either died or stood aside, allowing him at last to take the throne. It is popularly believed that Thutmose was so enraged about having waited on the sidelines for so long that he took revenge by the systematic removal of Hatshepsut's mark from Egypt's monuments: her likenesses were hacked out of reliefs, her statues destroyed, her name cleanly chiselled away and sometimes replaced by his own or his father's as if she had never existed. Even her glorious obelisks at Karnak were hidden out of view behind high sandstone walls.

In reality, the *damnatio memoriae* of Hatshepsut began some twenty-five years later towards the end of Thutmose's reign and was continued by his son, Amenhotep II (*c.*1427–1400 BC) – hardly the swift act of hot retribution from a furious wronged man. Indeed, there is nothing to suggest that Thutmose or his courtiers resisted or opposed Hatshepsut at any time during her reign. It is more likely that he was preparing for Amenhotep II's succession and attempting to block any pretenders from among Hatshepsut's surviving relatives by erasing her record from history. Although expunged from the sacred king lists, Hatshepsut had made a deep enough impression to live on in folk memory at least until 300 BC when Manetho noted that the fifth ruler of the Eighteenth Dynasty was a female.

WOMEN

As pharaoh, Hatshepsut had been portrayed as a man, because the role of king was regarded as an intrinsically masculine one. This reflected a general truth about Egyptian society: women could be rich and powerful, and even become pharaoh, but their status was lower than that of men. Even so, Egyptian women enjoyed a degree of equality not often seen in the Ancient World, and in theory had the same rights as men in front of the law. A wife could represent her husband in business, at the market, or in the courts. She could buy, sell, own and inherit property. She could live or find work away from home.

Except for the very richest women, however, things were a little different in practice. Men had the greatest access to the best jobs and were more likely to be educated, while women were generally illiterate and left to look after the household. Only the highest born women were likely to receive a formal education and participate in government and administration, although it seems that there were never any female scribes. Neither was it a great boon to have property rights if all your worldly possessions amounted to a few rags and the odd pot, as was the case for the majority. Most ordinary married women would have been too busy to find work elsewhere, attending to the needs of their children, making clothes, washing them, and grinding grain for bread and beer. While her husband's business revolved around the outside world, the typical wife found herself within the confines of the small family hut; no wonder that men are often depicted in art as tanned and robust, while women seem pale and delicate. Double standards were also in evidence when it came to adultery. Though frowned upon, a married man could sleep with single women (or pay a visit to the country's thriving brothels), but an unfaithful wife could expect severe punishment.

But everyday Egyptians of both sexes cherished their families and preferred a harmonious domestic life above all things. While literature written by women is virtually unknown, pieces written on the subject of keeping a woman happy enjoyed long popularity, such as the *Instruction of Ptahhotep*:

> If you take a wife... let her be more content than her fellows. She will be twice as firmly attached to you if her chain is pleasant. Do not upset her; grant that which pleases her; it is to her contentment that she appreciates your work... If you are wise, look after your house; love your wife with all your heart. Fill her stomach and clothe her back... Make her happy as long as you live... Be not brutal; tact will persuade her better than violence...It is that which keeps her with you; if you repel her, it is an abyss. Embrace her, respond to her arms; call her, display to her your love.

Superpower

THE EGYPTIAN NAPOLEON

When sovereign power was finally his, Thutmose III (*c.*1479–1425 BC) had far more pressing matters to attend to than the damnation of Hatshepsut's memory. The overlords of Mitanni had steadily been extending their power base in the Levant, and while a handful of Mediterranean ports such as Byblos and Sidon still lay within Egypt's sphere of influence, important inland areas rich in tin, copper and cedar were falling under Mitannian control.

Thutmose quickly readied his army and set off for the Levant on the first of at least seventeen military campaigns during his rule. Between Egypt and Mitanni, the land was governed by numerous semi-independent and fortified city-states, which Thutmose picked off one by one as he tore his way north across the countryside. Ignoring his generals' advice he followed a dangerous mountainous route to Megiddo, where a formidable coalition of city rulers led by the hostile king of Kadesh was preparing to receive him. None had expected him to come by way of the difficult ground, and the Egyptians pulled off a devastating surprise attack. The king of Kadesh managed to escape, but Megiddo fell and a bevy of local potentates were forced to pay homage to the pharaoh, bearing gifts of silver, gold, lapis lazuli and malachite. Thutmose departed with fabulous spoils: almost a thousand chariots (the chiefs' own were wrought of gold), fine suits of bronze armour, hundreds of slaves, horses and many thousand head of cattle. In later centuries Megiddo became synonymous with momentous battles: the Biblical book of Revelations, written almost 1500 years later, sites the last battle between good and evil there – the Hebrew 'Armageddon'.

Unlike Nubia which had by now been Egyptianised, the Levant was a cultural and linguistic hodgepodge that would not be incorporated easily into the empire. Thutmose did not waste his time trying to make his conquered lands Egyptian, and was content to receive tribute and taxes from his new vassal states. He left garrisons which could quickly respond to any uprisings and took young Levantine princes back with him to Egypt for education alongside the elite so that their loyalties would be with the pharaoh. The princes were also, in effect, his hostages should their families at home attempt sedition.

In almost a decade of campaigning, Thutmose successfully strengthened his hold over coastal Palestine and Syria – including the subjugation of Kadesh – but he knew that sooner or later he would have to confront Mitanni to consolidate his gains. The time came in the thirty-third year of his reign. With admirable foresight, he went to Byblos, one of the centres of the timber trade, and had boats constructed, which he then transported on carts as his army journeyed eastwards towards Mitanni. Early skirmishes with Mitanni vassals went the pharaoh's way, forcing the enemy to retreat well into its hinterland, crossing the Euphrates at Carchemish and seeking the safety of the far bank. They had no idea that the Egyptians had come fully equipped with a portable fleet, which the pharaoh swiftly deployed to cross the water and continue the slaughter. It was a famous victory, which Thutmose celebrated by erecting a stela alongside his grandfather's and another that described the events at the other end of his empire at Kurgus in Nubia. Mitanni had suffered a humiliating defeat, but it was by no means vanquished as a power and Thutmose had to undertake at least six more campaigns to suppress Mitanni-sponsored agitation in northern Syria.

By the end of Thutmose's reign, Egypt was the overlord of hundreds of city-states and her superior power was acknowledged by the kings of neighbouring Assyria, Babylon and Hatti, who showered Thutmose with gifts to win favour and protection. Wealth and luxury goods poured in from across the Egyptian empire, soon making the pharaoh the richest and most powerful man on earth. Towards the end of almost fifty-four years as king, Thutmose at last had time to put his incredible riches to use, dedicating a good proportion of his rewards to work on many of the country's temples, not least, of course, the favoured Temple of Amun at Karnak. Among the enhancements were two new gateways (the Sixth and Seventh Pylons) carved with the huge images of him smiting foreign hordes in the ancient royal pose used since the time of Narmer; and the *akh-menu*, a key construction at the heart of the precinct, inscribed with the story of his reign. He outdid Hatsheput by raising at least seven obelisks in Karnak and two in Heliopolis, none of which remains in Egypt today. The most magnificent was 118ft (36m) high and now stands, slightly truncated, in Laterano, Rome as the world's tallest authentic obelisk. Others were taken to Paris and Istanbul; the pair at Heliopolis were moved by the Romans to Alexandria, and in the late nineteenth century to London and New York, where they are both known as 'Cleopatra's Needle', despite having little to do with Cleopatra.

Thutmose III's was a triumphant reign which firmly established Egypt as an imperial superpower, and Thutmose himself was long venerated as one of the civilisation's greatest warrior kings. He is sometimes called the Napoleon of Ancient Egypt; both shared a hunger for battle and empire, and both were of very short stature. The king's mummified remains, stripped of their valuables and badly damaged in antiquity, and disturbed a number of times since, are of a bald man with buck teeth and a slight physique, who stood around five feet tall.

THE ARMY

Egypt's emergence as a fearsome military power was thanks to its new permanent army of professional soldiers. The New Kingdom emphasis on the pharaoh's qualities as a warrior and conqueror had also trans-formed the status of the humble infantryman, up till then usually a reluctant and poorly trained conscript anxious to go home. Suddenly the army was glamorous and began to enjoy the same kind of respect as the priestly and scribal classes. The elite complemented their careers in the temples and civil service with a stint as an army commander (like everywhere else, the best jobs soon became hereditary), while the uneducated Egyptian also hurried to enlist. Opportunities lay open to him as a professional soldier that he could not hope for if he stayed in the fields or followed his father's trade.

The rewards could be great indeed, and some generals, such as Thutmose I, eventually became pharaohs. Others were given hand-some pay-offs for good service when they retired; one soldier of lowly birth, who had fought bravely alongside the pharaoh, received 'gold, slaves and many fields', with which he could live out the remainder of his days in luxury. Others amassed riches on the campaign trail through looting.

But the risks and hardships were also great. Many soldiers joined up as young boys and were sent to barracks where they were drilled and beaten 'like a piece of papyrus' (corporal punishment was a standard component of any education). As infantrymen they might be sent far from home to garrison the remote desert forts on the fringes of the empire. Around fifty ranks of officer separated the common private from the pharaoh. The danger of being killed in combat was an ever present worry, but not just for obvious reasons; dying outside Egypt and not receiving the correct funerary rites and burial could destroy one's claim to eternal life. As the satirical Papyrus Lansing noted, the soldier's lot was not a happy one:

> Let me tell you the woes of the soldier… He is awakened at any hour… and toils till the sun sets. He is hungry, his belly hurts; he is dead while yet alive…He is called up for Syria. He may not rest. There are no clothes, no sandals… His march is uphill through mountains. He drinks water every third day; it smells and is brackish. He falls ill. The enemy surrounds him with weapons. His body is weak and his legs falter… His wife and children are in their village; he dies and does not reach it.

PEACE WITH MITANNI

Having laboured for so long to transform Egypt into the world's first superpower, Thutmose III made sure there could be no confusion over who was the chosen heir at his death, so he asked his son Amenhotep to share the throne with him in the closing years of his reign. Amenhotep II (*c*.1427–1400 BC) was a dashing and gifted horseman, six feet in height, famous for his achievement of shooting arrows from his moving chariot through small copper targets – 'a remarkable feat...never seen before', according to a stela at Giza.

Twice he was called upon to suppress disturbances in Syria, the most serious of which involved an alliance of seven unruly chiefs. In a ruthless expression of Egypt's might, he personally clubbed each of them to death and hung the bodies head-down from his royal barge as he sailed home to Thebes, where he transferred six of them on to the city walls. The last festering corpse was taken all the way to Napata in Nubia where it was also paraded, 'so that his victories would be remembered forever throughout the land', as the Amada stela records. Among the substantial booty from the campaign was three-quarters of a ton of gold and over sixty tons of copper.

Shortly after his Syrian missions, Mitanni emissaries were sent to Egypt to proffer the hand of peace, which Amenhotep swiftly accepted, clearly preferring to spend his fantastic riches on monuments and temples rather than seeking glory far away from home on foreign battlefields. From this time on, Mitanni was portrayed as an ally rather than foe in royal art, and its chiefs are depicted meekly offering tribute to the pharaoh, but there is likely to have been a more diplomatic exchange of gifts between the two states.

The busy preparations and construction work for his thirty-year royal jubilee were ongoing when Amenhotep II died, after twenty-six years of largely peaceful rule. There was no shortage of young princes to take the crown, among the many children of an extended royal harem, and Thutmose IV (*c*.1400–1390 BC), the son of Tiaa, became king. Thutmose established his divine right to be pharaoh in the 'dream stela', impressively positioned between the paws of the Great Sphinx at Giza. The stela describes how the Sphinx visited Thutmose in a dream while he rested in its shadow, and begged him to clear away the sand that had blown over his limbs; in return for the rescue excavation, the Sphinx promised to grant Thutmose the crown of Egypt, a reward which was clearly realised back in the waking world.

Thutmose IV was a short-lived but dynamic ruler, who was able to cram into his reign quick campaigns in Syria to unseat disruptive vassals, and missions to Nubia to quash guerrilla action on transport routes from Egyptian goldmines. Sealing diplomatic relations with Mitanni, he persuaded Artatama, the ruler of the kingdom, to offer his daughter's hand in marriage. However, when Thutmose died, possibly from a wasting illness which left his body severely emaciated, it was the young son of his Egyptian-born wife Mutemwiya who became pharaoh.

AMENHOTEP III: APOGEE OF AN EMPIRE

Probably not even a teenager at his coronation, Amenhotep III (*c.*1390–1352 BC) inherited an empire approaching the summit of its greatness. The heroic warrior kings before him had won Egypt land, resources and respect, and his more recent forbears had made diplomatic approaches and strategic alliances with any neighbouring powers that could unsettle the status quo. After he crushed a few small ructions in Nubia and Palestine in the early years of his rule, demonstrating he was capable of upholding *maat*, Amenhotep III had little to concern him. The kingdom was secure, the throne was safe and there were no more enemies to face. All that was left for him to do was to keep the peace and spend the rest of his thirty-eight-year reign luxuriating in the stupendous bounty of his empire.

Consequently, the pharaoh launched into a huge building programme which emphasised his greatness and godliness, mainly focused around Thebes. At Karnak he tore down shrines and a court to make space for its grandest ever gateway, the Third Pylon, which he planned to cover in gold, new shrines for the goddesses Mut and Maat, and another pylon for their processional way. Not far to the south, he constructed the magnificent Temple of Luxor, where the god Amun, 'the hidden one', was concealed from view in a sumptuous shrine and paraded on his heavenly barque from his residence at

Karnak during the annual Opet festival. In the new temple, called Ipet-resyt ('temple of the southern harem') the holy congress between heavenly Amun and Amenhotep's mother, 'the god's wife of Amun', was staged in ritual as part of the festival to reaffirm the pharaoh's role as the personification of the god on earth.

Across the Nile and linked to the river by a specially built canal, he constructed a truly spectacular royal residence, which he called 'the Palace of the Dazzling Aten', known today as Malkata. Large enough to accommodate the entire royal family, the king's harem, palace servants and officials engaged on royal business, the site covered at least eighty acres and was as artfully decorated as it was lavishly furnished. His funerary temple was yet more grandiose, an enormous monument to himself embellished with gold and silver and fronted by two colossal quartzite statues looming 59ft (18m) into the air either side of

The Colossi of Memnon are almost 60 feet (18m) high and were built by Amenhotep III at the entrance of his funerary temple

the entranceway – the Colossi of Memnon, whose disfigured seated forms are all that remain of the site. (One of the colossi was badly damaged during an earthquake in 27 BC, producing a flaw in the stone which reputedly whistled each morning at dawn; in the third century, the Roman emperor Septimius Severus repaired the damage and silenced it forever.) Amenhotep raised hundreds of statues of himself, many of them equally colossal, though most were appropriated by later kings, particularly Rameses II, or destroyed for re-use in other monuments.

Amenhotep III was a consummate statesman and diplomat, and dramatically expanded trade to Greece and Crete, while maintaining regular friendly correspondence with his 'brother' kings in Mitanni, Assyria, Hatti, Cyprus and Babylon, as evinced in the Amarna Letters, clay tablets discovered by a peasant in the late nineteenth century, written in the cuneiform Akkadian script of Babylonia, then the international language of diplomacy. Goodwill gifts between kingdoms would be regularly exchanged, the pharaoh often receiving horses, chariots, lapis lazuli, copper and highly prized iron, while commonly being entreated in return to send large quantities of gold 'which is like dust in your country', as the Mitannian king reasoned. The reciprocity did not extend to royal daughters. The pharaoh happily wedded the princesses of neighbouring powers, marrying into wealth and reinforcing good relations, but he persistently ignored requests for his own, declaring that 'since the earliest times, no daughter of the king of Egypt has ever been given in marriage'. Amongst this brotherhood of kings, the pharaoh was 'more equal' than his peers.

The most important of his royal wives was the beautiful Queen Tiye, the daughter of a chariot commander, Yuya, and his wife, Tuya. Yuya has been equated by some to the Biblical Joseph, but there are many other theories that place Joseph to the earlier reigns of Senusret III (*c*.1870–1831 BC) or Amenemhat III (*c*.1831–1786 BC), or the Hyksos kings (*c*.1650–1550 BC), while certain names and details of the story may correspond to the much later Sais period (664–525 BC). However, the vagueness of the Biblical chronology and the difficulty scholars have in correlating it with the pharaonic historical record (not to mention the fact that the ancient Egyptians did not hold Old

Testament figures in the same high regard as the people of Israel, and may not even have made note of them), means that we are unlikely ever to know which pharaoh Joseph served.

Tiye's family was from Akhmim between Assyut and Thebes, and became respected and influential enough to be given a burial in the Valley of the Kings, an exceptional privilege for commoners. Queen Tiye was not simply Amenhotep's favourite but an active player in the affairs of state and depicted on monuments with far more prominence than the canons of royal art previously allowed. She survived her husband, but remained dear to her son, Amenhotep IV (Akhenaten) and grandson, Tutankhamun, who was buried with a box of her beloved hair – two of the most famous of all the pharaohs, standing at the centre of Ancient Egypt's most serious cultural and religious crisis.

SEEDS OF A REVOLUTION

The roots of this crisis can be traced back to the reign of Amenhotep III. Peace and prosperity stimulated fresh ideas in art and literature, and good international relations had opened the door to outside influences. The ancient formal styles of art that had been sacrosanct since the Old Kingdom began to be relaxed, making space for a freedom of expression that would blossom more fully during the Amarna period. The cultural revolution spread into fashion with the appearance of exuberant wigs tightly knitted with long curly tendrils and elegant, finely pleated robes in place of the functional linen garb of old. New ways of thinking seeped into the religious sphere too, and Amenhotep's curiosity about solar theology began to emerge. Furthermore, the priesthood of Amun, appointed with a glorious temple and by now immensely wealthy, was the only institution in the country that could remotely rival the pharaoh for riches and influence.

His immediate forebears, Amenhotep II and Thutmose IV, had already rekindled interest in the sun god Horemakhet, identified with the Great Sphinx, and Amenhotep III now turned his attention to the old solar cults of Lower Egypt too. Among them, it was the Aten, an unusual and obscure deity without gender or body, representing the disc of the sun itself, that seemed to have most appeal to him. He named his palace after the Aten and excavated a pleasure lake for Queen Tiye on which they would sail the royal barge, the *Aten Gleams*. Even at Karnak, he is depicted in carvings as a semi-divine being bedecked in solar-related finery. By the end of his reign, after three royal jubilees, the deified king was so strongly associated with the sun disc that he referred to himself as the 'dazzling Aten'.

Whether or not the rise of the Aten in Egyptian theology was part of the pharaoh's attempts to reduce the strength of the priesthood of Amun, Amenhotep III still honoured and worshipped the multitude of gods in the pantheon. Before he died, an obese man with terrible abscesses in his teeth, he can have had little idea that his passion for and association with the Aten would contribute to a critical and damaging spiritual convulsion in Egypt at the hands of his successor.

The Amarna Period

THE HERETIC KING

Amenhotep III's chosen heir, Thutmose, had been primed to take over the empire, trained in a series of high-powered posts in the administration. But he died before his time and his younger brother, Amenhotep, was plunged in at the deep end, unprepared and little known, taking the throne when the great pharaoh died. In the early months of his reign, he obediently finished the building projects of his father, and there was no reason to suspect that Amenhotep IV (*c.*1352–1336 BC) was not the safe choice that Egypt needed to preserve its unrivalled place in the known world.

Before long, however, eyebrows were raised as the royal workmen began to fashion new temples at Karnak not for the supreme deity Amun, but the god of the sun disc, the Aten, a clear attempt by Amenhotep to hijack the religious centre of the country for his own favoured deity. Other solar temples were built in the north and south, the cult was publicised in Karnak during a *sed* jubilee, a festival normally reserved for the thirtieth regnal year, but celebrated after just three years by the new pharaoh. No doubt it was also to show off the exceptional beauty of his young wife, Nefertiti, whose serene and superior face has been immortalised by the painted limestone bust held in Berlin. The king adored her and sought to promote her both in his new rituals and royal art.

Amenhotep IV's predilections and idiosyncrasies may have surprised his subjects, but the diversion of funds from the old state cults to his pet one, which forced the closure of many temples, must have severely upset priests across the land. His rejection of Amun and its powerful Theban priesthood was impossible to ignore when the pharaoh changed his name from Amenhotep ('Amun is content') to Akhenaten ('Efficacious for the Aten'). Even so, few Egyptians would have been prepared for his decision in the fifth year of his reign to abandon Thebes and found a new administrative and religious capital on pristine soil untainted by worship to other gods, which could be devoted entirely to the greatness of the Aten and the royal family. For this end he chose a forgotten spot on the Nile in Middle Egypt at modern-day Tell el-Amarna (from which the name for the period is derived), sheltered by a sweeping crescent of high cliffs. He named his new city Akhetaten ('Horizon of the Aten') and marked it with fourteen imposing boundary stelae before embarking on rapid construction works using small-sized, low quality sandstone blocks (*talatat*) that could be easily assembled and transported. Before long Akhetaten had the palaces, administrative offices, army barracks, royal workshops, labourers' quarters, and temples for the Aten, the largest of which occupied a site almost half a mile long and contained almost a thousand offering tables. Within a few years, his new city was ready and the royals, courtiers, key scribes, priests and administrators, not to mention thousands of lowlier officials, servants and workers, were uprooted from their homes and relocated.

Once installed in his new power base, a city idyll isolated physically and spiritually from the rest of the country, Akhenaten pressed ahead with his radical religious programme. All rival temples were closed, the cults disbanded, the priesthoods dispossessed. An army of Akhenaten's followers (the literal army according to some) swept the country, destroying images of the gods, and obliterating their names. Religious festivals were outlawed, processions prohibited and public holidays abolished.

CULT OF ATEN

The cult of Aten was the sole state religion and Akhenaten was its high priest and prophet. The Aten was the ultimate cosmic force, the creator of all living things, bathing the world in its life-giving rays, while the pharaoh fulfilled the role of its divine manifestation on earth. All other gods were now surplus to requirement and the mythology that linked them redundant. Replacing the centuries of literature, stories and utterances associated with the gods and carved on to temple walls, was the single text, the 'Great Hymn to the Aten' probably composed by the pharaoh himself, a celebration of the Aten as the universal creative force which has much in common with the later Psalm 104 of the Bible.

It is hard to imagine that Akhenaten's religion had much appeal to the masses. The Aten had no mythology to inspire or instruct, it had no corporeal form to identify with, no festivals when its image was paraded outside the forbidden temple sanctuaries to allow a personal connection. Akhenaten did ride his chariot along the grand processional way in the new capital so that the crowd could get a glimpse of the living god, but this solemn self-conscious affair had none of the joyful revelry of the old festivals. The long-standing belief in Osiris and the afterlife was also dispensed with, severing ordinary Egyptians from the eternity that their ancestors occupied. Instead the new theology made Akhenaten, not Osiris, the arbitrator of an individual's fate after their death in a return to Old Kingdom models in which the divine pharaoh was the only means by which Egyptians could grant the survival of the soul. Widespread unrest and rioting was probably only averted because the average Egyptian continued to worship the ever popular household gods such as Bes and Taweret, and probably did not care a great deal for the high-flown concepts of the new state religion. Whether Akhenaten ignored such deities as oversight or exigency is hard to tell, but their continued existence has led some Egyptologists to suggest that Egypt had not become a true monotheistic state, but a 'henotheistic' one, in which a single god was elevated far above the others.

AMARNA ART

The disembodied Aten, the solar disc, could not be depicted in the traditional postures associated with human or semi-human forms, so Akhenaten devised a new and original style of artistic expression. The Aten was carved in temple walls and nobles' tombs as the sun itself, casting rays of light ending in hands that bestowed heavenly goodness or the *ankh*, the sign of life, on the royal family basking beneath it. The pharaoh's family – his beloved wife Nefertiti and their six daughters – were also depicted with unprecedented candour and intimacy. Informal scenes of palace life included Akhenaten and Nefertiti in love, holding hands, touching and kissing; in others the parents bounce their daughters on their knees, play with them and embrace them, usually under the benevolent glow of the Aten.

It was not only the subject matter of royal art that had changed, but the subjects themselves. Rejecting the idealised physiques of all previous kings, Akhenaten demanded to be portrayed in a curiously androgynous manner that made him seem abnormal as either man or woman. His body had the voluptuous thighs, hips and buttocks of a child-bearing female, while his fleshy breasts and belly were certainly not those of the toned young kings of the past. His narrowed and elongated head, with its stretched eyes, heavy ears, fat lips and accentuated chin, perched on top of a swanlike neck, strike an almost inhuman, otherworldly quality. This may have been precisely the preternatural effect he wanted to create, a blurring of his sexuality in parallel with the genderless yet all-creating Aten. On the other hand, some believe these portraits to be realistic representations of a man suffering from some genetic disorder such as Fröhlich's Syndrome, which causes a feminisation of the male body much as Akhenaten displays in his portraiture. As it also causes sterility, however, it hardly seems an appropriate affliction for a pharaoh who sired at least six and possibly ten children. A better bet might be Marfan Syndrome, the symptoms of which include a tall, lanky body with a pigeon chest,

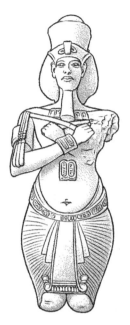

A curious androgynous statue of Akhenaten

overlong limbs, tapering spidery fingers, a gaunt elongated skull and an unusual jaw. This hereditary condition also weakens the eyes, perhaps explaining the king's obsession for the sun disc, possibly one of the few things he could see, and causes defects to the heart, making sudden death likely. Then again, the style was also used to depict Nefertiti and her princesses, as well as elite courtiers and lower classes in less pronounced forms, though it did become less extreme in the later years of the pharaoh's reign. Only Akhenaten's body holds the answer to whether these are fanciful or faithful portraits of the king, but his remains are yet to be found and there is a high chance they never will be, having perhaps been destroyed by angry mobs after his death or later by the tomb robbers who ransacked his grave.

AKHENATEN'S FINAL YEARS

Except for the quashing of a rebellion in Nubia, Akhenaten showed little interest in the international affairs of his empire, preferring the creative challenges of establishing his religion and art, and a happy family life at home. Lacking the diplomatic skills of his father, he fobbed off the Mitanni king with gold-plated wooden statues when solid gold was requested, and soon enough broke off correspondence altogether. He turned a deaf ear to the pleas of his vassal states in Syria, who were coming under increasing pressure from the Hittites and Assyrians, increasingly powerful and hostile forces in the region.

Unwilling to leave Akhetaten, but anxious to impress the world with his greatness, the pharaoh staged a grand international pageant at his new city in the twelfth year of his reign. Delegates came from afar bearing gifts exotic and luxurious including antelopes, copper and

Queen Nefertiti: her beauty immortalised for ever
in this painted limestone bust

incense from the Near East, gold, ebony, resins, rare animals and slaves from Africa. It was the highpoint of Akhenaten's reign, a sure sign that Egypt was flourishing without the gods of the past. He had made risky changes to the religious fabric of the country, but for his troubles the dazzling Aten had blessed him, his family, his people and empire.

But not long after the pageant, Akhenaten's life was turned upside down by a string of calamitous events that rocked the royal household and sparked countrywide instability. A virulent plague had been wreaking havoc in the Near East, and it is supposed that it may have been carried in to Akhetaten by the Levantine emissaries. In a matter of years, the pharaoh had lost his mother, Queen Tiye, at least three daughters, his second wife Kiya, and probably also his dear Nefertiti who suddenly disappears from the record. Bereft, the pharaoh vented his grief by ordering the image and name of Amun, whom he held responsible, to be defaced. In a manner far more thorough than in previous years, the god's image was hacked and chiselled from reliefs and monuments, from the high obelisks and doorways, while his statues were toppled and scarabs destroyed. At around the same time, the situation in Syria had reached crisis point with the fall of the Mitanni kingdom, a major upset to the regional balance of power that caused many vassal states to switch allegiance to Egypt's enemies. When Akhenaten died after seventeen years on the throne, Egypt's influence in the Near East was rapidly weakening and the empire teetered on the brink of collapse.

Restoration

AFTERMATH

The mysteries and controversies surrounding the Amarna period do not end with Akhenaten's death. The identity of his successor, the inscrutable Smenkhkara (c.1338–1336 BC), is a point of hot contention. In all likelihood he is Akhenaten's son or brother, though many believe the king is not a man at all, but Nefertiti reinvented as a male ruler as was Hatshepsut before her; after all, Nefertiti vanishes from history at about the time that Smenkhkara appears, and they do share a set of names. Whoever he or she was, Smenkhkara's reign was brief and obscure.

The only remaining male issue of the line – probably Akhenaten's son by Kiya – was Tutankhaten (*c.*1336–1327 BC), a boy of nine at the most, without the maturity to rule nor a queen mother to be his regent. Two of the most senior court officials stepped in as protectors: Ay (*c.*1327–1323 BC), a respected courtier of long standing, who had served under the great Amenhotep III and was probably brother of Queen Tiye as well as father of Queen Nefertiti; and General Horemheb (*c.*1323–1295 BC), a sophisticated and experienced army commander and politician possibly married to Nefertiti's sister.

With the prophet of Atenism buried in his Amarna tomb, Akhenaten's religious revolution quickly ran out of steam. Most people had converted for expediency rather than true faith, and were keen to go back to the familiar gods of Egypt. Early in his reign, the boy-king signalled a return to the old ways by changing the '-aten' element of his name, becoming Tutankhamun ('living image of Amun'), and abandoning Akhetaten to re-establish the administrative capital at Memphis and the religious one at Thebes. Only the most ardent devotees of Aten could have been sorry to leave Akhetaten, the capital set in sere and isolated land that soon reverted to obscurity. Egypt's temples were re-opened, their cults and priesthoods reinstated and finances appropriated by Atenism redistributed. The demolition of Akhenaten's monuments began, the start of a process that continued into the reign of Rameses II, until all memory of the heretic king was completely erased. The obliteration was successful for more than three thousand years, until Akhenaten's name was rediscovered at Amarna in the nineteenth century, provoking a whirlwind of interest and study that has made him the most written about of all pharaohs. Ingenious theories have linked Akhenaten to Moses and identified him with Oedipus; in more conventional discourse, the king now holds a key place in the history of religion.

For Tutankhamun and his court, the monotheistic (or henotheistic) experiment was over, and the young king erected the 'Restoration Stela', so all the kingdom should know that he had delivered the country from the evils of Akhenaten's reign. According to the inscription, Egypt had fallen into chaos, the temples were in disrepair and their sanctuaries left to choke with weeds, the army luckless on the battlefield, and the people abandoned by the gods who no longer answered their desperate prayers. In contrast, Tutankhamun had come as the nation's saviour and upholder of *maat*, the cosmic order of things. He was the righteous king who honoured Amun with a golden image, lavishly refurbished the temples, pleased the gods and brought joy and order back to the land. Such propaganda no doubt had its purpose in healing the state, but Egypt still faced problems, not least its new enemies in northern Syria, the Hittites who had recently helped vanquish the Mitanni kingdom. General Horemheb's skirmishes with them had so far been inconclusive and it was clear they should not be underestimated.

SUCCESSION CRISIS

When Tutankhamun died unexpectedly after ten years as king without an heir, the kingdom was once again plunged into crisis. Recent three-dimensional X-rays have contradicted the theory that he was murdered by a blow to the head, though a new possibility emerged that he broke his thigh and died from an infected wound. It seems, however, that the exact manner of Tutankhamun's death will forever remain a mystery.

His wife and half-sister, Ankhesenamun, who had borne him two stillborn infants, became the key to the succession – whoever married her would become king. Fearing for her life and distraught at the prospect of marrying a commoner, Ankhesenamun dispatched a frantic letter to the Hittite king, Shupiluliuma, requesting that he send one of his sons to be her husband and take the crown of Egypt. Initially highly suspicious of such an appeal from an arch-enemy, the king was eventually persuaded to send his prince, Zananza, who was duly intercepted by hostile Egyptian agents and murdered. This triggered a general escalation of enmity between the two powers, and the furious Shupiluliuma unleashed a wave of revenge attacks.

Ay, Tutankhamun's right-hand man ended up marrying

Ankhesenamun, his own granddaughter, and became pharaoh. He gave the dead boy-king a grand burial in the Valley of the Kings in a small tomb crammed full of his most precious objects, a spectacular repository for a king who had saved Egypt from 'heresy'; once sealed it remained virtually intact until its famous discovery by Howard Carter in 1922 (see p.306). Ay was already an old man when he came to the throne and ruled only for four years before his death brought Horemheb the crown.

Ever the military man, Horemheb swiftly stamped his authority on the country, imposing draconian penalties for criminals in his 'Great Edict'. Those guilty of corruption had their noses cut off and were exiled to Sile in the Delta, while thieves suffered the agonies of a hundred blows. At least as important to him was to make amends to the old gods for Akhenaten's wrongs, tearing down his sun temples at Karnak and beginning work on a new court and pylon in honour of Amun, the future site of the Great Hypostyle Hall. Horemheb also erased the heretic king and his immediate successors from the king lists, making it appear that he followed on directly from Amenhotep III, an attempt to excise the whole traumatic period from history. The fact that Tutankhamun's tomb was spared such treatment suggests that this was a political measure to bolster his own position rather than an act of genuine revenge or malice. Lacking an heir of his own, Horemheb chose another military man as crown prince. Rameses was an old friend and a trusted colleague who already had children and grandchildren – the ideal person to found a new dynasty to take Egypt back to greatness.

REASSERTING EMPIRE

Rameses I (*c*.1295–1294 BC) knew well what was expected of him and took seriously the great responsibility of beginning a new and triumphant dynasty (the Nineteenth, *c*.1295–1186 BC), basing his royal titles on those of Ahmose, the venerated founder of the Eighteenth Dynasty. Already advanced in years, Rameses accomplished little more than this in his sixteen months as king, but his son and co-regent, Sety I (*c*.1294–1279 BC) nursed the same ambitious vision, and immediately prepared the army, revitalised under Horemheb, for a series of campaigns to win Egypt back its empire.

Foiling an uprising of desert nomads (Bedouin) in Sinai, he secured land routes there for the passage of his troops into the Levant. As he marched up the coast, he recaptured a string of ports, once again gaining control of important shipping channels and much-needed Lebanese cedar for the service of his country, halting only at the strategic buffer states of Amurru and Kadesh at the very doorstep of the mighty Hittite kingdom. Sety knew that he would not be able to hold these two states once his army had returned to Egypt, so a truce was agreed between the two powers, whereby Amurru and Kadesh would stay with the Hittites, but Egypt would have unmolested control of the Levantine coast.

The benefits of Sety's firm and energetic leadership was soon evident up and down the Nile, as the treasury – virtually bankrupt from Akhenaten's skewing of the economy to favour his religion – was replenished with tax and tribute. The armies and workmen were well provisioned, and the mines and quarries were re-opened to supply Egypt's craftsmen with materials to make beautiful monuments. First among these was Sety's immaculate temple at Abydos, a huge edifice built in the finest pale limestone and exquisitely carved in raised relief, the most elegant and time-consuming form, by the kingdom's best artists. His 450ft (137m) rock tomb in the Valley of the Kings was also the deepest and longest ever cut, with the some of the most beautiful reliefs and paintings.

Rameses II, King of Kings

Sety's young son, Rameses II (*c.*1279–1213 BC) showed considerable promise on the battlefield from an early age. As a teenager he was allowed to ride against Libyan tribes fleeing famine and threatening Egypt's western borders, as well as command a mission to quash a rebellion in Nubia. When his father died, it was quickly clear that Rameses had a taste for warfare and was far from content with the 'gentleman's agreement' his father had struck up with the Hittites. Thutmose III, the great warrior king of the Eighteenth Dynasty, had won Amurru and Kadesh for Egypt, and if the empire was to be great again, Rameses would need to win them again.

THE BATTLE OF KADESH

Having strengthened his Libyan front with a string of forts on the western Delta, Rameses set off in the fourth year of his reign (*c.*1275 BC) for the Near East. At the sight of the large Egyptian army, Amurru quickly switched allegiance to the pharaoh. Muwatallis, the Hittite king, was furious at the breach of Sety's peace agreement and assembled a huge force drawn from the many provinces and allies of his kingdom, numbering close to forty thousand men. Undaunted, and perhaps showing the inexperience and bravura of youth, Rameses swallowed disinformation fed to him by enemy agents that the Hittite army was over a hundred miles away to the north, and rushed forward with a light vanguard division to snatch Kadesh city from under Muwatallis's nose. In reality the bristling Hittite army was lying in wait just behind the city; Rameses had walked straight into a trap.

The Hittites swooped down on the Egyptians, splintering a second following division before turning on the pharaoh's vanguard. According to the inscriptions Rameses commissioned to describe the battle, the young king fixed his armour, harnessed his warhorse and called on Amun to protect him before he charged into the fray screaming his battle cry. Like a god he fought off the enemy, single-handedly cutting a swathe into the Hittites until Amun appeared in the form of Egyptian reinforcements from Amurru that hit hard into the Hittite chariotry. The pharaoh's armies rallied and stabilised, forcing the enemy back across the River Orontes and taking whatever spoils and prisoners were left on the battlefield. As night fell the two armies disengaged and stood on opposite banks of the river in stalemate. Again a truce was agreed, and the rival kings both returned home in triumph.

In the propaganda war, however, Rameses was surely the victor. The story of the pharaoh's 'victory' was told at great length on the walls of all the major temples as well as in various manuscripts in a masterstroke of public relations that made the battle one of the best known in ancient times and elevated Rameses to the level of a hero king. The reality was a little different, as the Hittites quickly mopped Amurru and Kadesh back up into their empire when the Egyptians departed. The two powers eyed each other warily for sixteen years, until a peace treaty was signed on a silver tablet, guaranteed by the collected Hittite and Egyptian pantheons, that called for a cessation of hostilities. This ushered in an era of fraternity and international trade comparable to that during Amenhotep III's reign. Relations had improved so much thirteen years later that the new Hittite king, Hattusilis, offered Rameses his daughter with a fabulous dowry, whom the pharaoh promptly added amid much ceremony and celebration to the extensive harem of beautiful women that Sety had amassed for him while he was still a boy.

THE EXODUS

The pharaoh's large royal household was based at a resplendent new capital at Piramesse ('house of Rameses') near Avaris in the eastern Delta, an enviable spot surrounded by abundant freshwater lakes and fertile fields. This was the city 'Ramses' of the Bible, apparently built by Hebrew slaves shortly before Moses led them out of Egypt in the Biblical exodus. It is unlikely that they crossed the Red Sea, a mistranslation of the Hebrew *Yam Suph*, meaning 'Reed Sea', which probably referred to one of the papyrus marshes near the capital.

There were many foreigners in the eastern Delta at the time including the *apiru* or *habiru* (a term referring to prisoners in general rather than a people, but which may be connected to the word 'Hebrew'), who would have been forced to labour on the pharaoh's building projects. A further link with the Biblical story is the premature death of Rameses' firstborn son, an echo of the final and most dreadful of the seven plagues. No doubt some *apiru*, who were also members of the tribe of Israel mentioned fleetingly in an inscription by Rameses' successor Merenptah, did escape Egypt to start a new life. However, Egyptian records make no mention of an exodus, and what was an epoch-making event for the Hebrews failed to register on the Egyptian radar.

RAMESES, BUILDER

Although Piramesse was by contemporary accounts 'a very beautiful place without equal', Rameses had no intention of locking himself away in his city as Akhenaten had done. Something of a megalomaniac, he wanted the world to know of his greatness for all time and travelled between Byblos in the Levant and Gebel Barkal near the Fourth Cataract in Upper Nubia commissioning buildings, monuments or inscriptions at practically every ancient site along the way. To achieve this undertaking, he cut corners by routinely usurping his forebears' monuments and by using low-quality limestone pieced together with generous quantities of plaster. He also had no patience for the exacting raised relief carvings of his father and opted for the quicker sunk relief which had the added advantage of being harder for his successors to erase.

Among his finest architectural achievements were a series of eight rock-cut temples in Nubia, of which the pair at Abu Simbel for the pharaoh and his wife Nefertari are the most celebrated today, dramatically hewn out of a towering cliff-face and fronted by banks of

The celebrated Abu Simbel temple in Nubia commissioned by Rameses

imposing colossi. At Karnak, he completed the Great Hypostyle Hall, an awe-inspiring jungle of more than 120 gigantic carved columns. Its central passage is embraced by six pairs of 75ft (23m) pillars, so broad that it would take at least six people to encircle them hand in hand. At the Theban necropolis he busied himself with three grand tombs (as well as several others for lesser family members): two in the Valley of the Kings, one of which is the largest ever discovered in Egypt, rediscovered in 1987 and found to contain many dozens of burial chambers for the pharaoh's sons; and a third in the Valley of the Queens for Nefertari, regarded as among the most beautifully decorated of all ancient Egyptian tombs. The Ramesseum, the pharaoh's funerary temple, was yet another large-scale monument to his glory, featuring a massive seated granite statue of the king, whose broken torso was the inspiration for Shelley's famous sonnet *Ozymandias* (the name is a Greek corruption of Rameses' prenomen 'Usermaatre', one of his five royal names).

Rameses' extensive building works, colossal statues and masterpieces of grandeur made him a legend during his own reign, which itself – so fitting for a king prone to exaggeration – stretched to sixty-seven years and was celebrated with thirteen jubilees. It was the longest since Pepy II back in the Sixth Dynasty. He survived his twelve eldest sons and probably dozens of others among a brood that could have numbered over a hundred. His death in about 1213 BC was the end of a golden age, but his name endured for centuries to come as a byword for greatness and Egyptian might, qualities that his successors would find increasingly difficult to emulate.

The Defence of Egypt

THE SEA PEOPLES

During Rameses' reign, Egypt seemed to exist in a bubble in which the pharaoh could do no wrong and his kingdom could not be touched. At his death, the bubble burst. Suddenly the parlous state of the world outside pressed in and could not be ignored. On the other side of the Mediterranean, famine and plague had been sweeping across the Aegean, contributing to the collapse of the Mycenaean civilisation, uprooting hundreds of communities and triggering mass migrations of people seeking a better life. The Egyptians called these displaced groups the 'Sea Peoples', an umbrella term for various tribes from the Aegean and Asia Minor that were loosely allied and campaigned together. Among them were the Denen and Ekwesh, now linked with the Greek Danaoi and Achaeans of the *Iliad*; the Shekelesh who probably either originated from or ended up in Sicily; the Sherden associated with Sardinia; the Lukka with Lycia in Anatolia; and the Peleset with the Philistines of the Bible. In their search for a new home, the Sea Peoples had been causing intense upheaval in the Eastern Mediterranean as they attacked the Levantine city-states and ravaged the western reaches of the Hittite empire.

Egypt so far had been spared the invasions, the strife and the crop failures that were devastating its neighbours. In fact, Rameses' thirteenth son, the new pharaoh Merenptah (*c.*1213–1203 BC) had enough food at his disposal to send shipments of grain to his father's old allies, the Hittites, who were struggling to cope. But it was only a matter of time before the hungry marauders made for Egypt's abundant land, and in the fifth year of Merenptah's reign, the Sea Peoples landed on the North African coast, joined forces with Libyan tribes and headed eastwards towards the rich Nile farmlands. It did not take long for them to infiltrate the western Delta and oases, nor to stir up trouble in Nubia to incite rebellion, but Merenptah faced them down in a six-hour battle, slaughtering around six thousand and imprisoning many thousands more. The invading hordes had been checked but the danger would return.

Meanwhile, a more urgent problem was developing within the royal household. Rameses II's procreative feats had produced dozens of young princes who jockeyed for the throne, the result being that the Nineteenth Dynasty quickly disintegrated into a rapid succession of short-reigning monarchs. When Merenptah died, the crown was somehow usurped from his oldest son and heir by his cousin Amenmessu (*c.*1203–1200 BC). Eventually Sety II (*c.*1200–1194 BC) managed to reclaim the throne, and had just enough time in his short reign to wipe out all trace of the usurper's image from the kingdom's monuments, before his own demise precipitated another succession crisis. His only son, Saptah (*c*.1194–1188 BC) was too young to rule and was also crippled from a severely deformed left foot probably from polio, so Sety's wife, Queen Tausret (*c*.1188–1186 BC) became regent and then sovereign after the young king's early death. She could only govern Egypt with the help of the powerful chancellor Bay, a murky character, possibly a Syrian who had worked his way up through society by graft and guile. Tausret's death marked the end of the Nineteenth Dynasty and the line of Rameses. With no heir to oppose him, Bay may have tried to take full control, plundering the country as it descended into lawlessness.

INVASION AND DECAY

Out of the turmoil, a new king emerged to found the Twentieth Dynasty (*c*.1186–1069). Little is known of Sethnakht's (*c*.1186–1184 BC) provenance or how he came to power, but he managed both to stabilise the country and provide a fit and capable heir. Rameses III (*c*.1184–1153 BC) looked to the great Rameses for inspiration, copying his royal titles and giving his children the same names as his role model's offspring. They may have shared names, but the two kings occupied quite different times; although Rameses III would prove himself to be an able warrior king like his forebear, it was in the desperate defence of his realm rather than its proud expansion.

He was tested three times in his reign, twice by Libyan tribes in about 1179 BC and 1173 BC, but his sternest challenge was to repel the Sea Peoples' double-pronged attack on the Nile Delta by land and water in about 1176 BC. By then the Sea Peoples had sacked the Hittite capital and toppled its once mighty empire, laid waste to several of the great Levantine cities and had managed to settle across the eastern Mediterranean. Rameses saw that Egypt was still threatened and when he heard that the Sea Peoples were advancing on two fronts, he prepared a large army to defend the Nile Delta and his north-eastern border. The attacks came but Rameses was an able commander and forced the invaders out of the Delta and back from Palestine, a triumphant feat celebrated on the walls of his magnificent mortuary temple at Medinet Habu modelled, of course, on the Ramesseum of his hero.

In happier times Rameses III might have been able to amass a broad portfolio of impressive monuments like his namesake, but as it was he could only point to this Theban temple, still beautifully preserved today, as his one grand edifice. Egypt was in an economic mire and the king simply could not fund further building works. The ructions during the closing years of the Nineteenth Dynasty had damaged the efficient collection of taxes and tribute. Worse still, corruption had crept into the administration, haemorrhaging state resources, while the temple estates, especially the Temple of Amun at Thebes, which by now employed eighty thousand people, controlled almost a third of Egypt's farmland making it difficult for the crown to manage the economy. Rameses III did not even have the grain to pay the builders working on the Theban monuments, based at the village of Deir el-Medina, which had been inhabited by west bank labourers for much of the New Kingdom. They registered their displeasure by downing tools and staging the world's first recorded strikes. Discontent pervaded the country and by the final years of Rameses' reign it had even seeped into the royal harem, where a plot was hatched to murder the king. The plan was uncovered, and the various conspirators forced to commit suicide or executed.

End of the New Kingdom

The next eight kings after Rameses III each took the name 'Rameses', using it like a talisman to will the revival of Egypt's fortunes. They prayed to the gods for reigns as long and fruitful as their idol, Rameses II, but only two ruled for more than ten years – hardly the solid foundations for Egyptian renewal. On the contrary, the kingdom slowly began to unravel, the hard-won territories in Syria-Palestine were allowed to slip out of Egyptian control, and the authority of the king fatally weakened. The speed of the decline was hastened by corruption spreading through the bureaucracy and temple priesthoods, and a succession of low Nile inundations that resulted in food shortages and hyperinflation of the price of grain. Even as early as Rameses IV's reign (*c*.1153–1147 BC), the king had to rely on the increasingly powerful high priest of Amun – by now a virtually hereditary position outside royal control – to pay his builders' wages, and by the time of Rameses IX (*c*.1126–1108 BC), the high priest was depicted at the same size as the pharaoh on temple reliefs, a clear sign that his status now rivalled the king's.

The last pharaohs of the Twentieth Dynasty had never seemed so mortal and ungodly. In years of poor harvests when the spectre of famine hung over the land, the sheen of kingship had tarnished sufficiently for Thebans to plunder the sacred tombs and temples of their old rulers. In this period the Ramesseum was denuded of its gold, and a spate of tomb robberies swept the west bank; royal sarcophagi were broken into and the precious amulets and jewellery stashed between mummy bandages were filched. Those who were caught were dealt with severely, but the underlying reality was plain: Egyptians struggled to respect the divinity of their rulers and were not going to starve while the country's greatest riches lay buried with the dead.

During Rameses XI's troubled thirty-year reign (*c*.1099–1069 BC), the New Kingdom fell into a crisis from which it could not be extricated. In what became known as the 'year of the hyenas', famine gripped the land, Libyan raiders terrorised the Theban area, and a rebellion broke out there in which priests looted temples and the workers of Deir el-Medina ransacked tombs. The viceroy of Nubia, Panehsy, marched into Upper Egypt to restore order, dislodging the high priest of Amun in the process; he then tried to unseat the king too, a coup attempt that was unsuccessful. Rameses XI had all but lost control and his top military men emerged to rule on his behalf, such as General Piankh, who managed to assume the titles of vizier, high priest of Amun, and viceroy of Nubia, an unprecedented combination of Egypt's most powerful military, religious and administrative roles. In about 1080 BC a period optimistically called the 'Renaissance' was initiated to signal a return to glory after a time of chaos.

Under the 'Renaissance', Herihor, an army generalissimo of Libyan extraction who inherited power from his father-in-law Piankh, governed Upper Egypt from Thebes, while Smendes, probably

Rameses' son-in-law, ruled Lower Egypt from the Delta. Meanwhile Rameses carved out his share of Middle Egypt from Memphis. Herihor was effective in rounding up tomb robbers – Deir el-Medina was dissolved around this time – and it was under him that the process of gathering up, restoration and safekeeping of desecrated mummies began. Eventually, the remaining grave goods and mummies from virtually every royal tomb would be assembled, accounted for, labelled and then hidden in secret places. The fourteen mummies stashed in Amenhotep II's tomb in the Valley of the Kings and the twenty others stowed in a cache cut deep into cliffs near Deir el-Bahri, were only discovered in the late nineteenth century (see p.275).

The unbalanced triumvirate of Rameses, Herihor and Smendes divided the country into separate polities and ended the unified mode of governance in operation for almost five centuries since Ahmose. There was no way the new system could easily be reversed and when Rameses XI died after thirty difficult and ineffectual years as king, the New Kingdom died with him.

CHAPTER FIVE

Fragmentation and Repair

The Third Intermediate Period and the Late Period (*c.*1069–332 BC)

Tanis and Thebes: the Twenty-first Dynasty

After the demise of Rameses XI, the last pharaoh of the New Kingdom, Egypt in theory remained a unified state under a single ruler. In reality power was divided between a line of kings, the Twenty-first Dynasty (*c.*1069–945 BC), based in Tanis in the north-eastern Delta, and a string of military commanders who also held the post of high priest of Amun at Thebes. Smendes (*c.*1069–1043 BC) was the first of these northern kings, acknowledged as such by his southern counterpart Herihor (see also p.123), who nevertheless ruled Upper Egypt as a separate state.

In a sense, however, the real authority was the god Amun himself, who had ultimately benefited most from the riches and glories of the preceding imperial age and now emerged at the head of a theocratic system of government. Amun was consulted on all matters of policy and his will was communicated by oracles to Egypt's rulers.

As Thebes was Amun's principal cult centre, Smendes found it prudent to build a parallel centre in Lower Egypt and established a new capital at Tanis near Piramesse, which was silting up and had lost its river access. In Tanis, he began works on a temple to Amun and other important state deities and developed the site as the burial ground for the dynasty's kings.

Smendes had nothing like the wealth of the New Kingdom pharaohs. The empire had been allowed to disintegrate and Egypt had lost control of international trade. Luxury goods and the best raw materials were difficult to procure, and Smendes had no access to the

goldmines and quarries of Nubia. Much of the fabric of Tanis, therefore, was taken from Piramesse and Avaris, and refashioned for its new
location.

Nor could the Twenty-first Dynasty kings mobilise the kind of
workforce and concerted labour effort needed to make huge monuments. Their tombs were relatively modest while a good proportion
of the royal funerary equipment, the fine jewellery and precious metals
may have been sourced from the necropolis at Thebes. The granite
sarcophagus of Psusennes I (*c.*1039–991 BC), for example, was usurped
from the Nineteenth Dynasty pharaoh Merenptah, and Psusennes'
splendid silver coffin and golden mask (held in the Egyptian Museum,
Cairo) were probably made from materials recycled from the looted
tombs of dead kings at Thebes.

The fractured remains of Tanis comprise one of the best preserved
sites in the Delta, where much archaeological evidence has been
hidden or destroyed by the movements of the Nile. Even so, relatively
little is known about the Twenty-first Dynasty kings based there.
Siamun (*c.*978–959 BC) is mentioned in the Old Testament (I Kings
9:16–24) for his small-scale action on the Philistine city of Gezer,
which he apparently gave to King Solomon of Israel along with his
daughter's hand in marriage. But what a contrast this was with the
Egypt of the New Kingdom, when the Asiatic kings sent their
princesses with magnificent dowries and the mighty pharaoh could
refuse to return the compliment. Clearly Egypt's low standing in the
Near East had yet to recover from the tail end of the previous dynasty,
when Herihor sent an ambassador to Byblos to procure cedar for a
sacred barque for Amun. The story, recounted in the *Tale of Wenamun*,
has the eponymous protagonist suffering the ignominies of being
robbed en route, being snubbed and slighted by the prince of Byblos,
and then having to pay exorbitant prices for the wood – hardly the
kind of treatment the agent of a respected foreign power would
expect.

It was a straitened Egypt, but the universal acknowledgement of the
supremacy of Amun and intermarriage between the rulers of Tanis
and Thebes encouraged stability. In one instance, the Theban ruler
Pinudjem I, who was powerful enough to have his name written in a

cartouche like a pharaoh, managed to install his son Psusennes I as king of Egypt at Tanis. But such close ties between the two cities did not result in the reunification of the realm. On the contrary, around this time fortresses were built throughout Upper Egypt, especially around modern-day el-Hiba south of the entrance to the Fayum, which marked the frontier between the spheres of Theban and Tanite control. Many settlements along the Nile Valley show signs of fortification, and in Thebes itself, even the priests and administrators felt it necessary to protect themselves within the defended enclosures of the temple at Medinet Habu. The threat was less likely to be an attack from Tanis, than aggression from the Libyan tribes that had steadily been infiltrating Egypt.

The Libyans

Despite the celebrated victories of Merenptah and Rameses III against invading Libyan tribes (principally the Meshwesh and the Libu), a steady trickle of Libyans managed to settle in the western Delta, an area of poor grazing land that was ultimately of little concern to the pharaohs. The xenophobic rhetoric so common in the inscriptions of the warrior kings belied the fact that foreigners could actually do very well in Egypt. The army had a large Libyan contingent during the Ramessid era, and Merenptah, for instance, employed Libyan merce naries to secure the Kharga Oasis, funnily enough, against attacks from Libyan invaders. The army was a passage into Egyptian society; foreigners could work their way up the ranks to positions of high authority, while good service was rewarded with plots of land.

The breakdown of centralised government during the Third Intermediate Period (*c.*1069–661 BC) gave the Libyan settlers an opportunity to establish power centres and mini-chiefdoms throughout Lower Egypt. Gradually their strength and autonomy grew, aided by political marriages with the ruling houses of Upper and Lower Egypt and soon members of the royal household bore Libyan names. By the latter half of the Twenty-first Dynasty, the crown itself was held by a Libyan – Osorkon the Elder (*c.*984–978 BC), the son of the Meshwesh chief based in Bubastis, strategically positioned midway between Memphis and Tanis. He may not even have been the first Libyan ruler as his predecessors may have chosen to adopt Egyptian names to disguise their foreign origins.

SHESHONQ I

The period of Libyan dominance proper in Egypt was begun by Osorkon's nephew, Sheshonq I (*c.*945–924 BC), marked by Manetho as the founder of the Twenty-second Dynasty (*c.*945–715 BC). When Psusennes II (*c.*959–945 BC), the last king of the previous dynasty, died without an heir, Sheshonq was well placed to take the throne. In addition to his links with Osorkon the Elder, Sheshonq had made a tactical marriage between his eldest son (who would become Osorkon I, *c.*924–889 BC) and Psusennes' daughter. He immediately implemented measures to increase his authority over the whole land by installing another son, Iupet, as high priest of Amun and military governor of Upper Egypt while power in Thebes was at a low ebb, and by forging marriage alliances between his family and the Theban ruling classes as well as other influential Libyan chiefs in Lower Egypt. The autonomy of Thebes had been successfully curbed and the oracular pronouncements of the god Amun could now be treated as advice rather than prescription giving Sheshonq greater freedom to follow his own policies.

Sheshonq had elevated the power of the king, but he also had ambitions to boost the prestige of Egypt abroad. To this end he renewed trade links with Byblos sending a handsome statue of himself to King Abibaal there to sweeten relations – and to lubricate the flow of wood to Egypt that had probably dried up since Wenamun's hapless journey under Herihor. In a far less diplomatic manner, Sheshonq impressed himself on the Near East with a full-scale military assault on the Hebrew kingdom, which had recently split into Israel and Judah after the death of Solomon. According to the Old Testament (I Kings 14:25–28 and II Chronicles 12:1–12), 'Shishak king of Egypt' stormed the land with 1200 chariots, 3000 cavalry and innumerable soldiers, and invaded Jerusalem pillaging it of its treasures, most notably 'all the shields of gold which Solomon had made'. Before his campaign was out he supposedly knocked off more than 150 other cities, including Megiddo and Gaza in Palestine, later commemorated in the triumphal victory relief on the 'Bubastite portal' overlooking a vast new court at Karnak, one of the key historical records of the period. The image of him carved in stone, smiting the Asiatic foe in time-honoured pharaonic style harked back to an age of imperial greatness.

FRAGMENTATION

Had Sheshonq lived more than a year after his campaign in Syria-Palestine, he might have consolidated his domestic and international gains, and the wealth and influence of his successors might have endured better. As it was, his reign was the high-water mark of the Third Intermediate Period and Egypt's imperial aspirations soon dissipated after his death. The conquered Levantine lands regained their sovereignty, and international relations were limited to commercial exchanges with Byblos. Back at Tanis a succession of Libyan kings named Sheshonq, Osorkon and Takelot presided with ever dwindling authority over a country that was rapidly fragmenting into independent local power centres. Sheshonq I's policy of installing his sons into key posts and encouraging intermarriage with local elites proved to be a short-term measure. Local clans holding high office in the army, clergy and bureaucracy fused together and transmitted their power to their children, bypassing royal appointments, while efforts by the king to win back their loyalty with gifts of large estates only served to hasten the decline of royal authority.

Osorkon II (*c.*874–850 BC) was the last of these kings with the resources and influence to undertake major construction works at Tanis and Bubastis, where he built a new hypostyle hall and festival court (again by re-using the stone from Piramesse) to celebrate his *sed* jubilee. Even his reign had its difficulties, however, particularly after he failed to make his son a high priest of Amun at Thebes. His cousin, Harsiese, took the post and quickly declared himself king and the crisis only ended with his death. Trouble broke out again between Tanis and Thebes in the eleventh year of Takelot II's reign (*c.*850–825 BC), when the king's son, Prince Osorkon, was rejected as chief priest by the

Thebans, who favoured the grandson of Harsiese. Osorkon marched into Thebes and made an example of the rebels by killing them and burning their bodies to destroy their souls for eternity, but four years later trouble broke out again and this time Prince Osorkon found himself fighting a civil war which continued on and off for more than a decade. When Takelot II died, Prince Osorkon suffered the double blow of losing Thebes – and with it Upper Egypt – while his younger brother, Sheshonq, sneaked in to usurp his throne at Tanis.

It is from the reign of this king, Sheshonq III (c.825–773 BC), that the political situation in Egypt gets particularly confused and fragmented – made all the harder to piece together because of the repetitive profusion of Libyan names. The civil war had sapped the kingdom of its cohesive strength, and rival chiefs in the Delta were now emboldened to proclaim themselves king. The first to do so was Pedubastis I (c.818–793 BC), who is thought to have ruled from Leontopolis in the central Delta, and is the founder of Manetho's Twenty-third Dynasty (c.818–715 BC), ruling simultaneously with the Twenty-second.

By 730 BC, the cracked pieces of the Egyptian state were governed by two official dynasties in Tanis and Leontopolis, two more kings at Herakleopolis and Hermopolis in Upper Egypt, the 'Great Chief of the Libu and Prince of the West' based at Sais in the western Delta, another Prince Regent and four 'Great Chiefs of the Meshwesh' elsewhere in the Delta, and a number of other potentates who controlled the interstitial splinters in the margins.

In addition to this was a line of Nubian kings based at Napata in Kush, downstream of the Fourth Cataract, who had steadily been expanding their territory northwards to rule at least as far as Elephantine and probably much further.

Out of this mêlée of contemporaneous dynasties, kings, chiefs and princes, two main powers emerged: the resourceful king of Sais, Tefnakht (c.727–720 BC), the founder of the Twenty-fourth Dynasty (c.727–715) who had gathered an alliance of Delta leaders under his command for a territorial push southwards; and the Kushite king Piy (also called Piankhy, c.747–716 BC), the founder of the Twenty-fifth Dynasty (c.747–656 BC) who had come to control much of Upper Egypt.

The Nubians

Piy mobilised his garrisons and marched north to counter Teknakht, who withdrew to Memphis where he prepared to make a final stand, but fled just before Nubian troops stormed the city. The other Delta kings soon fell into line and brought tribute to Piy, who was happy to keep them on as long as they recognised him as their overlord. He then returned to Nubia to spend his newly acquired spoils restoring and enlarging the Temple of Amun at Gebel Barkal, originally established by Thutmose III as the god's residence in Nubia. In Piy's absence, Tefnakht returned to Sais and swiftly regained his former territory over the western Delta as far as Memphis. His son and successor Bakenrenef (*c.*720–715 BC) was no less determined than his father to add southern Egypt to his realm, but his Nubian counterpart, Shabaqo (*c.*716–702 BC) who followed his brother Piy, proved to be his nemesis. Shabaqo rushed north from Napata, captured Bakenrenef and had him burned alive, and then appointed his own man to govern Sais, effectively subjugating all of Egypt to Nubian control.

Despite the passing of 350 years since Nubia slid out of the grasp of the pharaohs, the Kushites of Napata still bore obvious marks of Egyptian influence. Indeed, the Temple of Amun at Gebel Barkal was probably the core of cultural and political activity from which these kings of Kush emerged. And now that a Nubian king ruled all Egypt – albeit with the prevailing decentralised administration and continued existence of Libyan chiefdoms – he and his successors were keen to show off their respect for traditional Egyptian values. Shabaqo went around the kingdom renovating and enhancing temples, notably at Bubastis, Athribis, Abydos, Dendera, Esna, Edfu and especially Thebes, where he undertook work at Karnak, Luxor and Medinet Habu. Returning to the very roots of a culture, he established the chief royal residence at Memphis, the ancient seat of the Old Kingdom, and reasserted the importance of the city's great god Ptah by building a limestone chapel there. Furthermore, he had the *Memphite Theology*, the religious doctrine of Memphis and Ptah written on a frail, worm-eaten papyrus, carved onto a basalt stela for posterity. It remains one of the key sources of our knowledge of this theology, even though the stela was at one point used as a millstone. The Nubians also drew on the formal styles of the Old Kingdom to decorate their temples, and though they preferred to be buried in their homeland with their ancestors at el-Kurru, they nevertheless had pyramids constructed over their tombs.

While they championed the age-old forms of Egyptian art and religion, they also brought distinctly Nubian flourishes with them. The single-*uraeus* cobra worn on the king's headband now appeared as a double *uraeus*, perhaps symbolising their rule over the combined kingdoms of Kush and Egypt; and the blue (*khepresh*) crown so popular during the Nineteenth Dynasty when Nubia was firmly under Egypt's heel, was abandoned for a close-fitting cap crown resembling Ptah's own headgear. Ptah was undoubtedly important to the Nubians, but Amun was still the dominant god, and under them the office of 'god's wife of Amun', always held by a royal princess, became the spiritual focus of the cult. The role took over the economic and political authority of the high priest, who by now had been all but stripped of his military and administrative powers. One of the innovations of the post of 'god's wife' was celibacy, which prevented these women from transmitting the office to their daughters and creating a rival power base within the dynasty. The more prominent role of women in religion and their association with divine royal children developed into one of the central elements of Egyptian theology over the next millennium.

THE ASSYRIAN QUESTION

With the notable exception of Sheshonq I, for most of the Libyan period the pharaohs had neither the ambition nor the wherewithal to turn their attentions to the goings-on beyond Egypt's borders. Meanwhile, the Assyrians had steadily been extending their power and territory, ravaging the land from northern Mesopotamia to the Syrian coast with breathtaking cruelty – burning and dismembering their enemies as they went, or flaying and hanging their skins around purpose-built pillars. By the time the Nubians held the Egyptian crown, the motley collection of states of southern Syria-Palestine was all that lay between the Nile and the Assyrian Empire. The Kushite

Sphinx of Taharqo *c.* 690-664 BC

kings recognised it was a dangerous situation for Egypt and they veered between policies of aggression, sending troops to aid Philistine resistance, and appeasement; when a Philistine rebel sought safety from the Assyrians with their erstwhile allies in Egypt, Shabaqo immediately delivered him into the hands of his enemies, 'loading him down with chains, fetters and iron bands' to curry favour. On the other hand, his successor Shabitqo (*c.*702–690 BC) was quick to dispatch a force led by his younger brother Taharqo (*c.*690–664 BC) to support a co-ordinated uprising between Phoenician and Palestinian states against the Assyrians. The rebellion collapsed before the Egyptians could engage and Taharqo returned home rather than taking the superpower on alone. The Assyrians also withdrew, diverting their armies to a new revolt at the other end of the empire, leaving Egypt space to breathe again – but Taharqo had marked himself out as an enemy.

THE INVASION OF EGYPT

Everything went well for Taharqo in the first half of his twenty-six-year reign, and few suspected that this was to be the last glorious gasp of the Nubian period. In his sixth year, the Nile flooded to the highest levels in memory, bringing a bumper crop and wiping out the country's pests, rats, snakes and locusts; it was interpreted as a blessing of divine approval from Amun. Taharqo ruled over a prosperous land and built across his realm, erecting a series of major temples and monuments in Nubia, and enhancing many existing temples in Egypt, not least Karnak, where he was responsible for the sacred lake and its temple, and processional colonnades in front of the main entrances. The pharaoh was also confident, perhaps overconfident, of his military prowess and enjoyed successful expeditions to Libya and the Palestinian coast, where he was able to take advantage of the demise of Assyrian influence following the assassination of King Sennacherib in Nineveh.

However, the new Assyrian ruler, Esarhaddon (681–669 BC), proved himself every bit as bellicose as his forebears and would not stand to see his African enemies making gains in the Levant. His decision to march against Egypt was the beginning of the end for Taharqo, even though he forced the Assyrians back from the Delta on their first confrontation in 674 BC. Three years later, Esarhaddon returned. He crushed Egypt's border defences and stormed Memphis in half a day, capturing the queen and royal family and transporting them off to Assyria as chattels. Taharqo fled for his life back to Napata, while Esarhaddon installed new men at every level of the Egyptian administration, particularly favouring Nubia's old rivals from Sais in the north, the descendants of the vanquished Tefnakht.

Content with the changes they had made, the Assyrians departed, clearly underestimating the persistent Taharqo, who wasted little time retaking his old realm. The death of Esarhaddon in 669 BC delayed the response, but his son, Ashurbanipal (669–627 BC), appeared with his armies in 667 BC, once again forcing the pharaoh to flee to the safety of Napata, where he died three years later. Still unwilling to rule Egypt directly, the Assyrians chose Nekau I (also called Necho) of Sais (672–664 BC) as governor in Memphis, and his son, Psamtek, who had already been taken to Nineveh to learn Assyrian customs, to rule at Athribis in the Delta. Again the invaders withdrew and again the Nubians rose up, this time led by Taharqo's son, Tanutamani (664–656 BC). He recaptured Memphis and defeated Assyria's vassals in the Delta, killing Nekau in battle. It was the final straw for Ashurbanipal, who determined to end these seesawing actions against the Nubians once and for all. With a huge force he attacked Egypt and rapidly advanced through the Delta up the Nile towards Thebes where Tanutamani had taken refuge. The climax of the campaign came in 663 BC, when Ashurbanipal achieved what had been unthinkable since the beginning of the Middle Kingdom – the sack of Thebes, the wholesale looting of its magnificent temples, the desecration of its sacred precincts, the ravaging of the religious heart of Egypt. It was a cataclysm that must have deeply affected the Egyptian psyche and undermined confidence in the seemingly timeless values that underpinned the civilisation.

The Kings of Sais

Tanutamani escaped but spent the rest of his days in the relative obscurity of Kush, a kingdom too far even for the Assyrians to conquer. Ashurbanipal called on Psamtek I (664–610 BC) to administer Egypt from the latter's stronghold at Sais in the western Delta. Psamtek had obviously impressed him as a very capable and astute man and the Assyrians trusted him to look after Egypt while they attended to developments elsewhere in their empire. Capable and astute he was, for he recognised that Egypt would always be vulnerable to foreign domination if internal power was divided between warring factions and numerous principalities. He took it upon himself to unify the land under the centralised rule of one king – the model of government that had always served Egypt best.

With the help of foreign mercenaries particularly from Greece and Caria (south-western Turkey), in just a few years he had control over the whole Delta. By the ninth year of his reign his influence was such that Thebes was willing to adopt his daughter, Nitocris, as 'god's wife of Amun'. Dressed in fine white robes and adorned with brilliant turquoise jewellery, she was received amid much fanfare and bestowed with fabulous gifts of land and produce. The festivities represented more than just her marriage to Amun: in return for giving away his daughter, Psamtek's reward was dominion over Upper Egypt – her successful reception ceremony in Thebes was tantamount to his coronation as King of the Two Lands. The era of unified rule from the Twenty-sixth Dynasty (664–525 BC), headed by Psamtek, to the conquest of Alexander the Great in 332 BC at the end of the Thirty-first is known as the 'Late period'.

Egypt's economy had been badly damaged by war and invasion. Nubia and the Assyrian-occupied Near East were still sensitive regions, so Psamtek looked north for trading partners and found enthusiastic and enterprising merchants in the Greeks, who quickly established themselves in bustling commercial centres such as Naukratis in the Delta. As business contacts blossomed across the Mediterranean, Psamtek developed an extensive seafaring fleet, which would eventually form the basis of a national navy, soon to be an important component of Egypt's military strength. Psamtek also sought to overhaul his land forces; he had at his disposal large numbers of native Egyptian soldiers (the Greeks called them *machimoi*), militiamen who might switch loyalties at a moment's notice if called on by local potentates. Psamtek found it far more reliable to employ mercenaries, many of whom were now offering their services to states all around the eastern Mediterranean. In addition to the Libyans and Nubians who had long padded out the Egyptian army, garrisons of Greeks, Carians and Phoenicians began appearing at strategic places on the eastern and western borders of the kingdom, while a unit of Jews was positioned on Egypt's southern frontier at Elephantine.

Eventually the opportunity presented itself to move against the formidable might of the Assyrians. With the empire under considerable pressure on other fronts and with the support of Gyges of Lydia, Psamtek managed to wrest Egypt from the Assyrians. The fruits of his labours were enjoyed for the rest of the dynasty, which would in more troubled times come to be remembered warmly for its prosperity, independence and traditional Egyptian values.

The trend begun by the Nubian kings of reclaiming the styles of the past was continued and expanded, perhaps in a kind of nationalistic reaction to the influx of Mediterranean immigrants. Ancient sites such as Djoser's Step Pyramid at Saqqara were restored and the idealised forms of Old Kingdom statuary and reliefs were imitated. One of the best-known constructions surviving from the period is Psamtek's

A mummified cat from the Late period when animal cults reached the peak of their popularity

addition of the Greater Vaults to the Serapeum at Saqqara, where sacred Apis bulls, believed to be manifestations of the god Ptah's spirit, were entombed in magnificent stone sarcophagi.

Animal cults reached the peak of their popularity during the Late period. They were managed by their own priesthoods who would breed, mummify and bury sacred animals such as falcons, associated with Horus and Osiris, and ibis, linked to Thoth, in their thousands. Pilgrims would show their piety by paying for the embalming of animals, which would be mummified and stored in long underground galleries. Many other species were also accorded funeral rites in this way, including baboons, dogs, cats, jackals, rams, fish, snakes and crocodiles.

As far as human tombs are concerned, some of the grandest of the Saite period were built by nobles rather than kings. The Theban mortuary complex of Mentuemhat, an erstwhile priest of Amun and governor of Thebes, must rank as one of the most imposing private tombs of Ancient Egypt for its large and elaborate design and fine carved reliefs.

THE NEW WORLD ORDER

As Psamtek's glorious reign unfolded, the troubled Assyrian empire unravelled. The decline rapidly gathered speed after Ashurbanipal's death in 627 BC, when the Babylonians, the Scythians, the Medes and the Persians smelled decay and began to circle the dying kingdom. Psamtek realised that Egypt's fortunes had risen as Assyria's had dipped, but he also knew that the empire's total collapse would destabilise the region and create newer, more powerful opponents. He therefore sent his armies to assist the Assyrians against the Babylonians in 616 BC, but his efforts were to no avail. Within four years, the Assyrian capital Nineveh had fallen and its royal line had been terminated.

Inheriting this volatile situation from his father, Nekau II (610–595 BC) strove to capitalise on the upheaval. He marched into the Levant, deposed the king of Jerusalem and demanded tribute from his new vassals in the manner of an omnipotent New Kingdom pharaoh. However, his triumphs turned out to be more a flash in the pan than the dawn of a new golden age. Nekau held on to his foreign possessions for only four years before a reorganised Babylonian army set upon the Egyptian outpost at Carchemish in 605 BC, scattering the pharaoh's soldiers and hunting them down to the last man. Having inflicted this humiliating defeat, the Babylonian king, Nebuchadnezzar II (605–562 BC) decided to take the battle to Egypt. This time Nekau successfully held him off at Egypt's eastern border, but by 597 BC, Nebuchadnezzar had taken Jerusalem and most of Egypt's territories in the Near East.

Though Nekau had been beaten back, he was a man of great vision with a passion for things nautical. He greatly enlarged his father's embryonic navy, equipping it with trireme warships and hired the services of expert Ionian captains, who were far more accomplished mariners than their riparian Egyptian counterparts. Herodotus, who is a key source of information for this period – admittedly sometimes lurid and unreliable – tells us that Nekau sent a fleet of Phoenicians to circumnavigate Africa, which they apparently achieved, embarking from the Red Sea and returning via the Straits of Gibraltar two years later. The last impassable stretch, the Suez Isthmus, the pharaoh had previously sought to defeat by digging a canal along the Wadi Tumilat from the Nile to the Red Sea. According to Herodotus, the circuitous waterway cost the lives of 120,000 men and even then was abandoned unfinished after an oracle warned Nekau that only foreigners would benefit from it. The prediction turned out to be correct; almost a century later Darius completed it to the advantage of the Persian Empire.

In addition to his fruitless and costly canal scheme, Nekau was

blamed for the loss of Egypt's holdings in Syria-Palestine. His unpopularity was such that his son, Psamtek II (595–589 BC), excised his
name from inscriptions. He was even more zealous in defacing the
monuments of the Nubian kings, following a successful expedition to
Kush to crush the dynasty's old foes – not that there is any evidence
that they had provoked such action. Greek and Carian mercenaries in
the army etched graffiti onto the leg of a colossal statue of Rameses II
at Abu Simbel to commemorate the campaign.

But there was no question that the real threat to Egypt still lay in
the Near East, and Psamtek urged the king of Judah to rise up in
rebellion against the Babylonians, impressing his case further by
touring the region in 591 BC. The resulting revolt was an unmitigated
disaster, culminating in the fall of Jerusalem in 587 BC, the capture and
humiliation of its king, the murder of his heir, and the forced expatri-
ation of thousands of Jews to Babylonia; the lucky ones (including the
prophet Jeremiah) escaped to Egypt.

The failure of Psamtek's son, Apries (589–570 BC) to lend adequate
support to the rebellion triggered an insurrection by the Jewish
garrison stationed at Elephantine, but this upset was just the beginning
of the new pharaoh's troubles. When he answered the call of his Libyan
allies in Cyrene to help drive Greek settlers away, his native Egyptian
army, the *machimoi*, were soundly beaten, and on their return the
survivors promptly mutinied against Apries' Greek mercenaries, at a
pitched battle at Momemphis in 570 BC. The *machimoi*, heavily
outnumbering the mercenaries, walked away victorious and
proclaimed their general, Ahmose, king. Meanwhile, the deposed
pharaoh was captured, strangled and buried.

Ahmose II 'the drunkard' (also known as Amasis, 570–526 BC) is
colourfully described by Herodotus as a man from humble origins
with a common touch that endeared him to his subjects. He applied
himself to affairs of state from dawn to mid-morning, after which time
he turned his mind to more pressing matters such as drinking and
merry-making. After all, he likened himself to an archer's bow:
'Archers string their bows when they wish to shoot, and unstring
them after use. A bow kept always strung would break, and so be
useless when it was needed.' And he may have had a point because

under his relaxed style of leadership Egypt greatly prospered. The rift between Egyptian Greeks and the indigenous population was swiftly healed in a masterful compromise strategy that gathered Greeks and other colonists in one place, Naukratis, out of the resentful eye of a nationalistic public. It was an authoritarian measure considerably sweetened by the granting to the city of exclusive trading privileges that made it by far the most important commercial centre in the country. The economy boomed and Ahmose's relations with the Greek world became so good that he regularly donated to their temples, even funding the full renovation of the great buildings of the oracle of Apollo at Delphi after it had been ravaged by fire in 548 BC.

In light of the latest developments in the Near East, it was propitious timing that Ahmose had made so many friends in Greece; he well knew that close economic ties often prefigured military alliance. A new imperial power was rapidly emerging in Persia under Cyrus II the Great (559–529 BC) of the Achaemenid house, sending shockwaves of alarm throughout the eastern Mediterranean. An alliance was hurriedly agreed between Egypt, the Greeks of Lydia and Sparta, and even Babylonia, but even this united front was insufficient to stop the advancing Persians, who steamrollered into Lydia in 546 BC demolishing the linchpin of the coalition; seven years later they had sacked Babylon.

Egypt was without allies in the Near East and dangerously isolated, but the country clung on till Ahmose's death in 526 BC. At this precarious moment the Persians pounced, putting Ahmose's inexperienced son Psamtek III (526–525 BC), who had been pharaoh for just a few months, to the test. At Pelusium, which marks the eastern entrance into Egypt, Psamtek's soldiers fought bravely but were eventually overwhelmed. The pharaoh fled to Memphis, but the city fell and he was captured, thrown in chains, deported and later murdered. Egypt had become just another province of the Persian Empire.

The Persians

The man that had subjugated all Egypt, Cambyses (525–522 BC), the son of Cyrus and first king of Manetho's Twenty-seventh Dynasty, was not remembered kindly by classical authors. According to Herodotus, the king desecrated Egypt's temples, broke into the ancient tombs around Memphis to gawp at the bodies of dead pharaohs, removed Ahmose II's recently embalmed corpse to inflict every indignity on it before having it burned, and slaughtered the sacred Apis bull. The army he sent to face down the Ammonians at Siwa Oasis in the Western Desert was swallowed by a sandstorm and never seen again. However, the sensational accounts of a cruel tyrant touched by madness, are more than likely to have been exaggerations of later Greek propaganda, as the discovery of an Apis bull buried by the king himself at the Serapeum with full customary ceremony would suggest.

Nevertheless, Persian dominion over Egypt was unpopular enough to spark an instantaneous revolt on Cambyses' death, which his successor Darius I (522–486 BC) only managed to suppress after three or four years. Darius was sensitive to the feelings of the population and was careful to demonstrate a keen respect for Egypt's religion and traditions. Adopting the titles of a pharaoh, he restored temples that had fallen into disrepair, built a new temple to Amun at Hibis in the Kharga Oasis, and ordered the codification of all of the country's laws, a task that took over a decade. At the same time, he screwed the new province firmly into his empire, finishing off Nekau II's canal to the Red Sea so that tribute could be carried back to the motherland as easily as soldiers could be sent in. Darius and his successors ruled *in absentia* while the actual governing of the satrapy (a province of imperial Persia) was left to a satrap, who exercised complete control. The satrap was kept in check, however, by frequent monitoring from the king's spies.

Relegated to a satrapy, Egypt paid its taxes and tribute, sent its best craftsmen and artisans, supplied its food and best materials, and added its army and navy to the forces of the Persian Empire. Egyptian men and warships were regularly mobilised in the long and bitter wars against the Greeks, including the battles of Marathon (490 BC) and Salamis (480 BC), both of which the Persians lost. Nonetheless, Egypt seized every opportunity that came along to throw off the Persian yoke. In 486 BC, the empire was still reeling from its unexpected loss at Marathon when a revolt erupted in the Delta, which the despised and merciless Xerxes (486–465 BC), Darius's son, was forced to crush. The assassination of Xerxes in Persia triggered another insurrection led by Inaros and Amyrtaios, both probably descendants of the kings of Sais. With the help of Greek allies, they managed to gain control of the Delta as far as Memphis, before Artaxerxes I (465–424 BC) reasserted Persian authority in 454 BC. A restless peace followed lasting thirty years (during which time Herodotus visited Egypt), broken only by another flare-up when Darius II (424–405 BC) ascended the throne. At the next accession, the plotting and strife at the heart of the Achaemenid dynasty degenerated into armed conflict between Artaxerxes II (405–359 BC) and his younger brother Cyrus. This time the Persians were in no position to quell a rebellion nor mount a bruising campaign to win Egypt back.

Independence Restored

Amyrtaios of Sais (404–399 BC), the grandson of the rebel leader who had fought Artaxerxes I half a century previously, picked away at the Persians in a six-year guerrilla war and finally succeeded in overthrowing them in 404 BC. He declared himself king and was soon accepted the length of the land, becoming the first and only ruler of the Twenty-eighth Dynasty. It was the beginning of the final period of Egyptian independence in the pharaonic age, enduring for just over sixty years to 343 BC. This was a troubled time, however, in which the persistent manouevring between Delta princes for the throne was set against the ever-present danger of a Persian retaliation. Fortunately for Egypt, for much of the time the Persians were too thoroughly entangled in wars against Sparta for an assault on the Nile.

Amyrtaios's reign was cut rudely short when a rival family based at Mendes in the northeastern Delta headed by Nepherites I (399–393 BC) seized power and founded the Twenty-ninth Dynasty (399–380 BC). Instability dogged the dynasty: of its four kings, two only lasted for a matter of months, and at least three were deposed, perhaps by violence. The longest-serving and most significant of them was Hakor (393–380 BC), who was noted as being 'generous towards the temples', undertaking a wide-ranging programme of renovation across the country. A major peace treaty between Sparta and Persia was convened in 386 BC, which gave the latter control over the Greek peoples of Asia Minor in return for the autonomy of the other Hellenic states, provided that they refrained from aggression against the empire. This immediately put Egypt in a worrisome position: its Greek alliances were rendered useless at just the moment that Persia was free to channel its full might against what it still considered to be its mutinous satrapy. However, Hakor managed both to forge a crucial alliance with the rebel king of Cyprus and reinvigorate his military machine, assembling an imposing fleet and hiring crack Greek troops under the command of the brilliant Athenian general, Chabrias. Thus prepared, he succeeded in staving off repeated Persian attacks between 385 and 383 BC. Frustrated, the Persians diverted their forces towards Cyprus instead, which they defeated in 381 BC.

THE FINAL FLOURISH

Hakor's services to his country were not rewarded by the smooth transmission of power to his chosen heir, Nepherites II (380 BC), who was swiftly ousted by a military coup. Its leader, Nectanebo I (380–362 BC) of Sebennytos (modern Samannod on the Damietta branch of the Nile) was the founder of the Thirtieth Dynasty (380–343 BC), the last native dynasty of pharaonic Egypt. The final indigenous kings would oversee a prosperous and relatively peaceful country, but first Nectanebo had to defend Egypt against a combined Greek and Persian task force in 373 BC. The enemy sidestepped Nectanebo's best defences around Pelusium at the eastern gateway to the kingdom, and found scant resistance as they bore down on Memphis via a poorly protected branch of the Nile. Luckily for the pharaoh, the Greeks and Persians still distrusted each other intensely after decades of war and dallied in their advance, allowing Nectanebo to reposition his armies. His counterattack just as the Nile inundation made marshland out of the Delta was too much for the invaders, who were forced into full retreat. Shortly afterwards the Persians became embroiled in uprisings across the empire, which kept them out of Egypt for twenty more years.

During this window of freedom, building works were carried out from the Mediterranean coast to the Nubian borders. Buoyed by a healthy exchequer, Nectanebo oversaw more temple construction and restoration projects than any pharaoh since the collapse of the New Kingdom. His best-known surviving work is the Avenue of the Sphinxes at the Temple of Luxor, but he was also responsible for the early phases of the temple at Philae, and the First Pylon at the Temple of Amun at Karnak, and is attested at numerous other sites.

After a brief hiatus marked by the reign of his son Teos (362–360 BC), who undertook a botched campaign against Persia and was subsequently removed by his cousin Nectanebo II (360–343 BC), the cultural renaissance continued. The second Nectanebo's devotion to refurbishing temples was as ardent as his namesake's, and his hand has been detected at more than a hundred sites across the country. It is therefore a shame that Nectanebo II, a highly creative man who was in the process of engendering a massive revitalisation of art and literature, is forever remembered for losing Egypt's independence, bringing to a close the unique native civilisation of the pharaohs which had spanned almost three millennia.

Surfacing from years of internal turmoil, the Persians once again surveyed their old territories and eyed Egypt hungrily. Artaxerxes III (r. in Egypt 343–338 BC) personally spearheaded the expedition of 350 BC against Egypt, which Nectanebo II managed to rebuff. It was a victory that bred a fatal overconfidence in Egypt and spurred Artaxerxes to redouble his efforts. When the Great King of Persia returned seven years later, he came with the best generals in the known world, including Mentor of Rhodes who had defected from the Egyptians and knew the details of their defences. Learning from past mistakes, he also launched his attack outside the time of the Nile inundation. The Egyptians were overrun at Pelusium and were soon compelled to abandon their fortifications further inland. As the Persians pressed down on Memphis, Nectanebo realised that the game was up and fled to Nubia where he lived out the remainder of his days.

The Second Persian Period

If Cambyses had been given harsh treatment by the Greek historians, Artaxerxes III fared little better, accused like his predecessor of butchering sacred animals, plundering Egypt's temples and forcing the priests to buy back their holy objects at great expense from looters. While Artaxerxes set about reincorporating the old satrapy into the empire, few could have suspected that the Persians would be in Egypt for barely a decade before being swept away by a younger and more vigorous force.

In 338 BC, Artaxerxes and almost his entire family were poisoned, except for the king's young son Arses (338–336 BC), whose authority in Egypt may have been challenged by the little-known Khababash – a native rebel who seems to have taken control of portions of the country for a couple of years. Arses himself was soon murdered and succeeded by Darius III (336–332 BC), the last Achaemenid ruler of Egypt. When the power of the Persian army was uncontested, upheavals at the top of the empire could be absorbed. In its weakened state such ferment could not pass without consequence, especially when the ailing empire was faced with an irrepressible new foe, Alexander the Great.

CHAPTER SIX

Alexander and the Ptolemies

332–30 BC

Alexander and his legacy

Tutored by Aristotle and renowned for his military genius, the young king of Macedonia, Alexander the Great (r.332–323 BC) was bent on destroying the Persian Empire. He crossed the Hellespont in 334 BC and defeated Darius III at the Battle of Issus in northern Syria the following year, before brushing aside the Persian satraps on his ineluctable advance southwards. In 332 BC he marched into a jubilant and expectant Egypt, where the reviled Persian governors surrendered without a fight. Alexander was embraced as liberator and crowned pharaoh in Memphis. His position was sealed when the ancient oracle of Amun at Siwa Oasis proclaimed him son of god. Before long even the locals were whispering that he was also the long lost son of Nectanebo, giving him a direct link to royal Egyptian blood.

Alexander's conquest of Egypt was a spectacular and popular success. It added a large and important new chunk to the Macedonian Empire which already encompassed most of the eastern Mediterranean. For a man whose military genius was matched only by his ambition, however, this was but a prelude to even greater achievements. In 331 BC, he and his fearsome army left Egypt to finish off the Persians, a task that occupied them for only a few months, before they initiated a series of brilliant campaigns that extended their frontiers far eastwards beyond the Hindu Kush to the Punjab and down the Indus valley. Driven by their young leader to the fringes of the known world, it was only the reluctance of his exhausted soldiers to continue that persuaded Alexander to turn back. But this was no cause for shame; by the age of thirty Alexander had been proclaimed god on earth and amassed the largest empire ever known.

His sudden death in Babylon from fever (323 BC) was the unforeseen setback to the master plan. There was no obvious successor among either his family or his generals, no one with a claim so strong, the ability and vision so exceptional, that all could agree to him. As the story goes, his advisers huddled around his deathbed and anxiously asked to whom his empire should go. '*To kratisto*', ('to the strongest') was Alexander's gasped reply. Some thought he actually said, '*to Kratero*', ('to Craterus'), Alexander's favourite and leading general, who was crucially absent in Macedonia at the time. Either way, it was not answer enough; the result was four decades of fighting in the 'Wars of the Successors' and the break-up of the Macedonian Empire.

From his family, there were two possible royal successors: his simple-minded half-brother Philip Arrhidaeus (r.323–317 BC), who would never be able nor allowed to rule alone; and his son, later to become Alexander IV (r.317–305 BC), borne after his death by his Persian wife, Roxane. Alexander's second-in-command, Perdiccas, took it upon himself to act as guardian for the 'joint kings', while he allocated portions of the empire to the supervision of his generals. Among them was Alexander's boyhood friend, Ptolemy (r.305–285 BC) son of Lagus, who was given governorship of Egypt. He had long been attracted to the country for its abundant natural wealth and inaccessibility; and he knew well that he could carve out a comfortable kingdom for himself there.

Ptolemy wasted little time asserting himself. While Alexander was alive Egypt had been entrusted to the hands of Cleomenes, a Greek from Naukratis, who had since robbed, cheated, extorted and embezzled his way to a considerable personal fortune. Ptolemy had this unpopular man tried and executed, deftly removing Perdiccas's key agent from government, and used the appropriated riches with ingenious zeal to firm up his position and ingratiate himself with the population.

Before long, Perdiccas realised that some of his generals, not least Ptolemy, were straining to take their territories out of the empire. Ptolemy's hijacking of Alexander's embalmed body as it was being transported from Bablyon to Aegae, the customary burial ground for

Macedonian royalty, was a brazen affront and an obvious attempt to link his rule to the divine king. Perdiccas had to act, but his invasion of Egypt in 321 BC could hardly have gone worse. Hundreds of his troops were drowned or eaten by crocodiles in the Nile and his enraged army mutinied and murdered him.

The episode marked the beginning of the Wars of the Successors. For the first twenty years of the Wars, those that wanted to keep the empire intact fought those that were trying to break it apart. By 305 BC, Ptolemy's power was such that he declared himself king, and within a few years there was no question that the rest of Alexander's imperial lands would be divided. During the last twenty years of the Wars, the intermittent battling would decide where the frontiers fell. Three major empires eventually emerged from the mêlée: the Antigonid (after Antigonus) of Macedonia; the Seleucid (after Seleucus), controlling much of Syria and Mesopotamia; and the Ptolemaic, centred on Egypt. Competition between the Ptolemies and the Seleucids over Syria and Phoenicia were behind six more Syrian Wars between 274 BC and 168 BC (see p.163), though the region was effectively lost to Egypt at the end of the Fifth after their defeat at the Battle of Panion in 200 BC.

Building on the kingdom that Ptolemy I Soter 'saviour' had secured for his dynasty (all the kings of which were called Ptolemy, usually followed by an epithet name), the empire reached its height during the reigns of his successors Ptolemy II Philadelphus (r.285–246 BC) and Ptolemy III Euergetes (r.246–221 BC). The core of the kingdom consisted of Egypt, Cyrenaica (coastal Libya), Cyprus and substantial tracts of Syria and Judea, but at its greatest extent the empire also controlled dozens of cities along the coast of Asia Minor, southern Thrace, and numerous Aegean islands. For a brief time, Ptolemy III pushed the boundary as far east as the Euphrates, before native disturbances against the Greeks demanded his withdrawal. In terms of raw land area it was nothing like Alexander's original empire, but its extensive network of possessions around the eastern Mediterranean seaboard enabled the early Ptolemies to dominate trade in the region and accrue vast profits. In addition to its commercial power, the far-flung territories provided a defensive cushion around its Egyptian

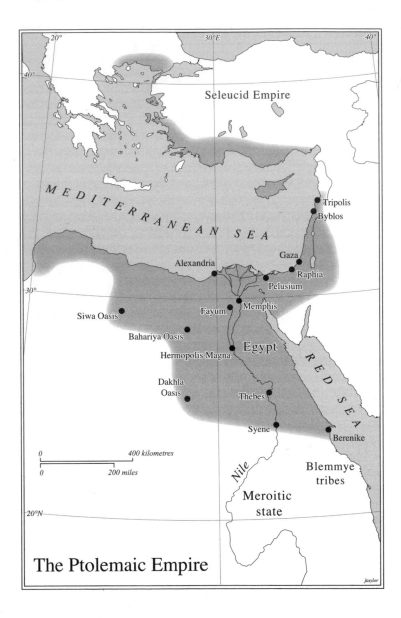

The Ptolemaic Empire

heartland. This was particularly important in light of the vulnerable coastal position of the new capital, the first and greatest of many cities founded by Alexander during the course of his campaigns.

Alexandria

The ramshackle fishing village of Rhakotis lying 16 miles (26km) west of the Canopic mouth of the Nile was hardly an auspicious venue for the foundation of a great imperial city. Yet with characteristic flair and foresight, Alexander, inspired by a dream about nearby Pharos Island, marked out the boundaries of his namesake city on the site. He had no chalk for the task and used grain instead, which his soothsayers claimed was a good omen for the future abundance of the city. When a flock of birds flew down to devour the grain, Alexander was concerned, but his soothsayers reassured him; it was a portent of how Alexandria would nurture and enrich immigrants from across the Mediterranean.

Sure enough, Alexandria quickly became the jewel of the Ptolemaic Empire, and for centuries was unsurpassed in the Mediterranean as a centre of learning, culture, commerce and architectural beauty. By the early third century BC, the immensely wealthy city boasted two glorious harbours and canal links to the Nile. It was a hive of international trade attracting people from all quarters of the Greek–speaking world, from Marseilles and Sicily to Sinope on the Black Sea coast. Its streets and markets bustled not only with Macedonians, Greeks and Egyptians, but Persians, Syrians, Libyans, Nubians, Jews and Arabs. As the poet Herondas wrote in around 270 BC, the lure of Alexandria was irresistible:

> Whatever is, or was, is there in Egypt:
> Great wealth and wrestling-grounds, power, clear skies, glory,
> Gold, goddesses, philosophers and young men,
> The temple of the holy sibling-couple,
> The noble sovereign, and the great Mouseion;
> Women (I swear by Korê, spouse of Hades!)
> More than the stars, heaven cannot boast so many,

> All looking like the goddesses who flaunted
> Their splendid charms at Paris for his judgement...
>
> Herondas, *Mimiambs*, 1.23–34

Ptolemy I was noted by the classical authors for his extraordinary largesse, modesty and talent for civic affairs, and he did more than anyone to transform Alexandria's rude foundations into a majestic imperial capital. As soon as the government buildings were ready, he moved his administration from Memphis. Facing the rest of the Mediterranean, Alexandria was ideally positioned to bring Egypt into the Greek world and to counterbalance the enduring power of the ancient Egyptian capital. But Ptolemy had other ambitions too; he wanted to make his capital the envy of the other Successors and the seat of Hellenistic civilisation.

The Sema (or Soma), the mausoleum for the body of mighty Alexander, lay at the heart of the city from where it seemed to radiate his divine power across the empire. Though lost to us today, the tomb was long thought to have been at the intersection of the two principal thoroughfares, Canopic Way running parallel to the shore and Sema Street perpendicular to it, magnificent boulevards more than 100ft (30m) wide. In the Brucheion, the royal district to the northeast, Ptolemy located his sprawling palace complex (which by the Roman period occupied up to a third of the entire city), and the celebrated Mouseion with its Great Library, where the greatest thinkers of the time congregated. A second 'daughter' library was kept at the Serapeum on the other side of the city, a sumptuous temple to the god Serapis (see p.158) built in the Greek style and conspicuously fronted by colossal Egyptian sphinxes. A great causeway, the Heptastadion, extended almost a mile from the mainland out to the Pharos Island, where Alexandria's famous lighthouse beaconed the city's greatness to the world.

Alexandria soon earned the title 'Queen of the Mediterranean' and the historian Diodorus Siculus, who visited in 60 BC, recorded that 'many reckon it to be the first city of the civilised world, certainly far ahead of all the rest in elegance and extent and riches and luxury.'

THE MOUSEION

Foremost among the new institutions was the Mouseion (or Museum, a temple to the Muses, the Greek goddesses of the arts and sciences), based on Aristotle's Lyceum in Athens, which it arguably outperformed. The Mouseion's centrepiece was its library, which became by far the best-stocked academic repository in the Ancient World. Its collection of as many as 700,000 volumes (papyrus rolls) was gathered largely with the help of the benevolence and patronage of the early Ptolemies – and laws that allowed the confiscation of all literature that came into the city; the originals went to the library, while copies were made and returned to the owners.

With such formidable resources at its disposal, the Mouseion attracted the top scholars of the age, a remarkable number of whom had a deep and lasting impact on Western thought. During the early third century alone, the many distinguished alumni included: Euclid (*fl. c.* 300 BC), who brought together the strands of Greek mathematical knowledge in his definitive work, *Elements*; Eratosthenes (*c.* 276–194 BC), who estimated the Earth's circumference to within 50 miles (80km) by comparing the angle of the sun between Alexandria and Aswan at noon on the summer solstice; Aristarchus (*c.* 310–230 BC), whose theory that the Earth went around the sun predated Copernicus by 1800 years; Archimedes (*c.* 287–212 BC), famed inventor of the eponymous screw, still used for raising water, founder of the science of hydrostatics and discoverer of the formulae for the volume and areas of spheres; Herophilus (*c.* 335–280 BC), the father of anatomy; Erasistratus (*fl. c.* 250 BC), a pioneer of modern medicine who was the first to trace arteries and veins to the heart; and Ctesibios (*fl. c.* 270 BC), who discovered the elasticity of air and invented hydraulic and compressed air pumps. Among the poets and literary scholars were Theocritus (*c.* 310–250 BC), whose pastoral *Idylls* deeply influenced others from Virgil to Tennyson; Zenodotus of Ephesus (*fl. c.* 290 BC), the grammarian and critic; Apollonius of Rhodes (*fl.* third century BC), author of the epic *Argonautica* about the quest for the Golden Fleece; and Callimachus (299–210 BC), who championed more succinct and erudite forms of poetry, while simultaneously compiling a 120-volume catalogue for the library.

Alexandria did not serve Greek culture alone. Ptolemy II encouraged the Egyptian priest and historian, Manetho, to write a history of the pharaohs to the end of the Thirtieth Dynasty, which is today preserved only in excerpts through other authors, but forms the basis of the chronology of Ancient Egypt (see p.27). The same king, it is said, also summoned the greatest Jewish scholars from Jerusalem to translate the Old Testament into Greek. As the legend goes, the seventy-two translators, six from each of the twelve tribes of Israel, working for seventy-two days in separate cells, produced identical texts, known as the *Septuagint* (Latin for seventy).

THE LIGHTHOUSE

The academic brilliance of the Mouseion flooded the Classical world with light of scientific and artistic knowledge, but even it was surpassed in fame and appeal by an architectural marvel which cast a

. The Lighthouse of Alexandria completed in 280 BC. It towered at least 400 ft (120m) into the air at the entrance to the Great Harbour

real beam of light far out into the Mediterranean. The Lighthouse of Alexandria towered at least 400ft (122m) into the air at the entrance to the Great Harbour on the eastern tip of the Pharos Island, a name that has become synonymous with lighthouses (for example, French *phare* or Italian *faro*).

Designed by Sostratus the Cnidian and dedicated to the 'Saviour Gods', Ptolemy I Soter (the saviour) and his wife Berenice, in 280 BC it was completed, like so many of the city's great institutions, by Ptolemy's son and successor Ptolemy II. It was built in three tapering storeys. At the bottom was a square block containing three hundred rooms, upon which was an octagonal layer and finally a cylindrical one holding the flames, topped by a huge statue of Poseidon. It is thought that fuel was carried up via pulleys, lifts, and a double spiral staircase at its centre, to feed a fire whose light was amplified by the judicious positioning of mirrors. Apparently, the blaze could be seen 35 miles (56km) away, a remarkable accomplishment which made it one of the Seven Wonders of the World. The lighthouse provided guidance to seafarers through the rocky approach to the harbour for over a thousand years, until rough seas and damage after the Arab conquest caused irreversible damage to the structure in the eighth century. It finally collapsed to the ground in its entirety in the fourteenth century after an earthquake.

The Prime of the Ptolemies (331–221 BC)

As if the fame of Alexandria's celebrated monuments and hallowed institutions were not sufficient to arouse the envy of his rivals, Ptolemy II founded a four-yearly festival, the Ptolemaeia, in honour of his father and the dynasty, which he hoped would match the Olympic Games in status. No expense was spared to wow his Hellenistic visitors. The displays of exuberant wealth and power included military march-pasts of more than eighty thousand servicemen, a mechanical giant that could sit, stand and pour libations, and enormous party pavilions decorated in the finest and most exotic animal skins, floral displays and *objets d'art*.

PTOLEMY PLC: ECONOMY AND ADMINISTRATION

The funding of projects like the Ptolemaeia, not to mention the construction and maintenance of the great new capital, demanded that the Egyptian economy ran at the limits of its capacity. To achieve this, the first two Ptolemies strove to maximise the productive potential of the land while introducing an all-embracing bureaucracy that enabled them to siphon off as much of the country's profits as possible into the royal coffers. To this end, the government controlled every aspect of the economy – agriculture, textiles, the production of papyrus and vegetable oil, currency and banking, mining, construction, manufacturing and trade – down to the smallest detail and employed a sizeable workforce of bureaucrats, administrators, managers, census takers, data collectors and accountants to ensure the smooth running of the system. The state owned monopolistic rights over most economic sectors, but auctioned them off to private concerns in exclusive contracts. The Ptolemies also stitched up the currency exchange markets by forcing foreign traders who wished to do business in Egypt to change all their money into Ptolemaic coinage, for which privilege they were charged a hefty commission. Taxes were high and widely applied; the considerable task of collecting revenue was auctioned off to tax farmers, who were personally liable to pay what was due but could usually expect to reap handsome profits themselves.

Agriculture, as ever, was the most important component of the national economy, and under this highly regulated regime farmers were forced to follow government schedules for crop selection, sowing and harvesting. Every scrap of arable land was put to use, and in the Fayum substantial swathes were reclaimed from the desert margins using sophisticated new irrigation techniques, such as the *saqiya* (see p.5), an ox-driven waterwheel. Cultivable land increased threefold and around forty new Greek settlements sprang up in the region, the inhabitants of which brought with them new strains of wheat, fruit and other crops as well as choice breeds of cattle, goats, pigs and sheep. Many other new towns also appeared in the Delta and Nile Valley to accommodate the influx of Greek immigrants; Ptolemais in Upper Egypt was founded by Ptolemy II to curb native power in Thebes as Alexandria had done in Memphis. The country's population swelled to as much as eight million and agricultural productivity jumped to levels not reached again until the industrial age.

The king, in theory, owned all the land; in reality, he was the owner of some very substantial estates, farmed by tenants, and the rest was 'on lease' to the temples, the new cities and fortunate private individuals. Prized officials were granted prime pieces of land in recompense for service, while soldiers were accorded smaller holdings (*kleroi*) in an attempt to keep them tied to Egypt. This was hoped to solve the problem of reliance on travelling mercenaries, who would only serve for limited periods and demanded payment in familiar money. It was hoped that the cleruchs (people who held *kleroi* or allotments) would develop into a reproducing military class, permanently settled on the land, that could be called upon to fight without delay. The allotments were sometimes found in marginal and previously uncultivated areas and such grants encouraged the maximisation of Egypt's agricultural potential. In most of these cases, the cleruchs themselves did not get involved with the cultivation of their holdings, but would sub-lease them at high rents to Egyptian peasants, who were left with the back-breaking task of making them productive; they also had to pass on a share of the harvest to keep their landlords in food.

THE GELLING OF TWO CULTURES

Under the early Ptolemies, Egypt once again became a rich and respected nation – at least for the Graeco-Macedonian elite that governed and owned it. The Greeks had successfully transposed them-selves at the apex of Egypt's society, taking the best jobs and making the most money. The splendid new capital was unmistakably Greek. Its many Greek inhabitants wandered its orthogonal streets (a grid layout designed by Dinocrates of Rhodes, a typically Greek form) clothed in Greek dress and speaking the Greek tongue. Known as *Alexandria ad Aegyptum*, Alexandria-by-Egypt, it was an Hellenic city transplanted whole, from where one travelled 'to Egypt'. Meanwhile the Egyptian natives, a conquered people, found that they paid the highest taxes, had diminished rights to land, livelihood and property, suffered discrimination under Greek law (though a subordinate

Egyptian legal system still co-existed with it) and were treated generally as second-class citizens.

However, the Greeks had long revered Egypt for its antiquity and culture. From the beginning, Alexander was keen to show his respect for the religion, not only to distinguish him from the sacrilegious Persians, but so he could play the role of pharaoh, the semi-divine representative of the gods on earth. His successors were quick to grasp the value of this too and commonly sought to legitimise their position as pious pharaohs, upholding order and defending the realm from chaos. It was therefore in their interest to support the temples and their estates, as well as the priests who, after all, conferred honours on the royals, devised their royal titles and crowned them as pharaohs. Consequently, the Ptolemies lavished vast sums on the temples, embellishing old ones and building new, many of which now constitute Egypt's best preserved and most impressive temples. Karnak, long the engine-room of state religion and ideology, received substantial additions, while the fine Temple of Horus at Edfu, Temple of Isis at Philae, Temple of Hathor at Dendera, Temple of Sobek at Kom Ombo and Temple of Khnum at Esna were extensively developed. At each, the Ptolemaic kings portrayed themselves on the temple walls in time-honoured style offering to the various gods of the Egyptian pantheon. In return, the priests showed their gratitude in such inscriptions as appear on the Rosetta Stone. This was written in Greek, Egyptian demotic and sacred hieroglyphic script to celebrate the first anniversary of the coronation of Ptolemy V Epiphanes (r.205–180 BC) on 27 March 196 BC:

> Since King Ptolemy is wont to do many favours for the temples of Egypt and for all those who are subject to his kingship, since he has given much money and much grain to the temples of Egypt in order to create peace in Egypt and to establish the temples; he had new temples, sanctuaries, and altars set up for the gods, and caused others to assume their proper condition…it has seemed fitting to the priests of all the temples of Egypt to increase the honours which are due to King Ptolemy, living for ever, the Manifest God whose excellence is fine…

Egyptian gods were also repackaged to make them more appealing to Greeks without alienating the native population. Ptolemy I in consultation with Manetho devised the god Serapis, based on the Egyptian cult of Osiris-Apis (whence the name), which was linked to Dionysus and depicted as a kindly-looking Zeus or Hades carrying a fruit-basket on his head, a reference to his associations with fertility and the harvest. Worship of the cult swiftly spread from its centre, the Serapeum at Alexandria, throughout the Mediterranean. Isis, the sister-wife of Osiris, did not require much of a makeover as she incorporated elements from many venerated Greek goddesses and came to command near-universal appeal, eventually outshining Serapis in popularity.

On another level, the Greek and Egyptian notions of kingship had also to be reconciled. Emulating ancient pharaonic practice, Ptolemy II married his full sister, Arsinoe II. It went against the customs of the Greeks and caused a scandal, but he successfully rode it out by emphasising the divine precedents of such a union. In Egyptian religion there was the brother-sister couple Osiris and Isis, the heavenly models of the earthly king and queen, and the Greeks too could not deny that their own great god Zeus had wed his sister Hera. Ptolemy's consanguineous marriage therefore emphasised the divine qualities of the royal couple and enabled him to establish a dynastic cult acceptable to both Greeks and Egyptians, which his descendants were careful to maintain. A consequence of such marriages was that the royal sister-wives were far more than mere consorts and took very prominent roles in the affairs of state. In some instances, like their pharaonic predecessors, they acted as regents for their young children – and the seventh and most famous of the Cleopatras became a queen in her own right – thus becoming the first women since the New Kingdom to wield absolute power over Egypt.

The Ptolemies were keen to use Egyptian royal art and iconography, and adapt characteristics and traditions of native religion for Greek consumption, but a true synthesis of cultures was never achieved. Just as the two populations generally co-existed with only occasional intermingling, their styles of art also occupied largely discrete spheres with only occasional borrowing by Egyptian artists of Greek cultural attributes (such as the inclusion of hair under the traditional head-dress). In this way, a statue of a pharaoh could take an entirely traditional Egyptian form and style, yet still have a few subtle features of Greek portraiture that linked it to the statuary more familiar with the ruling class.

There were marriages between Greeks and Egyptians but the first inter-racial wedding does not appear in records until 250 BC, more than eighty years after the conquest of Alexander. Most occurred among the lowlier Greek classes in the poorer backwaters of the country. Their offspring took on both Greek and Egyptian names, finding it more advantageous to use the former in official situations and the latter in domestic.

But in general, the division between the native Egyptian population and the favoured Greek-speakers was entrenched, and there were few ways that the average Egyptian could hope to get ahead. One was to learn Greek and find work in local administration, though promotion to ranks of high status were rare and slow-coming. During the reign of Ptolemy IV Philopator (r.221–205 BC), who found himself scrambling to assemble a large force to see off a threat from the Seleucids, it also became possible for Egyptians to join the army, but the government was careful to restrict the privileges enjoyed by native soldiers lest their Greek counterparts complained. Few Egyptians were allowed to become officers or join the prestigious cavalry, and they were given far smaller land-holdings in payment than the Greeks.

Ptolemaic decline

Had the later Ptolemies been able to maintain the zeal of the early rulers and the energy of the huge bureaucracy that served them, then the successes of the empire might have been longer lasting. But the leaders became increasingly myopic and entangled in the dynastic intrigues; the strength of central authority began to crack; controls over the bureaucracy slackened, allowing corrupt officials to extort with impunity; the economy stagnated causing the oppressed, impoverished natives to clamour for change; and worst of all, the Ptolemies' prized empire was lost.

The Greek historian Polybius laid the blame firmly at the door of the fourth Ptolemy, a man he described as 'negligent and lazy...inattentive and unpleasant to deal with'. It was, he maintained, 'due to his shameful philanderings and incoherent and continuous bouts of drunkenness [that he] found in a very short space of time both himself and his kingdom to be the object of a number of conspiracies'. Of course, it was far more complicated than Polybius cared to admit, but the signs that all was not well within the Ptolemaic state surfaced during Ptolemy IV's reign.

At the Battle of Raphia (217 BC), Ptolemy IV won a decisive victory over the Seleucids with the help of an extensive native army. The victory emboldened the native population and rekindled nationalist sentiments led to an outbreak of civil disobedience in the Delta. The unrest spread into Upper Egypt where it gathered intensity, until the region fell into the hands of two successive native 'pharaohs' ruling from Thebes (206–186 BC). Although the uprising was eventually suppressed, insurrections were episodic throughout the period, and there were at least ten serious native revolts between 245 BC and 50 BC. Anti-Greek, pro-native feelings also surfaced in Egyptian literature during this period in the *Demotic Chronicle* which eulogised the lives of the old pharaohs, and the later *Oracle of the Potter*, a prophetic work describing the imminent destruction of outsiders and their city Alexandria: 'That will be the end of our evils when Egypt shall see the foreigners fall like leaves from the branch.'

The emergence of the 'Alexandrian mob', a violent rabble that was quick to take offence and could rarely be calmed without bloodshed, was another expression of domestic disaffection. The mob first appeared at Ptolemy IV's death when it tore 'limb from limb' the court conspirators who had attempted to cover up the king's death in order to deny the accession of the boy-king Ptolemy V, and reappeared regularly throughout the rest of the Ptolemaic period. The mob made another particularly dramatic intervention when it killed Ptolemy XI Alexander II (r.80 BC), having tolerated him as king for only a few days, in revenge for his ill-judged assassination of his wife and co-ruler Cleopatra Berenice III.

It was in this atmosphere of uprising and riots that the land began to slip into lawlessness. Robberies became commonplace and Nile traffic was frequently preyed upon by thieves. Corrupt and ruthless local officials similarly preyed on ordinary people, breeding disillusionment and despair and leading peasants and workers to strike and abandon their homes to take refuge in temples. The disruptions had a severe effect on both the economy and food supply. Towards the end of a wretched reign that lurched from crisis to crisis and took Egypt to the brink of calamity, Ptolemy VIII Euergetes II (r.170–116 BC) tried to rectify matters, introducing tax exemptions and amnesties, and urging his officials to treat his subjects with moderation. The measures did improve the immediate condition of the country, but it was too late to stem Egypt's overall decline.

Nor can matters have been helped by the constant infighting amongst the Ptolemies themselves, a family for whom squabbles were all too frequently resolved by murder. The debilitating effect of this was further exacerbated by a string of disastrous regents and guardians who invariably put their own interests far above those of the state. Two spectacularly inappropriate guardians of the six-year-old Ptolemy VI Philometor (r.180–145 BC), one a former Syrian slave and the other an Asian eunuch, entered into a catastrophic war with the Seleucids that very nearly brought the kingdom to its knees. Disaster was averted thanks to Roman intervention (see p.163), but the country ended up with two rulers, Ptolemy VI and his younger brother Ptolemy VIII Euergetes II. The rivalry between them led to a crippling civil war that rumbled on in fits and starts for two decades, destabilising the country and advertising Egypt's precarious condition to hostile powers abroad.

After Ptolemy VI was mortally wounded in Syria, Ptolemy VIII took his chance to seize the throne, repressing his opponents and exiling the great intellects of the Mouseion – snuffing out at a stroke Alexandria's reputation as a beacon of erudition – and marrying his brother's widow, Cleopatra II, who was also his own sister. At the wedding celebrations, he killed his bride's young son (his nephew), Ptolemy VII Neos Philopater (r.145), the heir to the throne, while he lay in her arms. He went on to sire a son by her, Memphites, but ruined the chance of a straightforward succession by marrying his niece, Cleopatra III. The predictable antagonism between the two queens, who each strove to make her child heir to the throne, plunged the country once again into civil war. During the struggle, the king murdered Memphites and sent the dismembered body to his first wife as a birthday present. For these and other atrocities, the people changed his name from Euergetes 'benefactor' to its opposite, Kakergetes 'malefactor'; a physically obese repulsive man, they also mocked him as Physcon, 'fatty'. This sordid history exemplifies the behaviour of the later Ptolemies.

The Creeping Rise of Rome

Internal difficulties were considerably aggravated by the loss of Egypt's empire, which deprived the state of the crucial trade revenue and sparked off a string of economic crises. As the Ptolemaic star dwindled during the first and second centuries BC, a bright new one was rising in the west. Through a mixture of clever diplomacy and brute force, Rome had steadily been growing in power and had come to dominate the region's politics. Eventually it would effectively steal Alexander the Great's inheritance from under the noses of his squabbling successors.

The relationship between Egypt and Rome began in 273 BC when Ptolemy II dispatched gifts and an embassy to Rome, a diplomatic courtesy between two broadly equal powers. The Romans were 'pleased that one so far away should have thought so highly of them' (Dio Cassius) and returned the compliment. Gradually and virtually imperceptibly, the balance of power shifted. The friendship between independent nations became increasingly lopsided as the weakened Ptolemies sought assistance in times of crisis, eventually turning to Rome for support or arbitration in every little dispute. And when serious emergencies arose – as when Egypt lost its possessions in Syria to the Seleucids in 200 BC and those in Asia Minor four years later – they were suddenly utterly reliant on Rome. The Romans appeared to act in the interests of their old friends by securing peace for Egypt, but no attempt was made to regain its territories. Rome had extended its influence to the eastern Mediterranean while making Egypt unhealthily dependent.

During the Sixth Syrian War against the Seleucids the very survival of the Ptolemaic kingdom itself rested with the Romans. The Seleucid monarch, Antiochus IV, successfully invaded Egypt in 170 BC and again in 168 BC when he captured Memphis and threatened Alexandria. This was more than the Romans were prepared to accept, and the Senate issued a decree that Antiochus must withdraw from Egypt. Gaius Popilius Laenas was sent with the news and met the Seleucid king at Eleusis, a suburb of Alexandria. Having handed him the decree, he drew a circle around him in the sand, forbidding him to leave it until he had answered. At first Antiochus was outraged at such arrogance, but realising he faced a stronger power, he quickly recovered his composure and agreed to do all that the Romans ordered.

It was a bold move that succeeded in humbling Antiochus and establishing the dominance of Rome in the politics of the Mediterranean. The Ptolemies owed their kingdom to Rome, and although they continued to rule independently, Roman senators were increasingly treated like the patrons of a client state. From the Senate's point of view, there was no need to be over-assertive. The bickering amongst the Ptolemies and the outbursts of the Alexandrian mob would provide plenty of opportunity for it to intervene in the future. Furthermore, the Romans did not want an Egypt so weak it would be advantageous to their main rivals in the region, the Seleucids.

The relationship between Egypt and Rome had changed, but in general it remained one of *amicitia et societas* (friendship and alliance). Bit by bit, however, the Roman administration expanded around the eastern Mediterranean: the Macedonian kingdom (annexed in 168 BC) and Pergamum in Asia Minor (133 BC) constituted major territorial additions, and the Romans displayed their awesome military might in 146 BC, when they razed Carthage to the ground (ending the Third Punic War), and destroyed Corinth, the principal city of the Achaean League.

The murder of Ptolemy XI Alexander II (80 BC) at the hands of the Alexandrian mob put Egypt in a precarious position. Ptolemy XI had taken the throne with full support from Rome and news that his reign had lasted just eighteen days did not play out well in the Senate. His successor Ptolemy XII Neos Dionysus, also known as Auletes, 'the flute-player' (r.80–51 BC), found himself in an uncomfortable position between the hot-tempered Alexandrians, who had brought him to power, and Rome, which had yet to accord him formal recognition. He did all that he could to win the latter's favour, plundering state coffers to furnish Roman potentates with huge bribes, and did little when Rome took over Cyprus in 58 BC. Such acquiescence enraged the mob, which forced him from the throne and he withdrew to Rome where he ran up enormous debts buying military support to regain his kingdom. He successfully returned three years later and promptly murdered his daughter, Berenice IV, who had been ruling in his absence.

But his efforts could not halt the ever tightening hold of imperial Rome which was killing Egypt by slow strangulation. Cyrenaica was annexed in 75 BC, Crete in 65 BC, the rump of the Seleucid kingdom in 63 BC, and the Ptolemies' last foreign holding, Cyprus, in 58 BC. Egypt now owed its survival to the splintered politics of the Senate; none of Rome's most powerful players could afford to let another make the annexation.

Cleopatra

At his death Ptolemy XII left two boys and two girls, and a will guaranteed by the people of Rome that the first of each sex should ascend the throne as co-regents, a practice dictated by Ptolemaic custom. The eldest son was the ten-year-old Ptolemy XIII (r.51–47 BC), who swiftly became the pawn of his guardians; the eldest daughter was the striking Cleopatra VII (r.51–30 BC), a girl of seventeen whose youthfulness belied the precocity of a quick and hardened mind. The cruel experiences of her childhood – the murder of her sister at the hand of her own father, the suicide of her uncle in Cyprus when the Romans seized the island – had coloured her outlook and stiffened her resolve. No foreign king nor army could hope to challenge Rome and win, but Cleopatra had other means to recapture the glory of her house. The weapon of her irresistible womanhood was more powerful than any in a general's armoury, and with it she succeeded in disarming and enchanting two of the most important Romans of the age. And before her own demise at the hands of the third, she had managed to garner

Probably bust of Cleopatra VII, the legendary queen of Egypt

an empire beyond the imaginings of the first Ptolemies.

A QUEEN'S BEAUTY

For such an enduring icon of femininity, it is refreshing, if somewhat surprising, that Cleopatra's beauty 'was not of that incomparable kind which instantly captivates the beholder' – the assessment of Plutarch, whose account some two hundred years later is the closest thing we have to an eyewitness description. No sculptures survive that can be said with absolute certainty to be of Cleopatra (although there are a couple of strong contenders), while her two-dimensional portraits are almost all the formal, non-realistic representations, such as the temple reliefs at Dendera, that follow age-old conventions and give few clues to her true appearance. Her coin portraits, thought to be more naturalistic, are so unflattering – thanks to a famously prominent nose and flaring nostrils – that commentators of the past have pleaded to ignore them:

> If we are to believe the medals, this nose is out of all proportion; but we will not believe them; no, not if people should put before us all the collections of medals in the Bibliothèque Nationale, the British Museum, and the Cabinet of Vienna…The features which caused Caesar to forget the empire of the world were not spoilt by a ridiculous nose.

Anatole France, preface to *Cleopatra* by Théophile Gautier, 1899.

A more kindly interpretation might be that she had the strong features of a strong and royal woman, but few would deny that her principal attractions lay elsewhere. As Plutarch had it, 'her conversation was so delightful that it was impossible to avoid being enthralled by it; and, combined with her beauty, the charming grace which she displayed in talking, the sweetness and liveliness of her disposition, which set off all her words and actions, was a sting which pierced keenly'. Her voice, we are told, was pure sweetness and utterly seductive, while her wit, self-assurance and intelligence commanded broad admiration. She was a gifted linguist too, and the first of the Ptolemies to speak Egyptian fluently.

JULIUS CAESAR

In 48 BC Julius Caesar came to Egypt in hot pursuit of his adversary Pompey, whom he had just defeated at Pharsalus. He found a country on the verge of civil war and a reception committee bearing the head of Pompey. Caesar burst into tears at the sight of his dead rival; he was a merciful man who had honourable intentions to reconcile Pompey, a former friend and son-in-law, to his position. Ptolemy XIII had been responsible for the murder, an ill-judged attempt to curry favour. Earlier, Ptolemy had also driven his elder sister, Cleopatra, from Egypt, who had been on the point of fighting her way back at Pelusium when Pompey's sudden arrival there had stopped the armies from engaging.

Now Caesar took up residence at the palace in Alexandria and summoned Ptolemy to him. Cleopatra could only gain an audience by being carried into the compound at dusk in a bed-linen sack (or in later versions, a carpet) to be unfurled before him. Such coquetry delighted the Roman and, succumbing to her considerable charms, he reinstated her as queen. The young Ptolemy was furious and seeing that his army outnumbered Caesar's by five to one, had the palace surrounded and stirred up the Alexandrian mob. During the ensuing fighting, Caesar set fire to the enemy fleet in the harbour and the flames spread, engulfing some of the book depositories of the Great Library, if not the entire complex itself. Ptolemy was drowned in the Nile and his two principal guardians, the power figures of his court, were also killed. Cleopatra had become sole ruler, but to uphold the tradition of dual rule, she married her younger brother, Ptolemy XIV (r.47–44 BC), who at eleven years old could offer little resistance to her will, nor protest about her condition, heavily pregnant as she was with Caesar's son, Ptolemy Caesarion 'little Caesar'.

Caesar and Cleopatra embarked on a Nile cruise, no mere pleasure trip but a flotilla of four hundred ships impressing on the populace the might of Rome – and by extension, the strength of their queen. What better ally could Cleopatra have had than the most powerful man in the known world, a man so smitten that he dedicated a gold statue of her in his new temple of Venus, right under his wife Calpurnia's nose? What misfortune then that the same man should be assassinated in Rome on the Ides of March 44 BC. Cleopatra had been in Rome at the time too, trying among other things to get her son recognised as Caesar's only male heir. Now without a protector, she scurried back to Alexandria. Still, she knew Caesarion could serve as a bargaining chip in the future and made him her co-regent as the fifteenth Ptolemy (r.44–30 BC) after engineering the disappearance of her brother, Ptolemy XIV.

ANTONY

After two years of civil war, in 42 BC Mark Antony defeated Caesar's murderers at Philippi and the empire was divided between the members of the Second Triumvirate. Octavian, the great-nephew and adopted son and heir of Caesar, took the territories to the west, while those in the east fell to Antony; Lepidus was given 'Roman Africa', Carthaginia and neighbouring territories, before he was forced to retire from public life in 36 BC.

In 41 BC Antony summoned Cleopatra to him at Tarsus in Cilicia (southern Turkey) to upbraid her for her alleged support of his enemies. Her magnificent entrance as Isis–Aphrodite reclining under a golden canopy and waited on by beatific cupids was immortalised by Shakespeare (who drew heavily on Sir Thomas North's translation of Plutarch):

> The barge she sat in, like a burnish'd throne,
> Burnt on the water. The poop was beaten gold,
> Purple the sails, and so perfumed that
> The winds were love-sick with them; the oars were silver,
> Which to the tune of flutes kept stroke, and made
> The water which they beat to follow faster,
> As amorous of their strokes…

She softened his anger, melted his defences and 'purs'd up his heart'. Three years after losing Caesar, she had won a second great Roman with the power to fulfil her instinctive desires: to safeguard her dynastic line and to restore Egypt's empire.

Wintering with her in Alexandria, Antony let the affairs of state slip while he threw himself into a life of unbridled pleasure. No feast was too lavish, no party too expensive for the lovers' self-styled club, the 'Society of Inimitable Livers', which could not be outdone for opulence and regal luxury. In this atmosphere of passion, revelry and abandon, Cleopatra bore him three children: in 40 BC, the twins Alexander Helios 'sun' and Cleopatra Selene 'moon', and four years later, Ptolemy Philadelphus.

But Antony was no lovestruck fool and hoped to win major dividends from his alliance with the Egyptian queen. With Cleopatra's support, he wanted to expand his eastern territories into Parthia (east of the Roman province of Syria), a project that made Octavian uneasy. In 40 BC, Antony left Egypt to repair his relations with Octavian, marrying his sister, the dignified and much-respected Octavia, to cement the bond between them. The tensions did not die away. After three years apart, Antony returned to Cleopatra's welcoming arms. As a reward for her loyalty, he reorganised his provinces, gifting her a kingdom that resembled the empire of her forebears, including large portions of the Levant and areas of Cilicia. The territory was richly forested; in return for his generosity he wanted her to build a substantial navy and tap Egypt's wealth to fund his eastern conquests.

Unfortunately Antony's expedition to Parthia in 36 BC ended in humiliating retreat and the loss of over a third of his army. Despite the pleas of Octavia, who was still keen to mend the ever widening rift between her brother and her husband, Octavian did little to help, and offered his colleague only the barest of reinforcements.

Antony's dependence on his oriental queen grew. A second campaign to Armenia (34 BC) met with some success, and Antony celebrated the triumph in Alexandria as if it were the Rome of his empire. The festivities had a strong Hellenistic flavour and climaxed in the ceremony of 'the Donations' in which their children were crowned and given extensive realms, some of them yet to be conquered. Caesarion was named 'King of Kings' and Cleopatra 'Queen of Kings'. Of course, Antony as Roman triumvir stood above them all – and in his honour Cleopatra began work on a spectacular temple to him on the shore of the Great Harbour, which was later known as the Caesareum. (The New Kingdom obelisks that were borrowed from Heliopolis in about 12 BC to adorn the entrance, long outlived this grand monument and became known as 'Cleopatra's Needles', even though she had nothing to do with them. They were eventually transported to Victoria Embankment in London and New York's Central Park where they were erected in 1879 and 1881 respectively.)

Antony's exaltation of a foreign queen and her family disturbed the Romans, but he still had a sizeable following in the Senate. It was only the concerted efforts of Octavian and his supporters to smear his reputation, largely through a sustained and vitriolic attack on his relationship with Cleopatra, that opinion began to turn. Antony issued counter-propaganda and denials, but did not help his case by divorcing Octavia (32 BC), a woman who had behaved impeccably and had unstintingly sought to further her husband's interests. In Rome, Cleopatra was blamed for the divorce, and even the fair-tempered poet Horace was incited to rail against her, writing that 'the deranged queen and her gaggle of filthy disease-ridden degenerates, was hatching the ruin of the Capitol and the destruction of the empire'.

But the hammer blow came later in the same year, when Octavian seized Antony's will from its place of safekeeping with the Vestal Virgins and disclosed its key clauses: that Caesarion was Julius Caesar's son, meaning that Octavian's adoption by Caesar and position as heir was severely compromised; that his children by Cleopatra should receive large legacies, contrary to Roman law which prohibited foreigners from being beneficiaries of Roman wills; and that he should be buried in Egypt. Of the clauses, which may well have all been fabricated by Octavian, it was the last that caused the loudest outcry, feeding on widely-held fears that Antony wanted to transfer the Roman capital to Alexandria, the exotic home of the parasitic schemer, Cleopatra. Though Antony himself still had some support, Roman animosity towards his 'harlot queen' was almost universal. As a result, Octavian was able to declare her an enemy of the Roman state, and because Antony would not leave her, war between the two men was inevitable.

ACTIUM

The great clash came on 2 September 31 BC at Actium in western Greece. In the months before the battle, Octavian's outstanding general and admiral Agrippa had already scored some key successes against Antony's outlying naval bases, cutting off crucial supply routes to his enormous army and fleet stationed at Actium. As early attempts to break Octavian's blockade failed, the morale of Antony's ill-fed soldiers plummeted. It has been supposed that Antony decided his best hope was to break out of Actium by sea with as much of his fleet as possible, while his army withdrew towards Macedonia until they could regroup to fight another day.

If this was the case, the first part of the plan worked beautifully. While the opposing navies were engaged, Cleopatra's fleet of sixty ships slipped through the weakened centre into open waters, and Antony was able to follow shortly behind. However, his tactics had been betrayed to Octavian the night before, who saw to it that the rest of the navy would be too deeply embroiled in fierce deck-to-deck fighting to break out; around 170 of Antony's ships failed to get away and surrendered or were sunk.

When Antony and Cleopatra reached North Africa several days later to make arrangements for a counter-attack, they were probably still unaware that all was already lost. During the course of their voyage, the nineteen legions comprising Antony's land force had begun their planned retreat, but Octavian had caught up with them and offered terms that the demoralised soldiers could not refuse. With their surrender, what had seemed a reasonable outcome at Actium swiftly transformed into a crushing defeat; Antony had lost his army, his navy and his empire. All that remained was Egypt, Cleopatra and her small fleet.

If history rewards the victors, Actium was no exception. How well it suited Octavian to paint Cleopatra as the cowardly traitor, fleeing the battle at its most critical moment to save her own skin. How neat it was that Antony's flight behind her could be presented as the actions of a man blinded by love, willing to forsake his loyal troops and all hope of victory for this woman.

THE END OF THE PTOLEMIES

The pair waited in Alexandria for their inevitable demise. While Octavian's armies closed in, they lived with the same extravagance they had enjoyed together ten years earlier – but now they renamed their 'Society of Inimitable Livers' the 'Society of Partners in Death'. Antony hoped to be killed honourably in battle but what was left of his army deserted him at the final stand outside Alexandria on 1 August 30 BC. The same day Octavian marched into the ·city. Barricaded into her mausoleum with all her treasures, Cleopatra let it be known that she was dead. At the news, Antony fell on his sword – but when the truth emerged he begged to be taken to her in his death throes. He died in her arms and she took her own life a few days later by poison, as the story goes, from the bite of an asp.

Their children were paraded in Octavian's Triumph at Rome, but survived. Cleopatra Selene was married off to King Juba II of Mauretania, while Alexander Helios and Ptolemy Philadelphus were taken in by the magnanimous Octavia. Ptolemy Caesarion was not so lucky; Octavian was advised that 'too many Caesars would be a bad thing' and had him murdered.

Having annexed Egypt for Rome, Octavian – 'one of the most odious of the world's successful men' according to E. M. Forster – paid his respects to the mummified remains of Alexander the Great, whose nose he is reported to have broken off by accident. He had no such intention of honouring the dead Ptolemies and refused to visit their tombs, saying, 'I wished to see a king, not corpses'. It was truly the end of the Ptolemaic age.

CHAPTER SEVEN

From Rome to Byzantium

30 BC – 641 AD

The Roman Administration

Emperor Augustus (r. in Egypt 30 BC–14 AD), as Octavian was known from 27 BC, wrote that he had 'added Egypt to the empire of the Roman people'. But he knew that Egypt could not be just another province, governed by an appointed senator responsible to the Senate and People of Rome. Its extraordinary natural wealth could easily be misused by ambitious and unscrupulous politicians as a base to threaten his empire. His solution was to entrust the administration to someone of the equestrian order; that is, a man of substantial wealth but prohibited from a political career in the Senate, who would be personally answerable to the emperor rather than to the state, effectively making it his personal estate. Moreover, he forbade any senator or any other leading Romans from even entering Egypt without his prior authorisation. Even with this degree of control, Augustus remained highly suspicious of the man left in charge, his *praefectus Aegypti*, prefect of Egypt. The first, Cornelius Gallus, boasted too loudly of his success suppressing an uprising in Upper Egypt and subsequent invasion south into the kingdom of Meroe, and was swiftly recalled by the emperor only to be forced to commit suicide.

For ordinary Egyptians, the transition from independent Ptolemaic realm to a province in the Roman Empire was relatively smooth. Their new rulers were foreign, like the Ptolemies, and lived on the other side of the Mediterranean, but they still decorated the temples with traditional portraits and inscriptions, carving their names in hieroglyphs enclosed in the royal cartouche. The broad organisation of the country was largely unchanged from the Ptolemies, with its administrative division into around thirty 'nomes' each run by a *strategos* accountable to four regional administrators, the *epistrategoi*. Augustus, however, did feel it necessary to strip the *strategoi* of their military powers, preferring to place control of the army firmly in the hands of the Roman officers. Three legions were assigned to Egypt, one for Alexandria, one near Memphis, and the third distributed between numerous forts and outposts to police key roads, mines, quarries and grain depots. In the rule of Tiberius (r.14–37), the country was deemed peaceful enough to require only two legions, and by the time of Hadrian (r.117–138), this was further reduced to one.

CLASS AND RACE

Towards the end of the Ptolemaic period, the division between the Greek ruling class and the Egyptian population had begun to soften, with the latter group able to acquire status through intermarriage and other means. Augustus was no champion of such social mobility and quickly imposed a rigid social structure based on class and race which made it difficult, if not impossible, for the lower ranks to get ahead. At its top were the Roman citizens, exempt from most of the taxes and duties imposed on the rest of the country. Next were the citizens of the three predominantly Greek cities of Egypt: Alexandria, Naukratis and Ptolemais (and later, the Roman Antinoopolis in Middle Egypt, founded by the grief-stricken Hadrian in 130 for the memory of his young lover Antinous who had drowned there during their tour of the Nile). Anyone living in Egypt who was not a Roman, a citizen of one of the four cities, or a Jew, was classified as an Egyptian (including the rural Greeks). These were the masses, the humble and the poor, with few rights and low status, prohibited from advance by repressive legislation that outlawed or heavily penalised intermarriage. Nor did Caracalla's (r.198–217) extension of Roman citizenship to all inhabitants of the empire in 212 improve their position: the discrimination continued as if the edict had never existed. Only one section of society had it worse. Slavery flourished under the Romans, with abandoned female babies comprising much of the new stock; around two-thirds of Egyptian slaves were women.

GREEKS AND JEWS

Of the favoured cities, Alexandria should have enjoyed the highest status, but apparently because of the city's previous support for Antony, Augustus abolished its council (*boule*). At the same time, he granted the Jews – who, according to the Jewish philosopher Philo, dominated two of the city's five districts – all the freedoms they had had under the Ptolemies plus their own council of elders. It was a situation that unsurprisingly fuelled tensions and resentment between Greeks and Jews, leading to a Jewish massacre in 38 AD. Appeals and embassies were made in vain to Caligula (r.37–41), but the matter simmered on until Claudius (r.41–54) ordered both sides to end the feuding. This did not stop episodic rioting over the years, for example, in 66 when many thousands of Jews were killed. Notwithstanding such horrors, the relatively good conditions enjoyed by the Jews under the Romans lasted until 115, when a huge Jewish revolt erupted across Egypt culminating in the most serious and bloody event of the first two centuries AD. It may have been the appearance of a 'messiah' in Cyrene that triggered the insurrection, which rapidly spread to Egypt, Cyprus, Mesopotamia and Judea. Although it was swiftly put down in Alexandria by Trajan (r.98–117), Jewish gangs terrorised the country-side, unleashing their wrath with particular vehemence against the Greeks, whom they drove from their homes and slaughtered. The guerrilla warfare lasted for two years until it was quelled with ferocious retribution. The Jewish population was all but wiped out, and it did not begin to recover until the end of the second century.

TAX, TRADE AND EXPLOITATION

One of the many burdens borne by the Egyptians was the array of swingeing Roman taxes and imposts, plus the 'liturgies', obligatory public services performed by (mainly) Egyptians at their own expense. The rates were far higher than anything the Ptolemies had imposed, and collected with relentless Roman efficiency. Tax farmers would stop at nothing to get payments from their charges, even if it meant illegally 'racking their bodies with twistings and tortures or killing them off with newly contrived modes of death', as Philo claimed. The revenues that flooded back to Rome were so far above the expected quota that Tiberius remarked, 'I want my sheep shorn, not skinned alive.' Much of it was collected in grain, Egypt's prime product, and before long the country's downtrodden peasantry was providing Rome with a third of its food supply.

Neither was the province plundered only of its agricultural resources. The Romans went to considerable trouble to extract fine stone, minerals and precious metals from remote mines and quarries in the Eastern Desert. The exceptional stone (granodiorite) quarried from Mons Claudianus, for example, was used almost exclusively to make columns for some of Rome's most important buildings, including the Forum, the Colosseum and the Pantheon. In addition to produce, raw materials, and manufactured items such as glass, pottery and papyrus, Egypt was also an invaluable nexus of world commerce at Alexandria and a prime conduit for luxury goods imported from India and the Far East via desert caravans and the Red Sea.

SOCIETY AND CULTURE

Although most of Egypt's assets leached straight out of the country for the benefit of the emperor and Rome, Alexandria continued to be by far the richest and most important city in the eastern Mediterranean. As ever, there were periodic outbursts and disturbances, but the Romans were still keen to encourage Greek culture and supported the great institutions of learning such as the Mouseion and Library. It was during the Roman period that Alexandria nurtured the historian Appian (*fl. c.*120), and the mathematician, geographer and astronomer, Ptolemy (also known as Claudius Ptolemaeus, *fl. c.*140), who compiled the highly influential *Almagest*, a synthesis of all Greek astronomy that had gone before – even if it did contradict earlier insights that the earth went around the sun. His geocentric conception of the universe which was named the Ptolemaic system after him, was dogmatically adhered to in the West until the sixteenth century. Less celebrated than Ptolemy, but no less brilliant was Heron (*fl. c.* 62), the geometrician and inventor who came up with the world's first steam-powered engine and coin-operated machines, as well as dozens of formulae for

Anubis as a Roman soldier

the properties of polygons. The great physician Galen (*c.*129–216) finished his training in Alexandria, which had by then become the foremost centre of contemporary medical knowledge. Greek cities throughout the country also featured smaller scale centres of culture and learning, theatres, schools and gymnasia; from Naukratis came the grammarian Athenaeus (*fl. c.* 200), and from Lycopolis, the philosopher and founder of Neoplatonism, Plotinus (205–270).

While the Greeks and other 'foreigners' were laying the foundations for the flowering of art and literature during the Byzantine period, native Egyptian culture and religion was withering away. Ironically, at much the same time it was in decline at its source, the cults of Isis, Serapis, Osiris and Anubis were gathering popularity throughout the Roman world; indeed, Isis cropped up as far afield as Hadrian's Wall in Britain. The well-to-do of Egypt, which excluded the huge majority of the indigenous population, were still happy to appropriate the traditional practices of pharaonic times. They embalmed and mummified their dead, and commonly depicted the native deities associated with death on tombs and funeral stelae, albeit with a strong classical flavour. Egyptian gods appeared in Roman dress or had traditional postures but Hellenic faces, as can still be seen in the catacombs of Alexandria. Similarly, their mummies – such as those of this period recovered from the Fayum – often bore beguiling, realistic portraits painted in a very non-Egyptian style. Such charming adaptations aside, there was initially plenty of support from the top for Egyptian art and culture (in modified form at least) and the earlier emperors were keen to fulfil the ancient role of pharaoh in temple decoration and construction – the most famous example being the exquisite Kiosk of Trajan at Philae.

However, the appearance of new buildings and inscriptions tailed off rapidly after about 160 AD and Decius (r.249–251) was the last emperor to have his cartouche carved on to a temple wall. Crippling taxation of the indigenous population, the steady reduction of government subsidies to the temple priesthoods, the centralised control of the temples under Roman officials, the drop in status of the priesthoods and their role in society, the sharp decline in the number of scribes who understood hieroglyphic script and demotic (the Egyptian cursive script since the Twenty-sixth Dynasty), and the withdrawal of support from local elites more concerned with emphasising their Hellenistic identity, all worked together to hasten the demise of indigenous traditions. The last known hieroglyph was carved on 24 August 394 and the last demotic inscription in 452, both at Philae. By then, the ancient religion and culture that had underpinned more than three thousand years of Egyptian civilisation were rapidly being lost or subsumed into dominant new forms.

POLITICAL OUTLINE

Locked into the Roman Empire and treated as the provisioner of Rome, Egypt was not at the cutting edge of international politics, but followed the fortunes of its masters. At peace, under little or no threat of invasion, and only infrequently visited by the emperor, the country lived out a broadly uneventful existence for the first two centuries of Roman rule. That is not to say that discontent was not simmering away beneath the lid of imperial domination; there were intermittent revolts as well as the Jewish rebellions, outbreaks of plague, and spats with the Blemmyes and other Nubian tribes. And the dissatisfaction steadily increased during this period as over-taxation, mismanagement of resources, and lack of maintenance of irrigation systems began to affect productivity and local prosperity. The extensive damage and depopulation caused by a peasants' revolt in the Delta (171–172), which had to be put down with reinforcements from Syria (whose leader then proclaimed himself emperor and had to be killed), compelled Commodus (r.180–192) to supplement his corn supply from other parts of the empire.

From this point on the economic situation in Egypt only deteriorated. Hyperinflation, the strictures of the liturgies and punitive tax collection drove large numbers of peasants off the land and into a life of brigandage. Anti-Roman sentiment had never run higher. Caracalla's visit to Alexandria in 215 was met with hostile crowds that jeered and accused him of murdering his brother Geta (r.209–212). His vengeance was savage; for several days his troops rampaged the streets in an orgy of slaughter and plunder.

As the third century progressed, Rome's control of its territories was severely tested, particularly in the east. Unrest in Syria allowed Zenobia, Queen of Palmyra, 'perhaps the only female whose superior genius broke through the servile indolence imposed on her sex by the climate and manners of Asia' (Edward Gibbon, *Decline and Fall of the Roman Empire*) to seize power in Egypt from 270–272, until Aurelian (r.270–275) was able to regain control, destroying much of Alexandria's royal quarter including possibly the Great Library and the Soma (the tomb of Alexander) in the process. Twenty years later the revolts continued and the Roman response intensified in its severity. Galerius (r.293–311) personally oversaw the obliteration of Koptos, the gateway town for desert routes to the Red Sea, following an insurrection in 293, and Diocletian (r.284–305) laid siege to Alexandria for eight months after the usurper Lucius Domitius Domitianus had been proclaimed emperor there (297). When the city fell, Diocletian rode in on horseback, swearing that he would not stop the carnage until the blood stained his horse's knees. To the relief of the Alexandrians the horse 'trod on a man's corpse and stumbled and knelt on it so that the horse's knee was bloodied. The emperor noticed this and granted a pardon.' The citizens were so grateful they put up a bronze statue of the horse in thanks; Diocletian himself celebrated the victory by erecting a gigantic column in the Serapeum, later misnamed 'Pompey's Pillar', one of the rare classical monuments in the city to survive the centuries.

To govern better its fraying frontiers and quell the regular revolts that threatened to break out anywhere from Britain to the Persian Gulf, Diocletian divided the empire into east and west (293). It was to be ruled by the 'Tetrarchy', two emperors with the title 'Augustus' and two junior colleagues and heirs called 'Caesar'. Diocletian took the eastern half and appointed Maximian (r.286–305) to the west.

Diocletian was also a religious man, anxious to defend the Roman pantheon against new cults that refused to be assimilated into it. In his eyes, the worst of them all was Christianity, a monotheistic and evangelical religion that not only denied the pagan gods and his divinity as emperor, but sought to convert those that worshipped them.

Early Christianity in Egypt

By the time Diocletian came to Egypt in 297, Christianity was well established there. According to Matthew 2:13–20, the infant Jesus and his family slipped out of Judea to the safety of Egypt after Joseph was warned in a dream that King Herod intended to kill the Christ-child. There they remained until after Herod's death; traditionally they sheltered during their journey under a sycamore at Heliopolis (now called the Tree of the Virgin) and stayed in the area that is now Old Cairo. It could therefore be supposed that Christianity took root in Egypt among those that had come into contact with the Holy Family even while Jesus was a babe-in-arms. We are also told in Acts 2:10 that Egyptian Jews were among the congregation in Jerusalem when the Holy Spirit descended during the first Pentecost, nine days after Christ's crucifixion (c. 30 AD); perhaps they were the first to bring the faith to Egypt.

As tradition has it, however, St Mark the Evangelist, who came to Egypt in the early 40s AD, was the founder and first Patriarch of the

Church of Alexandria, the first to convert an Egyptian to Christianity (a Jewish cobbler named Ananias), and the first of Egypt's many Christian martyrs. The new religion must have quickly found followers among the Jews of Alexandria, the poor and disaffected; its message struck a chord with many who resented the rule of imperial Rome and the arrogance of the Greek-speaking upper classes. Within a couple of decades Christians had become prominent enough to arouse the suspicions of pagan Alexandrians, who were enraged to find Mark leading an Easter service on the same day as the feast of Serapis. As the legend goes, they dragged Mark by a rope through the city streets until he died but were thwarted in burning his body by a miraculous cloudburst which doused the flames. Christians spirited his body away, burying it under the altar of his church. It was apparently stolen by Venetian merchants in 828, placed in a basket of pork to deter the probes of Islamic officials, and smuggled back to Venice where it became the principal relic of the Basilica di San Marco. A small relic of St Mark was returned to Egypt by the Vatican in 1968, on the nine hundredth anniversary of his death.

ANCIENT EGYPTIAN RELIGION AND CHRISTIANITY

It is no coincidence that ancient Egyptian religion withered away precisely when Christianity began to blossom. As its rapid spread throughout the country testifies, Egyptians found the new religion relatively easy to accommodate beside long-held native beliefs. For example, the Christian promise of an afterlife conformed with ancient, dearly cherished convictions – and improved on them. Eternal life was available to all without the rigmarole and expense of mummification, tombs, spells and votive offerings; paradise was no longer the domain of the rich and powerful but available to the poor and humble.

On another level, the ancient religion found a new expression in Christianity and influenced its early theological development. One striking example is the concept of the Holy Trinity as three-in-one, a formula which had existed only in Egypt beforehand. From the New Kingdom onwards, Egyptians began grouping gods into 'triads', a divine family of father, mother and child such as Osiris, Isis and Horus, different parts of a single holy entity. Linked also were Egyptian ideas about the soul, which they believed to be comprised of the *ba*, *ka*, and *akh*, each of which represented elements as well as the totality of the individual. The resonance of these ancient beliefs was surely felt during later disputes about the nature of Christ which eventually rent Christendom; it is telling that many of the leading theologians who wrestled with these problems came from Egypt.

There are many other details that point to continuities between old and new religions. In iconography, for example, the sign of the cross cropped up in Egypt in the form of the *ankh*, the native symbol of life, which chimed well with its connection to the resurrection. We can also draw a line between Isis nursing the infant Horus (or Harpocrates as he was then known) and early depictions of the Virgin Mary nursing the baby Jesus. Similarly, many have commented on the relationship between the cult of Isis and the Christian emphasis on the veneration of the Mother of God. In early Egyptian Christian art, Jesus is portrayed as shepherd and winnower, carrying the same crook and flail that Osiris held. Furthermore, the Christian notion of 'the resurrection of the flesh' is not found in the Old Testament, yet has much in common with the cult of Osiris and mummification, and the mentions of the 'second death' in Revelation closely resemble the ancient Egyptian concept that terrified believers in the pharaonic age (see p.72).

THE WORD AND COPTIC LANGUAGE

The world's earliest known fragment of the New Testament, a scrap of the Gospel of St John written in Greek on papyrus, was found in Egypt and dates to around 125 AD. Its provenance from Oxyrhynchus, where thousands of papyrus fragments were found, suggests that Christianity had begun to spread throughout the countryside.

About a century later, translations of the Bible began to appear in the native Egyptian language using a new system of writing. It was based on the Greek alphabet with some additions derived from demotic for unfamiliar sounds. The language came to be known as Coptic and was the principal medium for Egyptians, spoken and written by Christians and pagans alike and used in secular as well as sacred texts. The term 'Copt' itself derives from the Greek *Aiguptios*, which originally referred to a native Egyptian as opposed to a Greek or Roman living in Egypt. With the arrival of the Arabs in the seventh century, the word was corrupted to *qibt* and was eventually used only for the Christian population of the country, as it is today.

The dispersal of sacred texts written in a new native script and the appearance of missionaries preaching in the Egyptian vernacular pushed the message of Christianity far outside Alexandria. Its early appeal to the Jews and intellectuals of the metropolis crossed the boundaries of class and culture, and began to attract the uneducated and disenfranchised, the native majority in the towns and villages of the countryside.

CATECHETICAL SCHOOL OF ALEXANDRIA

Christianity primarily flourished among the Jewish communities of Alexandria and was probably regarded by outsiders as just another sect of Judaism until as late as the second century. But after the near total annihilation of the city's Jews between 115 and 117 under Trajan (see p.177), the Judaic influence on Christianity quickly diminished while Greek elements came to the fore. It was during the second century that the Catechetical School was established in the city, which drew on the intellectual rigour of Greek culture and philosophy – while rejecting its pagan underpinnings – to develop the doctrines of Christianity. Two of the most important early leaders at the school were Clement (d. *c.* 215) and his brilliant pupil Origen (*c.*185–254), eminent scholars whose erudition and treatises were very important during the early Christian period.

They strove to counter the influence of the Alexandrian philosophers and the Gnostics, who preached a mystical version of Christianity which dwelt on the struggle between good and evil and drew on diverse sources including dualistic Asiatic religions, Platonic philosophy and ancient Egyptian magic, particularly the arcane writings of the *Hermetica*, attributed to Hermes Trismegistus, a Hellenised version of the Egyptian god Thoth. (The *Hermetica* would become the key text in alchemy, which itself would be known as the 'Egyptian art', or *al-Kemi* by Arabs, from the Coptic word *kemi* 'Egyptian', ultimately deriving from the ancient name for Egypt, *Kemet*.)

Clement and Origen aimed to harness the instruments of scientific and philosophical reasoning to develop a systematic theology and the basis of a Christian orthodoxy. As it turned out, their works were not thought orthodox enough by later generations; Clement was denounced as a heretic and had his sainthood removed by the Orthodox Church, while Origen, who was reputed to have written over six thousand texts, was deemed to have grown excessively famous by the Alexandrian Patriarch Demetrius and excommunicated for heretical teaching.

PERSECUTION

The religion at large apparently had a profile low enough to have gone unnoticed by the Roman authorities until 202 when Septimius Severus (r.193–211) prohibited Christians from proselytising, a move that affected the Catechetical School and forced Clement to flee the country. The penalty for transgression was banishment or hard labour in the mines; in the early years, the faithful deliberately had to seek execution if they were to be martyred. But such leniency did not last long. The persecutions of 249–251 under Decius exhibited all the cruelty of a systematic eradication, and even Origen, who was widely respected outside Christian circles, was brutally tortured; he died from his injuries four years later. Another Alexandrian martyr, Apollonia, had her teeth pulled out before her execution and later became patron saint of those with toothache. A purge to root out church leaders came in 258 under Valerian (r.253–260), but his son, Gallienus (r.253–268), issued an edict that tolerated the religion and allowed the church to establish itself throughout the country.

By the time Diocletian initiated the Great Persecution on 23 February 303, Egypt had seventy-two bishoprics, including eighteen in the Thebaid (Thebes and its environs). The devastation of this infamous persecution was so severe that the Coptic Church, as the Christian Church of Egypt became known, named the period the 'Era of Martyrs' and still dates its calendar from the first day of Diocletian's reign (29 August 284) to commemorate the many thousands that were sent to their deaths. Poor health led to the emperor's abdication, but the persecutions soon resumed under the fanatically anti-Christian Galerius and Maximinus Daia (r.305–313), and once again Egypt bore the brunt of Roman fury. The historian Eusebius gave an eyewitness account of the atrocities:

> Some were scraped, racked, mercilessly flogged, subjected to countless other torments too terrible to describe in endless variety, and finally given to the flames…
>
> But words cannot describe the outrageous agonies endured by the martyrs in the Thebaid. They were torn to bits from head to foot with potsherds like claws till death released them. Women were tied by one foot and hoisted high in the air. Others again were tied to trees and stumps and died horribly; for with the aid of machinery they drew together the very stoutest boughs, fastened one of the martyr's legs to each, and then let the boughs fly back to their normal position; thus they managed to tear apart the limbs of their victims in a moment. In this way they carried on, not for a few days or weeks, but year after year…
>
> Some victims suffered death by beheading, others punishment by fire. So many were killed on a single day that the axe, blunted and worn out by the slaughter, was broken in pieces, while the exhausted executioners had to be periodically relieved.

The History of the Church, 8.8–9

But none of the brutalities dented the ardour of the faithful 'who would jump on to the platform in front of the judge and proclaim themselves Christians'. There should have been some respite from the slaughter after Galerius, on his deathbed, had a change of heart and issued the Edict of Toleration in 311, which granted Christians the freedom to worship, but Maximinus Daia would not relent and continued the purges with renewed ferocity for a further two years until he was deposed.

CONSTANTINE THE GREAT

Not all Romans despised Christians as Maximinus Daia did. Constantine the Great (r.306–337) renounced paganism and became a Christian after he had a vision of a flaming cross in the sky with the words 'under this sign you shall conquer'. He claimed Christ had also appeared to him with the advice that he should take the symbol as his standard. Marching under this banner, Constantine saw off rivals to the throne and took complete control of the western empire by 312. The following year he issued with Licinius (r.308–324), the emperor of the east, the Edict of Milan, which gave freedom for all to worship any god. Later, Constantine made special dispensations to Christians too, by making them eligible for public office and by returning property confiscated from them during the persecutions.

In 324 Constantine defeated Licinius and became the sole ruler of the Roman Empire. The same year he established Constantinople on the site of ancient Byzantium as the 'New Rome', which was formally dedicated as administrative capital of the empire on 11 May 330. It was a momentous development for Egypt, as this new seat of power in the eastern Mediterranean would eventually undermine the long-standing pre-eminence of Alexandria.

MONASTICISM

In the new climate of religious freedom under Constantine, Christianity rapidly took hold throughout Egypt. While missionaries roamed the country to preach the Word, others led by example through the rejection of worldly comforts to devote their lives to God in ascetic isolation. Hermits (from Greek *eremites* 'man of the desert') and anchorites (*anachoretes* 'one who withdraws') were nothing new in Egypt. There had been the reclusive Katachoi who lived off charity in the catacombs of the Serapeum at Saqqara in the second century BC, and then the fugitives who fled into the desert to escape tax collectors or religious persecution. And now with Christianity and the instruction of Jesus to 'go and sell that thou hast, and give to the poor, and thou shalt have treasure in heaven' (Matthew 19:21), holy men and women all over Egypt rid themselves of their possessions and walked off into the desert to dedicate themselves to a life of spiritual contemplation. If martyrdom was no longer an option to heroic Christians, the devout could still commit their lives to Jesus through 'mortification', the denial and deadening of their former needs, appetites and desires. These hermits and ascetics, holed up in caves or ancient tombs in the barren deserts and mountains of Egypt were the 'fathers' of Christian monasticism. It was a movement which spread throughout Europe to the remotest wind-beaten extremities of Britain and Ireland, developing into a form of devotion that is still practised today.

The first Christian hermit was St Paul of Thebes (*c.*234–347), who apparently spent almost ninety years in cave-bound meditation. The traditional founder of monasticism, however, is regarded as St Anthony (*c.*251–356). His simple life, his battles with the demons who tried to tempt him, his miracles and his feats of endurance, made him the prime model for aspiring hermit monks (from Greek *monachos*, 'solitary man'). Other anchorites occupied caves nearby to learn from his wisdom, and soon informal communities of monks appeared around him, bound by their commitment to God. The first of these monastic communities was at Pispir in Middle Egypt (modern day Deir el-

Icon of the errant hermit, Abu Nofer

Maymun), which became so popular that Anthony withdrew for renewed solitude to a cave above the Wadi Arabah in the Eastern Desert. After his death, his fame spread far outside Egypt with the publication of the *Life of Anthony* written by Athanasius (*c.*293–373), the Patriarch of Alexandria. The hermit's followers built a monastery in his name near his cave, which is still flourishing today. Anthony's disciple St Macarius (*c.*300–390) established many others in the Wadi Natrun, west of the Delta, four of which have survived to modern times. *The Sayings of the Fathers*, a work that has inspired generations of monastics, was largely written in the Wadi Natrun monasteries.

The enclosed, self-sustaining monasteries staffed by a fellowship of monks who wore the same clothes and shared the benefits of each other's labours, who ate together in a refectory and prayed together in a chapel – in other words, the monasteries familiar to us today – were developed by St Pachomius (*c.*292–346) in Upper Egypt. Applying his earlier career as a soldier to his religion, Pachomius developed highly disciplined and organised monastic communities, demanding his monks adhere scrupulously to strict rules governing day-to-day life. This popular and enduring formula was taken to Europe by St Jerome as the *Rule of Pachomius* and formed the blueprint of Western monasticism in later centuries.

Few were as disciplinarian as Shenoute (*c.*334/350–452/466), who ran the enormous White Monastery near Sohag, which was home to well over four thousand brethren (not to mention the twenty thousand people who took refuge there at one point after the Blemmyes from Nubia had ravaged the region). Infractions of the regime were severely punished; in one unfortunate incident, he reputedly lost his temper and beat a monk to death after he was caught with a woman. Shenoute is better remembered, however, for his prolific writings, his letters, instructions, homilies, polemics and sermons, which elevated Coptic literature to new heights and established Shenoute's Sahidic dialect of Coptic as the classical standard idiom for Copts for the following centuries.

Before the arrival of Islam in the seventh century, there were more than a hundred monasteries in Egypt and many tens of thousands of monks; travellers commented that the deserts were more populated than the towns. The monastic movement was decisive in bringing Christianity to rural Egyptians, and even those who chose not to become monks or hermits would voyage to these communities to seek advice and guidance from the famous holy recluses. Meanwhile it was from the ranks of these monks that the bishops and leaders of the Egyptian Church would be selected. Ever since the early fifth century most Coptic Patriarchs have been recruited in this way, and from 1525 onwards, all have had monastic experience.

EARLY SCHISMS

The rapid expansion of the early Church did not come without disputes. Even during the persecutions of the late third century, a row erupted in Egypt about how best to deal with Christians who had renounced their faith to evade financial ruin, torture or martyrdom, leading to the formation of the breakaway Meletian sect. However, few arguments were as bitter – and abstruse – as those that centred on the nature of Christ, which ultimately sundered the native Egyptian Church from the others.

The argument was started by an Alexandrian priest named Arius (*c.*250–336), who challenged the established dogma by maintaining that God was superior to Christ, who had a human element and was therefore not of the same substance. He reasoned that to see them both as divine suggested that there was more than one God. On the other hand, his opponents claimed that to stress Christ's humanity was to diminish his divinity, leaving him vulnerable to attack from those who saw him as just a 'special man'.

Constantine attempted to resolve the dispute at the First Ecumenical Council of Nicaea in 325, which ruled that Christ was 'the only Son of God, eternally begotten of the Father...true God from true God, begotten, not made, one in Being with the Father', thus making the Arian position heretical. The Nicene Creed, developed further at future councils, is still regarded as the only ecumenical statement of Christian faith, accepted by the Catholic, Orthodox, Anglican and other major Protestant churches. Its main champion at the First Council was another Egyptian theologian, Athanasius, whose impressive analysis of the matter before an assembly of over three hundred top ecclesiastics won him the argument and the Patriarchate of Alexandria three years later.

But the quarrel did not end there and many were opposed to the ruling, not least the Arians, the Meletians, and Emperor Constantine himself. The dispute dragged on for at least sixty years until Emperor Theodosius (r.379-395) at the Second Ecumenical Council of Constantinople in 381 reaffirmed the Nicene Creed, effectively ending Arianism in Egypt.

RIVALRY WITH CONSTANTINOPLE

At the same council, however, Theodosius presided over a serious setback for the international standing of the Alexandrian Patriarch and the Egyptian Church when he decreed that the Bishop of Constantinople stood second only to the Bishop of Rome. By the late fourth century Egypt had become predominantly Christian, and the Patriarch of Alexandria, who controlled the appointment of all bishops in Egypt, Libya and the Pentapolis (five cities of North Africa) as well as the considerable wealth of the See, held powers to rival even the prefect. The See of Alexandria – home to the Catechetical School and the leading theologians of the age, dozens of monastic communities, and a devout native laity – was also arguably the most important in Christendom. Theodosius's challenge to its primacy was not well received and triggered a power struggle against Constantinople which coloured much of the country's history over the next few centuries.

In 391 Theodosius prohibited paganism, unleashing waves of persecutions and the closure of the temples to Egypt's ancient gods. It had taken less than eighty years for the persecuted Christian minority to transmute into the persecuting majority. In Alexandria, the patriarch Theophilus (*fl*.384–412) agitated his flock against the unfaithful until fanatical rioters tore down the Serapeum, smashing its idols and destroying its library (the 'daughter' or subsidiary library of the Great Library of the Mouseion) of forty thousand books. His nephew and successor, Cyril (376–444), was even more zealous in his purges, driving Jews out of the city in 412, desecrating pagan sanctuaries and inciting Christian mobs to street violence that ultimately led to the murder of the gifted female mathematician and Neoplatonist philosopher Hypatia (*c.*370–415). A teacher of great renown, she was the torchbearer of scientific learning and philosophy, fields which had come to be regarded by Christians as deeply pagan concerns; her death persuaded many other scholars to leave the city, initiating the city's decline as the supreme centre of ancient learning.

Ambitious and aggressive, Cyril also employed the tactics of force and intimidation to resolve doctrinal arguments with other theologians, especially if they were associated with Alexandria's great rival Constantinople. He unleashed a vitriolic attack on Constantinople's patriarch, Nestorius (d. *c.* 451), who had managed to reopen the controversy surrounding the nature of Christ by insisting that the Virgin Mary should not be called 'Mother of God' (*Theotokos*) since she bore not God but the human Jesus. To Cyril this smacked of old Arianism in its attempt to separate Christ's divine and human natures. In the Third Ecumenical Council at Ephesus in 431, he commandeered proceedings before most of his opponents had even arrived, cowing those present with a large band of rowdy supporters until the assembly agreed to condemn Nestorius as a heretic.

Cyril was followed by another imposing patriarch in 444, Dioscorus (d. 454), whose powers and tyrannical authority were sufficient to earn him the epithet 'Pharaoh of the Church'. But it was a gross overestimation of his strength that precipitated a calamity for the Egyptian Church that led to permanent isolation and loss of influence.

MONOPHYSITISM

When a new quarrel erupted Dioscorus took on the combined might of the patriarchs of Rome, Constantinople and Antioch in favour of a monk from Constantinople, Eutyches, who had developed Cyril's anti-Nestorian views by preaching that Christ had only one nature after the incarnation, his humanity having been subsumed into his divinity, 'dissolved like a drop of honey in the sea'. It was a form of what came to be known as 'monophysitism' (one nature), a belief that Christ has a single nature. Presiding over the Council of Ephesus in

449, dubbed the Robber Council on account of the unruly and dishonourable conduct of many in attendance, Dioscorus bullied the assembly into vindicating Eutyches, excommunicating the Roman Pope and deposing the Bishops of Antioch and Constantinople, the latter dying shortly afterwards from his harsh treatment.

CHALCEDON

The Patriarch of Alexandria had asserted his primacy but in the process had outraged a substantial portion of the Christian world. The backlash was not long in coming. At the Council of Chalcedon in 451, the rulings of the Robber Council were annulled and Dioscorus was excommunicated and exiled on grounds of misconduct (rather than heresy); he died three years later. Monophysitism and Nestorianism were condemned and the official orthodox doctrine took a 'diphysite' stance recognising Christ as having one person and two perfect, indivisible and distinct natures – the view of the majority of Christian churches today.

In the aftermath of the council, acrimonious struggles over the Patriarchate of Alexandria broke out between Chalcedonians (dubbed 'Melkites', from the Aramaic word for king, for their support of the imperial line) and Coptic 'anti-Chalcedonians'. The theological differences between the two sides were extraordinarily subtle but they were exaggerated to the greatest extremes by rival political factions. As much as anything, it was the fierce political nationalism of the native Egyptians forcing a wedge into a hairline theological split that created an irreparable rupture with the Roman and Byzantine churches. It should be noted that many different monophysite positions exist and most Copts have rejected the label 'monophysite' and now prefer the term 'anti-Chalcedonian' as a more accurate way to describe their position.

THE FORMATION OF THE COPTIC CHURCH

The emperor Justinian (r.527–565) made extra efforts to win over the anti-Chalcedonians, tempting the Alexandrian Patriarch Theodosius (d.567) to accept the Council's rulings with entreaties of power. When the patriarch refused, Justinian deposed him and assigned a succession of imperial appointees to the post, all of whom were unacceptable to the native population. Theodosius was exiled but curiously was able to take up residence in the court of Justinian's wife, Theodora, who was herself a monophysite.

After 570, Alexandria had two coexisting patriarchs, one for the Melkites and another for the anti-Chalcedonians. The former were never Egyptians and were imposed on Alexandria from abroad, while the native anti-Chalcedonian patriarchs were forced initially to take up residence in monasteries outside the city. Similarly, the adherents of each group broadly followed existing fault lines in Egyptian society – between Greek speakers and Coptic speakers, landowners and peasantry, imperialists and nationalists. In the country at large there were thought to be about 200,000 Melkites but six million anti-Chalcedonians. The schism was never healed and the result was the separation of the native Egyptian Church, which became known as the Coptic Orthodox Church, from the Churches of Rome and Constantinople. The Melkites became part of the Eastern Orthodox Church.

The Byzantine Empire

In 395, Emperor Theodosius divided the Roman Empire between his two sons, who ruled eastern and western halves from Constantinople and Rome respectively. The west was soon in tatters; Rome was sacked by the Visigoths in 410 and the last western emperor was deposed in 476. Barbarian hordes soon overran Italy and the Vandals seized North Africa. The east, on the other hand, which became known as the Byzantine Empire, was faring much better, even though Bulgars and Slavs probed and harried the northern frontier and the Persians menaced the east.

When Justinian became emperor in 527, he harboured a grand vision to return the Roman Empire to its former greatness, and quickly succeeded in recovering North Africa from the Vandals (533) and Rome from the Ostrogoths (536). He also felt that the unity of empire depended on unity of faith.

In Egypt this meant the enforcement of Chalcedonian principles. It also meant the eradication of the final pockets of paganism, principally the closure in about 535 of the Temple of Isis at Philae, where the Blemmyes and Nubades, Nubian tribes that inhabited areas around the cataracts beyond the southern frontier, continued to worship the ancient gods. Justinian resolved to convert them, but his wife Theodora sent a rival monophysite mission that arrived far sooner thanks to her Egyptian associates. Justinian made other attempts to establish Chalcedonian doctrine in the countryside too, founding the Monastery of St Catherine in the Sinai peninsula (*c.*530), now a famous Greek Orthodox monastery and repository for exquisite illuminated manuscripts.

THE USURPER AND THE REVOLUTIONARY

Justinian's achievements in extending and consolidating the Byzantine Empire were squandered by his successors who battled to prevent the collapse of its economy and the disintegration of its territories. The tyrant Phocas (r.602–610), who murdered his predecessor Maurice (r.582–602) and his family in the first bloody overthrow since the time of Constantine, lost the Balkans to the Avars and Syria-Palestine to the Persians.

Seeing the empire fall to pieces around them, members of the Byzantine government appealed for a new leader and found Heraclius (r.610–641), the son of the governor of Carthage. Heraclius identified the strategic importance of Egypt as the base for an attack on the emperor. It was the granary of Constantinople, and in the dockyards of Alexandria he could simultaneously cut supply lines and assemble a fleet. Egypt was also a hotbed of nationalism and overripe for insurrection against Constantinople and the hated Phocas. From his base in Carthage, he ordered his general, Niketas, to march into Alexandria. In 610, Phocas's army was cut to pieces outside Alexandria's gates and later that year Heraclius, master of Egypt, was able to take Constantinople and the crown.

PERSIAN OCCUPATION

The coup sparked off unrest all over the empire and it took time for Heraclius to assert his authority. Making the most of the instability, the Persians captured Jerusalem in 614 and looted it of the 'True Cross', on which Christ was crucified. In 616 they marched into Egypt and seized Alexandria three years later. They indulged their contempt of Christians by despoiling churches and butchering monks in their monasteries; stories of the cruel Cambyses, the reviled Persian conqueror of more than a millennium past, began circulating in Coptic literature.

After methodical preparations, Heraclius responded with a series of brilliant campaigns in Asia Minor, Armenia and Mesopotamia between 622 and 628, that forced the Persians back from Byzantine lands.

CYRUS, THE PERSECUTOR

The entire Christian world rejoiced in Heraclius's triumph against Persia. News that the holy sites and relics had been returned to Christendom drew Christians of all sects and persuasions together in collective thanks. A united Church galvanised against schism well suited the emperor, as it would present a formidable front against enemies of the empire. With this in mind, he formulated a compromise doctrine (monothelitism – that Christ had one will) that he hoped would bring the anti-Chalcedonians back into the imperial religious fold while they were still well disposed to Byzantium.

He imagined he could achieve this through gentle persuasion but his disastrous appointee for the task, Cyrus, had none of the charm, patience nor sensitivity that such an operation required. Cyrus was made Melkite patriarch of Alexandria and given the civil and military powers of a viceroy. When his first clumsy attempts to propose the compromise fell flat in 631, he hastily resorted to violence, initiating a decade of savage persecution against the Copts.

With canny percipience, Benjamin, the Coptic patriarch went into hiding in the desert monasteries of Upper Egypt as soon as Cyrus touched the Alexandrian shore. His brother had no such luck and was captured, tortured with burning torches pressed against his flesh 'till the fat dropped down from both his sides on the ground', then tied in a sack of sand and drowned. Many others were beaten, tortured, imprisoned and murdered for refusing to accept Chalcedon, though many more were lost to the Coptic Church through bribery and extortion.

The result was precisely the reverse of that which Heraclius had intended. Through cruelty and force his agents had turned native Egyptians against Byzantium for good. The belief that their Church had no future within the empire can only have opened their eyes to extraordinary developments in Arabia, where the Prophet Muhammad (*c.*570–632), had united virtually all the tribes of the peninsula behind his One Omnipotent God.

The Coming of the Arabs

In 622, the same year that Heraclius began his counter-offensive against the Persians, Muhammad made his flight from Mecca to Medina. The *hijra*, as the migration became known, marked the foundation of the Muslim community and the first year of the Islamic calendar. After eight years of sporadic raiding and warfare against his enemies in Mecca, Muhammad seized the city in 630. He put an end to profane worship there by destroying the pagan idols and shrines of the Kaaba, Mecca's holy site, and rededicated it to Allah. By his death in 632, he had unified the Arab tribes and transformed Arabia into a formidable powerbase from where the new faith could spread east and west.

For the Byzantines, the timing could hardly have been worse. The wars with the Persians had been enervating, and the imperial armies were exhausted and overstretched, quite unable to occupy and secure the large territories that the Persians had evacuated. In contrast, the invigorated Muslim forces were inspired by faith and prepared to die for Allah.

> Let those who would exchange the life of this world for the hereafter, fight for the cause of God; whoever fights for the cause of God, whether he dies or triumphs, on him We shall bestow a rich recompense.
>
> The Koran 4:74

Muhammad himself had promised that his followers killed in holy war would be taken to paradise: 'The fire of hell shall not touch the legs of him who shall be covered with the dust of battle in the road to God.'

THE STRUGGLE FOR EGYPT

The Muslim armies surged out of Arabia in 634 in a full-scale invasion of Syria and Palestine. Indecision and delay undermined the lacklustre defensive efforts of the Byzantines, and during the Battle of Yarmuk (636), their numerically superior army was cut off, surrounded and slaughtered almost to a man. Syria, Palestine and Upper Mesopotamia had to be abandoned to the Arabs.

Egypt was seriously vulnerable. Its land communications with the rest of the empire were severed; its governors were disorganised and inexperienced in matters of war; and its people were unwilling to fight for the sake of Byzantium. The Arab general, Amr ibn al-As, anticipated the battle for Egypt, commenting that no place in the world was so wealthy and so defenceless.

Late in 639, he set off with a small force of four thousand cavalry for the fortified frontier town of Pelusium, the great bastion on the road from Palestine, regarded as the key to Egypt. The emperor had long been aware of the threat to Egypt, and still on the eve of invasion no preparations were made, no reinforcements sent for its defence. After a siege of one month, Pelusium fell without a battle worthy of its importance, and the door to Egypt was opened.

For the next few months Amr could do little but temporise, instigating desultory skirmishes in the eastern Delta and the Fayum, until a legion of twelve thousand reinforcements which included some of the finest fighters of the Arabian army reached him at Heliopolis. Even so, they were heavily outnumbered by the huge imperial force that had been massing at nearby Babylon-in-Egypt, the formidable fortress on the Nile constructed by Trajan near the site of an old Persian stronghold. Babylon was originally built to guard the confluence between the Nile and Nekau's canal to the Red Sea (see p.138); it now lies within Old Cairo, and is therefore considered by many to be where the modern city began.

Amr had no siege engines but managed to lure the Byzantines from the safety of their high walls out into the open at Heliopolis, where he caught his foe in a deft trap, ambushing them with hidden troops in the height of battle. Some escaped the onslaught and made it back to Babylon, many fled in panic towards the Delta and Alexandria, many more were cut down.

THE FALL OF BABYLON...

Among those holed up in Babylon was the man in charge of Egypt, Cyrus. He had little stomach for warfare and sued for peace, but the Muslim terms of surrender were fixed by scripture and not open to negotiation. Cyrus was offered three alternatives: convert to Islam and become equals with the invaders; take inferior status and pay tribute (*jizya*) for protection; or fight to the death. To the disgust of his soldiers, Cyrus was happy to accept subjugation and tribute, and wrote to Heraclius for his approval. But the aged emperor, veteran warrior and skilled military leader, was enraged at the suggestion and exiled Cyrus on charges of treachery. He then promised his meagre garrison clinging on at Babylon that he would dispatch the legions needed to sweep the Arabs away.

In February 641, however, Heraclius died and the reinforcements were never sent. As Egypt dangled in the jaws of defeat, morale crashed inside Babylon. Stricken with despair the Byzantine soldiers surrendered the fortress and with it control of the Nile. The day before, they dragged Copts held in the fort's dungeons and amputated their hands – an act of blind malice against fellow Christians even in the face of Muslim conquest. To the Copts the fall of Babylon was the divine punishment Byzantium had long deserved. The Bishop of Nikiu wrote: 'God punished the Greeks thus for not having respected the vivifying passion of Our Lord. That is why God rejected them... Their religion was debased... Everyone knows that the defeat of the Greeks...by the Muslims was in punishment for the tyranny of Emperor Heraclius and the wrongs he inflicted on [the Copts] through the patriarch Cyrus.'

...AND ALEXANDRIA

The country was virtually under Arab control – with one crucial exception. Alexandria, still one of the finest cities in the world, was heavily defended, cradled by virtually impregnable ramparts, protected by long-range artillery, well provisioned and easily replenished by sea. The Arabs had no fleet to make a blockade and could not get close enough to fire their arrows without being flattened by a storm of rocks and stones catapulted over the walls. But in the distance they could see the supreme prize that awaited them:

> Beyond and above them gleamed domes and pediments, columns and obelisks, statues, temples, and palaces... Even these half-barbarian warriors from the desert must have been strangely moved by the stateliness and grandeur, as well as the size and strength, of the city they had come to conquer.
>
> *The Arab Conquest of Egypt*, A. J. Butler (1902)

In normal times, the Byzantines would have had no cause to fear the loss of the city. But these were not normal times. The death of Heraclius precipitated a power struggle in Constantinople that dramatically worsened after his son and successor, Heraclius Constantine (r.641) died of tuberculosis after a reign of barely two months. In the confusion, the fresh troops that Constantine had been readying for Egypt's rescue were sidelined again and Cyrus was recalled from exile with a mission to make peace with the Arabs.

It was a double blow that sealed Egypt's fate. On 8 November, 641, Cyrus surrendered Egypt to the Arabs. The treaty stated that hostilities should cease; that the Byzantine armies would leave within eleven months; that the Egyptians would pay tribute to their new masters; and that the Jews and Christians should not be interfered with. Cyrus, it is said, died shortly afterwards from grief and dysentery. Some of his officials converted to Islam and stayed on, but the Byzantine garrisons withdrew. The wealthiest Alexandrian nobles and merchants gathered up their possessions, took to their boats and cast off for Cyprus, Rhodes and Constantinople. The Byzantine Empire would survive elsewhere for eight more centuries, but its time in Egypt was over. In September 642, the gates of the great city were flung open and the Arab horsemen rode in.

CHAPTER EIGHT

The Arab Age

642–1250

Under Arab Rule

Soon after the capture of Alexandria, Amr ibn al-As, the Arab conqueror of Egypt, reported back to the caliph (the 'successor' to Muhammad and leader of the Muslim community):

> It is impossible for me to describe the variety of its riches and beauty; I shall content myself by saying that it contains 4000 palaces, 4000 baths, 400 theatres or places of amusement, 12,000 grocers and 40,000 tributary Jews.

His awe-struck soldiers wandered the great colonnaded avenues, shielding their eyes from the dazzling glare of bright marble, dumbfounded at the affluence of the city. But they resisted the temptation to pillage. After all, the treaty agreed with Byzantium guaranteed them handsome tribute; spoils could only be gathered once, but taxes could be collected year after year. Nor did they rampage the streets in an orgy of blood-letting and destruction and contrary to the histories that emerged more than five centuries later, they were not responsible for the ruin of Alexandria's Great Library, which had probably already been destroyed during the Roman period.

Amr no doubt believed that Alexandria would make him a fine capital, but Caliph Umar (r.in Egypt 642–644) had his concerns. He, like most Arabs at the time, was wary of any place that could not be reached by camel, and felt the interminable rivers, marshes and irrigated lands of the Delta a barrier to communications. Besides, without a navy and still deeply suspicious of sea travel, the Arabs were ill-equipped to defend the port capital from invading fleets. According to legend, Amr returned from Alexandria to his encampment outside Babylon-in-Egypt to find a dove nesting in his tent (*fustat*), which he took to be a sign from God that this was an auspicious site for a new capital. After the dove's brood had flown, he erected a simple mosque on the spot, the first in Egypt, which still exists today by name though its original structure has long been replaced by rebuilding and enlargement. Around the Amr Mosque grew the city of Fustat, or Misr al-Fustat; Misr was the ancient Semitic word for Egypt, and it was soon used to refer to the capital itself as well as the country, as it is today.

Amr's next priority was to improve trade and transport links with Arabia for the passage of Egypt's plentiful produce and tribute. The ancient canal connecting the Nile to the Red Sea begun by King Nekau II twelve centuries earlier was cleared within a couple of years – by forcing the Copts to work on it. After years of suffering and persecution under the Byzantines, they complained bitterly of such treatment at the hands of their new masters:

> And the yoke they laid on the Egyptians was heavier than the yoke which had been laid on Israel by Pharaoh, whom God judged with a righteous judgement, by drowning him in the Red Sea with all his army after the many plagues wherewith He had plagued both men and cattle. When God's judgement lights upon these [Muslims] may He do unto them as He did aforetime unto Pharaoh!
>
> *The Chronicle of John, Bishop of Nikiu*

Fortunately such privation was the exception rather than the rule and Amr proved to be a wise and just governor. He well remembered Muhammad's words that the Copts were his uncles and brothers-in-law, allies against his enemy and helpers in his religion: 'So take good care of the Copts, for they are your kinsmen and under your protection. They shall relieve you of the cares of this world, so that you shall be at leisure for religious worship.' The Muslims knew little and cared less about the bitter arguments of Chalcedon and were content to let the 'People of the Book' whether Copt, Melkite or Jew, practise their religion. The Coptic Patriarch Benjamin, who had by now spent thirteen years hiding in the desert wastes of Upper Egypt, was reinstated in 644 and accorded the full respect due to a holy man, while his

Church, released from the strictures of Byzantium, breathed freely and flourished. The Muslims, however, had new limitations to impose: the construction of new churches and synagogues was outlawed; distinctive clothing had to be worn; the ringing of church bells was prohibited; only asses rather than thoroughbreds could be ridden; worship had to be done discreetly; and preaching to Muslims was punishable by death. Neither could converts to Islam go back to Christianity; apostates would also pay the ultimate price.

ADMINISTRATION OF ARAB EGYPT

Under Islamic law the *dhimmis*, the people of tolerated religions, received protection and a recognised but inferior status in society in return for payment of the *jizya*, a poll tax. In addition to this was a land tax, the *kharaj*, payable in kind (principally grain) at the time of harvest according to size of holding and level of the inundation. Further imposts were made for the maintenance of Muslim troops. New converts to Islam (*mawali*) were treated better but did not achieve full equality with Arab Muslims; they were exempt from the poll tax but still paid the land tax. Women, children, beggars, the elderly, insane and terminally ill were exempt from both taxes unless they had an independent income. The collection of the taxes and matters of general administration was virtually the same as in the Byzantine system, with many of the old officials keeping their jobs and Copts filling empty posts.

At the top were the Arab Muslims who were initially prohibited from owning land outside the peninsula. The idea was that the subjected peoples would work the land, people the civil service, and pay taxes enough to support the Arabs as an elite warrior caste, freed from everyday concerns to worship Allah and to expand and defend the Islamic Empire. But as Arab settlers poured into Egypt after the conquest, the ideal became unworkable and permission was granted for them to hold landed property.

The bounty of the land, the taxes and tribute were divided between the Arab Muslims according to status, military prowess and knowledge of the Koran, with the largest portion destined for the caliph back in

Medina. A register (*diwan*) of people eligible to receive payment, effectively a census of Arab Muslims, was compiled in order to make the
necessary calculations and distributions. The privileges granted by the
diwan were fiercely guarded. The resistance of those on the *diwan*
towards new Arab settlers, who also wanted to be included, and the
caliphs, who regularly demanded larger slices of the revenue, lay at the
root of much of the political unrest and violence during the early
period of Arab rule.

EGYPT, A CAMEL TO MILK

The first signs of such tensions did not take long to surface. Amr had
won Caliph Umar a rich and fertile new dominion and sent him ships
and caravans laden with grain and gold, but still his master berated him
for bringing in less than half of the revenue that the 'unbelieving
pharaohs' had extracted from the land. Perhaps it was a similarly
grinding attitude at court which led to the caliph's murder by one of
his slaves, a Persian Christian, but the tenor of his complaints persisted
under his successor, Uthman (r.644–656), who replaced Amr as
governor of Egypt with his half-brother Abdallah.

The outcry in Alexandria after Abdallah raised taxes, breaking the
terms of the treaty of surrender, was long and loud. Nevertheless, the
people had no choice but to pay and Abdallah is said to have gloated
to Amr, 'The camel gives more milk now.' Amr replied, 'Yes, but you
are starving her young.'

However, Constans II (r. in Egypt 641–642) the Byzantine emperor
noted the distress of his former subjects and in 645 dispatched a fleet
of three hundred warships to win Egypt back. The Byzantines put
Alexandria's small defending garrison to the sword before leading an
undisciplined rampage across the Delta. Caliph Uthman was forced to
reinstate Amr, the most gifted general of the Arab army, who duly
drove the Byzantines back to Alexandria after a ferocious battle
beneath the walls of Nikiu, his own horse having been killed under
him. Once again Amr found himself on the wrong side of Alexandria's
insuperable ramparts. His fears of a long siege were short-lived
though, as one of the gatekeepers betrayed the Byzantines and opened

the heavy doors to his army. This time Amr's troops stormed in, killing, looting and laying waste all before them. Amr vowed that he would never again have to face the city's great walls and reduced them to rubble.

It was a momentous victory but the caliph repaid Amr by again replacing him as governor by Abdallah. But he could not deny Amr's value on the battlefield and tried to get him to stay on as army commander. Amr rejected the offer and left Egypt, replying, 'I would be the man holding the cow by the horns while another milked her'. Abdallah's military skills were far below his abilities to wring tax out of the population; his expedition to Nubia in 651 was driven back by tribal bowmen and the frontier was effectively fixed at Aswan.

DIVISION IN ISLAM: SUNNI AND SHIA

Caliph Uthman's attempts to impose rigid centralised control over the empire and demands for ever larger shares of the tribute were deeply unpopular with his Arab subjects. In the uprising of 656 a few hundred rebels from the Arab army in Egypt travelled to Medina to air their grievances. They forced their way into the caliph's compound and in a scuffle fatally wounded him.

Ali, the cousin and son-in-law of Muhammad, was elected the new caliph, but this was not to everyone's liking – not least Uthman's relatives in the powerful Umayyad clan whom Ali subsequently removed from office. Ali had little choice but to march against the assorted malcontents against him, scoring an impressive victory at the Battle of the Camel outside Basra (656), but he still had to face Muawiya (r.661–680), the cousin of Uthman and the governor of Syria, who continued to challenge his authority. Muawiya had also enlisted the support of the redoubtable Amr.

Having captured Egypt in 658, Amr met Ali in battle at Siffin on the west bank of the Euphrates. The balance went against Amr until he ordered his men to fix pages of the Koran to their spear points, the sight of which led the caliph's army to refuse to fight, since the holy book forbids Muslims to shed each other's blood. It was therefore decided to put the matter to a debate; according to legend Ali's advocate was tricked by Amr into deposing Ali, who was then assassinated with a poisoned sabre in 661 by a faction of his own disgruntled supporters. Shortly afterwards Muawiya was made caliph. By appointing his own son as his successor he founded the Umayyad dynasty and introduced the hereditary principle to the caliphate.

The party that had supported Ali, called the Shia (from *Shiatu Ali*, 'the faction of Ali'), who believed that Muhammad had designated him as successor from the outset, refused to recognise the Umayyads, considering them usurpers of the caliphate from Ali's line. They invited Husayn, Ali's son by Fatima, the daughter of Muhammad, to be caliph but he was captured and killed by Umayyad troops at Karbala, Iraq (680). All Muslims were affected by his murder; brother Muslims fighting each other was bad enough, but to kill Muhammad's grandson for political gains was an affront to Islam. For the Shia, however, the martyring of Husayn held deep spiritual significance that set them apart from the rest of the Islamic world. To this day a rift exists between the Shia, who insist that Ali's descendants are the legitimate leaders of Islam, and the Sunni majority, who reject this.

The Umayyads (661–750)

Amr was granted undisputed control over Egypt as a reward for helping the Umayyads win the caliphate. He was entitled to pocket all its surplus revenue and amassed a vast fortune before his death in 664. However, he did not establish a dynasty of Egyptian rulers – in legend his sons rejected his treasure-filled coffers considering them the fruits of a sinful life – and the subsequent governors of the province were appointed and deposed by the Umayyad caliphs based in the imperial capital, Damascus.

The Umayyad period saw the introduction of administrative initiatives that would eventually change Egypt from a Coptic-speaking Christian society into an Arabic-speaking Islamic one. In 706 Arabic was made the official language replacing Coptic and Greek, meaning that Copts (and other non-Arabs) working in the administration had to become proficient or lose their positions. Over time, Arabic gradually squeezed Coptic out of private life as well as public, until the sixteenth century when the Coptic language was confined only to church liturgy. Tax increases and the substitution of Coptic collectors for Muslims triggered an uprising among the Copts in 725–726. The revolts never really threatened Arab dominion, but were savagely crushed all the same. Repression and over-taxation pushed some Copts into converting to Islam, but the Arab Muslims did not encourage them to do so as mass conversions meant fewer poll tax payers and a decline in revenue.

The old Byzantine coinage was replaced with Islamic currency minted in Damascus, which was itself linked to the provincial centres by a new and efficient postal system. The migration of Arabs to Egypt picked up speed, particularly during the reign of Caliph Hisham (r.724–743) when thousands of Bedouin (Qays) settled on the land, being among the first Arabs to colonise areas outside Fustat and Alexandria. Islamic ways were also felt more keenly in society: wine merchants were closed down and their supplies destroyed; churches and monasteries lost certain financial exemptions; and Christian village headmen were replaced with Muslims.

THE UMAYYADS IN THE WORLD

The Umayyads were energetic conquerors and extended their borders to the fringes of India and China in the east as well as North Africa, Spain and southern France until their advance was halted at Poitiers by Charles Martel in 732. Having developed a navy, they also continued to harry the Byzantines, laying siege to Constantinople twice (668–673 and 717–718), though they failed to clinch the victory that would have made them masters of the Mediterranean.

The Arabs had little traditional knowledge of architecture, but it was under the Umayyads that the expertise of subject cultures was assimilated and reinterpreted for the glory of Islam. Some of the greatest and most sacred mosques surviving today were built by the Umayyad caliphs, apparently using the skills of Greek-speaking Christians in Syria. The Dome of the Rock (687–691) and the al-Aqsa Mosque (693–705) in Jerusalem, and the Umayyad Mosque in Damascus (706–715, incorporating the older Cathedral of St John the Baptist) number among them, while the great mosques of Mecca and Medina were also aggrandised and beautified during this period.

Such buildings represented the zenith of Umayyad power. However, after the death of Hisham the dynasty began to collapse under the weight of a faltering economy, corruption and internal dissent. An insurrection led by Abbas al-Saffah 'the slaughterer' (r.750–754), a descendant of Muhammad's uncle, broke out in Persia resulting in the overthrow of the governor there (747) before it spread westwards to unseat the caliph, Marwan II (r.744–750). Marwan fled to Egypt but was captured in Busiris and decapitated; his head was sent back as a trophy to Abbas, the new caliph.

The Abbasids (750–868)

The Abbasids had been helped to power by many groups antipathetic to the Umayyad caliphate. These groups were not thanked for their efforts. First the Abbasids rounded up and disposed of their enemies, then the various factions that had supported them. Finally even the brilliant general, Abu Muslim, who had co-ordinated their crowning victory, was put to death. The result of such ruthless sangfroid was the foundation of the longest surviving and most celebrated Arab dynasty in Islam. But the choice of Abbas's brother and successor al-Mansur (r.754–775) to found a new capital at Baghdad (762) in Iraq, distancing himself from the Mediterranean, contributed to its relatively short-lived influence on Egypt and the western provinces.

Where the Umayyads had discovered the potential of architecture, the Abbasids demonstrated a thirst for intellectual knowledge in fields for which there had been little or no Arabic tradition. As translations of the great classical texts and treatises were made into Arabic, a door was opened to new worlds of creative and scientific inquiry. Discoveries that had taken the Greeks (and other more ancient civilisations) many centuries to conceive in philosophy, astronomy, mathematics, medicine, astrology, geography, history, fine arts and literature were absorbed and advanced by the Arabs in a matter of decades. In later times, this reinvigorated channel of knowledge would stream back into Europe and help stimulate the Renaissance.

The reign of Harun al-Rashid (r.786–809) marked an early high point in the power, wealth and cultural achievements of the dynasty. His court provided the backdrop for the stories of the *Arabian Nights*, written in the mid-tenth century and subsequently embroidered further with fables drawn from many cultures before appearing in its completed form in fifteenth-century Egypt.

REVOLT AND CIVIL WAR

While Abbasid fortunes were flourishing in Baghdad under Harun, it was a time of growing instability and discontent in Egypt. The caliph and his predecessors had attempted to reverse the drop in Egyptian revenues by raising taxes and using the resident Arab army (*jund*) to quell the rebellions that consequently broke out in 754, 763, 784, 802 and 806. The system could only operate as long as the *jund* was content, but during this period their grants were being reduced and their authority eroded by new Arab settlers who refused to pay the land tax. When they were no longer willing to do the caliph's dirty work, imperial troops would be sent in. The governors of Egypt also depended on the goodwill of the *jund* as well as the local Arab aristocracy (*wujuh*) to rule. During Harun's reign they enjoyed little such support: of twenty-two successive governors none lasted much more than a year.

Smouldering tensions between the *jund* and the imported troops, between the established aristocracy and the new Arab migrants erupted at Harun's death in 809 and a war of succession between his sons added fuel to the fire. In the confusion, control of Egypt drifted into the hands of Yemeni migrants in the north, and imported Abbasid armies who controlled the south, while a body of 15,000 exiled *mawali* (non-Arab Muslims) from Spain flooded into Alexandria and became masters of the city in 815. The long-established Arab families of the *jund* and the *wujuh* who had dominated Egyptian society since the conquest, fell from power while the *mawali*, the new Muslims, and others scrambled for the prize.

It was not until 826 that Egypt was returned to the control of Caliph al-Mamun (r.813–833) by his much-feared Turkish troops.

These soldiers were 'mamluks' (from Arabic meaning 'owned'), non-Muslim slaves captured in the Turkic regions of the Caucasus and Asia Minor and given complete training in military skills, indoctrinated into Islam and taught to fight for their masters with unflinching loyalty. In adulthood they were freed and could gain positions of high power in the service of the court.

The province continued to be restless with further insurrections in 830 and 831, the latter involving an unprecedented coalition of local Arabs and Copts against the government. Al-Mamun personally oversaw the suppression, a rare visit to Egypt of a reigning caliph, when according to legend he also broke into the Great Pyramid in search of gold, but only found an empty sarcophagus; (today visitors to the pyramid still enter through 'Mamun's hole'). The Coptic rebels were killed and their women and children thrown into slavery, while their Arab counterparts were removed from the *diwan* and lost their influence. The Egyptian historian al-Maqrizi (1364–1442) wrote, 'from then on the Copts were obedient and their power was destroyed once and for all; none were able to rebel or even oppose the government, and the Muslims gained a majority in the villages'.

This put the lid on the situation until 862 when another uprising broke out among local Arabs who turned government tax collectors out of the Delta. It was only quelled, and with difficulty, four years later by the caliph's crack Turkish troops. But they themselves were becoming aware of their power, and as an enfeebled caliphate in faraway Iraq descended into a chaos of palace intrigues, Egypt's Turkish governor moved to establish his own dynastic line.

The Tulunids (868–905)

The Turkish soldier, Ahmad Ibn Tulun (r.868–884), had served under Caliph Mustain (r.862–866) with such flair that he was given the governorship of Egypt in 868. Soon problems in Baghdad gave him the opportunity to assert himself. He bought an independent army of 66,000 Greek, Turkish and black soldiers and while he still recognised the spiritual leadership of the caliphate, for the first time since Cleopatra, Egypt was ruled as an autonomous state. With no tribute to

Minaret of the Ibn Tulun Mosque

pay to the caliph, Ibn Tulun reduced the poll tax – instantly winning the favour of Jews and Christians – and ploughed money into public works such as repairing the country's ailing irrigation system. He also built up a large navy and by 878 he had extended his rule into Syria.

Egypt's economy swiftly recovered and he embarked on magnificent building projects to create an imperial capital to rival Baghdad and Samarra (the Abbasid capital from 836 to 892). The showpiece was the vast Ibn Tulun Mosque (878–880), which was large enough to hold his entire army during Friday prayers. It borrowed from Mesopotamian style with its brick and stucco construction, and its spiralling minaret recalled the ziggurats of ancient Babylonia. Its location north of Fustat became the focus of a new capital called al-Qatai (the Wards), a square mile reputedly consisting of a thousand plots for the various ethnic groups of his mongrel army. Here he also built a sumptuous palace, a hippodrome, an aqueduct and a hospital, but only his mosque survived the systematic destruction wrought on the city by the Abbasids when they regained control in 905.

At his death, Ibn Tulun left his son Khumarawayh (r.884–896) a stable and prosperous Egypt, an empire stretching to the Byzantine border and a treasury worth 10 million dinar (the gold coin of the period). Unfortunately, Ibn Tulun's talent for good government was not hereditary. Khumarawayh had no gift for military nor civil affairs, but a limitless capacity for profligacy. He spent inordinate amounts embellishing his father's palace, decking its halls with gold and gilding its pleasure gardens, the glittering trees of which encircled a lake of sparkling quicksilver designed to catch the light of the sun, moon and stars. There the dissolute ruler was fond of passing the hours, apparently floating across its radiant surface on a gigantic air-filled cushion while a blue-eyed lion kept watch at his side. He married his daughter off to the caliph with a fantastic dowry and assembled for himself a huge harem of beautiful young women. But his indulgences were eventually his undoing and he came to a violent end at the hands of his court eunuchs. His luxurious tastes had left the treasury empty and the dinar devalued, and his three successors could not reverse the dynasty's decline.

ABBASIDS RECAPTURE EGYPT

The Abbasids stormed into Fustat and al-Qatai in 905 and inflicted damage in proportion to the incredible affluence they found. In the thirty years of their rule, the country reverted to the miserable state it had been in when Ibn Tulun had taken over. The Abbasid governors of Egypt faced persistent internal disorder and the threat of invasion from the Fatimids in the west, a Shia dynasty originally from Syria but based in Tunisia, and could only maintain control with the co-operation of the local army. However, with much of the tribute heading back to Iraq, they seldom had funds to pay the troops and extorted whatever they could from their subjects. The soldiers themselves supplemented their income by plundering the country and robbing the very people they were supposed to protect.

The Ikhshidids (935–969)

It took another governor of Turkish military descent, Muhammad Ibn Tughj (r.935–946) to re-establish order in the province and force Fatimid invaders out of Egypt for the third time in twenty years. Ibn Tughj was rewarded with the Persian title *al-Ikhshid* 'prince' in recognition that Egypt was best governed as an autonomous principality. Following the example of his role model Ibn Tulun, he added Syria to his territories and by 944, as the Abbasid Empire began to fracture into petty provincial dynasties, he also seized the Hijaz including the great cities of Islam, Medina and Mecca.

MUSKY CAMPHOR

Ibn Tughj was succeeded by his sons, Unujur (r.946–961) and then Ali (r.961–966), but the real power in court lay with a black eunuch, Abul Misk Kafur (r.966–968), who had risen from the humblest origins in Nubia to command the Ikhshidid armies. Eventually he usurped the throne of Egypt. A deformed and clumsy man reeking of musk (*misk*) and camphor (*kafur*) whence his name, he struck a peculiar figure at court, but his odd appearance belied his considerable abilities on the battlefield and in civil life. He successfully repelled incursions from the Fatimids in the west, the Nubians in the south and the Hamdanids in Syria, while also entertaining at court the most eminent Arab poet of the time, al-Mutanabbi. Nevertheless, a series of terrible natural disasters racked the country: low Nile floods brought devastating famines (949, 952, 955, 963–969); plague swept the land in 967; a fire tore through Fustat in 955; and violent earthquakes hit in the same year – Kafur's sycophants claimed they were caused by the earth dancing with joy at his greatness. He was not a popular ruler, taxing harshly to pay for extravagances while his subjects starved, and poets such as al-Mutanabbi, who had once heaped praise on him later wrote scathing diatribes.

With no heir, a succession crisis was inevitable at Kafur's death. Ahmad (r.968–969), the eleven-year-old son of Ali was the last of the dynasty, a weak ruler of a weakened Egypt who could do little to resist the rising power of the neighbouring Fatimids.

The Fatimids (969–1171)

The Fatimids, a Shia dynasty from Syria, regarded the conquest of Egypt as the first step in their mission to rid the Islamic world of the rival Sunni caliphs. They traced their origins to Fatima, the daughter of the Prophet and wife of the fourth caliph Ali, and were the religious leaders of the Ismaili sect of the Shia branch of Islam. Having established their own caliphate in Tunisia from 909, they had repeatedly tried to expand eastwards towards the centres of Sunni strength before their successful invasion of Egypt in 969. Unlike their predecessors, they did not profess even nominal allegiance to the Sunni caliph in Baghdad; to the Fatimids he was no more than a usurper, while they were the rightful and divinely ordained guardians of Islam.

As the apocryphal story has it, when the Fatimid caliph al-Muizz (r. in Egypt 969–975) rode into Fustat he was asked by an upstanding citizen to prove his claim to the caliphate. 'There is my lineage,' he said brandishing his sword. Then he reached into his purse and showered the onlookers with gold coins, saying, 'And there is my proof.' Whether true or not, the images of the sword and coins summed up the first glorious century of Fatimid rule. On one level, they acquired by force an empire that far eclipsed the powers of the Sunni caliphs. At its height it included North Africa, Sicily, Syria, Palestine, the Hijaz, the Red Sea coasts and Yemen – and for a short time, the name of the Fatimid caliph was even read out at Friday prayers in the mosques of the Sunni capital Baghdad. On another level, the people of Egypt – consisting mainly of Sunni Muslims in the cities with large numbers of Christians still in rural areas and the south – found it easy, like the onlookers in the story, to accept their Shia masters in view of the immense wealth they brought to the country.

The Fatimids overhauled the administration to end the destabilising depredations of corrupt tax officials. They had no qualms about employing the services of Jews and Copts, who like them represented religious minorities. The Copts were keenly sought for their expertise in record keeping and bureaucracy, not to mention their skills as weavers, artists and architects. Unlike the Sunni, the Shia did not treat representational art as taboo and happily decorated their buildings, ceramics, glassware, metalwork and carvings with animal figures and people, often borrowing directly from the Coptic idiom.

FOUNDATION OF CAIRO

As soon as the Fatimid commander Jawhar, a Greek or Sicilian convert to Islam at the head of a modest force of loyal Berber troops, had taken Fustat (969), he began marking out a new royal city a few miles to the north. It was named al-Qahira (the Conqueror) because, as tradition has it, al-Muizz wanted a city that would rule the world. In European mouths 'Qahira' became 'Cairo'.

Jawhar also founded the great Azhar Mosque ('the Resplendent'; 970–972) as the core place of Fatimid worship; in 988 it was made into a seminary for the propagation of the faith, and to this day is the most important institution for religious learning in Islam as well as the

Azhar Mosque

oldest continually functioning university in the world.

In just fifteen years of Fatimid rule, Cairo had become the most magnificent city in the Islamic world. The Arab geographer Maqdisi, who visited in 985, noted, 'Baghdad was once an illustrious city, but it is now falling into decay and its splendour has gone. I found nothing pleasurable, nothing there to impress me. Cairo today is what Baghdad was in its prime, and I know no more illustrious city in Islam.' In time the new city could boast four cathedral mosques, nine imposing gates and houses rising to five or six storeys built amongst colourful gardens and orchards. Some even had rooftop pleasure parks irrigated by large waterwheels. The royal palace alone, separated from the hubbub of the bustling metropolis by a generous swathe of open ground, was reputedly large enough to accommodate thirty thousand people.

If Cairo was an awe-inspiring royal capital, its nearby counterpart Fustat was the commercial engine of the empire and eventually the two would fuse. Travelling in Egypt during 1047–1048, the Persian traveller and polymath, Nasir Khosrau, was astounded by the range of produce he saw in Fustat's seething bazaars on a single day:

> I found red roses, lilies, narcissi, oranges, lemons, apples, jasmine, basil, quince, pomegranates, pears, melons, bananas, olives, plums, fresh dates, grapes, sugar-cane, aubergines, squash, turnips, radishes, cabbages, fresh beans, cucumbers, green onions, fresh garlic, carrots and beetroot. No one would think that all of these fruits and vegetables could be had at one time, some usually growing in autumn, some in spring, some in summer, some in winter.

But no mere greengrocers, Fustat's bazaars were the nexus of an enormous trade network that spanned the known world, and its souks were the best-stocked of the age, overflowing with exotic luxury goods. Khosrau noted that a shopper could buy fine porcelain, aromatics, silks, ink and cinnamon from China; spices, tin, fragrant sandalwood, coconuts, carved teak from India; elephant ivory from Zanzibar; rubies from Sri Lanka and pearls from the Gulf of Oman; slave girls and drugs from Constantinople; delicate crystal from the Maghreb; furs and amber from the pine forests of Scandinavia; textiles from Spain and Sicily; steel weaponry from Damascus; carpets from Armenia; leopard skins, gold and ostrich feathers from Abyssinia. Locally manufactured wares held their place among the imports: diaphanous linens of

Damietta and Fustat (from which we get the word fustian) as light as the membrane of an eggshell; iridescent cloths of Tanis, which changed colour depending on the height of the sun, reserved for the rulers of Egypt and the envy of royalty around the world; flawless glass and crystals; and porcelain 'so fine and translucent that one can see one's hand behind it when held up to the light'. Paper, a Chinese invention which had reached Egypt in the beginning of the ninth century and had become a linchpin of contemporary publishing and record-keeping, was being produced and sold locally in large quantities. And underpinning this booming economy was the Fatimid currency, the gold dinar minted in the city that became the most internationally respected and accepted coinage of the period.

Sustaining such prodigious commerce was an all-pervading sense of security. According to Khosrau, the merchants, jewellers and money-changers never locked their shops (a net being sufficient to keep light fingers at bay), a sure sign of general well-being and abundance: 'I saw such personal wealth there that were I to describe it, the people of Persia would never believe it. I could discover no end or limit to their wealth, and I never saw such ease and comfort anywhere.'

CALIPH AL-HAKIM 'THE MAD'

The grandson of al-Muizz was the most notorious of all the Fatimid caliphs. Al-Hakim (r.996–1021) was an innocent blue-eyed boy of eleven when he assumed the caliphate. His choice to spurn the trappings of his position by wearing modest white robes and getting around only on a donkey, was an early clue to a deep-rooted puritanism in him, but it took a few years for his erratic and brutal character fully to emerge. Its first expression was with the murder of his Slavic tutor, swiftly followed by the assassinations of his most senior ministers and advisers. Throughout his reign, those closest to him were the most at risk from his capricious moods which swung without warning from generous praise to murderous rage.

Nor were his subjects safe. Despite having a Christian mother and two Greek Orthodox bishops for uncles, and despite being part of a dynasty that generally treated other religions well, al-Hakim persecuted the Christian faithful, levelling thousands of churches and forcing worshippers to wear black robes and bear crosses a yard long and a yard wide. Jews were made to wear a wooden yoke and Sunni Muslims were also occasionally maltreated. In 1009 he ordered the destruction of the Church of the Holy Sepulchre in Jerusalem, an outrage that lingered in European minds and eventually served as a pretext for the First Crusade. Women too were discriminated against, their freedoms gradually curtailed until they were prohibited from appearing in public altogether; his ban on cobblers from making women's shoes was supposed to help restrict their movements.

Other arbitrary laws were passed. Dogs were killed because he found their barking irritating. A vegetable (mallow) was banned because it had been a favourite of Muawiya, the man who defeated the Shia figurehead Ali. Frivolities, games, music and pleasure trips were outlawed, alcohol was poured away, and stocks of grapes, raisins and honey destroyed in case anyone tried to make liquor out of them. Merchants dreaded his appearances at the markets. Anyone found to be cheating – and al-Hakim's judgement was at best eccentric – was publicly sodomised by Masoud, the huge black slave who accompanied him; the caliph himself would contribute to proceedings by standing on the victim's head.

Despite or, more likely, because of such behaviour, his efforts to foist Shia Islam on the population were fruitless. Nevertheless, the Hall of Science which he instituted in Cairo for the promotion of Shiism quickly became one of the prime locations for general intellectual inquiry in the Islamic world, and the impressive al-Hakim Mosque, finished after his death in 1013, was the second largest of the dynasty. Al-Hakim's personal interest in astrology also led to the construction of a lavishly equipped observatory on the Muqattam hills overlooking the city. He issued grants to learned men such as Ibn Yunus, the astronomer whose tabulations were still in use well into the nineteenth century, and Ibn al-Haytham (Alhazen), the great mathematician and physicist who was the first to give an accurate account of the mechanics of vision. When Alhazen failed to regulate the Nile inundation for the caliph, he feigned madness and went into hiding until his master's death.

Al-Hakim developed a conviction towards the end of his reign that he was an incarnation of God, a belief which disposed him to rescind his former persecutory policies, but which also provoked unrest among his orthodox subjects. After one protest he flew into a rage, turning loose his soldiers on Fustat. For three days the city blazed as they pillaged houses, ravished women and slew anyone who resisted. By the time his fluid emotions filled him with the deepest regret at the suffering he had caused, half the city had been looted, and a third was left in smouldering ruins.

The mad caliph mysteriously disappeared while taking his customary night-time stroll in the Muqattam hills. His ass was later found mutilated and his clothes cut up. Many suspected his sister, Sitt al-Mulk, of involvement in his death. However, his body was never found and the Druze sect (now based mainly in the Levant), who accept his claims to divinity, still maintain that he will one day return to usher in a new golden age. His mosque was shunned as a place of worship and used for profane purposes – as a prison for crusaders, a stable, a warehouse and a museum for Islamic art in the nineteenth century – until 1980 when it was restored by a Shiite sect from Brunei.

FATIMID DECLINE

Al-Hakim's successors were ineffectual and allowed the glory of the dynasty to ebb away. They faced problems in three main areas which ultimately proved insuperable. First, the political climate outside Egypt was rapidly changing, causing the Fatimid Empire to unravel. As early as 1048, their influence in North Africa had diminished sufficiently for local officials to renounce Shiism and return to the Sunni fold. In Syria too, Fatimid interests were squeezed by the Seljuk Turks, who had emerged as the supreme military power in the Near East since their capture of Baghdad in 1055 and their victory against the Byzantines at Manzikart (Armenia) in 1071. In the same year, Sicily was lost to the Normans, the first hint of the Western European menace that would trouble Egypt for much of the twelfth and early thirteenth centuries.

The second problem was famine brought about by a series of low Niles, first during the reign of al-Zahir (r.1021–1036), but even more seriously in the time of al-Mustansir (r.1036–1094). In the first decades of the latter's long rule, Egypt actually enjoyed enormous prosperity, but from 1065 to 1072 a terrible drought and low river levels caused a famine so devastating that Cairenes ate their horses, mules, cats and dogs. When the animals were finished, they turned on each other, ambushing lone walkers in the quiet streets or even catching passers-by on hooks let down from windows. Food could be bought only by the very richest – a loaf of bread went for the small fortune of fifteen dinar, while a few bags of flour could buy a house. Even the caliph, a few years before one of the richest men on earth, was forced to sell his most treasured possessions. His stable of ten thousand fine horses dwindled to three scrawny animals.

The third debilitating problem was recurrent warring within the army between its different ethnic groups, principally Berbers, Turks and Nubians. The infighting escalated under al-Mustansir and the only way the caliph could control his marauding men was through large bribes which he could ill afford. In one street battle, the royal library was looted and its priceless illuminated manuscripts scattered. It is said that Turkish officers tore up countless books, using their pages for tinder and their vellum bindings to repair their slaves' shoes.

The caliph could only regain control in 1073 by summoning the governor of Acre, the Armenian Badr al-Jamali, who commanded his own army. Badr was remarkably successful in reimposing order, aided in no small part by a good Nile and a bumper harvest. He won popular approval through his emergency tax relief measures. But Badr's services cost the Fatimids dearly. Badr was made vizier and effectively became ruler of Egypt; from this point, the Fatimid caliphs were governed by their own viziers.

THE FIRST CRUSADES

The final fatal onslaught against the flagging Fatimid state came as a consequence of the crusades. Pope Urban II's call to 'enter upon the road to the Holy Sepulchre, wrest it from the wicked race and subject it' captured the imagination of Western Christendom and initiated the first in a series of eight major crusades between 1095 and 1270.

Initial forays into Syria and Palestine made the most of divisions within the Muslim world. The Seljuk Empire, which had reduced Fatimid possessions in the Levant to a sliver along the coast, had fragmented into rival successor states too weak to check the Christian advance. The Fatimids themselves were willing to side with the crusaders, no doubt blinded by their hatred of their erstwhile Sunni enemies. Their perceptions quickly changed, however, when the crusaders stormed Jerusalem (which had just been taken from the Seljuks by the Fatimids) on 15 July 1099 and ran amok inside the city walls, mercilessly slaughtering almost all of its inhabitants. Before long, the first 'crusader states' had been carved out of the Levant: the Kingdom of Jerusalem, the Counties of Tripoli and Edessa, and the Principality of Antioch.

The Muslim backlash was spearheaded by the Seljuk governor of Mosul, Zangi, who recovered Edessa, sparking off the Second Crusade of 1147–1148. His son Nur al-Din (Nureddin) seized Damascus (1154) in its aftermath, from where he was able to launch offensives against the Kingdom of Jerusalem. Even had the Fatimids wanted to help Nur al-Din, their military strength was sapped to the point of uselessness by ongoing divisions between the caliph, vizier and competing cliques within the army. In the 1160s the fighting between Nur al-Din and Amalric, King of Jerusalem, drifted into Egypt. The Fatimids clung to power by changing sides according to the run of battle, a tactic which ultimately alerted both to the extent of Fatimid debility.

Nur al-Din seized the opportunity to invade Egypt in 1167. Predictably, the vizier called on Amalric for assistance and their combined troops were able to force a stalemate. As soon as Nur al-Din withdrew the following year, Amalric launched his own offensive on Egypt, prompting the Fatimid caliph to offer Nur al-Din a third of his revenues to send his army back in. Meanwhile the vizier ordered the burning of Fustat as a precautionary measure against the crusaders; it blazed for fifty-four days and never quite recovered its former glory. Nur al-Din's commander Shirkuh eventually forced Amalric out and was made vizier by the Fatimid caliph, a post he held for only two months before his death. He was replaced by his nephew Salah al-Din (better known in the West as Saladin), whose Kurdish father Ayyub, from whom the line derived its name, was a confidant of Nur al-Din.

The Ayyubids (1171–1250)

SALADIN

Saladin (r.1171–1193) began with no army, few supporters and scant resources, but his victory in expelling the last crusaders from Damietta brought him respect and money, which he sagely used to buy influence and an army, and in 1171 when the caliph died, he was strong enough to

Saladin who expelled the last crusaders and proclaimed himself
Sultan of Egypt in 1174

depose the Fatimid line and reclaim the country for Sunni Islam.

At the death of Nur al-Din in 1174, Saladin proclaimed himself sultan of Egypt and added Damascus to his domain. His run of luck continued later that year with the death of Amalric, whose weak, young, leprous son, Baldwin IV, became the focus of interminable plots and manoeuvrings in the Latin states. With the crusader states distracted, Saladin was free to pursue his main aim of uniting the Muslim territories of Syria, northern Mesopotamia, Palestine, the Hijaz, Yemen and the Maghreb — a feat he achieved through clever diplomacy backed up whenever necessary by the surgically precise use of force. Initially he was criticised for directing his considerable skills on the battlefield against brother Muslims, but his repeated acts of virtue, generosity, gallantry, piety and fair judgement brought him wide admiration and ultimately focused the efforts of a previously fragmented and dissenting Islamic world against the 'true foe', the Christian invaders.

By 1187, he was ready to face the Latin kingdom with his largest ever army, a force of thirty thousand men, including twelve thousand cavalry. He lured his enemy from the safety of their city-fortresses into a long march across the desert to the Horns of Hattin near Galilee, where on 4 July he surrounded and destroyed the exhausted Latin army (capturing in the process the relic of the True Cross, which was never seen again). The kingdom was left virtually defenceless and soon Saladin mopped it all up save for a few minor castles and the heavily fortified coastal cities of Antioch, Tripoli and Tyre. In October Jerusalem itself was back into Muslim hands after eighty-eight years of Christian control, a trauma to Christendom that precipitated the Third Crusade (1189–1192) led by the three most powerful kings of Western Europe. In his celebrated struggles against Richard I the Lionheart of England, Saladin neutralised the invaders' greatest efforts to regain ground, limiting their advance to the coastal strip, while maintaining the highest standards of chivalry and decorum. Peace was agreed in November 1192 with Jerusalem still in Islamic hands, but the hard campaigning seasons had taken their toll on Saladin and he died from fever three months later.

Although barely six of his twenty-two years as ruler were spent in

Egypt, Saladin put the country at the heart of his empire, and by extension the Muslim world. He transformed the capital, opening the Fatimid royal quarter to the public and giving the palaces to his officers, and built a new fortified royal residence, the Citadel (begun 1176), on the site of Ibn Tulun's 'Dome of the Air', a retreat away from the heat and clamour of the city on top of an imposing spur in the nearby Muqattam hills. The Citadel remained the royal residence and governmental seat of Egypt until the mid-nineteenth century. He also started work on a 12 mile (20km) defensive wall to encircle Fustat and Qahira (still separate cities at this time), apparently sourcing some of his material from the small pyramids at Giza. But Saladin's contributions were not purely military in nature. He courted scholars and theologians, encouraged public works and founded hospitals and *madrasas*, theological schools. His exemplary character and exceptional achievements made Saladin one of the great heroes of the medieval East.

THE AYYUBID SUCCESSORS

Saladin's was a hard act to follow, made harder still by his decision to divide the empire between his sons and relatives. The subsequent backbiting between them threatened to tear the realm apart until al-Adil, Saladin's brother, (also known as Safadin, r.1200–1218) settled the disputes at the battle of Bilbeis and proclaimed himself sultan. He was a wise ruler and promoted trade and peace with the crusader states, and led Egypt to a quick recovery after a double calamity at the beginning of his reign, an earthquake in 1200 and a terrible famine (1199–1202), at least as grave as the one a generation before. Hunger-crazed parents were driven to roast their own children for food and those that were caught were burnt alive – and their charred flesh put on sale in the markets. A doctor visiting Cairo at the time reckoned that many more than 110,000 people had died of starvation.

Egypt bounced back, and by the time of the Fifth Crusade (1217–1229), it had been identified as the hub of Islamic power and the key to recapturing Jerusalem. A successful attack on a key fortification on the Nile mouth at Damietta was an excellent start to the

Christian campaign, one considerably sweetened by the death of al-Adil, apparently caused by the shock of its loss. But the crusaders were unable to keep up their early momentum, and not even the persuasive powers of St Francis of Assisi, who vainly attempted to convert the new sultan, al-Kamil (r.1218–1238), during a special audience, could avert failure. After an ill-planned advance on Cairo through difficult waterlogged terrain, the Latins were driven from the country in 1221. The threat had gone but al-Kamil still perceived menace beneath the fragile alliances with his Ayyubid rivals, and in 1229 made a notorious agreement with the Holy Roman Emperor Frederick II in which he ceded Jerusalem in return for Latin military aid. It inflamed Muslim opinion that the Holy City should have been lost so cheaply.

His son al-Salih Ayyub (r.1240–1249) was equally preoccupied with challenges to the sultanate from his relatives and sought a solution in the purchase of unprecedented numbers of mamluks, soldier slaves loyal only to him (see p.211). He housed his hardy Kipchak Turks, who hailed from Crimea and the windswept Eurasian steppes, in purpose-built barracks on Roda Island by Cairo, from which location they came to be known as the Bahri Mamluks (*bahr* meaning river). It proved to be a wise precaution because Egypt was the target of yet another crusade, the Seventh (1248–1254), this time led by Louis IX, King of France. It was in response to the recapture of Jerusalem in 1244 by the Khwarezmian Turks, a people recently displaced from Central Asia by the Mongol hordes.

In an echo of the Fifth Crusade, the crusaders took Damietta (1249), but their progress through the Delta was severely hampered by the boggy ground which disrupted supply lines and spread disease. Had they known that the sultan had already died, they might have recovered the spirit to fight on for victory. But al-Salih's demise was kept secret for two months by his formidable widow, Shajar al-Durr ('Tree of Pearls'), until the only surviving heir, Turan Shah (r.1249–1250), could return from Mesopotamia to take the throne. In the meantime, the Mamluks destroyed the French army at Mansura; the king himself was taken prisoner and ransomed for a million dinar. The Bahri Mamluks had saved the realm and defended Islam, but the price for the Ayyubids was great. Turan Shah finally arrived in Cairo to take the crown, but could not establish his authority, and the Bahris in collusion with Shajar al-Durr had him murdered. It proved to be the end of the Arab dynasties and the beginning of a long period of Turkic rule. Egypt had fallen to the Mamluks, who were to rule as sultans for more than two hundred and fifty years and as Ottoman vassals for almost three hundred years more.

CHAPTER NINE

Mamluks and Ottomans

1250–1798

The Bahri Mamluks (1250–1382)

UNSETTLED BEGINNINGS

The first ten years of Mamluk rule were tortuous and turbulent. Shajar al-Durr (r.1250), a former slave concubine and the widow of the Ayyubid sultan al-Salih, was proclaimed sultana and ruled alone – the first and only Muslim sultana of the Middle East and one of the very few in all Islamic history. She had her image struck on coins and her name read in Friday prayers like a male sovereign. But her position was precarious. The idea of an independent female ruler did not play well in Cairo, nor with the caliph in Baghdad, the Sunni spiritual leader, whose response to the news was, 'Since no *man* among you is worthy of being sultan, I will have to send you one. Woe unto nations ruled by a woman.' Shajar's reign lasted for just two months before she abdicated and married the mild-mannered general, Aybak (r.1250 and 1254–1257), a Mamluk but not a Bahri, who was consequently made sultan. Aybak himself stood aside a few days afterwards and al-Salih's six-year-old cousin took the throne; no one was fooled that he was anything more than a puppet of Aybak, and Aybak himself a pawn of Shajar.

This tottering arrangement was threatened from all sides. First there were the Bedouin tribes (Arab nomads) of Upper Egypt who made it clear they would never be lorded over by Turkish slaves and concubines and revolted in an uprising lasting three years. Then there were the Ayyubid princes in Syria who felt they had a legitimate claim on Egypt and prepared for war. They were beaten back from the eastern Delta in

1251 with the help of the Bahri Mamluks, the prime military force in Egypt. The Bahris also had their eyes on the crown and having relied on them in both matters Aybak moved against them. He summoned the Bahri leader on the pretext of a meeting, but had him executed, and flung his head from the Citadel down to his brothers-in-arms waiting below. Most fled the country and all was now ready for Aybak to dispense with the young puppet sultan and resume the throne.

But Aybak had not reckoned on his wife, Shajar, who had caught wind of his plans to take another bride, the princess of Mosul. In a fit of jealous rage she arranged his murder, but almost before the fatal blows were struck, she knew she had made a terrible mistake, that his death would be hers also. As the story goes, she locked herself away in the tower of the Citadel and readied herself for her fate by grinding her priceless jewels to powder so no other woman could wear them. When she emerged, Aybak's furious concubines beat her to death with their wooden bathhouse clogs and tossed her body over the battlements as food for pariah dogs. Her remains were buried in a sumptuous tomb she had already built, under the inscription, 'O you who stand over my grave, do not be surprised at my state. Yesterday I was as you, and tomorrow you will be as I.'

Aybak's teenage son, Ali (r.1257–1259) was made sultan, but his purpose was little more than to present a serene front while Mamluk commanders jockeyed for power behind the scenes. Qutuz (r.1259–1260), who had killed the Bahri leader for Aybak a few years earlier, eventually outflanked his rivals and usurped the throne. No doubt the urgent need to find a strong leader for Egypt aided his rise – because there was a terrifying menace on the horizon. An insuperable army of 120,000 Mongols was marching over the face of Asia laying waste all in its path.

THE MONGOLS

In 1258, the Mongols led by Hulagu, the grandson of Genghis Khan, sacked Baghdad, reducing it to ruins, and massacred most of its inhabitants including the Abbasid caliph, the spiritual leader of the Sunni faith. Only the stench of the festering corpses littering the streets brought the carnage to an end, driving the invaders away. By 1260, the Mongols had crossed the Euphrates and had begun their devastation of northern Syria, levelling the great citadel of Aleppo before turning south to seize Damascus and squash other Ayyubid princedoms. Egypt was next.

Mongol ambassadors were sent to Cairo to demand the surrender of the 'upstart Mamluk slaves'. Qutuz replied by having them killed. The bold move won him the support of the exiled Bahris, now led by the charismatic Baybars (r.1260–1277), who decided it was better to side with an old Mamluk enemy than let the Mongols turn Cairo to rubble.

Fortunately for the Mamluks, the death of the Mongol Great Khan back in their central Asian heartlands prompted the withdrawal of the bulk of the Mongol forces along with their fearsome commander Hulagu. The remaining rump army was attacked and routed by Qutuz and Baybars at Ayn Jalut near Nazareth (1260). The few that had not been chased down by Baybars were flushed out of their hiding places in the reed beds on the banks of the River Jordan when the Egyptians put them to the torch. It was a decisive victory that halted the Mongol offensive, handed much of Syria to the Mamluks and shattered the aura of Mongol invincibility. Twice the Mamluks had saved Egypt and Islam from the infidels (first the crusaders, now the Mongols), a fact that was not lost on a grateful population.

Qutuz had demonstrated admirable leadership qualities in battle, but in its aftermath his talents deserted him. He had made many promises to his generals before fighting, which as victor he was either unwilling or unable to honour. Baybars who thought he had been promised the governorship of Aleppo was particularly disgruntled and as Qutuz rode back to Egypt, he was ambushed by a group of his unhappy subordinates, Baybars among them, and stabbed to death. Baybars was proclaimed the new sultan.

BAYBARS

The Mamluk era was firmly established under Baybars (r.1260–1277). Rejected by his first owner for the cataract in one of his blue eyes, Baybars nevertheless found his way into the royal army of Sultan al-

Salih (r.1240–1249) and quickly rose through the ranks of the Bahris. His disability was more than compensated for by his robust build and his boundless energy that inspired the confidence of his subordinates. Now as sultan of Egypt, he also proved to be an astute politician, cutting taxes to win popular approval and buttering up the rich and powerful by granting them places in his court; all the while, he slipped his own loyal Mamluks into positions of power.

The next problem for him as slave-turned-sultan was one of legitimacy. If his assertions that he had inherited the kingly qualities of his former master al-Salih, through education and association rather than heredity, were not entirely convincing, he concocted other solutions. One was to produce a man claiming to be the uncle of the last Abbasid caliph and to pronounce him the new caliph amid much pomp and ceremony. In return, the caliph formally invested Baybars as sultan and set up residence in Cairo, making it the spiritual centre of the Sunni world and applying a veneer of respectability to the Mamluk sultanate. However, the caliph turned out to be more ambitious and less malleable than Baybars had hoped, so he was sent with a small force on a suicide mission to recapture Baghdad from which he never returned. His replacement, another supposed relation, and his successors were installed in a palace just outside Cairo, but were kept under virtual house arrest, being wheeled out only when needed for state and religious ceremonies.

More effective than any of this in justifying his rule though, were his exploits on the battlefield, which served to portray Baybars – and the Mamluks in general – as the saviours of Islam. He spent much of his reign campaigning to consolidate gains in Syria and Palestine, as well as adding Berber and Nubian territories west and south of Egypt to his domain. The Mongols had been seen off, and having tightened his borders on the Euphrates against their occasional raiding parties, he directed his energies against the other infidel power of the region, the crusader principalities. By siege, assault, the scorching of crops and pasture, and the occasional judicious truce, Baybars managed to steal a string of crucial ports, towns and castles from the clutches of the Latins. The filleting away of their prize positions left the crusaders without the muscle to resist further Mamluk depredations after

Mamluk cavalry

Baybar's death. Qalawun (r.1279–1290) died on the eve of battle against Acre, the last and most tenacious Latin stronghold, leaving his son, Khalil (r.1290–1293), to take the final honour of chasing the crusaders from the Holy Land in 1291. However, Baybars was recognised as the architect of their downfall, and for this and other victories in Armenia and Anatolia, he occupies a place alongside Harun al-Rashid and Saladin as one of the great heroes of Islam.

THE MAMLUK WAY

For all Baybars' glory, for all his measures to justify his elevation to the throne, the Mamluk system did not lend itself to stable rule. The fact was that a Mamluk sultan could only rule for as long as he was able to maintain the upper hand over the Mamluks on whom he depended for power. Baybars and his successors buttressed their reigns by importing large numbers of personal Mamluks from the Kipchak region in the Caucasus, the original home of most Bahris. Later Mamluk sultans drew from a bigger basket; Tartar boys were most sought after, followed in descending order of value by Circassians, Greeks, Slavs and Albanians. Enslaved and shipped to Egypt with the compliance of foreign powers, the Turkish-speaking, pagan Mamluks were put into barracks with older Mamluks, taught Arabic and educated in the ways of the Koran and Islam. Their primary training, however was in the military arts; a rigorous schooling in everything from horsemanship to archery which transformed crude youths into the most respected and feared fighters of the age. Plucked from their homes and families as youngsters, these Mamluks were loyal to no one except their masters and brothers-in-arms within their households. At maturity, they were freed and if they had proved themselves ambitious and capable enough, they were given the rank of emir (commander) and a land grant (*iqta*), which paid for them to set up their own Mamluk households. The size of endowment and the number of troops under an emir's command increased with rank, but promotions could be won as much by conspiracy and violence as ability and experience; factionalism and rivalry between households underscored the set-up. Eventually some might reach the highest military and administrative offices of state; the ultimate goal for any determined emir, however, was to become sultan.

One of the more unusual but fundamental features of the system was a ban on inheritance. The point was to sustain an elite military caste joined not by familial ties but only by bonds of loyalty to master and household, something that was not compatible with the transmission of wealth and power between father and son. As one official had it, 'one obedient slave is better than 300 sons; for the latter desire their father's death, the former his master's glory'. When Baybars died after drinking tainted *qumiz* (fermented mare's milk) during a polo match, his son Berke Khan (r.1277–1279), was said to have been overjoyed. Nevertheless, the hereditary urge was strong, and many Mamluk sultans tried to ensure their sons would succeed them. Berke Khan himself had been groomed for the sultanate but was soon deposed, and his younger brother fared even worse, lasting for only a couple of months before Qalawun, by far the strongest emir of the time, seized control. Qalawun was arguably the most successful dynast as he was followed to the throne by seventeen of his descendants (amongst others) between 1290 and 1382, and his second son al-Nasir Muhammad I (r.1293–1294, 1299–1309, 1310–1341), enjoyed one of the longest aggregate reigns in medieval Islamic history despite being twice deposed. However, this was no dynasty in the conventional sense; heirs were routinely unseated by their brothers or by leading Mamluk commanders.

In the past, historians puzzled over the apparent failure of the Mamluks to reproduce more than two or three generations, often disapprovingly ascribing it to their predilection for handsome young boys. Emmanuel Piloti, a Venetian merchant living in Cairo at the beginning of the fifteenth century, wrote:

> several great heathen merchants who deal in no other merchandise than little male slaves of the right age to suit the sultan and to be brought to Cairo... When they are brought into the presence of the sultan in Cairo, there are old practised valuers who are expert in judging a boy's appearance.

Mamluk emirs also craved the choicest boys for their pleasure, the 'shameful custom', according to the French historian Volney, which 'is the first lesson [young Mamluks] learn from their masters of arms'. While 'the vice of Greeks and Tartars' was undoubtedly part of the Mamluk system, it was hardly responsible for the failure of Mamluks to produce dynasties.

The truth is more prosaic. Succeeding generations tended not to follow a military career, favouring more comfortable civil appointments, while those that did found themselves at a disadvantage to freshly imported Mamluks, who had much greater prestige and frequently won out in power struggles. Revenues and land grants issued to emirs reverted to the state after death and were not passed on to their children, who would have to compete with the new intake of power-hungry Mamluks. Wealth and status were gained not by inheritance but by machination and violence, so it is not surprising that after Baybars only ten out of more than fifty Mamluk rulers had the luxury of dying from natural causes while still in power; the rest were murdered or deposed.

Notwithstanding the assassinations, coups and violence that brought in as many as fifty-five rulers in 267 years, the system was remarkably effective and fostered long periods of prosperity, artistic achievement and architectural splendour. As the historian Ibn Khaldun remarked:

> When the Abbasid state was drowned in decadence and luxury and donned the garments of calamity and impotence and... had become deficient in energy and reluctant to rally in defence [of Islam]... then, it was God's benevolence that He rescued the faith... by sending to the Muslims, from this Turkish nation and from among its great and numerous tribes, rulers to defend them and utterly loyal helpers, brought from the House of War to the House of Islam under the rule of slavery, which hides in itself a divine blessing. By means of slavery they learn glory and blessing and are exposed to divine providence; cured by slavery, they enter Muslim religion with the firm resolve of true believers and yet with nomadic virtues unsullied by debased nature, unadulterated with the filth of pleasure, undefiled by the ways of civilised living, and with their ardour unbroken by the profusion of luxury. The slave merchants bring them to Egypt in batches, like sandgrouse to the watering places... Thus, one intake comes after another and generation follows generation, and Islam rejoices in the benefit which it gains through them, and the branches of the kingdom flourish with the freshness of youth.

> *Ibn Khaldun, d. 1406*

ARTISTIC EFFLORESCENCE

In times of stability Egypt certainly did benefit from Mamluk rule. With control of Egypt and Syria, the Mamluks cornered the spice trade between Europe and India and made huge profits, which they invested – as befitted their image as pious defenders of Islam – in mosques, *madrasas* and religious and charitable buildings in Cairo (as well as Damascus and Aleppo). This coincided with the influx to Egypt of skilled artisans and learned men driven from the east by the Mongol advance, which also made the country the main repository of Islamic culture.

The Mamluks were ruthless men but they delighted in art and architecture as much as the cold-blooded intrigues, cruel tortures and brutal executions that festooned their reigns. As the Victorian historian Stanley Lane-Poole saw it:

> A band of lawless adventurers, slaves in origin, butchers by choice, turbu-

lent, bloodthirsty, and too often treacherous, these slave kings had a keen appreciation for the arts which would have done credit to the most civilised ruler that ever sat on a constitutional throne. Their morals were indifferent, their conduct was violent and unscrupulous, yet they show in their buildings, their decoration, their dress and their furniture, a taste which it would be hard to parallel in Western countries even in the present aesthetic age.

Perhaps all too aware of the likelihood of an untimely end, they dedicated their fortunes into grand monuments, embellishing them for posterity with the most exquisite Arabic tracery, sumptuous marble mosaic, stained glass and the most eye-catching yet graceful adornments that their craftsmen could create. They decorated their households with the finest and most lavish furniture and fabrics, and dressed in colourful voluminous silks; as they rode on horseback through Cairo's dusty streets, they shone out against the grime like flashing jewels. They built grandiose mosques, *madrasas* and mausoleums, advertised by stripy *ablaq* masonry and graced with tapering minarets and lofty domes, conjuring up the dreamy medieval skyline that formed the backdrop of the *Arabian Nights*, which was completed during this period. In 1345, the traveller Ibn Battuta was moved to write that Cairo was 'the mother of cities…boundless in the multitude of buildings, peerless in beauty and splendour'. Ibn Khaldun was even more effusive as he looked on the capital:

> I saw the metropolis of the world – orchard of the Universe, beehive of nations… human anthill, gateway of Islam, throne of royalty, sparkling within with palaces and gates, shining on the horizon with monasteries and schools, illuminated by the moons and stars of its learned men – appear on the bank of the Nile, river of paradise.

The Mamluks were connoisseurs with vast riches at their disposal – riches that could be lost instantly with a seditious swipe of a scimitar; it is not so much of a paradox that such murderous men from barbarian origins should also be such aesthetes.

COPTIC DEMISE

Al-Nasir Muhammad I was perhaps the most spendthrift (and most cruel) of the Bahri Mamluks. His huge court and harem, his mosque on the Citadel hill (the only building to survive there from the Mamluk era), and other buildings which were among the most beautiful of the time, incurred colossal expenses. To fund it all, he had to find new sources of revenue. He ordered surveys of the country for redistribution of land grants for the benefit of the royal coffers; he forced merchants to buy his stock at inflated prices and foisted devalued currency on them at unfavourable rates; he increased taxation on flourishing private enterprises; and most of all, he expropriated the fortunes of his most wealthy officials, hundreds of whom he tortured or killed.

Of course, none of this was popular, but the downtrodden Arabic-speaking Muslim Egyptians vented their fury not on the ruling Turkish-speaking Mamluk caste, but on the Copts, many of whom staffed the financial ministries and were deemed to be responsible for the economic misery. The Mamluks were glad to have scapegoats – especially Christian scapegoats – for the economic mire in which they now found themselves, and fanned the flames of intolerance and ill-will. The old discriminatory laws of the Arab era – distinctive clothing, having to ride backwards on an ass, the closure of churches – had already been re-introduced by the time that violent anti-Christian riots broke out in 1321. Churches were looted and destroyed, holy relics burned, and Copts massacred. Further rioting in 1354 and then an attack on Alexandria (from which the city struggled to recover) in 1365 by the Christian ruler of Cyprus, Peter I of Lusignan, only heightened anti-Christian sentiment. Having lived alongside Muslims in roughly equal numbers for centuries, the situation was now so serious that there were mass conversions to escape the strife. The Coptic community shrank to only a tenth of the total population – roughly where it has remained to this day.

After al-Nasir's death from old age in 1341, the economic and social problems were intensified by a political meltdown as feuding emirs battled for control behind the throne. The quick-fire succession of twelve sultans that followed al-Nasir to 1382 were basically the puppets of the emirs; the oldest was twenty-four at his accession, but most were young children who were deposed or murdered when it suited the emirs. Those that ruled for more than a few months often proved to be dissolute wastrels more interested in idle pleasures and cruel tortures than government.

BLACK DEATH

The regime was dealt a catastrophic blow with the arrival of bubonic plague, the Black Death, in 1347. Egypt was already in the grip of a severe famine which lowered resistance when the plague first appeared in Alexandria, brought there on merchant ships from the Black Sea. Within a year the disease had devastated communities throughout Egypt, killing about a third of the entire population before the epidemic subsided in 1349. In Cairo, one observer estimated that over a thousand people were dying each day. The Egyptian historian al-Maqrizi recorded its ravages:

> Cairo became an empty desert, and there was no one to be seen in the streets. A man could go from the Bab Zuwayla to the Bab Nasr without encountering another soul. The dead were so numerous that people thought only of them. Rubble piled up in the streets. People wore anxious expressions. Wailing could be heard on all sides, and you did not pass a house without being assailed by shrieks. Corpses lay piled along the public way, burial trains jostled one another, and the dead were carried to their graves amidst commotion.

Egypt's recovery was thwarted by frequent and repeated returns of the disease, sometimes in the even deadlier form, pneumonic plague. There were at least fifty-five more outbreaks before the arrival of the Ottomans in 1517, twenty of which were major epidemics, followed by a further thirty-three epidemics before the end of the nineteenth century. Whereas Europe's population bounced back from the Black Death during the fifteenth century, Egypt's did not. Even by 1800, the population was only a third of the level it had been in the seventh century during the Arab conquest.

The economic repercussions were enormous; widespread labour shortages left fields and workshops abandoned, and productivity slumped. While this added considerably to the suffering of the surviving population, the twelve-year-old Sultan Hasan (r.1347–1351 and 1354–1361), who came to the throne after the assassinations of

Sultan Hassan Mosque, Cairo

all five of his brothers, actually profited from the catastrophe. Tens of thousands of families and individuals had perished leaving no inheritors and their estates automatically went to the crown. Hasan blew much of his windfall on the immense Sultan Hasan Mosque (1356–1361), to assuage what was seen as God's wrath in the calamity of the Black Death. The complex included a *madrasa* and a magnificent tomb then unrivalled for splendour in all Cairo, but Hasan's demonstration of piety did not save him from murder in a court intrigue; his body went missing and never occupied its intended place of rest in his grand tomb.

The Burji Mamluks (1382–1517)

After Hasan's death, a group of Mamluks from Circassia in the Caucasus dominated the tools of government behind a series of enfeebled sultans. Their barracks were in the towers of the Citadel, from which they became known as Burji Mamluks from the Arabic *burj* for tower. In 1382, the Circassian emir Barquq (r.1382–1389 and 1390–1399) topped off his meteoric ascent through the Mamluk ranks by seizing the sultanate at the age of ten to establish a new period of Mamluk rule.

The Burji or Circassian Mamluks were at least as bloodthirsty, grasping and unscrupulous as their Bahri predecessors. Their heirs were invariably ousted by stronger emirs, who had to suppress their rivals with unflinching brutality. A great part of the state's resources was spent buying large corps of new Mamluks to shore up these fragile regimes, but the rapid influx of raw and uncultured recruits caused as many problems as it solved. They took time to be integrated into the system but were quick to demand the full privileges of their caste. When these were not forthcoming, they could hold the sultan to ransom for better pay and conditions by rioting and terrorising the local population. The recruits of a recently deceased sultan could also present an awkward obstacle to any incoming ruler, most of whom found a short-term solution in buying their own new recruits – which in turn only contributed to the long-term instability of the regime. As the fifteenth century progressed, fighting on the streets of Cairo between the various factions of new and established Mamluks became serious enough to inflict fatal wounds on the Burji state.

TAMERLANE

Initially the Circassian Mamluks were equal to any external threats to their empire, despite the incessant political turbulence at home. The first Burji sultan, Barquq, had to protect his realm from Tamerlane (1336–1405; also called Timur Lenk) and his ferocious horde, who had blown over from Transoxania (modern Uzbekistan) like a vortex of destruction, devastating lands from Delhi to Georgia, razing cities and making mountains out of the heads of their vanquished foes.

In 1399, they advanced on Mamluk possessions in Syria. Aleppo was ravaged and Barquq was persuaded to withdraw to Cairo, leaving Damascus to a similar fate. Fortunately the lure of Baghdad, sacked in 1401, and the Ottoman army, crushed at Ankara the following year, were distractions enough to keep Tamerlane out of Egypt until his death in 1405. Again the Mamluks had escaped Mongol fury, and this time had also watched while their neighbouring rivals, the Ottomans, suffered a major setback.

CIRCASSIAN DECLINE

The machinery of the Mamluk system needed the lubrication of a healthy economy to run smoothly. Buying large numbers of new recruits, bribing influential allies, erecting beautiful monuments for posterity, and maintaining the luxurious lifestyle for which the Mamluk sultans had become famous throughout the Middle East, required a brimming treasury. But recurrent plagues and famines every few years continued to batter the devastated economy; as revenues declined, the sultans struggled to cover their costs.

Sultan Barsbay (r.1422–1438) looked to international trade for new sources of wealth and encouraged merchants travelling from India to unload their rich cargoes at Mamluk ports in the Red Sea. Heavy duties were charged on the majority of goods which proceeded on to Europe via Cairo and Alexandria, but the sultan did not stop there, also imposing a royal monopoly on the highly lucrative trade in spices. He reaped huge profits from the measures, but in the end his meddling put Egypt's traders out of business, angered foreign merchants and impoverished the people. Their wretchedness was exacerbated in leaner times by currency devaluations, high inflation, rampant corruption, neglect of public works and the imposition of swingeing taxes often collected by force – plunder in all but name – as well as confiscations and extortions, and the periodic looting of Cairo by unruly Mamluk recruits. Alexandria, once the trading centre of the Mediterranean, was also in chronic decline; its textile industry boasted twelve thousand looms when the Circassians took over, but by 1438 there were only eight hundred.

Political instability added to the misery; of the twenty-five sultans that ruled during the 134-year period of the Circassian regime, sixteen barely totted up a decade at the helm between them. The average reign of the nine remaining sultans was around fourteen years, and Qaytbay (r.1468–1496) was easily the longest serving and most successful of them. With an iron fist he kept the squabbling emirs in line, establishing an episode of stability and renewed prosperity. Soon he could afford to finance magnificent public works, including the harbour fort at Alexandria built from the ruins of the ancient lighthouse, and a glorious mosque and mausoleum in the capital decorated with the finest arabesque ornamentation, *ablaq* masonry and a gilded ceiling.

But the summer of Circassian rule was brief indeed. By the 1480s, Qaytbay's new Mamluks, hastily recruited to counter the Ottoman threat in the north, began to riot over their low pay. Meanwhile the Bedouin took the opportunity to revolt and could not be suppressed. Qaytbay's death in 1496 triggered another round of vicious internecine fighting between the Mamluk clans which brought the state to the brink of collapse. The sultanate briefly surfaced from the chaos under the stewardship of Qansawh II al-Ghawri (r.1501–1516), but the regime had failed to keep pace with changes overseas and by now it was too late for even the most gifted Mamluk ruler to rescue it.

MAMLUKS OUTMODED

At the turn of the sixteenth century the international order was rapidly changing; European powers were on the threshold of modernity but Mamluk Egypt looked ever more like a relic from the medieval past.

Vasco da Gama's successful navigation around the Cape of Good Hope in 1498 opened up a new sea route between India and Europe that bypassed Egypt altogether. The fall in trade was bad enough, but the Mamluks had no war fleet and the Portuguese began to prey on Muslim merchant ships in the Red Sea and Indian Ocean. As the royal coffers began to run dry, Sultan al-Ghawri scrambled to prepare fleets on both Egyptian shores to protect Mamluk ports and the holy cities of Islam in Arabia from the Portuguese menace. Even their rivals, the

Ottomans, moved to assist them against the European threat, sending arms, gunpowder, timber, iron and shipwrights. But the Mamluk was not a naval culture, and in any case, Western technology had begun to outstrip Eastern. The Portuguese warships were designed to survive Atlantic storms; they were superior in build, equipped with more sophisticated tools of navigation and far more powerful cannonry.

On land too, firearms were revolutionising warfare, but the Mamluks turned their noses up at them, considering guns unbecoming weapons for the chivalrous business of battle. Their skills as horsemen, swordsmen and archers could hardly be shown off in a gun battle; horsemanship in particular was a measure of a Mamluk's power, superiority and privilege. But al-Ghawri knew he would be lost without artillery and began casting cannons in the foundry at Cairo in 1507; it was not until 1511, however, that his test pieces actually withstood a detonation without exploding in a shower of shrapnel. His soldiers were also hostile to using firearms and lugging heavy artillery to the battlefield, and it was only in 1511 that a dedicated corps of arquebusiers was drawn up. Significantly, it was of non-Mamluk stock, made up of low-status and poorly paid reservists, Persians and Turkmen who were known to their comrades as the 'false' or 'motley army'. Complaints from established Mamluks over the (relatively modest) amount of money spent on the arquebusiers led to another bout of crippling riots in 1514 and the unit was never used in conjunction with the conventional Mamluk personnel for fear of sparking a revolt.

THE OTTOMAN CONQUEST

The Ottomans had no such scruples about gunpowder. They had recovered from their massive defeat at the hands of Tamerlane in 1402 to become a great regional power, which snuffed out the Byzantine Empire after the capture of Constantinople in 1453. Soon they were pressuring Mamluk borders too, but it was not until 1481 that the strain was really felt, after Sultan Qaytbay welcomed a deposed crown prince from Constantinople, sparking off a series of conflicts over the next decade. Peace was secured in 1491 after the Mamluks advanced into Anatolia as far as Kayseri, but victory came at a price: it was the new Mamluks recruited to fight these battles, as we have seen, that caused the sultanate immense problems at home.

In contrast to the Mamluk sultan's difficulties, the Ottoman ruler was by now immensely wealthy and oversaw an empire that stretched from the Caucasus to the Balkans. The Egyptian diarist Ibn Iyas noted that when the Ottoman ambassador called on Cairo in 1514 'he brought with him a sumptuous present: twenty-five loads of lynx, sable and ermine, of Bursa velvet, of coloured fabrics from Samarkand, of silver vases, to say nothing of twenty-five Mamluks of outstanding beauty.'

In the same year, the belligerent Ottoman ruler Selim the Grim (r. in Egypt 1517–1520), a religious zealot bent on the destruction of 'heretical' forms of Islam, demolished the Shiite Safavid army of Persia at Chaldiran in Anatolia. Al-Ghawri, who shared Selim's distaste for Sufism and Shiism, had initially enjoyed excellent relations with him, but on the pretext that the Egyptians had not helped against the Persians, the Ottomans attacked. The battle took place at Marj Dabiq, north of Aleppo in August 1516. Engulfed by an Ottoman army at least three times its size, blown to pieces by cannon and gunfire (the small unit of Egyptian arquebusiers was garrisoned on the Red Sea), and betrayed by Khayrbak, the Mamluk governor of Aleppo, who had secretly agreed to withdraw his troops while battle was in full swing, the Egyptian army was all but destroyed. Al-Ghawri died in the heat of battle from an apoplectic seizure; his body was never found, starting the legend that it had been whisked away by spirits.

As Syria fell to the Ottomans, al-Ghawri's nephew, Tumanbay II (r.1516–1517) was hastily proclaimed sultan in Cairo. The Mamluks could not have asked for a better leader. Bold, determined and just, Tumanbay organised a swift resistance, drumming up support and filling out his depleted forces with even the most unsavoury riff-raff of Cairo. Despite his best efforts to prepare the capital's defences and equip his men with guns, the hodgepodge army was no match for the Ottomans. When they met outside the city on 23 January 1517, the Egyptians were overrun in a matter of minutes, and Cairo was ransacked for three days. Ottoman soldiers rampaged the streets, slaughtering as many Mamluks as they could find.

Tumanbay escaped and fought against the Ottomans twice more, being defeated on both occasions. He was finally betrayed by a Bedouin who owed him his life, sold to the Ottomans, and hanged like a lowly criminal at the Bab Zuwayla, the great gateway leading to the vast Mamluk cemeteries, the Cities of the Dead. Twice the rope snapped, but Tumanbay maintained his dignity to the end.

Ottoman Egypt (1517–1798)

The transition to Ottoman rule was traumatic. Selim the Grim rounded up hundreds of Mamluks and executed them, spiking their heads on poles. Ottoman troops terrorised Cairo's narrow streets. The country's most gifted scholars, entrepreneurs, officials and artisans were shipped off to Constantinople. New Ottoman laws enraged the people who considered them against the nature of Islam. A debased coinage was introduced that robbed Egyptians of a third of their wealth. Mosques and palaces were stripped of their marble and fineries, which locals were forced to haul onto Ottoman ships while others were press-ganged to be the rowing crews. Far more psychologically damaging, however, was Egypt's relegation to a province, one of thirty-two in the Ottoman Empire, a loss of status that was further emphasised by the deportation of the Abbasid caliph from Cairo to Constantinople, ending the city's role as the centre of the Sunni spiritual world.

Even so, the Mamluk fire had not been extinguished. The traitor Khayrbak, a Mamluk himself, was made the pasha (viceroy of the province) – a recognition that the Ottomans would need Mamluk collaboration to rule Egypt effectively. Shortly before Selim's departure from the country, all surviving Mamluks were pardoned. As they reappeared from hiding, the Circassians were employed in a new cavalry unit to go alongside the six Ottoman regiments garrisoned in the province. Unsurprisingly they were little trusted and given Ottoman commanders, ordered to wear Ottoman clothes, go clean-shaven like their Ottoman counterparts, and adopt other Ottoman customs in an attempt to integrate them, lessen the risk of mutiny, and defuse tensions with the other regiments. Ottoman attitudes towards them gradually improved, not least after their performance at the siege of Rhodes (1522), where Selim's son and successor, the famous Sulayman the Magnificent (r.1520–1566) expressed his disbelief that his father had killed and squandered the talents of such extraordinary warriors.

After Khayrbak's death in 1522, it quickly became apparent that members of the old Mamluk elite still harboured ambitions to rule Egypt. A revolt in May 1523 underestimated the resolve of the youthful Sulayman and the strength of the nascent empire, and was swiftly crushed. A second rebellion a few months later, led by the Circassian viceroy Ahmad Pasha made better running. By extortion, confiscation, dismissals and promotion of his own coterie, Ahmad was able to proclaim himself sultan, mint his name on coins, and rule the land for several months before he was captured and beheaded in March 1524. His limited success inspired sporadic unrest amongst the Bedouin for another year until Sulayman's Grand Vizier, Ibrahim Pasha, quelled them and instituted a new administrative system for the province in an edict called the *Qanunname*.

CONSOLIDATION AND QUIESCENCE

The *Qanunname* edict recognised Egypt's position as the richest and most important province of the empire, and being a special case, blended the existing Mamluk system with some elements of Ottoman imperial administration. For the next sixty years, the formula worked well. Under the high command of the pasha, taxes and custom duties were collected to fund the local garrison, the civil service, and regional units for expeditions overseas, while anything left over was sent on to Constantinople along with sizeable shipments of produce. Grain, sugar, lentils and rice were distributed across the empire from Egypt, but it was trade in coffee that proved to be the province's most lucrative export during the sixteenth century, filling the gap left by disruptions to the spice trade. Beans were grown in Yemen and traded from Cairo with European merchants keen to satisfy an ever-burgeoning demand in the north. Caravanserais sprang up around the capital to house travelling merchants, and the city port at Bulaq thronged with ships and traders.

Good administration encouraged a period of stability and prosperity, but there was no royal household to stimulate the manufacture of luxury items and fine art, or to commission the construction of splendid mosques and mausoleums in the grand Mamluk manner. Notwithstanding this fall from former glory, viceroys and wealthy Cairenes continued to embellish the capital through endowments and charitable foundations with new mosques, schools, bathhouses and fountains. The port of Suez also benefited from resurgent commerce, even though the Ottoman plan of 1568 to build a canal across the isthmus came to nought.

As well as its economic importance, Egypt was a valuable base for Ottoman military actions overseas. It was the launching pad for a failed expedition of 1538 to end Portuguese naval superiority in the Indian Ocean. After the defeat, operations focused on securing Red Sea shipping routes and the holy cities of Mecca and Medina from Portuguese attack. Garrisons in Egypt were frequently called upon for defensive campaigns in Yemen and along the African Red Sea coast, or to protect pilgrim routes to the Hijaz – soldiering work that was deemed an easy detail compared to the hardships endured on other Ottoman fronts. As a result, the province attracted many foreign mercenaries in addition to 10,000 regular troops already stationed there. Political dissidents and immensely wealthy African eunuchs, who had been in charge of the sultan's harem in Constantinople before being ousted, also felt that a new and better life could be found in Egypt.

DISSENT AND DISOBEDIENCE

By the 1580s, a flood of cheap silver from the New World had seriously disrupted the Ottoman economy. The subsequent inflation sparked a crisis in the empire as soldiers, who enjoyed a fixed salary, found that their wages were worth only a fraction of their former value. From 1586 riots and revolts led by unhappy soldiers broke out with debilitating regularity, ushering in a long period of political instability. Most of the anger was directed at the viceroy, who could do little but take refuge in the Citadel or give in to the mutineers' demands.

The violence climaxed in 1604 when rebels ambushed and executed the pasha, and hung his head from the Bab Zuwayla. Even this did not placate the soldiery for long and they sought to make up the shortfall in their pay by illegal means, not least the extraction of an illegal levy (*tulba*) on the rural population. A new strong-arm viceroy, Muhammad Pasha, was sent to set matters right; but his suppression of the *tulba* provoked a massive insurrection in 1609 during which the rebels produced their own sultan and ministers. The pasha put a bloody end to the rebellion, exiling some but beheading many more, leading one chronicler to describe it as 'the second Ottoman conquest of Egypt'.

Muhammad Pasha's reassertion of vice-regal strength did not endure. A hundred pashas followed him in only 187 years of Ottoman rule. A pasha's term of office was admittedly short – usually a year and often renewed for two or three years – but many of these governorships were cut short by the machinations of the beys.

The Beys

The beys were military commanders of high rank not belonging to the garrisoned Ottoman regiments, most of whom were Circassians and descendants of the old Mamluk emirs. As their forebears had done, they were allowed to continue with the practice of importing, training and keeping their own Mamluks. The beys had far greater local experience and knowledge than the Ottomans, who came to rely on them for overseeing fundamental security tasks such as keeping marauding Bedouin in check; protecting the hajj pilgrimage caravan from raids; accompanying the yearly tribute payments to Constantinople; commanding Egypt's contingent of troops called up to fight for the empire; and ensuring that that the province's dams and waterways were well maintained. By the end of the century, these jobs had become some of the most important offices in the administration, virtual ministries, and the beys had assumed exclusive rights to lead them.

The beys also built up an economic base after they were allowed to become tax-farmers, bidding for the right to collect revenues for a given area or enterprise. Officials and impoverished garrison officers also sought to supplement their meagre salaries in this way. The introduction of tax-farms throughout the Ottoman Empire has been seen as a symptom of its decline, and in Egypt there is no doubt that they weakened imperial authority while handing power to local interests. Furthermore, the tensions and conflicts between the beys and other officers over control of tax-farms coloured much of the rest of the Ottoman period. All the while, the representatives of Constantinople, not least the pasha, became increasingly isolated and impotent, their political survival depending on their ability to play one side off against the other.

In 1623, the beys and garrison officers refused to accept the appointed viceroy, and in 1631 they deposed the incumbent with the official approval of the sultan in Constantinople. This established a legal precedent for the beys to remove pashas as they pleased, which they did with increasing regularity. From this moment, the beys were the effective masters of Egypt and as long as the sultan's sovereignty was recognised, the annual revenues were paid, and troops were provided when needed, Constantinople acquiesced.

INTERNECINE STRIFE: FIQARIS, QASIMIS AND JANISSARIES

Factionalism had been an endemic problem for the Mamluk rulers, and now it plagued the beys as well. For about a century from the 1630s, Egypt was racked by internecine struggles between beys of two main households, the Fiqaris and Qasimis. The exact origins of the two households are unknown but they may have derived from tribal rivalries in Yemen that became applied to Ottoman (Fiqari) and non-Ottoman (Qasimi), especially Mamluk, groupings within the military. Eventually the factions not only divided the military, but also Cairo artisans, the rural Bedouin and various other sections of Egyptian society.

From 1631 to 1656, the Fiqaris had the upper hand thanks largely to the efforts of their immovable leader, Ridwan Bey, who survived several revolts and attempts by the sultan and pashas to unseat him. His death was a spur to the Qasimis who had started to enjoy the support of the desperate central government. A massacre of Fiqari leaders in 1660 followed by the murder of the Qasimi leader two years later created a brief hiatus in their struggles.

Officers of the Janissary regiment, the elite Ottoman infantry corps and the largest, wealthiest and most influential unit of the garrison, emerged into this power vacuum and took control during the late seventeenth century. Over time Janissary officers had built up connections with foreign coffee merchants and acquired some of the most lucrative tax-farms in the province, siphoning off grain from charitable trusts for purchase of coffee, as well as control of highly profitable customs duties for many of Egypt's ports. But in the absence of a single powerful leader, the squabbling continued – not only between Fiqaris and Qasimis, but now also between higher and lower Janissary officers.

In 1711 rows broke out simultaneously within both the Janissary corps and the Fiqari household, and rapidly escalated into a miniature civil war that pitted all the vested interests against each other. Fierce fighting erupted on the streets of Cairo and the Citadel was bombarded by cannonfire, which streaked the night sky 'like lightning'. The Qasimis, aided by the Azab regiment, the second largest garrison corps, won out but the turmoil dragged on sporadically as each household attempted to pick off rival leaders with assassination and counter-assassination. The tables turned in 1730 when another bout of conflict shattered Qasimi power for good. Six years later their Fiqari counterparts were caught out in an ambush organised by the pasha, which left them without ten of their top emirs. By then, the sparring between Fiqaris and Qasimis had utterly exhausted both sides, allowing a new power faction to appear, the Qazdagli household, whose roots lay in the Janissary regiment.

QAZDAGLI HOUSEHOLD

The Qazdagli household managed to remain dominant in Egypt until the Mamluk system was expunged in the early nineteenth century by

Muhammad Ali (see p.264). During the middle years of the eighteenth century, an attempt to centralise control in the province in a single leading bey, known by the new title of *sheikh al-balad* or 'head of the city', engendered a period of stability and renewed commerce after years of factional violence that sapped morale, drained national resources and hampered economic growth. The coffee trade with Europe, especially France, was booming, the currency fluctuations of old had dissipated, and the province was momentarily spared any devastating outbreaks of plague.

In this more peaceful climate, the wealthier beys did not need to spend their cash on waging war, but ploughed it into monument building. Cairo in particular enjoyed a spate of construction activity, with new mosques and ornate public fountains springing up across the city. The size of the population increased, western Cairo rapidly expanded and the monied classes treated themselves to enormous luxury residences on the tranquil shores of the Ezbekiya lake away from the dust and hubbub of the city centre. As the contemporary historian al-Jabarti observed, contentment seemed at last to pervade the country: 'Egypt was then dazzlingly beautiful...The poor led an ample life, the small as well as the great lived comfortably...Well-being was spread over the whole city, security reigned, prosperity had set up its abode there.'

ALI BEY

The good times came to end during the rule of Ali Bey (1767–1772), the Mamluk of a ruling Qazdagli bey, who had risen to the post of *sheik al-balad* after his master's death. Nicknamed the 'Cloud-catcher' for his high-flying ambitions, Ali Bey had grand plans to extend his rule far beyond Egypt's provincial borders. He dreamed of recreating the Mamluk sultanate, taking Egypt out of the empire, and winning back the country's old territorial possessions of Syria and the Hijaz.

His first step was to secure his position, which he did by neutralising his enemies, whether real or imagined. Opponents, allies and even benefactors were deposed, forced into exile or killed, while Ali inserted his own Mamluks into the administration. In 1769 he wrested

Upper Egypt and its considerable agricultural resources from the sway of tribal Bedouin chiefs, who had ruled there for decades. To augment his wealth further he expropriated the customs houses of the country's major ports, ousting the Jews that operated them and replacing them with Syrian Christians, who advocated stricter tax control and higher revenues.

When a request came from Constantinople for Ali Bey to mediate in a dynastic squabble in the Hijaz, he snatched the opportunity to expand his power there, informing European merchants that they were welcome to bring their trade directly to Egypt in contravention of existing Ottoman laws. Embroiled in an enervating war with Russia, the Ottoman government did not have the reach to react when Ali started to mint his own coins and withhold remittance payments to Constantinople.

In 1771 the stage was set for Ali Bey's invasion of Syria. At the head of a large army, his deputy, Muhammad Bey, deftly captured Damascus. However, a few days later he abandoned the city and returned to Egypt, probably having accepted a large Ottoman bribe to turn against his master. Ali Bey's brief performance as an independent ruler came to an end when his second deputy turned against him as well, forcing his flight from Egypt in 1772. He died from battle wounds the following year while attempting to re-enter Cairo.

INTO THE MIRE

Muhammad Bey (d.1775) repaired the relationship with the Ottoman government, while continuing to pursue interests in Syria and Palestine, and making further trading partnerships with European powers, not least the East India Company of Britain. For a moment, Ali Bey and Muhammed Bey had pulled Egypt out of the shade of Ottoman hegemony and back into the bright lights of the international arena – a prelude to the country's crucial role in foreign affairs from the end of the century onwards.

But the grasping Mamluk grandees who followed them returned the country to the exploitation and short-sighted, destructive misrule of the past. Al-Jabarti rued their ascendance, commenting: 'their inclination was away from justice and towards the ways of folly. They accustomed themselves to tyranny and thought it gain; they persevered in injustice and continued their oppression without interruption.'

IBRAHIM BEY AND MURAD BEY

Two of Muhammad Bey's Mamluks, Ibrahim Bey and Murad Bey, outmanoeuvred their competitors and, finding neither was powerful enough to eliminate the other, formed an uneasy duumvirate that lasted off and on for twenty years until 1798. Motivated by greed and the blind desire not to be outdone by the other, they plundered the country's economy and resources, gaily embezzling funds earmarked for Constantinople, the civil service, religious foundations and for the general upkeep of the country. Their depredations brought the country to its knees.

When the Bedouin failed to receive their customary payments, they attacked pilgrim and merchant caravans. Travellers were killed, cargoes

Murad Bey, one of the Mamluks who plundered Egypt's economy and resources

stolen, and the land slipped into lawlessness. Ibrahim placed duties on coffee and spices that dried up international trade, while Murad's taxes on farmers and peasants were so excessive that they deserted the land. In savage retribution Murad razed countless villages in the Delta; fields were left untilled, irrigation canals fell into disrepair and agricultural output slumped at just the same time as droughts hit and rebels in the grain-rich south disrupted and withheld food shipments. Famines gripped the country, but the misery of the population was multiplied many times by pestilence that repeatedly annihilated livestock and recurrent plagues that swept through towns and cities, killing many tens of thousands of people.

The self-enrichment of these beys carried on regardless. Murad was fond of extorting huge sums from European merchants and bank-rupted some French companies in the process. The French govern-ment threatened to retaliate if the sultan failed to act against the duo. The response from Constantinople finally came in 1786, when an Ottoman task force led by Hasan Pasha drove Murad and Ibrahim into Upper Egypt and installed another Mamluk as the *sheikh al-balad*, who proved to be just as rapacious as the duumvirs. Hasan was recalled the following year for an imminent war against Russia before he was able to prise Murad and Ibrahim from their hideouts in the south. In 1791 another ferocious bout of plague wiped out the new government, allowing the two beys to resume their dreadful rule.

They had no mercy for a country ravaged by disorder, dearth, famine and disease, and no compassion for their wretched subjects, whom they continued to overtax, tyrannise and defraud. But this time their depredations on French merchants would not go unpunished. They arrogantly brushed off a warning from France in 1795 to respect its commercial interests, little suspecting that there would be any consequences to pay.

When Napoleon Bonaparte landed near Alexandria on 1 July 1798 with a fleet of 400 warships and 33,000 well-equipped and battle-hardened troops, Murad and Ibrahim were completely unprepared. As they hurried to muster a resisting force, they had no idea that Napoleon's arrival heralded the end of Mamluk society. Egypt's days as a neglected province in a declining realm were over; it was about to become the key piece in the game of empire between European superpowers.

CHAPTER TEN

The Dawn of the Modern State

1798–1882

French Occupation

Decades of neglect and civil strife had reduced Alexandria to a dirty and decrepit town of just a few thousand inhabitants by the end of the eighteenth century. Its dilapidated fort and crumbling ramparts were manned by only a handful of Mamluks with just a single barrel of gunpowder, hardly equal to the 33,000-strong French Army of the East, led by the twenty-eight-year-old Napoleon Bonaparte (1769–1821), the rising star and hero of the young Republic. Within three hours on 2 July 1798, the day after the French landed, the city had fallen.

Napoleon immediately issued a proclamation, read aloud through the city as well as distributed in Arabic, Turkish and French:

> People of Egypt, you may have been told that I have come here to destroy your religion. This is a flagrant lie. Do not believe it. Tell those deceivers that I have come to restore your rights to you and punish the tyrants, and that I serve God more than the Mamluks do; that I revere His Prophet Muhammad and the glorious Koran…

> Once you had great cities, large canals, a prosperous trade. What has destroyed all this, if not the greed, the iniquity, and the tyranny of the Mamluks?…

> May God preserve the glory of the Ottoman Sultan! May God preserve the glory of the French army! May God curse the Mamluks and bestow happiness on the Egyptian people!

Napoleon was prepared to say anything to win an empire; the idea of invading Egypt had been hatched several years before, and had as little to do with freeing Egyptians from the Mamluk yoke as it did with any veneration for Muhammad on Napoleon's part. Nor was it a direct response to the complaints of the small French expatriate business community who had suffered under the Mamluk beys. Rather, in this new age of empire-building, Egypt's unique strategic and economic value had been recognised. If well governed it could be fabulously wealthy and yet it was a poorly defended and hopelessly managed possession of the ailing Ottomans. It was also the perfect vantage point from which to attack British interests in India, the best means of hurting Britain considering that its naval superiority precluded an invasion of the island itself. Quite apart from this, colonising an exotic realm appealed to Napoleon's own brand of romantic megalomania. He dreamed of ruling an eastern empire, and spoke of 'marching into Asia, riding on an elephant, a turban on my head and in my hand the new Koran that I would have composed to suit my needs'. He was as keen on the Egyptian mission as the Directory in Paris, the revolutionary government, was keen to see the back of a terrifyingly ambitious young general.

BATTLE OF THE PYRAMIDS

Napoleon was impatient to get to Cairo and overthrow the Mamluks. Without giving them time to organise supplies, he sent his troops in the blistering heat of July along the dried-up bed of the canal linking Alexandria to the Nile. The wells along the route had been sabotaged and soon his thirst-stricken men were driven to madness by the mirages that shimmered and evaporated in the near-distance. Some soldiers lost their minds and shot themselves, while stragglers were picked off by Bedouin who harried the troops all the way to Cairo, leaving a 'trail of corpses' behind them.

The losses were not enough to upset the enormous numerical advantage Napoleon enjoyed over the Mamluks, whose leaders were still unaware that centuries of Mamluk traditions were about to end. In fact, Murad Bey was positively optimistic when he learned that the French hardly had a cavalry: 'I will trample them under my horse's hooves and slice them up like water-melons!'

The sides met at Imbaba across the Nile from Cairo within sight of the pyramids, where the Mamluk cavalry were arrayed in breathtaking splendour, their jewel-encrusted weaponry glittering in the sun, their bright silk robes and colourful pennants fluttering in the breeze beneath a cloudless sky. Galloping at full tilt they charged, reins clenched in teeth as they first emptied their guns and pistols which they flung over their shoulder for their foot-servants running behind to gather. At closer range they drew their scimitars to scythe down the enemy – a single swing was enough to sever a head clean off.

Against a less-organised foe this type of blitz charge was devastating. Against the well-drilled, tactically and technologically superior French army, it was disastrous. Quickly forming ordered squares, Napoleon's men tore the Mamluk horsemen apart with musket balls, shells and grapeshot before they could get close. Within an hour, the battle had become a massacre. Murad Bey turned and fled south with his survivors; he was hotly pursued by General Desaix across Upper Egypt and all the way into the Sudan, but would not be caught before his death from plague two years later. Ibrahim Bey who had been watching from the other bank of the Nile escaped to Palestine.

ABUQIR, THE BATTLE OF THE NILE

Napoleon marched victorious into Cairo on 24 July 1798. On 1 August, Lord Nelson took Napoleon's fleet by surprise at Abuqir Bay east of Alexandria, destroying all but two ships. Late in the evening the British had deftly sailed close to the shore behind the French defensive line and raked its unprotected side with cannonfire; the climax came when the bruising French flagship *L'Orient*, a 120 gun brute far bigger than any other vessel in the bay, exploded in a gigantic fireball with the admiral and his company on board.

The sinking of his armada was a massive blow to Napoleon, who now found himself cut off from the motherland with no easy means of reinforcement or retreat. Furthermore, the defeat encouraged the Ottomans, already piqued by the invasion of their territory and unconvinced by Napoleon's propaganda, to break their ties with

France and enter into an alliance with Britain and Russia to remove them. The loss of the sultan's complicity was at least as disastrous for Napoleon as the sinking of his battleships; in a single night his Egyptian campaign was undone.

THE FRENCH IN EGYPT

Napoleon did his best to brush off the bad news of Abuqir and set about establishing a colony. He fully intended to impose a new administration that would fund itself and create revenues for the Republic. To keep the people on his side, he set up local governing councils (*diwans*), staffed by handpicked notables from the native religious and mercantile classes, who it was hoped would provide a sheen of legitimacy to the new regime. However, the conceit that the French had come as liberators was seriously undermined by a range of oppressive fiscal measures that Napoleon was forced to introduce to finance the colony. Cash could not now be sent from Paris, and the treasures intended to fund the campaign – gold and diamonds stolen from Switzerland – had gone down with his flagship in Abuqir Bay.

At first Egyptians were intrigued by the peculiar habits, customs and clothes of their new masters, not to mention the 'immodest' behaviour of the unveiled Frenchwomen. Cairenes were delighted to find they could sell their wares to the soldiers at vastly inflated prices. But a wave of property confiscations, forced loans on artisans and merchants, and a new tax based on urban buildings rapidly soured the public mood.

When the Ottoman sultan declared war on France in September 1798, popular resistance began to crystallise, its leaders mainly coming from the mosques, particularly the Azhar Mosque. Calls from the minarets of Cairo to bear arms against the infidel French were heeded on 21 October when an insurrection broke out and barricades were erected across the city. The troops were sent in but the fighting only stopped the next day after Napoleon ordered the shelling of the Azhar Mosque, which was later stormed and desecrated. Around three thousand Cairenes were killed in the suppression compared to about three hundred French. But the Egyptians had made their point – the French hold on the country could only be maintained by force.

Unfortunately, their point was all too readily understood by Napoleon who had no qualms in forcing his authority. 'Every night we have about thirty heads chopped off, many of them belonging to the ring-leaders. This I believe will serve them as a good lesson,' he wrote to one of his generals.

Despite their unpopularity, their isolation, and the low morale of the French troops – who had come to Egypt expecting a promised land only to find a hostile and impoverished nation – Napoleon remained resolutely optimistic. He still believed he could found an eastern empire and conquer Constantinople and India.

DESCRIPTION DE L'ÉGYPTE

In the new spirit of the Enlightenment, he also hoped that the conquest would benefit the arts and sciences. To this end, he gathered 167 'savants' – the cream of France's young generation of mathematicians, chemists, engineers, architects, astronomers, botanists, zoologists, geologists, cartographers, economists, Arabists, artists and writers – to measure, describe, record and catalogue all aspects of Egypt.

The fruits of their exhaustive labours were published between 1810 and 1828 as the *Description de l'Égypte*, a monumental 24-volume work containing more than eight hundred engravings, three thousand illustrations and detailed text describing the minutiae of Egyptian life, geography and culture. The *Description* immediately aroused a fascination for Egypt in the West that has never diminished and provided the sturdy basis for the emergent new science of Egyptology. As such, it was unquestionably the great and enduring achievement of the brief and dramatic French encounter with the country.

FACING THE OTTOMANS

Napoleon led a force of 13,000 men into Syria in February 1799 to head off the imminent Ottoman invasion. He seized al-Arish, Gaza and Jaffa with relative ease, but his advance into Syria was beset with difficulties. Water was scarce and plague began to break out amongst his malnourished troops. They arrived in a woeful condition at Acre, a coastal stronghold known as 'the key to Palestine' because of its natural strategic position, to find a garrison of resourceful British marines and Turkish irregulars manning the fort and aiming captured French cannons down at them from the ramparts.

For ten weeks Bonaparte threw everything he had at 'that miserable hole', as he called it, with terrible losses, but could not break through. Of Sir Sidney Smith, who led the British at Acre, he later reminisced, 'That man made me miss my destiny'.

His retreat to Egypt presaged the horrors he would suffer in Russia: hundreds of his men were abandoned to die from thirst or illness along the way. None of this stopped him from proclaiming victory and staging a triumphal entry into Cairo, though his haggard soldiers 'had neither hats nor boots' and the air of defeat hung heavily over them.

There was genuine cause for celebration a month later when the French crushed a Turkish invasion aided by the British fleet at Abuqir in July. Napoleon knew it would not be enough to salvage his Egyptian project, but it did at least cast a thin patina of success over his imminent exit. The news – mischievously given him by Sir Sidney Smith – that French armies were in retreat across Europe and the Directory was in turmoil, presented the opportunity Napoleon needed to begin a new chapter. He stole out of the country on 23 August 1799 without even telling his designated successor, General Kléber. Three months later he had become dictator of France. Napoleon never returned, but in the twilight of his life he remarked: 'I should have done better to remain in Egypt; by now, I would have been Emperor of all the East!'

WITHDRAWAL

When General Kléber discovered he had been left with the task of extricating the French from Egypt he was furious: '*Ce petit salaud a foutu le camp avec ses culottes pleines de merde!*' he reputedly railed against his former commander.

Kléber was eager to bring the doomed campaign to a quick and clean end. Unfortunately the terms for withdrawal that he agreed with the Ottomans at the Convention of al-Arish (January 1800) were rejected by the British, bringing about an extension of the French presence in Egypt by almost two years. More revolts broke out and Kléber was assassinated by a Syrian Muslim while taking the air in his garden. Again French retribution was brutal: troops ran amok in Cairo, ringleaders were beheaded and the assassin had his offending right arm burnt off to the elbow before being impaled.

The dumpy and derided General Menou succeeded by seniority. To the dismay of his soldiers, he was in no hurry to quit the faltering colony. After all, he had already converted to Islam, changed his name to Abdullah, and married the daughter of an Egyptian bathhouse keeper in the mistaken belief she was a member of the native aristocracy.

The British at last decided that 'something ought to be done' about the French in Egypt and sent General Abercromby to invade. In March 1801, the British expeditionary force landed at Abuqir and scored a resounding victory at the Battle of Alexandria, even though Abercromby himself was killed. With additional Ottoman and British divisions bearing down on Cairo from Syria and the Red Sea, the French capitulated on 27 June and were evacuated within a couple of months.

The artefacts collected by Napoleon's savants were all confiscated, among them – and after some argument from Menou – the Rosetta Stone. It had been discovered in 1799 by a Lieutenant Pierre Bouchard (1771–1822), who immediately recognised that its as yet indecipherable hieroglyphic and demotic inscriptions might be unlocked by the accompanying Greek text. Wax impressions of this and other important items were made before the handover, allowing the Frenchman, Jean-François Champollion (1790–1832) to unravel the enigma of hieroglyphs before his rivals in 1822 (see also p.273).

The French Occupation had been too brief to bring about sweeping transformations to Egyptian society. On the other hand, the encounter shook Egypt from the torpor of an isolated and conservative past and left a lingering impression. Imported technology and ideas revealed new possibilities for government and economy that had been unimaginable under the Mamluks – who had also revealed themselves to be obsolete as the guardians of Egypt. Even if many in Egypt held an ambivalent attitude to European science, politics, administration and philosophy, it was accepted that the miserable, debilitating rule of the Mamluk beys was over.

The Rise of Muhammad Ali, the Moderniser

Egypt was handed back to the Ottomans after the departure of British forces in 1803, but with no overarching power to establish itself lawlessness prevailed. Ottoman governors could not control or pay their troops, who responded by plundering homes and businesses and terrorising the population. Meanwhile the surviving Mamluks, although weakened, enjoyed the underhand support of the British, and added to the maelstrom of violence in a vain bid to regain their former privileges, a restoration that most Egyptians were anxious to avoid.

Among the various Ottoman military units garrisoned in Egypt was a corps of Albanian irregulars, famed as much for their unruliness as their fighting prowess. An exceptional young commander had recently become their leader, a man with the warm intelligence to gain men's trust and a cold ambition that would just as soon break it. With characteristic shrewdness Muhammad Ali (b. *c.*1769, d.1849; r.1805–1848) managed to play all sides to his advantage; he won the confidence of the long-suffering public by highlighting the excesses of the Ottomans and Mamluks, even though he led an Ottoman force himself and had forged a tactical alliance with some Mamluks. By 1805 the public clamour for him to take over forced the incumbent governor out of office and to persuade the sultan in Constantinople to elevate Muhammad Ali to the post.

Having come to power at the age of thirty-five, this former tobacco dealer from the small port of Kavalla in Macedonia used every possible means to ensure he never lost it. He fended off Ottoman plots to oust him, and demolished a poorly conceived British invasion at Rosetta in 1807, adorning the streets of the capital with the spiked heads of His Majesty's soldiers.

MASSACRE OF THE MAMLUKS

By far his most dramatic coup was against the troublesome Mamluks,

Muhammed Ali (r. 1805–1848) who massacred the last of the Mamluks

the last menace to his rule. For several years he had chased them into ever remoter pockets of Upper Egypt, but in 1811 he changed tack and offered them their former palaces in Cairo in a masterstroke of false magnanimity. The deception deepened when he invited 480 Mamluk beys to take their places alongside all the great sheiks and notables at a sumptuous ceremony in the Citadel. Like a cat toying with his prey, Muhammad Ali 'received them with great pomp and courtesy', offering coffee and delicacies and engaging in polite small talk. His guests were then asked to form a column for a grand procession to the city. As the Mamluk contingent picked its way in single file down a steep and winding passageway, Muhammad Ali's soldiers suddenly flung the gates shut at either end, while more men appeared in the high buildings flanking the alley, muskets trained to unleash a hailstorm of shot on their helpless targets. The dust had barely settled on the beys' blood-soaked robes before the order was given to go through the country putting every last Mamluk to the sword. At least two thousand were killed in the extermination. Where the Ottomans and French had failed, Muhammad Ali had rid Egypt of the Mamluks forever.

LANDLORD OF EGYPT

The massacre handed Muhammad Ali total political power in Egypt, although he was technically still a vassal of the Ottoman sultan. Piece by piece he extended his power into the economy too, taking direct control of the agricultural system by placing government monopolies on most crops and knocking aside the grasping middle-men who impeded the flow of wealth from the producers, the fellahin (the rural peasantry), to the state. The economy had long been stifled by corrupt and inefficient tax-farms which he now swept away, confiscating huge portions of the countryside for himself including many of the land endowments that had succoured the great mosques and religious schools for centuries. Soon Egypt had virtually become his own private farm and he its 'universal master, universal landlord, universal merchant'.

Like the best chief executives, Muhammad Ali always sought ways to improve his business, expand revenues and maximise profits. He embarked on a series of highly ambitious public works which he could only complete by forcing peasants to do hard labour. The largest projects were the construction of a grand new mosque on the Citadel (1824–1844) and the repair of the ancient canal between Alexandria and the Nile, renamed the Mahmudiyya Canal in honour of the Ottoman Sultan Mahmud II. It fostered the rebirth of Alexandria which had by then shrunk to little more than a fishing village, spurring a recovery that saw its return as one of the busiest ports in the Mediterranean by the middle of the century. But it was at a price; at any one time more than 300,000 men, women and children had been displaced from their homes to work on it and when it was finished in 1820 after three grinding years of toil, many thousands had perished in its construction.

Much of the other work was in repairing the country's neglected irrigation channels, clearing new canals and deepening others so that large swathes of land could be watered throughout the year.

At the same time, the introduction of a new strain of long-staple cotton (having long fibres) revolutionised the Egyptian economy. The country became famous across the world for the quality of its cotton crop, and keen demand, not least from the English cotton mills, the centres of the nascent industrial revolution, fixed Egypt in the emerging mechanisms of global trade. The cotton crop fetched high prices and in the first fifteen years of Muhammad Ali's rule the country enjoyed a sixfold increase in national revenues. But much of the new wealth was channelled straight into the ruler's pockets and the suffering and poverty of the fellahin continued.

REFORM AND MODERNISATION

Muhammad Ali's daring economic and agricultural reforms were always secondary to his prime concern – staying in power. He had fought alongside the British at Abuqir (where he was apparently hauled from the sea to safety by Sir Sidney Smith himself), and was well aware that the old armies of the Ottoman Empire had long since been superseded by the well-trained and equipped modern forces of Europe. He wanted a similarly modern army for Egypt too.

Many of the reforms and innovations he introduced to realise this dream had major repercussions for Egyptian society as a whole. Factories were built to produce items for his military plans, from boots and uniforms, to armaments, sails and warships. Chemical plants, tanneries, sugar refineries and an enormous new arsenal at Alexandria (the *liman*) were also built to complement his burgeoning industrial-military complex.

A medical school was established under the auspices of the Frenchman Dr Clot to provide doctors and medics for service with military units; later Clot Bey, as he became known, was the driving force behind a national vaccination programme against smallpox, a quarantine service to counter the outbreak of plague and cholera, a school for midwives, and eventually a hospital for the civilian population.

Education, for centuries the preserve of the religious scholars of the mosques, was completely overhauled to furnish Egyptians with the skills and abilities necessary to maintain and people the apparatus of an efficient modern army. Military academies were set up in tandem with secular schools on the European model. At first they were staffed by Europeans, but eventually also by Egyptians, who had returned from technical and academic training overseas; they began to form a new native professional class.

An Arabic-language publisher was set up to provide these institutions with books, and a language school was founded to translate great European texts into Arabic. A state newspaper was published in Arabic, helping to inspire new indigenous interest in intellectual and political matters, and to elevate the language of the masses.

With an infrastructure in place for a great modern army, all Muhammad Ali needed was soldiers. Shunning the recruitment of Turks and Albanians, whose discipline and obedience were questionable at best, he sent a force into the Sudan in 1820 to capture 40,000 slaves who would form the basis of his new army. Thousands of prisoners were sent back to Egypt, but most died on the way from disease, hunger and ill-treatment 'like sheep with the rot'. After this failure, Muhammad Ali resorted to conscripting Egyptian peasants. Many doubted that the fellahin would ever make good soldiers, but the first trained units surpassed all expectations in quelling revolts of their own kind, which encouraged the pasha to draft ever larger numbers of natives. In a decade the ranks swelled to 130,000 reliable and disciplined troops, trained mainly by the French (there was no shortage of French officers looking for work following Napoleon's defeat at Waterloo in 1815) and commanded by Ottoman officers. It was a vast improvement on the old armies of the Ottoman mould with their volatile mix of ethnic groups and multifarious units that obeyed only their own officers and deserted at will.

An Empire but not a Nation

ARABIA AND SUDAN

Even before he had at his disposal a large army organised and maintained on European lines, Muhammad Ali had begun the process of amassing an empire. In 1811, he belatedly answered a request by the sultan to deal with the Wahhabis, a fundamentalist sect that had conquered Arabia. The holy cities of Mecca and Medina were soon recaptured, and after an arduous seven-year campaign that was belatedly rescued by the pasha's talented eldest son, Ibrahim, the Wahhabis surrendered their hold on Arabia and coastal Yemen.

The Sudan expedition of 1820 may have been fruitless as a slave-gathering (and to a lesser extent gold-finding) mission, but the conquest handed the pasha the Nile Valley all the way to the foothills of the Ethiopian mountains, albeit an area horribly denuded by his own men after a string of brutal massacres. More importantly, it gave him both shores of the Red Sea, a strategic triumph which rang alarm bells in Westminster and encouraged the British to frustrate the pasha's plans for further expansion.

GREECE

In 1824 the Ottoman sultan again called upon Muhammad Ali, this time to suppress the Greeks of the Morea and the Aegean islands who were agitating for independence. By now, the pasha's modernised army was ready. Commanded by Ibrahim, the Egyptian troops made easy work of capturing Crete, Cyprus and the Morea. But the successes came to a dramatic halt when an allied fleet of French, British and Russian warships sank virtually the entire combined Egyptian-Ottoman navy at Navarino Bay in 1827. Muhammad Ali had warned the sultan of the dangers of a European intervention, but the latter had stubbornly refused to listen, rejecting any mediation over the issue of Greek independence. Angered by Ottoman intransigence, and with his cherished fleet destroyed and his fine new army stranded, the pasha demanded Syria in compensation. The predictable refusal from Constantinople marked the end of Muhammad Ali's involvement in the sultan's schemes. From then on he acted independently, even though he still remained a tribute-paying vassal of the Ottomans.

AGAINST THE SULTAN

If the sultan would not give him Syria, Muhammad Ali resolved to take it by force. In October 1831 the attack was launched and within ten months Ibrahim had managed to occupy all of Syria, crushing

Ottoman resistance at Beylan outside Homs. The advance continued over the Taurus mountains into central Anatolia, where he scored another stunning victory at Konya (1833), inflicting massive losses on the Ottomans and capturing the grand vizier. Ibrahim pressed on to within a day's march of Constantinople, but with the ultimate prize in his grasp, Muhammad Ali quailed. The collapse of the Ottoman Empire could only incur the wrath of the European powers who would do anything to avoid a major war in the inevitable scramble over its disintegrating provinces. The pasha thought better of embroiling himself against superior forces. Instead at the 1833 Peace of Kutahia, he settled for official recognition of his new dominions, which now extended as far as the Taurus mountains – an Egyptian empire that recalled the greatest of ancient times.

The vassal had become far more powerful than his suzerain. Muhammad Ali craved independence but this was more than European governments were prepared to allow and no one was more opposed than Lord Palmerston (1784–1865), the British foreign secretary (and later prime minister). An excessively strong Egypt threatened British interests in the Mediterranean and communications with India, particularly if Muhammad Ali allied himself with the French as Palmerston suspected he would. Moreover, he simply detested Muhammad Ali the man, whom he considered 'an ignorant barbarian...as great a tyrant and oppressor as ever made a people wretched'.

The sultan's attempts to oust Muhammad Ali from Syria ended with the utter collapse of the Ottoman military at the Battle of Nezib in June 1839 and the subsequent defection of the entire Turkish fleet to Egypt. Independence was again for the taking, and again the pasha was frustrated, this time by the five European powers (France, Britain, Russia, Austria and Prussia) which rushed to make their support for the sultan known at the London Conference of 1840. Their position was underlined by the British bombardment of Beirut which sparked uprisings against the Egyptians throughout Syria, and the menacing arrival of the British fleet in Alexandria. Muhammad Ali could do nothing but climb down: he returned the Ottoman fleet, reduced his army to a mere eighteen thousand men and gave up all his conquests except the Sudan. In exchange the sultan issued a *firman* in 1841 granting him the Viceroyalty of Egypt for life and hereditary rights to the title by his male heirs. His empire was all but gone and his army reduced, but his oldest desires had been fulfilled: he headed a dynasty and Egypt was his for good.

THE EMPEROR'S DOWNFALL

Muhammad Ali's wings had been clipped, but the strain of his autocratic rule was already beginning to tell. The regime was deeply unpopular with an Egyptian people turned into paupers by excessive taxation, torn from their families for hard labour, and conscripted into the army for long periods; some feared the draft so much that they resorted to maiming themselves to avoid selection. Wars, high capital costs of industrial schemes and grand public works had stretched the country far beyond its means while his much-vaunted 'industrial revolution', powered in the end by no more than seven or eight steam engines, was in trouble even by the mid-1830s. A ban on monopolies imposed by an 1838 treaty between Britain and the Ottomans staunched the pasha's cash-flow and prevented him from bankrolling his mismanaged and inefficient factories; most were already failing from want of skilled management and labour, automotive power and fuel. As the edifice of his military-industrial complex cracked and crumbled, Egypt's economy subsided into a new configuration. No longer a manufacturer, it would supply agricultural raw materials – especially cotton – for export to industrialised Europe – especially Britain.

The strain also manifested itself on Muhammad Ali's ailing nerves. He became prone to fits of uncontrollable rage and collapse, and in 1847 he was forced to abandon his administration to convalesce in Naples. Ibrahim took over and was formally invested the following year but ruled only for six months before succumbing to tuberculosis. His father survived him by a few months, though by now a frail octogenarian, but was too ill himself to understand his son had died.

The Rediscovery of Ancient Egypt

While Muhammad Ali had toiled to transform Egypt from a backwater of a decaying empire into a modern industrialised country, in the European imagination it was being fixed as a paradigm of the Oriental world: an exotic concoction of ancient monuments and colossal statues engulfed by desert sands, winding medieval streets, mosques and minarets, harems and bustling markets.

'Egyptomania' had taken grip across Europe since the return of Napoleon's expedition. The 1802 account and drawings published by one of its members, the scholar, artist and aristocrat Baron Dominique Vivant Denon (1747–1825), was immensely popular even before the appearance of the magisterial *Description de l'Égypte*. For the next few decades adventurers, such as the Swiss explorer Johann Ludwig (or John Lewis) Burckhardt (1784–1817), who having rediscovered Petra in Jordan was the first European to stumble on the rock-cut temple of Rameses II at Abu Simbel in 1813, journeyed to Egypt and fed the growing hunger for travel narratives at home.

SNATCHING A COLLECTION

Other explorers came from among the swelling ranks of Europeans invited to Egypt by Muhammad Ali to help develop the country. Spurred on by their consuls, the boldest of them scoured the deserts and the Nile for the finest artefacts, statues and carvings which they hoped to sell to their governments for considerable profit. Having secured the pasha's authorisation, consul-collectors such as Britain's Henry Salt (1780–1827), France's Bernardino Drovetti (1776–1852), and Giovanni Anastasi (1780–1860) of Sweden and Norway, recruited fearless agents to locate, assemble and transport the antiquities. Competition was fierce between Salt and Drovetti, and pitched battles sometimes erupted between their agents amid the ruins, but the pieces gathered in these sorties formed the basis for the collections of the great museums of Europe.

The best agents became famous in their own right, most notably Giovanni Belzoni (1778–1823), a remarkable Italian who had previously studied hydraulics in Rome before exploiting his towering stature as weightlifter extraordinaire ('the Patagonian Samson') on the London stage. Under the auspices of Salt, he transported the colossal bust of Rameses II from Thebes to the British Museum in London, removed the enormous granite sarcophagus and lid from the tomb of Rameses III (now in the Louvre and Fitzwilliam Museums respectively), discovered the tomb of Sety I in the Valley of the Kings complete with its exceptional alabaster sarcophagus (now in the Soane Museum, London), opened Khafra's pyramid, cleared the drifting sand to reveal Abu Simbel, located the lost Ptolemaic port of Berenice, uncovered five other royal tombs, and put on a grand exhibition of his finds at the Egyptian Hall in Piccadilly (1822) which sealed his fame.

Noting the European fever for antiquities and underestimating their value, Muhammad Ali was content to see his antiquities go abroad in exchange for political and economic favours. So be it if monuments were smashed, tombs hacked to bits in the search for treasures, items wilfully destroyed to make remaining pieces more valuable, mummies desecrated, sarcophagi burnt for fuel in the stampede. Controls on excavation and removal were minimal until Muhammad Ali was finally encouraged by concerned onlookers to ban the export of antiquities in 1835.

Foreign treasure-hunters were not totally to blame for the damage. Egyptians living in the tombs at Qurna found 'it easier to live by selling dead men than by the toil of husbandry', and ground desiccated corpses for 'mummy powder' which was mixed with butter and sold for the cure of ulcers. Other locals broke up limestone monuments to burn in lime kilns or plundered ancient mud-brick for use as fertiliser; the authorities themselves dismantled ancient buildings to reuse material in new ones. During the 1820s alone, thirteen temples completely disappeared, and around the time of the pasha's export ban the Ninth Pylon of the Temple of Karnak was dynamited to build a factory.

THE BIRTH OF EGYPTOLOGY

The decipherment of hieroglyphs by Jean-François Champollion in 1822 led to a rush to record as many inscriptions as possible, a shift in emphasis away from treasure-hunting towards archaeology. Exhaustive information was gathered in expeditions led by Champollion, and later by the Prussian, Karl Richard Lepsius (1810–1884), in addition to work done by independent amateurs, namely Britons, Sir John Gardner Wilkinson (1797–1875) who spent twelve years surveying sites and copying reliefs before publishing the seminal *Manners and Customs of the Ancient Egyptians*, and Robert Hay (1799–1863), who made enough plans and drawings to fill forty-nine volumes during nine years of study in Egypt.

In these early years archaeological methods were still haphazard and rudimentary, often obliterating more information than was recorded. It is by the efforts of the French Egyptologist, Auguste Mariette (1821–1881), that the pillaging of ancient monuments was put in check. Sent on a mission from the Louvre to collect Coptic manuscripts, Mariette instead explored the necropolis at Saqqara, where in 1850 he made one of the great discoveries of Egyptology. Chancing upon a head of a sphinx poking through the sand, his exploratory excavations revealed the Serapeum (see p.137). One vault contained an intact burial of a sacred Apis bull, untouched since it was sealed during the reign of Rameses II in the thirteenth century BC; the ancient footprint of the workman who closed the tomb lay unblemished in the sand. Mariette enjoyed instant fame for his finds, but having been appointed the first Director of Egyptian Monuments by the pasha in 1858, his greatest achievement was to press for proper care of antiquities and monuments including a halt to their destruction or exportation. In the same year he was made head of a new museum of antiquities in Cairo, the first of its kind in the Near East, to which he dedicated his life. In 1902 the Egyptian Museum, as it is now known, moved into its present premises on Midan al-Tahrir, where it houses almost 200,000 pharaonic artefacts including some of the most cherished antiquities ever discovered. A memorial to Mariette stands outside. However, for all his support of Egypt's natural right to keep and protect its own heritage, it was not until 1952 that an Egyptian actually became director of the Antiquities Service.

His successor, Sir Gaston Maspero (1846–1916), built on Mariette's work and also oversaw some major discoveries, opening up three pyramids, and translating and publishing their inscriptions – the famous funerary spells known as the Pyramid Texts. As head of the Antiquities Service he also led the celebrated investigation into the provenance of a series of beautiful papyri and fine *shabtis* (small funerary statuettes) that had been appearing on the black market, suspecting they were from an illegal dig. Enquiries led him to the Abd er-Rasul brothers from the west bank village of Qurna opposite Luxor, who ten years earlier in 1871 had chanced upon a cache of royal mummies stashed in a crevice in the cliffs above Deir el-Bahri (see p.124), and had been slowly selling off its treasures ever since. Maspero immediately gave the order that the remains be moved to the Egyptian Museum in Cairo, and as some of the greatest kings of Ancient Egypt – Thutmose III, Rameses II and Sety I among them – were carried by steamer down the Nile, peasants lined the banks, the men firing shots out of respect and the women wailing and tearing their hair in mourning.

In the 1880s, the Briton, Flinders Petrie (1853–1942, knighted 1923), advanced archaeological method further with revolutionary new techniques, minutely recorded and painstakingly careful scientific excavation, systematic arrangement of pottery shards to estimate their relative age ('sequence dating' which is now common procedure), and the close observation of every scrap unearthed, however humble. In an archaeological career that spanned more than fifty-five years, he dug at more sites than Mariette and made more major archaeological break-throughs than any other archaeologist, including the discovery of Egypt's Predynastic past, till then unsuspected, and the tombs of the first pharaohs. Under Petrie, Egyptology and archaeology were elevated to true sciences, and though his ideas and techniques were eventually superseded, his core methods of excavation have remained the benchmark of good practice.

TOURISM

By the 1830s, travel in Egypt was no longer the preserve of explorers and the hardiest adventurers. The first guidebook to the country came out in 1830, written by the French consul's agent Jean-Jacques Rifaud (1786–1852) who in earlier times had battled 'quick as lightning and red as a turkey cock' with Belzoni for prize antiquities. By no means was it straightforward tourism: permission for travel had to be sought from the pasha himself; local dress was recommended; and the traveller was warned to hire bodyguards or at least carry a firearm. If it sounded daunting, at least the pioneering scholar, Edward William Lane (1801–1876) who 'lived among the people as one of them, assuming an Arabic name and even their opinions, so far as conscience would allow', had exploded the myth in his 1836 book *Manners and Customs of the Modern Egyptians* that the locals were dull and uncivilised. He found them instead to be a warm and vital people delighting in jokes, wordplay and satire.

With the advent of the steamship and spread of the railway, travel to Egypt became increasingly commonplace. By 1843, P&O steamers from Southampton were chugging into Alexandria after only fifteen days at sea; crossing France by train to Marseilles made the journey even shorter. 'Wherever the steamboat touches the shore, adventure retreats into the interior, and what is called romance vanishes, but this is a small price to pay for the spread of civilisation', noted the novelist William Thackeray, himself a visitor to Egypt in 1844.

After the explorers came the scholars, collectors, archaeologists and Egyptologists; but soon the specialists were giving way to writers (for example, Anthony Trollope, Gustave Flaubert, Théophile Gautier, Herman Melville, Mark Twain), painters (David Roberts and John Frederick Lewis), photographers (Francis Frith) and an ever-widening circle of people who wanted to experience the wonders of Ancient Egypt for themselves. 'Everyone has been to Egypt, it sometimes seems,' the novelist Penelope Lively has written. 'Everyone who was anyone, and a great deal more besides.' The ailing wealthy wintered in top hotels such as the renowned Shepheard's, hoping to find relief in the dry climate for their 'phthisical and bronchial affections' as one guidebook had it, while the healthy hired luxury houseboats (*dahabiyyas*) and cruised between sites along the Nile.

Industry and technology had revolutionised travel, but also helped create a middle class with time and money to spend on leisure. By the 1870s, Thomas Cook was extending the benefits of Egyptian travel far beyond the educated and moneyed classes down to the middling masses, with inexpensive package tours. Tourists thronged the great

Nineteenth-century European tourists encouraged by
Thomas Cook's package tours

sites as they do today, clutching the mass-produced guidebooks of the
time – Murray, Baedeker or Thomas Cook's own. They filled the decks
of steamboat cruisers, journeyed across the countryside by train and
picnicked atop the Great Pyramid, the ladies being hoisted up each
enormous block by sashes tied around their waists. And around them
swarmed crowds of natives, a nuisance of travel well covered by the
books:

> Everywhere, from morning till night, the traveller will be tormented with
> applications for backsheesh, which has been called the alpha and omega of
> eastern travel. It is the first word an infant is taught to lisp; it will probably
> be the first Arabic word the traveller will hear on arriving in Egypt, and the
> last as he leaves it.

Then, as now, some lamented the rise of package tourism, 'the multiplication of the hotels, the mass production of the peach-fed standardised tourist "doing" the whole country in ten days', as one civil servant of the time wrote. But tourism became and remains a crucial part of the Egyptian economy.

In the late nineteenth century, Britain sent the most visitors followed by the US, Germany and France, leading Théophile Gautier to remark, 'The English are everywhere except in London, where there are only Italians and Poles'.

Egypt in Europe

It is odd that one of the milestones in opening up Egypt to Europe, the introduction of the railway, was laid by Pasha Abbas Hilmi I (r.1848–1854), a grandson of Muhammad Ali, who nurtured an almost pathological dislike of Europeans. Often characterised as reactionary, secretive and suspicious, Abbas closed the new schools, neglected the factories and distrusted the European way of doing things, so it is not without justification that he has been called 'the dismantler of his grandfather's edifice'. Yet it was also Abbas who commissioned Robert Stephenson, son of George Stephenson, inventor of the *Rocket*, to design and build a railway between Alexandria and Cairo. It opened in 1855, the year after Abbas's murder, apparently at the hands of his personal servants after an altercation.

A new impetus towards development came from his successor, Said Pasha (r.1854–1863), a son of Muhammad Ali. He was ebullient where Abbas had been sullen, lenient and forgiving where the other was paranoid and intolerant. He extended communication links, revived his father's works in agriculture, irrigation and education, encouraged native Egyptians into positions of importance and made Arabic rather than Turkish the language of administration.

He also had many European friends and advisers, the very people his predecessor would have shunned. Perhaps a little too trusting and suggestible, it was under him that Europeans won a foothold as a privileged caste in Egypt. They had long been abusing the advantages accorded them by the sixteenth-century Capitulations, originally agreed between the Ottoman sultan and European monarchs to provide conditions by which foreign, infidel merchants could live and operate within the Islamic Empire. Said codified some of these abuses of power in law, for example, completely excusing Europeans from the jurisdiction of Egyptian courts and state by allowing them to be tried in their own consular courts. His misguided generosity extended to financial support of foreign projects and schemes, a sometimes wasteful benevolence which inadvertently began a cycle of debt and dependence that ultimately ended in the occupation of the country by a foreign power.

THE SUEZ CANAL

By far the most important of these projects was the Suez Canal. The concession to build it was granted by Said in 1854 to the Frenchman Ferdinand de Lesseps (1805–1894) on characteristically over generous terms that would sorely burden his successors and the country.

There was nothing new in the idea of linking the Mediterranean to the Red Sea by water. The pharaohs had achieved it by building a canal from the Nile Delta along the Wadi Tumilat, which was navigable during the inundation, but it fell into disrepair many times during the Roman and Byzantine eras until it finally silted up completely under the Arab rulers of the eighth century. Napoleon had also been interested in connecting the two seas, but his engineer's faulty calculations put the Red Sea ten metres higher than the Mediterranean and the idea was abandoned. (On the contrary, the finished 99-mile long (160km) canal became and remains the longest in the world without any locks.) Under Muhammad Ali the scheme once again surfaced, though the pasha wisely put his energies into building the politically neutral Delta Barrage rather than taking on the canal, a project that he believed was bound to attract international interference: France and Austria were keenly in favour, Britain and Russia adamantly opposed.

By granting the concession, Said blundered straight into this potentially troublesome conflict of interests. However, his man De Lesseps proceeded undaunted, skilfully eluding hostile forces determined to see the project fail. This entailed a certain degree of sharp practice: he

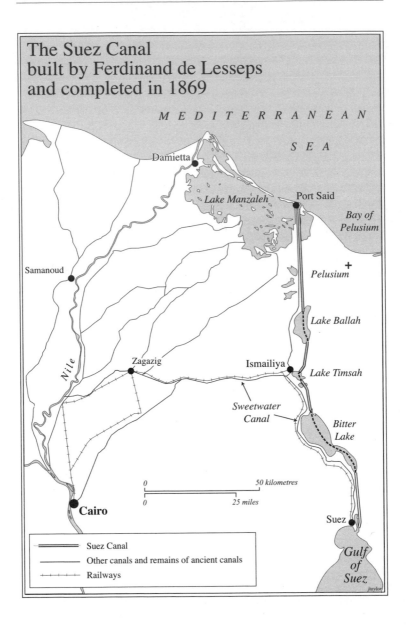

The Suez Canal
built by Ferdinand de Lesseps
and completed in 1869

M E D I T E R R A N E A N

S E A

Damietta

Lake Manzaleh

Port Said

Bay of
Pelusium

Samanoud

+ Pelusium

Lake Ballah

Nile

Zagazig

Ismailiya

Lake Timsah

Sweetwater
Canal

Bitter
Lake

0   50 kilometres

0   25 miles

Cairo

Suez

Gulf
of
Suez

	Suez Canal
	Other canals and remains of ancient canals
+++++	Railways

floated the Suez Canal Company, which had the 99-year lease over the canal, on the stock market with neither the authorisation of the Ottoman sultan (still technically the supreme ruler of Egypt) nor that of Said, then unloaded the remaining unsold shares, almost a quarter of the total, on to the pasha's account without telling him. The project was kept alive, but the enormous cost of building it was met in the main by the Egyptian people through high taxes and forced labour.

One of the most naïve of Said's agreements was that four-fifths of the workers be Egyptian. So it was that, after work began in 1859, around 60,000 to 80,000 peasants at any time were forced from their villages under the corvée (labour tribute) and the coercion of the *kurbash* (a rawhide whip) to toil on the canal at the expense of their own crops and families.

After Said's death, his nephew Ismail (r.1863–1879), came under heavy pressure to end the corvée from the Ottoman sultan, who was himself under the thumb of British politicians. While work was under way, the British did whatever they could to impede the Gallic scheme. They could hardly let France have the upper hand in managing a canal that was set to revolutionise the parameters of international shipping and cut travel times to India alone by more than half. The sultan's request resulted in a work stoppage, but it was only temporary and Ismail was forced to pay a huge fee in compensation to the Company, covered by another sizeable loan to add to the £10 million debt already racked up by his predecessor. Gradually the corvée workers were replaced by mechanised dredgers – but this did not stop the pasha, more an opportunist than a moralist, using forced labour on his many other projects across the country.

ISMAIL OPENS THE CANAL

To mark the opening of 'the greatest engineering feat of the century' on 17 November 1869, Ismail spared no expense, making it the extravagant highpoint of a profligate reign. The royalty of Europe and thousands of international dignitaries were transported and accommodated at public expense, and entertained with 24-course feasts, grand balls and firework displays. The Empress Eugénie of France, the undoubted star of the occasion, was housed in one of Ismail's many new palaces, described as 'of doubtful taste but madly sumptuous' – as well as a chalet specially built for her at the foot of the Great Pyramid. It was lit by magnesium flares and fireworks, and stood at the end of a 10 mile (16km) ceremonial avenue leading from the capital (also built just for her in record time by forced labour). Cairo was transformed into 'Paris on the Nile' and graced with grand new buildings, palaces, squares and avenues after the designs of Baron Haussmann. The main boulevard, Sulayman Pasha Street (now Talaat Harb) bulldozed its die-straight course through the heart of town, flanked by high Parisian-style shuttered apartment blocks and tree-shaded pavements. Music was to be supplied for the city's new opera house by Giuseppe Verdi, who was commissioned to write a piece that dealt with themes of imperial Egypt; as it happened, the sets and costumes for *Aida* were trapped in Paris under siege during the Franco-Prussian war and *Rigoletto* was performed instead.

The purpose of such extravagance was to show the civilised world that Egypt was a modern and cultivated country, not only on a par with but part of Europe. Yet Ismail had nagging fears that the glorious achievement of the Canal would bring Egypt trouble; his wish that the Canal 'belong to Egypt, not Egypt to the Canal' was not to be fulfilled for almost ninety years.

BORROWING MODERNITY

The Suez celebrations were spectacular and immensely costly but Ismail also lavished vast sums of borrowed capital on transforming Egypt into a modern Europeanised country. Enormous investments were made to the nation's infrastructure in the development of new canals, irrigation channels, harbours and lighthouses, the construction of more than 400 bridges across the Nile, the erection of 5000 miles (8047km) of telephone lines, the doubling of the size of the railways to 1100 miles (1770km) of track, the setting up of a national postal service, the improvement of municipal services in towns and cities such as water distribution, public transport, street lighting, parks and open spaces. He founded banking institutions, a legislative assembly, learned societies, public libraries, museums, and specialised schools for lawyers, teachers, technicians, administrators and other professionals, while extending state education to girls and the children of the fellahin. He helped abolish the slave trade in Sudan, Central Africa and across the Red Sea.

Towards the end of his reign, he reportedly said, 'My country is no longer in Africa, it is in Europe' and in 1876, *The Times* was so impressed it was moved to comment: 'Egypt is a marvellous instance of progress. She has advanced as much in seventy years as other countries have in five hundred.' The transformation he had wrought had relied on European expertise and above all European money; unctuous foreign bankers circled Ismail as eager to supply him with loans as he was eager to initiate new projects. Egypt had become a 'Klondike on the Nile', awash with money and Europeans flooded in to make the most of it. Under the khedive's encouragement the stream of a few thousand immigrants per year transmuted into a torrent of well over a hundred thousand. Fortunes were to be made; foreigners were exempt from paying tax because of the Capitulations and had the protection of the consular courts if something went wrong. The balance of power was changed slightly with the introduction of the Mixed Courts in 1875 by prime minister Nubar Pasha, which allowed Egyptians to bring civil cases against foreigners before European and Egyptian judges, but foreigners still enjoyed huge privileges under the new system. Nevertheless, an indigenous legal profession was born, which became the proving ground of many future nationalist politicians.

DEBT AND DEPENDENCE

Egypt had become a wealthy country during the global cotton shortage caused by the American Civil War (1861–1865). Prices had soared to around four times their 1860 level while acreage in Egypt expanded fivefold to keep up with the demand, particularly from the Lancashire mills whose supply from Louisiana had been cut.

The fantastic riches generated by the cotton boom dried up in 1866 with dozens of major projects still needing finance. Ismail's personal expenditure was also spiralling out of control – his astronomical private allowance was reputedly double that of his contemporary, Queen Victoria – and these expenses could not easily be extricated from the mounting national debt. Enormous bribes were regularly given to the Ottoman sultan in return for political favours, most notably the bestowal of the title 'khedive' in 1867, which hoisted his status above other viceroys almost to royalty.

Only a small fraction of the cost of his multifarious public projects and interest payments could be covered by taxing the fellahin into the ground; the tantalising riches hoarded by foreign residents were out of reach of his taxmen. Soon Ismail found he was entangled in a cycle of debt, being forced to take out new loans at usurious rates to make up the shortfall.

But by 1875, his creditworthiness was non-existent and the banks unwilling or unable to give any more hand-outs. His desperate need for cash that year led him to sell his controlling share in the Suez Canal to the British government under Benjamin Disraeli (1804–1881), an event that instantly redefined Britain's relationship with Egypt. The sale provided only temporary relief, however, and nothing could save the country from bankruptcy.

In 1876, international creditors moved in as a joint body called the *Caisse de la Dette Publique* and consolidated the total debt at £91 million, while French and British agents took over management of government revenues and expenditure in a system known as 'Dual Control'. More than half of national revenues were siphoned off to service the debts, representing an enormous drain on the economy. Gradually, Europe began to handle more and more of the economy, from revenues of the railways and customs to large tracts of the viceregal estates. Soon they moved into the political arena too, setting up the 'European ministry' in 1878, which included a French minister of public works and an English minister of finance, to administer the country independently of the khedive, who was not even allowed to attend its sessions.

Ismail struggled to return to the locus of power and to reduce the rate of interest on the colossal national debt. In 1879, he announced a new all-Egyptian cabinet to replace the European ministry in the name of putting the needs of the country before those of foreign creditors. This gave the Europeans the excuse they needed for the khedive's removal. They pressed the sultan to depose Ismail. Keen to reassert Ottoman authority in Egypt, he did not need much persuasion, and quickly issued the appropriate *firman* (royal decree). Ismail left the country for a gilded life in Naples in June 1879, never to return. Tawfiq (r.1879–1892), his timid and pliable young son, was his replacement, a man far more likely to co-operate with the foreign controllers and creditors who held the country's purse strings.

Ismail had intended to liberate Egypt from the ignorance, squalor and poverty of its medieval past; but in the process of funding its passage to modernity he had thrown the country into the shackles of foreign control. Egypt was now more a part of Europe than Ismail had ever intended.

NATIONALIST STIRRINGS

Under Ismail an educated and Europeanised Egyptian class had begun to emerge in government, education and the military. Native born, Arabic speaking, but influenced by ideas of patriotism and liberty imported from Europe, they became the main progenitors of nationalism and political reform in Egypt, and fostered movements that would eventually develop into full political parties in the early twentieth century.

Associated with this political awakening was the rise, from the late 1860s, of independent daily newspapers and academic, political and satirical journals published in Arabic, which helped shape public opinion and engendered a firmer sense of Egyptian national identity. Ironically, religious minorities and immigrants were particularly prominent in the formation of the private press: two Lebanese Christian brothers founded *Al-Ahram* in Alexandria in 1875, the first paper in the country to use the telegraph for news gathering and now the leading daily of the Arab world, while the satirical *Abu Naddara al-Zaraqa* (1877) set up by an Egyptian-Italian Jew was the first to feature the popular slogan of the era 'Egypt for the Egyptians'.

The latter organ was influenced by the political and religious agitator Jamal al-Din al-Afghani (1838–1897) whose appearances in Egypt during the 1870s crystallised nationalist opposition on the basis of international Islamic solidarity. His calls for the regeneration and modernisation of Islam, while keeping true to its core values, and the political liberation of Islamic countries greatly influenced generations of young Egyptian journalists, intellectuals, army officers and politicians.

The Urabi Revolution

The financial mess of Ismail's reign was bad enough, but the wound to Egyptian pride caused by the meddling of European controllers was even harder to soothe. The new khedive Tawfiq had little authority and dwindling reserves and decided to throw his lot in with the Europeans, enraging opinion further. He acquiesced to their demands to install a new prime minister to rule on his behalf. This man, the autocratic Riyad Pasha, felt no compunction in dismissing the assembly, importing ever greater numbers of high-salaried European officials, suppressing the nationalist press and exiling nationalist leaders.

By 1881, a large cross-section of the Egyptian population was agitating to see him go. Ahmad Urabi (1839–1911), an army colonel of peasant origin (like Nasser after him), emerged as the leader of a broad opposition movement which included indigenous army officers, businessmen, the fellahin, landowners, bureaucrats and intellectuals. They clamoured for some form of parliamentary government in which normal Egyptians could have a say in the running of the country. Above all, they were tired of the old Turkish and Circassian elites that had effectively owned and governed the country since Mamluk times, and Tawfiq and his Europhile dynasty sat at the summit of these 'foreign' power structures.

Urabi had already made a name for himself by agitating against the Turkish elite within the army, who 'hated the fellahin', insisted on keeping Turkish as the official language, and blocked the promotion of native soldiers. In a country where the ruling class and richest landowners were mainly of Turkish origin, such protests resonated far beyond military circles into the hearts of indigenous Egyptians of all classes.

In September, Urabi led a demonstration against the khedive and surrounded his official residence, Abdin Palace, with thousands of supporters. Tawfiq gave in to his demands: the dismissal of Riyad, a new constitution, the strengthening of the representative assembly and the enlargement of the army. Urabi was hailed as a national saviour and crowds gathered to cheer him wherever he went. Europeans, on the other hand, began to fear for their privileges, their investments and their safety.

Twice the French and British tried to strengthen the khedive's hand, and twice their attempts backfired. Their 'Joint Note' delivered to the legislative assembly which stressed their commitment to the khedive encouraged moderates to unite with Urabi, who was made minister of war. Then the appearance of French and British warships outside Alexandria provoked fears of an invasion and supercharged the atmosphere in a city that was already seething with tension. Europeans comprised a fifth of the population, held the best jobs and enjoyed the best terms of trade thanks to the Capitulations, and local bitterness against them was palpable. A simple altercation one hot June day between an Egyptian and a Maltese rapidly brought long-standing animosities to the surface, and the tussle degenerated into a city-wide riot that left around three hundred people dead.

The riot hardened British resolve to act against the Urabists. While a new government in Paris lost its nerve and withdrew the French fleet, the British began bombarding Alexandria on 11 July. Tawfiq imitated outrage and put up a sham resistance, but he took refuge with British marines only a few days later; after the khedive's troops retreated, Bedouin mobbed into the city, looting and burning from street to street before British troops landed to restore order.

It was left to Urabi to protect Egyptian sovereignty. He proclaimed a 'national struggle for liberation' and called for 25,000 conscripts, supplies and war materiel. The British prime minister William Gladstone (1809–1898) was soon persuaded to launch a full-scale invasion, and further troops under Sir Garnet Wolseley landed at Suez and Port Said in August with orders to crush the rebels using any means. The decisive clash with Urabi came on 13 September at

Tell el-Kebir where the Egyptians were overrun, losing around three thousand men to fifty-seven Britons. Cairo was occupied the following day, the remnants of Urabi's army dispersed, and he and his aides surrendered. Tawfiq was restored to the palace while Urabi was tried and sentenced to death, immediately commuted to exile in Ceylon.

In its efforts to maintain the status quo in Egypt, prop up the khedive, protect its creditors and the Suez Canal, Britain had become an occupying power. What was intended as a temporary emergency measure under Gladstone's ostensibly anti-imperialist government became a turning point in the modern history of Egypt. Britain's 'accidental' occupation was to extend into seventy years of domination.

CHAPTER ELEVEN

The British Occupation

1882–1952

The Cromer Years

At first the British regarded the invasion of Egypt as a brief 'rescue and retire' mission to restore the khedive's authority and protect foreign interests. But promises to evacuate as soon as possible, and by one count there were more than forty in 1883 alone, began to sound increasingly hollow as the months, then years ticked by. The fact was that the British were reluctant to withdraw until the problems that had triggered the intervention had been solved. Paradoxically the firm hand needed to set matters straight only embroiled them further in the day-to-day running of the country, making it ever harder to disengage. Before long it was taken for granted that Egypt was a 'veiled protectorate', not officially part of the British Empire but governed from the shadows by its agents and officials.

'SAVING' EGYPTIAN SOCIETY

The initial priorities were to win the 'race against bankruptcy', meet debt payments and restore political stability, goals difficult enough during the most clement circumstances let alone when impeded by the machinations of hostile French and Ottoman governments. It was to the considerable skills and efforts of Sir Evelyn Baring (1841–1917), Lord Cromer from 1892, who as 'British agent and consul general' was the *de facto* ruler of Egypt from 1883 to 1907, that the country's early financial recovery is credited. A member of the famous banking family, Baring had been the representative of British creditors in Egypt during the financial crisis of the late 1870s. Baring seemed uniquely qualified to extricate the country from its economic mess. He had a deep sense of duty and believed it was the 'Englishman's mission' to 'save Egyptian society'.

Relying on plain commonsense rather than flashy innovation, his judicious husbandry of the economy, based on improving productivity and marshalling expenditure, had saved Egypt from the perils of insolvency by 1887. The irrigation system was completely overhauled, improved and extended, so that farmers could benefit from perennial watering, multiple harvests and enhanced acreage. The faulty Delta Barrage built by Muhammad Ali was made functional and work began on the first Aswan Dam (completed in 1902). Productivity leapt, government revenues almost doubled and the value of imports jumped fourfold. Freed from the mire of debt, the country was showing profits by 1891 allowing Cromer to slash taxes that had so impoverished the fellahin and plough surpluses back into public works, drainage, railways and projects to yield further quick returns.

On the political front, the aim was stability. Britain's own status as occupier of a province of the Ottoman Empire, supposedly a friendly power, was fudged with typical Whitehall sophistry. They were not ruling over a vanquished people, merely acting in an advisory capacity to the government. The Dual Control was abolished (to the burning chagrin of the French), but the khedival system was kept more or less intact with one major change: British officials were inserted into key posts to give 'advice' to ministers, advice which had to be followed.

Khedive Tawfiq was pliant as ever and his prime ministers swallowed the bitter pill of British meddling with a few exceptions. Old-time politicians Nubar Pasha and Riyad Pasha objected to changes in the police and judiciary and resigned. Sharif Pasha (who like Nubar and Riyad had also been a prime minister before the occupation) stepped down over British proposals to abandon the Sudan, but for the rest of the lengthy Cromer period Mustafa Fahmi Pasha, who shared the khedive's capacity for docility, served loyally as an acquiescent prime minister.

Egypt was stable and in the flush of a minor economic miracle. The national estate had been rehabilitated and made profitable, and law and

Lord Cromer, the *de facto* ruler of Egypt from 1883 to 1907

order had simultaneously been re-established. The peasantry was better off too, excused at last the humiliation of the corvée and *kurbash* which were both abolished under Cromer. These were successes indeed. But from the Egyptian point of view there was much to resent.

PRICE OF 'SALVATION'

Cromer's answers to Egypt's problems were couched mainly in financial and administrative terms, and designed to create instant economic benefit. Other concerns, such as education and industrialisation which required large investments of time and capital, were subordinated and often ignored even though they were the cornerstones of long-term regeneration. Education was particularly badly neglected, receiving barely 1.5 per cent of total government expenditure. Having flourished during Ismail's reign, primary and secondary schools atrophied and technical colleges languished under Cromer; he was convinced 'subject peoples' had no call for schooling, and anyway, an uneducated country would need educated foreigners to govern it.

Industrialisation was similarly sidelined – and not only because of the slow returns such large-scale development entailed. An indigenous textile industry would compete with the English cotton mills, so Egypt was constrained as a monoculture economy supplying cheap raw cotton to Britain. Efforts were concentrated in maximising the country's cotton-growing capacity, which Cromer did expertly well, but even the move to perennial irrigation had serious problems. The damming of the Nile waterlogged the soil and deprived the land of its nutritious yearly silt deposits. New drainage systems had to be developed and farmers grew dependent on artificial fertilisers, while the soggy land became a breeding ground for bilharzia and malarial mosquitos which debilitated rural communities.

Neither was there a strategy for reform in politics, no urge to bolster indigenous political institutions, no preparation for a time when Egyptians would govern themselves. If anything, the reverse was true. Even as early as 1886, Cromer suggested that there should be no limit to the duration of British presence, and by 1889 Whitehall had buckled under his heavy influence, abandoning any plan to withdraw. Over time Cromer fed an increasing number of British bureaucrats into the system, simultaneously leaching authority from the khedivate, entrenching a sense of dependence, and creating a foreign interest-group which had everything to gain from maintaining the occupation indefinitely. With the flood of minor officials 'the classic process of colonisation had begun', as Ronald Storrs, himself a minor British official during this period, noted in his memoirs. 'Everybody and everything was becoming cleaner, richer, easier and more proper, but somehow... there was less fun. Once more we had multiplied the harvest but not increased the joy.' There was little mixing between the British and Egyptians, and the former were happier spending their free hours in the expat sporting clubs and at hotel dances than getting to know their Arab colleagues:

> The British official... was a hard and honourable worker, punctual and punctilious in his Department or Ministry from early morning until well after noon. He would then drive or bicycle to the Turf Club or his flat for

luncheon, play tennis or golf until dark at the Sporting Club, return to the Turf Club to discuss the affairs of the day and dine there or at his flat... It was with an air of virtuous resignation that [his wife] steeled herself to sacrifice an afternoon for a call upon an Egyptian or Turkish lady, as likely as not better born, better bred, better read, better looking and better dressed than herself.

Ronald Storrs, *Orientations* (1937)

The arch-imperialist, Baring, the man nicknamed 'OverBaring' by his colleagues, was a brilliant administrator but stiff and unimaginative, locked into the common – essentially racist – prejudices of the time that elevated his own (in his words) 'imperial race' far above 'poor, ignorant, credulous' Egyptians encumbered by 'sixty centuries of misgovernment and oppression', 'antique and semi-barbarous customs' and 'the Oriental mind' with all its proclivities to 'want of accuracy, which easily degenerates into untruthfulness'. Such a people, he considered, were far better served by good foreign government than self-government. At bottom, he believed Egyptians were incapable of ruling themselves.

Cromer could absorb languages quickly but during a quarter-century in Egypt he never bothered to learn Arabic; like the culture, religion and daily lives of native Egyptians, it was superfluous to the needs of the accounting book and balance sheet. Cromer was magisterial in style and incorruptible of character, but lacked the basic humanity that the building of a nation required.

OPPOSITION FORMS

If nationalism had been smothered with the fall of Urabi, the death of Tawfiq in 1892 was an opportunity to rekindle opposition to the British. The new khedive, Abbas Hilmi II (r.1892–1914), Tawfiq's seventeen-year-old son, was quick to assert himself, dismissing his father's submissive prime minister, Mustafa Fahmi, and replacing him with his own man to form a new ministry. Cromer had not been consulted and acted with typical heavy-handedness, demanding a reversal and a written promise that the khedive would follow British advice in future. Abbas could do little but relent. It was a sharp and humiliating lesson that he and his government were powerless to resist Cromer's unbending will.

Disillusioned, Abbas lent his support to the emergent new opposition, funding the anti-British newspaper *al Muayyad* and secretly subsidising Mustafa Kamil (1874–1908), a young lawyer and firebrand, to rejuvenate and reorganise the nationalist cause. Mustafa Kamil became the loudest voice against the occupation and the political successor to Urabi. He founded his own daily newspaper *al Liwa* and later the National Party, and was a constant thorn in the British side, pointing out at every opportunity the contradictions and hypocrisies of their position. He called for an immediate evacuation from Egypt, which for him, meant the entire Nile Valley including Sudan. This became the central demand of nationalists and the main sticking point in Anglo-Egyptian relations until 1956 when the British finally withdrew from Egypt and Sudan declared itself independent.

Sudan

THE MAHDI'S REVOLT

Sudan had been granted to Muhammad Ali by the Ottoman sultan in 1841, and Khedive Ismail had sent expeditions south to extend his territory to the uppermost reaches of the White Nile around the equator. Broadly speaking, the Sudanese were not well governed by their neighbours and during the turmoil of the late 1870s, discontent pervaded the country. Local bigwigs had also been enraged by the attempts of foreigners to abolish the Sudanese slave trade. The ill-feeling was exploited by Muhammad Ahmed (1844–1885), a Muslim mystic and self-proclaimed 'Mahdi' ('divinely guided one'), a messianic figure sent by God to spread justice, restore faith and defeat the enemies of Islam just before the end of time. In 1881, the Mahdi called his followers to a jihad against foreigners in their land.

The revolt was allowed to spread. The Egyptians had not the resources to crush it in its early stages and the British, having only just intervened in Egypt, had no desire to add Sudan to their burdens.

Muhammad Ahmed (1844–1885), a Muslim mystic and self-proclaimed
'Mahdi' or 'divinely guided one'

Eventually the Egyptian government sent a ragbag shower of '9000 infantry that 50 good men would rout in ten minutes, and 1000 cavalry that have never learnt even to ride' according to Cromer, under the charge of the British officer William Hicks, to quash the rebellion. It was annihilated almost to a man by Mahdists in November 1883.

By now Cromer was in charge. His recommendation was the immediate evacuation of all Egypt's remaining garrisons, a course of action that was highly unpopular with Egyptians, who maintained their territorial claims to the entire Nile Valley. The prime minister Sharif Pasha resigned in protest.

GORDON OF KHARTOUM

The British press clamoured for the hero General Charles Gordon (1833–1885), who had already served successfully in Sudan under the Khedive Ismail, to oversee the evacuation and put matters right. Cromer was reluctant; he knew that Gordon underestimated the power of the Mahdi and that he advocated strong measures against him rather than slipping away quietly.

Sure enough, it was not long after Gordon had ensconced himself in Khartoum (February 1884) that he began sending telegrams to Cromer urging that 'the Mahdi must be smashed up' and questioning the morality of abandoning the people of Sudan to the ferocious and fanatical Mahdist hordes. But by mid-March events had overtaken him; the tribes along the Nile to the north had risen with the Mahdi, river supplies had been blocked and the telegraph cut. Thirty thousand Mahdists encircled him in Khartoum.

Gordon himself still had several months to effect an escape, but refused to walk out on the garrisons and civilians in his charge. A proud and pious Christian with a keen sense of honour, he doubtless also wanted to avenge the death of Hicks and avoid being driven out of Sudan by a Muslim. If he would not budge, an expeditionary force would have to be sent to get him out. Gladstone, the British prime minister, vacillated and resisted, but in the face of intense pressure from the public, Parliament and even Queen Victoria, he finally agreed to dispatch a rescue mission in early August.

The expedition's progress up the Nile was painfully slow. As conditions in Khartoum steadily deteriorated, the situation took on all the inevitability of an unfolding tragedy. In October Gordon wrote, 'It is, of course, on the cards that Khartoum is taken under the nose of the expeditionary force, which will be *just too late.*' The relieving force arrived on 28 January 1885, but Gordon would never know it. Two days earlier Khartoum had been overrun and he decapitated.

RECONQUEST OF SUDAN

The Mahdi survived Gordon by only five months before he died from poison or disease, leaving a territory half the size of Europe to his successor, the Khalifa Abdallah (1846–1899), whose tyrannical and bloody rule depopulated the country by at least two-thirds. Inflamed by successive victories over the British and the myth of Mahdist invincibility willed by God, the Khalifa threatened to invade Upper Egypt and wrote a letter to Queen Victoria summoning her to submit before him and convert to Islam. She never deigned to proffer a reply.

It was a decade before the political climate was right for the British to excise the stain of the defeats and Gordon's death from the imperial copybook. By the 1890s, the occupation of Egypt was well established and rival European powers were scrambling to grab as much African territory as possible. Most alarmingly, the French were attempting to link up their colonies on the east and west African coasts by moving into Sudan and the Upper Nile.

It was decided that Sudan must be retaken and General Horatio Herbert Kitchener (1850–1916), the sirdar or commander-in-chief of a newly trained and reorganised Egyptian army, set forth from Wadi Halfa in May 1896. It took him over a year to build a railway at the rate of a kilometre a day across the desert to Abu Hamed (missing out the loop of the Nile) and another year to reach Khartoum, but just a few hours to flatten the Khalifa's army in the desert outside Omdurman (1 September 1898). Raked end to end by booming artillery and automatic Maxim guns, more than ten thousand spear-toting Mahdists littered the plain at a loss of about four hundred of Kitchener's men.

Not content with the 'good dusting' he had given the enemy, Kitchener disinterred and flung the Mahdi's body into the Nile, having removed the head as his own trophy. Reports that he intended to make it into an inkstand shocked Victorian England and he was forced to give it up for a discreet burial at Wadi Halfa.

His next mission was to see off the small French contingent that had recently reached the outpost of Fashoda about four hundred miles upstream after an intrepid trek across West Africa. Kitchener's arrival there with four gunboats and three battalions effectively ended French influence in the Nile basin and blocked their east-west link-up across Africa, while significantly contributing to completing the British corridor north-south.

ANGLO-EGYPTIAN CONDOMINIUM

British and Egyptian flags flew together over Khartoum. From January 1899 it was agreed that Sudan should become an Anglo-Egyptian Condominium, which at bottom gave supreme power to Britain under the guise of shared responsibility. The arrangement had the added advantage for Britain of precluding the kind of foreign interference from the Mixed Courts, Capitulations, and the Ottoman suzerain, that had to be endured north of the border.

Egypt, on the other hand, had funded the bulk of the cost of the reconquest, supplied most of the troops and suffered most of the casualties, but had little to show for the effort. Unsurprisingly, the Condominium was another source of grievance and most Egyptians considered it a major affront to national pride that they had been used by the British to forge another link in their imperial chain from the Delta to the Cape.

Cromer bows out

The hopes of Mustafa Kamil and the nationalists that France might one day help dislodge the British were dashed by the Entente Cordiale of 1904, which settled differences across the Channel and recognised Britain's special place in Egypt. Mustafa Kamil turned to the Ottoman Empire instead and attempted with some success to rally nationalist opinion behind the sultan during a territorial dispute (the Taba Incident of 1906) between the Ottomans and Britain over the Sinai peninsula.

Cromer supported a free press and tolerated the constant sniping at his regime in nationalist papers. The tirades, he considered, were a safety valve for opposition feeling, and at any rate only 20 per cent of the population could actually read. He had every confidence that while the educated elite grumbled the illiterate masses enjoyed and appreciated the British Agency's even-handed justice and corruption-free administration.

THE DINSHAWAI INCIDENT

The Dinshawai Incident of June 1906 shattered any illusions the British had about the goodwill of the masses. A party of British officers out on a pigeon shoot in the Delta village of Dinshawai had run into trouble with locals, who objected to them interfering with the birds, which were a part of their livelihood. Scuffles led to the death of one of the Britons. Retribution was swift and severe. Fifty-two Egyptians were rounded up and tried without appeal before a special court, four of them executed in front of their fellow villagers and the rest sentenced to imprisonment, hard labour or public floggings.

Anger and indignation swept the country, and Mustafa Kamil attracted a huge following among the masses with speeches that decried the brutality of a foreign ruling power out of touch with the needs of the nation. This time the British could hardly counter that they had the support and affection of the fellahin. Cromer had been on leave in England at the time but gave his backing to the court and its sentences. His resignation – officially due to poor health, but no doubt hastened by the affair – came a few months later in March 1907.

The Drive for Independence

Suddenly conditions seemed favourable for the political reform that was long overdue after a progressive Liberal government in London appointed Sir Eldon Gorst (1861–1911; consul general 1907–1911) as the new consul general. An intelligent man, receptive to change, Gorst had plenty of experience of Egypt, spoke Arabic and won the friendship of the khedive as quickly as Cromer had lost it. Gorst's feel for conciliation and diplomacy contrasted well with his predecessor's aloofness and autocracy.

In the nurturing early sun of an encouraging new administration, Egypt's first modern political parties sprang up, each striving to guide the direction of reform and the sentiments of the newly politicised masses. First was the Umma or People's Party, founded by educated liberals who felt that rational social development in co-operation with the British would provide the best route to full independence. Its newspaper *al-Jarida*, edited by the brain and driving force of the party,

Ahmad Lutfi al-Sayyid, advocated secularism over the pan-Islamic and Ottoman-leaning tendencies associated with more extreme nationalist groups such as Mustafa Kamil's National Party (*Hizb al-Watani*), hastily convened in response. The third major party of the period formed in 1907 was the Constitutional Reform Party (*Hizb al-Islah al-Dusturi*) of Sheikh Ali Yusuf, which represented the interests of the khedive and his court in the face of the Umma's calls for full parliamentary authority. It consequently enjoyed very little following in the country at large.

Gorst's attempts to liberalise the regime centred on fostering good relations with the khedive, giving indigenous consultative bodies more power and stripping down the number of Britons in the civil service. The first aim he achieved relatively quickly, the second backfired spectacularly, and the third made him deeply unpopular with his fellow countrymen within the administration.

His problems began with the appointment of a new prime minister, Butrus Ghali, an able and intelligent man whose broad government included Saad Zaghlul (1857–1927) of the Umma Party and a counterpart from the Constitutional Party. Nevertheless, he was hated by nationalists for his past record: he had signed the reviled Condominium Convention on Sudan and presided over the special tribunal that dealt with the Dinshawai affair. As a Copt he was also distrusted by many Muslims and was rabidly attacked as collaborator, traitor and infidel in the press of the National Party, which was sliding into Islamic fanaticism after the untimely death of Mustafa Kamil in 1908.

Another bigger mistake was the backing Gorst gave to the proposal in 1910 to extend the Suez Canal Company's ninety-nine-year lease for another forty years. The nationalists feared it would prolong foreign interference and whipped up a storm of protest which culminated in its nearly unanimous rejection in the newly empowered General Assembly and then the assassination of Butrus Ghali by a young Muslim extremist. This marked the end of Gorst's experiment in limited Egyptian self-rule which was deemed to have failed. Fatally stricken with cancer, the consul general resigned in 1911 and died shortly afterwards.

KITCHENER

The appointment of Lord Kitchener (consul general 1911–1914), the hero of Khartoum, was seen as a return to the strong, autocratic style of Cromer. Stamping on nationalist agitation with one heavy army boot, he kicked the attentions of the khedive and the politicians away with the other, and reverted to rule through British advisers and officials. Focus was redirected onto agricultural productivity, enhancing irrigation, raising of the Aswan Dam, and improving the lot of the fellahin in decrees such as the Five Feddan Law, designed to relieve peasant debt. Kitchener had little time for the chicanery of the political world, though his one nod to reform was the introduction of a new constitution complete with a new legislative assembly in 1913; the outbreak of war cut short its life – and Kitchener's consulship – after only five months.

FIRST WORLD WAR AND THE PROTECTORATE

The Ottoman Empire's entrance into the First World War in November 1914 on Germany's side presented an immediate problem to the British Agency over Egypt's unresolved international status. Technically Egypt was still a province under Turkish suzerainty and its people the subjects of the Ottoman sultan, all of whom would therefore be at war with Britain and legally sanctioned to commit hostile acts against British interests.

Unwilling to annexe Egypt outright, Britain improvised by declaring it a Protectorate in December, at last severing the ties with the Ottoman Empire which had lasted for almost four centuries. Khedive Abbas Hilmi, who happened to be in Constantinople at the time, was deposed and his uncle, Husayn Kamil (r.1914–1917), was installed with the new title of sultan. Further assurances that Britain would defend Egypt and not call on Egyptians to participate actively in the war defused a delicate situation.

Beyond this, Egypt's legal status under the Protectorate was not much clearer than it had been before, but it was obvious to nationalists that this was not a step forwards. The new legislative assembly had been closed and the ruling house had been aggrandised with the new royal title. The circumstances of war precluded active protest (thanks to the imposition of strict censorship laws and draconian security laws), but the opposition bided its time, plotting in secret until it would be able to execute plans to resist the occupying power. In the meantime, Egypt became a base for large numbers of Allied forces, including thousands of Anzac soldiers who launched the attack on Gallipoli from Alexandria in 1915.

By August 1916, the occasional forays of pro-Ottoman Bedouin from Libya in the Western Desert and the more serious Turkish attacks on the Suez Canal and Sinai had been neutralised. Egypt secure, the British organised a counter-offensive into Palestine which urgently needed men, animals and supplies. Egyptian provincial leaders and village headmen were left to round up 'volunteers', conscripts in all but name, while British confiscations of grain, fodder and animals were enforced insensitively without adequate recompense. To add to the privations of the fellahin, the war demand for large cotton crops came at the expense of food production, leading to shortages and high prices. Egypt smouldered with resentment.

ARMISTICE

On Armistice Day, 11 November 1918, there was reason to hope that Egypt might at last win complete independence. President Woodrow Wilson had introduced his 'Fourteen Points' for post-war settlement outlining the ideals of democracy and national self-determination. Britain had also promised sovereign status to Syria, Mesopotamia and the Hijaz whose Arabs had risen up against the Ottoman Empire during the war, a revolt forever associated with T. E. Lawrence, 'Lawrence of Arabia'.

If such places were ready for independence, Egyptians argued, how could Egypt possibly not be too? They had made substantial sacrifices and contributions to the war effort and borne the abuses and injustices of British military rule. Now was surely the time that they would be rewarded with freedom and democracy, the very things that they had apparently been helping the Allies fight for. The British, however, had come from the war convinced of the strategic value of controlling

Egypt and they had no intention of letting go.

SAAD ZAGHLUL AND THE WAFD

Two days after Armistice, a delegation (*wafd*) led by Saad Zaghlul (1857–1927) met the high commissioner (the new title for the consul general) of the Protectorate, Sir Reginald Wingate, to demand complete autonomy for Egypt. Zaghlul was the son of a village headman, an indigenous Egyptian of modest origins who had broken into the elite through talent, ambition and marrying into the Turco-Egyptian aristocracy. Having trained as a lawyer, he had moved into politics and won popularity with the public as education minister for insisting (against British advice) on the use of Arabic in elementary schools. Gradually he had become increasingly strident until, as vice president of the pre-war legislative assembly, he emerged as the voice of the opposition against the government and the British administration that instructed it.

Having been refused permission out of hand by the British government to present the case for Egyptian independence in London and at the Paris Peace Conference, Zaghlul resolved to make the Wafd the permanent national delegation and official representative of the Egyptian people. Within a few years, the Wafd was to become the most important political party in modern Egypt and its leader, Zaghlul, the 'Father of Egyptians'.

Using a network of secret printing presses to spread the nationalist message across the country, he swiftly garnered mass support for his project. As the Paris Peace Conference began in early 1919 without representation from Egypt, Wafdist agitation increased and the British grew nervous.

1919 REBELLION

Zaghlul was arrested in March 1919 and exiled to Malta. The backlash was immediate. Demonstrations and strikes broke out across the country, as all sections of Egyptian society took to the streets in protest; even the largest minority, women, till now an unheard voice, made their presence felt. The demonstrations soon degenerated into riots as the masses vented the fury that they had carried with them through decades of oppression. Telegraph and rail communications were sabotaged, and British soldiers murdered.

General Sir Edmund Allenby, the victor against the Turks in Palestine, was sent to replace Wingate and restore order which he did in April by releasing Zaghlul and allowing the Wafd to proceed to Paris. The gesture was disingenuous; Britain's allies, including the United States in which the nationalists had invested great hope, had already agreed to recognise the Protectorate. Another wave of civil disobedience washed over Egypt.

The British government felt vindicated in its intransigence, but it was patently clear to Allenby, the Wafd and the Egyptian people that the Protectorate could not continue in its present form. A commission under Lord Milner was sent to Egypt to consult on the form of a new constitution 'under the Protectorate', but the Wafd successfully orchestrated a nationwide boycott. In private talks with Milner in London (1920), Zaghlul was offered Egyptian independence with a continued British military presence and British financial and judicial advisers in the administration. This fell far short of Zaghlul's − and most Egyptians' conception of independence − and it was rejected.

British attempts to sidestep the Wafd by entering into treaty talks with the new prime minister, Adli Pasha Yakan were also fruitless. Adli was powerless without Zaghlul, the negotiations failed, Adli resigned and Egyptians again took to the streets. Zaghlul was deported for a second time, to the Seychelles. Allenby made quick use of his absence and pressed a reluctant British cabinet to grant a qualified independence, only persuading them after a personal trip to London and the threat of resignation.

INDEPENDENCE WITH RESERVATIONS

On the day of Allenby's return to Egypt, 28 February 1922, the British government announced the termination of the Protectorate and unilaterally declared Egypt to be an independent sovereign state. However, four matters were 'absolutely reserved to the discretion' of the British government: the security of imperial communications; the defence of Egypt; the protection of foreign interests and minorities; and Sudan.

These 'Reserved Points' as they came to be called, became the focus of protracted and bitter wrangling that dogged Anglo-Egyptian relations for the next thirty years.

The Kingdom of Egypt: the Liberal Era

THE 1923 CONSTITUTION

The declaration transformed Egypt from Protectorate to kingdom and Sultan Fuad (r.1917–1936), the son of Khedive Ismail, became King Fuad I. The country's best legal experts immediately set about preparing a constitution for a parliamentary democracy, deciding that Belgium's provided the most suitable model. After some wrangling between king and politicians, it was enacted in April 1923.

Something of a compromise document, the constitution pleased no one by trying to please all. The king was accorded considerable powers, including the right to dissolve parliament, appoint prime ministers and two-fifths of the Senate, the upper house in the new bicameral legislature that also included a Chamber of Deputies with members elected by the adult male population. But even this fell far short of the absolute rule that Fuad felt was his by birthright. To him, parliamentary democracy was tantamount to 'Bolshevism' and for much of his life he spent his energies thwarting the will of government and trying to dismantle the constitution.

On the other hand, the Wafd, whose leaders were still in exile, had rejected Allenby's declaration of independence, had had nothing to do with the constitution, and now suspected it gave far too much power to the king. Outbreaks of violence continued among their supporters until Saad Zaghlul and other nationalist leaders were permitted to return to Egypt and compete in the general election of January 1924. Reorganised as a political party, the Wafd won 90 per cent of the seats; they would always win whenever free elections were held. But by

participating they had also implicitly accepted the terms of both independence and the constitution, the first of many compromises in the
pursuit of power that would cumulatively erode the Wafd's credibility
and enormous popular support until the party was effectively superseded by extremist and radical groups in the early 1950s.

HIGH HOPES: OPTIMISM, TUTANKHAMUN AND PHARAONISM

Although Britain's military occupation continued, there were plenty
of signs that the 1919 rebellion had injected new spirit and optimism
into Egyptian life. In commerce, Talaat Harb founded Bank Misr
(1920), reputedly 'an Egyptian bank for Egyptians only', which soon
became the behemoth of national finance and the driving force
towards industrial development and economic independence,
investing in manufacture of textiles and pharmaceuticals, publishing,
printing, film production and air travel.

It was at this time too that Egypt began to dominate popular Arab
culture, as it does to this day. More books were published in Cairo than
all other Arab capitals combined; Egyptian periodicals flooded Arab
markets; film houses began producing silent movies; recording studios
opened; and Egyptian entertainers came to prominence, such as the
great singer Umm Kulthum (*c*.1904–1975), who in a career that
extended into the 1970s won the love and adoration of the Arab-
speaking world.

Howard Carter's sensational discovery of Tutankhamun's tomb in
November 1922 seemed the propitious climax to the year in which
independence was declared. As the tomb's lavish contents came to
light, all the wealth and sophistication of Egypt's past began to
symbolise the promise of a glorious Egyptian future. It was no coincidence that the official opening of the tomb in March 1924 coincided
with the inauguration of Egypt's first elected parliament. Suddenly the
ancient pharaonic history presented a new formula for a unique
Egyptian national identity, one that not only could be traced back to
the beginnings of history, but one that also transcended the modern
differences between Arab, Muslim, Copt and Jew.

Among the great advocates of this notion, known as 'pharaonism', was Dr Taha Husayn (1889–1973), the most influential of a new generation of philosophers, writers and intellectuals since the revolution. Taha Husayn also played down the Arab and Islamic components of the national identity, which he believed to be a consequence of just one of many invasions of Egypt including those of the Libyans, Nubians, Persians, Greeks, Romans, Turks, French and finally British. Instead he championed Egypt's many historical links to the Mediterranean and Europe, whose institutions, science and philosophy he deemed the key to becoming a modern liberal state.

A BAD START

As prime minister, Saad Zaghlul was no less determined to extirpate the British and secure Egypt's rights to Sudan. It was hoped that Ramsay MacDonald's Labour government might be the one to make the desired concessions, but during talks in London it soon became obvious that this was not the case.

After the rebuff, national frustration and anger focused on one Briton, Sir Lee Stack, who had the misfortune to be both the governor-general of Sudan and sirdar of the Egyptian army, the very personification of Egypt's continued subservience to Britain in key areas. Stack's assassination in Cairo by nationalist extremists on 19 November 1924 was taken very badly by his friend Allenby, who immediately, and without recourse to London, issued an ultimatum to the Egyptian government demanding stringent measures and large compensation. Zaghlul would comply only with the latter and resigned, and King Fuad quickly took the opportunity to suspend and dissolve parliament. The first democratically elected Wafdist government had sat for just nine months and Zaghlul, by far the most popular leader of his generation, would never again be prime minister.

TRIANGLE OF POWER

After this, politics became a three-way tug-of-war between the king, the Wafd and the British. Most of the time the battling was between

Fuad, who used his wealth and influence to undermine the constitution, and the Wafd, whose strength lay in free elections provided for by the constitution. Meanwhile the British fell behind whichever side served their interests best as the moment demanded. Occasionally, as after the murder of Stack, they steamed in and forced the issue without any care for Egypt's sovereign status or its democratic processes as if they still governed a protectorate. Allenby's successor from 1925 to 1929, the Tory imperialist Lord (George) Lloyd, threw his weight about by calling a gunboat to Alexandria at the slightest sign that things were not going his way; he managed to keep Zaghlul from the premiership in this manner after another election landslide for the Wafd in 1926.

There were also minority parties that contributed to the seesawing of power. Most were off-shoots of the Wafd, built around the personalities who had left the party after disagreements, but they rarely had much support from the population as a whole. The largest was the Liberal Constitutionalist Party (1922), moderate nationalists who had backed Adli Yakan against Zaghlul's radicalism. They upheld the constitution for the power it gave its members, mainly large landowners and wealthy intellectuals, who nonetheless were often used by the king in coalition governments with independents and other small parties to keep the Wafd from power.

The real losers in this ceaseless tussle were the Egyptian people and the infant democratic system, which never saw an elected parliament last its full four-year term. While the king and the British fought their own selfish corners, the Wafd, supposedly the party which held the interests of the population closest to its heart, put desperately needed social and economic reform a distant second to the goal of full independence from Britain. Moreover, the Wafd did little to nurture and fortify Egypt's fledging constitutional structure and democratic make-up. It was quick to mobilise public opinion, organise marches and stage rallies, but passed down opinion from above rather than stimulating and responding to political debate from below. Independent political thinking and activity were regarded with suspicion rather than encouraged as normal parts of a healthy democracy.

Even the charismatic champion of the people, Saad Zaghlul,

introduced patronage to public life. He did not tolerate differences of opinion within the Wafd and imposed absolute control over his party, a trait that has marked Egyptian political leaders ever since. Zaghlul's brief stint in power was hardly exemplary either, resorting to old censorship and security laws to stifle the opposition, and choosing to jail disgruntled factory workers rather than solve the problem through reform. Nevertheless Zaghlul was widely mourned after his death in 1927, and eulogised on all sides as a great Egyptian statesman and leader.

REPRESSION AND DEPRESSION

Zaghlul's successor as leader of the Wafd was Mustafa Nahhas (1879–1965), whose first term as prime minister lasted only three months before the king found a pretext to dismiss him in June 1928 and dissolve parliament. General elections the following year returned him and the Wafd to government, but again the king stepped in when treaty negotiations with Britain broke down over the Sudan question in June 1930, replacing Nahhas with the pro-palace strong man Ismail Sidqi.

Sidqi arrested Wafdist leaders, used British troops to disperse demonstrators, dismissed parliament and scrapped the 1923 Constitution, drawing up a new one that gave himself and the monarch even greater powers, and then proceeded to rule by decree for three years almost as a dictator. His harsh regime was not made any easier by its coincidence with the severe economic depression that gripped the world in the early 1930s. The value of Egypt's cotton crop slumped by two-thirds and agricultural wages declined by 40 per cent while the cost of living rose, forcing thousands of landless peasants to migrate to the cities for work. To his credit, Sidqi introduced import duties in 1930 to protect the embryonic national textile industry which consequently developed into the most important industrial sector by the end of the decade, but generally the privations of the Great Depression were sorely felt.

Pro-palace, but too autocratic for Fuad, Sidqi was himself ousted, and control fell into the hands of the king and his court flunkeys until the combined pressures of student riots, a united front of opposition parties, and the British, could no longer be ignored. The 1923 Constitution was reinstated and general elections called for May 1936, producing a Wafd majority. Fuad's death in April spared him the sight of Nahhas becoming prime minister for the third time.

ANGLO-EGYPTIAN TREATY OF 1936

Since the 1922 Declaration of Independence, Britain had been keen to formalise its position through a treaty with a freely elected Egyptian government that represented the wishes of the people. Negotiations had broken down three times (1924, 1927 and 1929–30), but storm clouds on the international horizon were now threatening enough to cause both sides to settle their differences. The fascist menace in Europe was gathering momentum and Benito Mussolini's successful invasions of Libya and Ethiopia made Italy a worrying presence in the region. Britain was eager to get Egypt on side, and Egypt needed Britain's protection without the exploitation and abuses that outraged the country during the First World War.

In August 1936, a twenty-year treaty was signed which was generally warmly received. Britain secured its right to protect its lines of communication during peacetime with ten thousand troops in the Suez Canal Zone, and to undertake the defence of Egypt against aggression and utilise Egyptian facilities in wartime. In return, Britain recognised Egypt's independence, agreed to remove British officials employed in the Egyptian government, and promised both to support its membership application to the League of Nations and bring about an end to the Capitulations. As pledged, in 1937 Egypt became a member of the League of Nations and established a diplomatic corps around the world. The same year, the Capitulations were abolished at the Montreux Convention, where it was also agreed that the Mixed Courts, which still gave foreign judges control over large swathes of domestic law, should be phased out in twelve years.

In short, the treaty was a move forward from the four 'Reserved Points' of 1922. The first two had been resolved and the third, concerning the protection of foreign interests, had been conceded by

Britain; but the troublesome fourth point on Sudan was deliberately set aside.

SOCIAL CRISIS AND THE RISE OF EXTREMISM

It seemed that a new dawn was rising over Egypt. The vexatious relationship with Britain had been soothed and settled. The Wafd was in power and the young and handsome Faruq (r.1936–1952), nicknamed the 'pious king' for his regular attendances at Friday prayers, had just succeeded his father Fuad to the throne. Faruq was immediately idolised among his subjects, not least because he could give speeches in Arabic, the first of his family to be able to do so. Foreigners were no longer protected by the Capitulations and Egypt, having opened embassies and consulates overseas, could at last follow its own foreign policy.

But not everyone was happy. Although the treaty had officially

King Faruq who reigned from 1936-1952

brought the occupation to an end, British troops were still in Egypt and now legitimately so. And while palace and parliamentarians continued their fruitless squabbles, nothing had been done to fight the poverty, illiteracy and disease that racked the countryside. A gulf lay between rich and poor. Over 60 per cent of land under cultivation was owned by 6 per cent of landowners and a tenth of it by just 270 people. The vast estates of the rich had been steadily increasing, squeezing the plots of smallholders. Meanwhile the landless rural majority suffered low wages and irregular work and lived without clean water, sanitation and healthcare. Bilharzia was endemic and infant mortality rates were among the highest in the world. Agrarian reform had been discussed, but the monarchy was the largest landowner and parliament represented the landowning classes, so there was no impetus for change. As governments came and went and the hardships continued, Egyptians began to believe that democracy was not serving them.

In increasing numbers, ordinary people turned to radical organisations outside the parliamentary system. One of the most effective of them was the Society of the Muslim Brotherhood, founded by the schoolteacher Hasan al-Banna in 1928, which advocated a return to orthodox Islamic principles in all areas of life. At first the Brotherhood concentrated on social action, providing schooling, healthcare and assistance in deprived rural areas and urban slums, which fast won the support of the poor. During the 1930s, it became increasingly political, blaming the country's woes on foreign infidels, particularly the British, and demanding the total rejection of secular politics, values and institutions imported from Europe, which were all regarded as sinful. The movement soon became a powerful political force, able to call on a wide base of followers from the disadvantaged underclass to the middle and professional classes.

Other radical groups sprang from the cracks in the system left by the shrinking power of the Wafd and the disillusionment of the 1930s. Fascism found its voice in Young Egypt (*Misr al-Fatat*), founded in 1933, which borrowed elements of similar European movements, such as militarism, socialism, xenophobia and extreme nationalism, and combined them with religious fanaticism. At the other end of the spectrum, the extreme left and communists protested against unemployment, city slums and the appalling conditions for urban workers in factories and industry.

Cairo University was also a hotbed of political discussion and dissent. Originally it had been the country's first private secular national university (1908), but it was reorganised as a state-run establishment in 1925 that could draw students from a far wider range of backgrounds. Women were admitted in 1928, the same year it moved to a campus location in Giza, and during the late 1930s its students and graduates were among the most politically active sections of society, regularly taking part in strikes and demonstrations.

The late 1930s also saw an increase in political violence, in no small part encouraged by members of radical groups aiming to destabilise the apparatus of state. Borrowing the idea of Mussolini's Black Shirts, Young Egypt developed a paramilitary section known as the Green Shirts, prompting the Wafd to set up a counterpart youth brigade of Blue Shirts. In 1938, the Muslim Brotherhood established a clandestine terrorist wing, committed to acts of violence, sabotage and assassination in its struggle to overthrow the secular order.

Facing student riots and anti-government demonstrations in the streets, strong opposition in parliament and hostility from the young king, the Wafdist administration buckled and was dismissed in December 1937. A rigged general election (April 1938) returned a majority for the Liberals and Saadists, a recent breakaway party from the Wafd, which called for a return to the principles of Saad Zaghlul. As the situation in Europe darkened, Egypt limped over the threshold of war governed by unstable coalition ministries backed by the palace.

The Second World War

The outbreak of the Second World War in September 1939 changed Anglo-Egyptian relations again. Under the terms of the 1936 Treaty, in the event of war Egypt had to provide all its facilities, ports, communications and airspace to an unlimited number of British troops, impose martial law and censorship restrictions, detain enemy residents and confiscate their property. All this Egypt duly did while maintaining a neutral stance. Few Egyptians wanted to get embroiled in what they considered a disagreement between Western powers. But as attention swung from continental battlefields to the North African desert, Egypt became the focus of one of the most important theatres of war. Only three years after the treaty had formally ended British Occupation, the country was re-occupied by around half-a-million Allied troops during the course of the war.

As ever, Egypt and the Suez Canal were of critical strategic importance to Britain. If they were lost, the Mediterranean would be in Axis hands and the backdoor into Europe would be closed. Britain would lose the Middle East and its oil, and vital supply lines, while other positions in Russia and Asia would be catastrophically weakened.

Italy entered the war in June 1940 and launched an invasion of Egypt from Libya on 13 September, reaching Sidi Barrani in three days. General Sir Archibald Wavell, the commander-in-chief of the Middle East, led a brilliant surprise counter-attack, capturing 38,000 prisoners, before driving the Italians back to El Agheila, halfway across Libya. German reinforcements under the dashing General Erwin Rommel revitalised the Axis offensive in March 1941 in a dramatic sweep back to the Egyptian border by May. The lightning advance of German panzer divisions sparked panic buying in Egypt and a run on the banks. Food shortages and price rises triggered riots against the British, who were accused of feeding their soldiers with Egypt's corn. Crowds took to the streets in Cairo and cheered for Rommel.

To many Egyptians it seemed the British yoke was about to be lifted, but the denouement of the seesawing Western Desert campaign would not be known for another year and a half. General Sir Claude Auchinleck, Wavell's replacement, succeeded in reversing the German advance as 1941 drew to a close. Rommel could not be contained, however, and bolstered by new shipments of tanks and fuel, he surged eastwards in early 1942. Again it seemed that Britain was on the verge of losing Egypt.

ABDIN PALACE INCIDENT

In Egypt pro-Axis sympathies were rising. In 1940, the British had persuaded the palace, itself tacitly in favour of the Italians, to remove the Fascist-leaning prime minister Ali Mahir as well as key army officers thought to have made friendly overtures to the Nazis. Now as the Afrika Korps bore down on Egypt and the king threatened to reinstate Ali Mahir, the British representative, Sir Miles Lampson (high commissioner from 1934, then ambassador after the 1936 Treaty), took drastic action. On 4 February 1942, British tanks surrounded Abdin Palace and Faruq was handed an ultimatum: either he appoint Nahhas at the head of a Wafd government or he abdicate. He had little choice but to comply.

The British had obtained the anti-Fascist government they wanted and the Wafd had the power they craved, but the incident proved to be irreparably damaging to all parties concerned. Britain had made a mockery of Egypt's sovereignty and – even more shocking to the population – with the Wafd's complicity. For so long the voice of Egyptian nationalism, the Wafd had not only acquiesced but gained from British interference. The party's credibility was further weakened by charges of corruption levelled at Nahhas by one of his closest and brightest associates, Makram Ubayd, in his *Black Book*. The king, meanwhile, had been insulted and humiliated, an affront to nationhood most bitterly felt by the army officers in his charge. Faruq's authority undermined, he began an infamous moral decline which saw him abandon the responsibility of his position for selfish pursuits, gambling, womanising and general excess.

EL ALAMEIN

As the summer of 1942 approached, Allied armies were in retreat across the globe and in North Africa, things were no different. Auchinleck had fallen back to a line west of Tobruk which soon disintegrated in the dust and confusion of a swirling Rommel attack. On 21 June, Tobruk itself fell and the entire Allied Eighth Army was in sudden headlong flight eastwards. The Afrika Korps swept into Egypt in hot pursuit, steaming to within sixty miles of Alexandria. Defeat looked imminent. Officials at the British embassy burned classified files and prepared to evacuate, and the Mediterranean fleet set sail from

Alexandria.

But this was the nadir of British fortunes in the Middle East. On 1 July Rommel's relentless advance ground to a halt at El Alamein, a natural 30-mile-wide bottleneck in the desert between the sea and the impassable Qattara Depression. Fighting continued throughout July, but Rommel could not break through; Auchinleck had held firm at the First Battle of El Alamein.

In August during a visit to Egypt, Churchill gave command of the Eighth Army to General Bernard Montgomery, a man whose freshness and brimming self-confidence energised his 'brave but baffled' troops. A few months later the Allied forces had been heavily reinforced and outnumbered a now exhausted and ill-supplied enemy by more than two to one.

After a slow start – which caused Churchill to wonder, 'Have we not got one single general who can even win one single battle?' – the Second Battle of El Alamein, fought between 23 October and 5 November 1942, went down as one of the great Allied victories of the war. Egypt had been saved, morale lifted, and the tide of war began to turn. Exaggerating only a little, Churchill later wrote, 'It may almost be said: before Alamein we never had a victory. After Alamein we never had a defeat.'

Soon Rommel was in flight across Libya and the war had left Egypt. The Axis forces were driven out of North Africa altogether on 13 May 1943.

WAR LEAVES EGYPT, TROUBLE REMAINS

The pressure off, the Wafd lost the backing of the British and was dismissed by Faruq in 1944. As the war drew to its conclusion, the new prime minister Ahmad Mahir, the brother of Ali Mahir, urged his colleagues to declare war on Germany, the only way a state could become a member of the future United Nations. As he left parliament, he was assassinated, but his successor, Mahmud Fahmi al-Nuqrashi made the formal declaration two days later on 26 February 1945. The assassination was the work of the Muslim Brotherhood, which had stepped up its terrorist activities. Any politician or public figure thought to be collaborating with the British or working against Egyptian nationalism was a target. It was the beginning of a new era of politics when extremists began to dictate the agenda by killings, bombings and violence.

The war had been a huge stimulus to the economy, and many Egyptians had made money by providing the goods and services that hundreds of thousands of Allied troops demanded. Factories had been built and jobs created to manufacture items that could not be imported from the West because of the fighting, and more than 200,000 Egyptians had found work on Allied bases. Victory had brought peace, but also massive job cuts and an end to the boom.

Unsurprisingly, Egyptians were impatient to see the full evacuation of British forces, even though the increasingly unpopular 1936 Treaty had more than a decade to run. Demonstrations and protests mobilised by radical groups gripped the country in February 1946, prompting the king to bring the strong man Ismail Sidqi back to the premiership. Hundreds of students, journalists, intellectuals and agitators of every political hue were arrested while political organisations and labour associations closed down, but the discontent could not be suppressed. Sidqi next attempted to solve the Anglo-Egyptian problem – the evacuation and the sovereignty of Sudan – in talks with Ernest Bevin in London. Though it was confirmed that British troops should withdraw to the Canal Zone in 1947 (as provided by the 1936 Treaty), the draft agreement went much further and would have given Egypt in 1946 what it eventually won in 1954 after a revolution. Unfortunately, the loose wording concerning the Sudan issue led to the collapse of the talks and Sidqi's resignation. Nuqrashi was returned to office and his referral of the matter to the United Nations for arbitration did not come to anything either.

The disappointment of these failures was completely overshadowed, however, by developments in neighbouring Palestine.

The Palestine War

ROOTS OF A CONFLICT

Zionism, a movement that sought the right to establish a Jewish national state in Palestine, had begun to gather momentum in Europe in the late nineteenth century. Large-scale Jewish immigration into Palestine, then a geographic area within the Ottoman Empire rather than a discrete administrative unit, began in 1882 and was mainly from Russia following pogroms and repressions. By 1914 around 85,000 Zionist pioneers had settled, owning around 2 per cent of the land, but comprising less than 8 per cent of the existing population of Arab Muslims and Christians.

The support for Zionism expressed by the British government in the Balfour Declaration of 1917, which favoured 'the establishment in Palestine of a national home for the Jewish people' was a cause of great alarm for Palestinians, for whom Zionism was a clear threat to their interests. However, Britain had also previously made arrangements with the Emir of Mecca (in the Hussein–McMahon Correspondence) that most of the Arab areas of the Ottoman Empire be returned to Arab sovereignty in return for a successful revolt against the Turks during the First World War.

Neither the Balfour Declaration nor the Hussein–McMahon Correspondence specified the borders of territory accorded to Jews or Arabs. The vagueness allowed both Zionists and Arab nationalists to believe Palestine had been promised to them.

Britain, the occupying power in Palestine, was granted the mandate over it by the League of Nations in 1922, but could not square the circle between the conflicting promises nor the differences of opinion within its own administration. The first Arab anti-Zionist riots erupted in 1920, but the increase in immigration triggered by the rise of Nazism in the 1930s greatly heightened tensions. As the Jewish population leapt from 164,000 in 1930 to 370,000 in 1936, Arabs feared that they would become a minority in their own land. In 1936 they staged a general strike and began a nationwide revolt that paralysed the country.

EGYPT, PALESTINE AND ARAB NATIONALISM

Up till this point Egyptians had been far more concerned with domestic problems than with the issues facing Palestine. Zionism held little attraction for the Jews of Egypt who had been prospering for decades if not centuries in Egypt's generally relaxed and cosmopolitan urban society. At the same time, Egyptian Muslims had been slow to identify themselves as Arabs. Their foremost loyalty was to Egypt and the Nile Valley, and Muslims and Copts felt bonded by the unique and glorious ancestry of a pharaonic past.

This was to change as the 1930s progressed. The growing mood of disillusionment, the emergence of a non-Westernised educated class, and the increasing level of interaction with neighbouring Arab countries caused a shift in perception away from Western-looking pharaonism towards Eastern-oriented Arab nationalism. Mixed up in this was a resurgence of Islamism, a revival of traditional Islamic values as espoused by groups such as the Muslim Brotherhood. By the end of the war, the Arab bond was formalised by six Arab nations (Egypt, Syria, Iraq, Transjordan, Saudi Arabia and Yemen) in the formation of the Arab League in Cairo in March 1945; Egypt was recognised as the leading member.

The 1936–1939 revolt by Palestinian Arabs aroused the sympathies of many Egyptians, who were by now in full support of people they regarded as their Arab brothers. In fact, on the eve of the Second World War the Palestinian question had become so important in the Arab world that Britain used it to win Arabs and their Muslim co-religionists away from a drift behind the Axis powers: the British White Paper of 1939 was pro-Arab, limiting Jewish immigration and land purchases, and calling for an independent Palestinian state in which Arabs and Jews would share authority.

PARTITION

Deteriorating conditions in Palestine after the war made it clear that the British mandate would not survive. The United Nations was called on to devise a new arrangement in January 1947. On 29 November, the UN General Assembly voted to partition Palestine between Arabs and Jews. The decision was vehemently opposed by Arab countries. On 14 May, 1948, David Ben-Gurion declared an independent state of Israel. A day later, when the British mandate officially ended, the armies of the Arab League invaded.

THE PALESTINE WAR: 1948–1949

On paper, winning a war should have been an easy job for the Arabs, whose combined wealth, territory and population of over 40 million people dwarfed those of the day-old Israel, inhabited by just 600,000. But the apparent advantages did not translate into victory.

Israel had an armed force of around 65,000, of whom about a quarter were hardened veterans who had fought with the British Eighth Army in the war, whereas the combined Arab force of 40,000 contained only around 5,000 who were actually ready for battle. Israel had one clear goal (its survival as a state), a well-organised command and internal supply lines. The Arabs had divided aims, long supply lines and a disastrously confused command structure; the soldiers were ill-equipped, poorly trained and sent to fight by generals who had no strategies for advance or retreat.

Egypt's army was the largest component of the combined Arab forces, but the government was only too aware that it was completely unprepared for battle. Despite the protestations of his ministers, King Faruq had committed his army to war mainly because he wanted to stop his rival, Abdallah of Transjordan, from annexing Arab Palestine for himself. Faruq supplied his troops with obsolete and defective stock procured from Belgium in a shameful deal that defrauded public funds and enriched the king and his cronies; meanwhile Faruq's generals had to borrow maps of Palestine from Cairo car dealerships.

Soon the Arab armies were in disarray and the Israelis had expanded into areas beyond those allotted to them by the UN partition; they probably would have stormed into the Sinai too had it not been under British protection. Around 725,000 Arab Palestinians fled their homes or were expelled by Israeli forces, but were prevented from settling in neighbouring Arab countries.

The Egyptian army held the area around Gaza, fighting tenaciously in defence of Faluja in a siege that lasted four months. Paramilitary units sent by the Muslim Brotherhood also distinguished themselves at Faluja, perhaps a little too well, because Nuqrashi realised that such zealous fighters under the command of a radical movement presented a serious threat to the security of the state. The Brotherhood were also carrying out attacks on Jewish properties in Egypt, and Nuqrashi outlawed the Society in December 1948. Within three weeks he was assassinated by one of their number. Hasan al-Banna, the supreme guide of the Brotherhood, was murdered in February, probably by government agents.

An armistice was agreed between Egypt and Israel on 24 February 1949. The repercussions of the defeat were to change the course of Egyptian history.

THE FREE OFFICERS

The disaster of the Palestine War was a signal to a secret society within the Egyptian army, known as the 'Free Officers', that something must be done quickly to rescue Egypt from chaos and corruption. In their eyes, dissolute politicians, a greedy king and British agents were all to blame for the defeat; the country had to be rid of them if it was to have a future.

Many of the officers in the conspiracy were among the first wave of graduates from the national Military Academy after its intake had been widened post-1936 to include bright school-leavers of the lower and middle classes, not just the sons of the wealthy. In 1939 a group of colleagues among them created the Free Officers, a clandestine revolutionary movement that would 'fight imperialism, monarchy and feudalism'. These men had few connections with the establishment but were patriotic and wanted to see the best for their nation. Some had links with the Muslim Brotherhood, some with Young Egypt, others with the communists and left-leaning groups. A few came with no ideological baggage but were moved by the arguments of the man at the centre of the movement, Gamal Abdel Nasser (1918–1970), who since his schooldays had been involved in anti-British protests and radical politics. Serious, thoughtful and charismatic, Nasser had earned respect in Palestine where he had been wounded in battle, and showed a gift for organisation and leadership. His appointment in 1943 as an instructor at the Military Academy allowed him to recruit the most promising new cadets to the movement.

Returning from Palestine, the Free Officers decided to crank their operations up a gear, drawing up a plan to seize power within five years. A nine-member executive committee was formed to command a network of secret cells within the army. Nasser's identity as president of the committee was known by very few, and he escaped detection when called in for interrogation by the prime minister himself in 1949.

Revolution

Having been fed stories of imminent Arab victory by the palace-controlled press, the Egyptian public was stunned by news of the defeat in Palestine. As the remnants of a humiliated army straggled home, reports of corruption and incompetence at the very highest levels gripped the country. Scandals surrounding the king's business dealings and private life seemed to surface daily. Faruq was hated, the government despised, and the value of the whole parliamentary system was in doubt. Egypt was ripe for revolution.

Elections in January 1950 returned Nahhas and the Wafd to government, but time was running out. Nahhas moved quickly to win back popularity and credibility with social reforms for the benefit of the urban and rural poor, as well as a renewed campaign to oust the British from Egypt and the Sudan. After months of unproductive negotiation with London, in October 1951 Nahhas formally abrogated the 1936 Treaty and the 1899 Anglo-Egyptian Condominium Convention, saying that, 'from now on the presence of British forces undeniably constitutes a forcible, and therefore illegal occupation of the Country'; Faruq was proclaimed king of Egypt and the Sudan.

Nahhas, perhaps unwisely, hoped that such a populist move would regain traditional popular support for the Wafd, which had been dogged by corruption allegations for years. Instead it unleashed a flurry of guerrilla attacks against British targets, the work of militant secret societies, extremist groups and radical organisations, which the Wafd tried to manage through aid and support, but which were ultimately beyond its control. At British installations in the Canal Zone, Egyptian workers downed tools and left offices; railways refused to move British supplies and personnel; customs officials, air transport workers and stevedores would not touch British cargoes. The government encouraged the uprising, urging groups of students, peasants and workers to harry British units. Muslim Brothers were released from jail, armed and sent into the fray.

Both the Wafd and the radicals underestimated how determined Britain was to keep its Suez bases. The British did not hesitate from entering into pitched battles with the guerrillas when necessary, and in one incident, they stormed a police station in Ismailiya killing more than fifty Egyptians.

'BLACK SATURDAY'

The next day, Saturday 26 January 1952, the news ignited a major riot in Cairo. Goaded by militants, mobs roamed the streets torching the capital's grandest buildings, especially those associated with foreigners. Shepheard's Hotel, the Turf Club, the luxury Cicurel and David Ades department stores, Barclay's bank, Groppi's restaurant, the Cinema Metro and the Opera House were among more than four hundred buildings set ablaze. Some foreigners were beaten to death by crowds as they fled the fires; more than thirty people lost their lives and many hundreds were injured. Neither the king, the government nor the police did anything until the evening, when the army finally stepped in, martial law was declared and the flames extinguished.

Within a few hours the 'European' capital built by Khedive Ismail had gone up in smoke – and with it, the European-style liberal democracy instituted almost thirty years before. Nahhas and the Wafd were dismissed by Faruq the following day. Over the next six months a succession of four prime ministers struggled to run the country, but it was the last gasp of a dying regime.

THE OFFICERS' COUP

The Free Officers had planned to seize control in 1954, but 'Black Saturday' had exposed not only the weakness of the old order but the public's eagerness for change. Furthermore, relations were now so bad between the government and the British that the latter were unlikely to intervene against a coup.

For these reasons the Free Officers decided they must act soon; they also knew that Faruq had heard rumours of an army conspiracy and was about to move against them. His authority as leader of the army had already been challenged when his candidate had been defeated for the presidency of the Officers' Club by General Muhammad Naguib (1901–1984), put forward by the Free Officers. General Naguib had fought bravely and been badly wounded in Palestine, and was popular with the young officers for his affable, avuncular manner. The king did not know, however, that Naguib was also to be the figurehead leader of the movement poised to depose him.

The proposed coup was moved forward to the night of 22 July 1952. Nasser had made careful plans and by the early hours of the following morning, key army headquarters, airports, the Cairo broadcasting station and telecoms centre, and major roads and bridges had been captured with little resistance.

At 7 a.m. on 23 July, Colonel Anwar Sadat (1918–1981) made a radio announcement to the people of Egypt, the first news that there had been a coup:

> Egypt has lived through one of the darkest periods in its history. The Army has been tainted by the agents of dissolution. This was one of the causes of our defeat in Palestine. Led by fools, traitors and incompetents, the Army was incapable of defending Egypt. That is why we have carried out a purge. The Army is now in the hands of men in whose ability, integrity and patriotism you can have complete confidence… Egypt will greet our Movement with hope and with joy, and she can be sure that the Army is pledged to protect the national interest… May God sustain us!

Three days later, Faruq was surrounded in his summer residence, Ras al-Tin palace in Alexandria and forced to abdicate in favour of his infant son Prince Ahmad Fuad (r.1952–1953). Like his grandfather Ismail before him, Faruq sailed from Alexandria on the royal yacht

Mahrusa into exile in Italy. Naguib was on deck to salute Faruq and hear his departing words: 'Your task will be difficult. It isn't easy, you know, to govern Egypt.'

Within a year the monarchy had been abolished, and after two years arrangements had been made for the full evacuation of British troops. For almost twenty-three centuries, ever since Pharaoh Nectanebo II was defeated by the Persians, Egypt had been under the yoke of a long succession of foreign rulers, including the dynasty of Muhammad Ali. Now Faruq had been flung out and no one was sorry to see the back of him. The British, who had propped up the monarchy by force, who had ruled for forty years and interfered for seventy, were soon to follow. At long last Egyptians ruled Egypt.

CHAPTER TWELVE

Nasser, Sadat and Contemporary Egypt

1952-

The Birth of a Republic

In a few hours during the darkness before dawn on 23 July 1952, the Free Officers carried out a *coup d'état* so painless that its success almost took them by surprise. The broad aims of the revolution were clear: stop the British Occupation and eliminate foreign meddling; break the power of the monarchy and landed classes; establish social equality; and chase corruption from political life. Exactly how these were to be achieved, and with what kind of government or programme, were matters still undecided.

In the meantime, they chose to maintain a semblance of continuity by setting up a regency council for the infant king and appointing Ali Mahir as prime minister, a patriotic, vehemently anti-British politician from the *ancien régime*. The real power lay in the Free Officers' executive committee, now restyled as the Revolutionary Command Council (RCC), fronted by the reassuringly benign, pipe-smoking General Naguib but effectively controlled by the shadowy Colonel Nasser at his side.

Pressure on the RCC came from all sides. The Muslim Brotherhood, with its many contacts among the Free Officers, pushed for an Islamic state. The Wafd called for a return to parliamentary government and free elections, which they knew they would win. Leftist groups urged for a radical overhaul of the system, and textile workers at Kafr al-Dawar outside Alexandria rioted and set fire to their factory on 12 August in the name of 'the people's revolution'. The RCC reacted harshly and snuffed out the revolt, killing eight in the ensuing clashes. Around two hundred people were arrested and two of the ringleaders were hanged, despite Nasser's vote for clemency. The revolution was not to be shared; its terms would not bubble up from the people but be prescribed by decree from above.

LAND REFORM: BREAKING THE ELITE

The first major decree, the Agrarian Reform Law of 9 September 1952, was an attempt to redress the gross inequalities in land ownership – and in the process break the political stranglehold of the big landowners who had dominated parliament and stifled reform since independence. It limited landholdings per individual to two hundred feddans (a feddan being just over an acre), or three hundred feddans if there were dependent children involved. Confiscated land was to be redistributed in small lots among the fellahin and rents were also reduced.

Land reform had weakened the capital basis of the old elites and now the RCC moved to destroy their political foundation too. Having abolished the 1923 Constitution, they undertook a series of purges and trials before a special 'Corruption Tribunal' which deprived leading politicians and palace officials of their political rights. A month later, in January 1953, the RCC sealed its power by banning all political parties, confiscating their funds, and replacing them with the 'Liberation Rally', an organisation designed to mobilise popular support for the new regime. A provisional constitution was promulgated in February which officially gave supreme authority to the RCC for a transitional period of three years.

Now the *coup de grâce* could be dealt. On 18 June 1953, the RCC abolished the monarchy and proclaimed Egypt a republic. The enormous estates of the royal household, totalling some 178,000 acres, were expropriated without compensation. General Naguib (1901–1984) became the republic's first president. He was also made prime minister, and Nasser emerged from the background to become deputy prime minister and minister of the interior, while other trusted officers were fed into ministerial positions.

POWER STRUGGLE

Unknown to most of the world, the architect and true leader of the revolution was not the mild-mannered General Naguib, but the tall and grave-looking colonel who stood at his shoulder. During the first year of the revolution, the general had played well with the public. His seniority and respectability had lent gravitas to what might have been regarded as an opportune putsch by a gang of ruthless young officers. But Naguib had not been a member of the Free Officers, and although sympathetic to the movement, he was far more conservative in outlook. He favoured returning the country to constitutional government and the officers to their barracks. Furthermore, he did not see himself as a mere figurehead; he had been asked to lead, he was the senior officer, and lead he would.

Colonel Gamal Abdel Nasser (1918–1970), on the other hand, brimmed with revolutionary zeal. He had grown up in a small house in Alexandria, where his father, who came from a poor peasant family

Gamal Abdel Nasser, a national hero who nationalised the Suez Canal

of Upper Egypt, had managed to find work as a postal clerk. At age seven the young Nasser had asked his parents during a meal, 'How is it that we are eating meat whereas the shepherds who look after the sheep do not?' At twelve he had been beaten over the head with a baton until he bled during an anti-British riot and at seventeen he was grazed by a bullet in another demonstration. He read widely in history and biography and was sure that Egypt had a destiny as glorious as its ancient past. His drive, vision and talent for organisation had been the engine behind the revolution, and he believed he was its natural leader; Naguib had fulfilled his uses.

By April 1954 Nasser's nimble political brain had outmanoeuvred Naguib, despite his backing from the Muslim Brotherhood, communists and outlawed political parties. Naguib lingered on as president for a few more months but his power had been extinguished. The same could not be said of the Muslim Brotherhood, whose tentacles of influence coiled into every section of the population, not least the Free Officers themselves. After clashes with the Liberation Rally in January 1954, the RCC found a pretext to round up Brotherhood leaders, dissolve the organisation and ban its activities. On 26 October, the Brotherhood struck back in an attempt on Nasser's life. As shots rang out about his head while he spoke at an Alexandria rally, Nasser defiantly cried, 'Let them kill Nasser; what is Nasser but one among many?'

In the aftermath of the failed plot, the police rounded up hundreds of Brotherhood members. Six ringleaders were executed, its supreme guide was sentenced to life imprisonment, and many others were given lengthy terms. General Naguib was not implicated in the plot, but he was known to have links with the Brotherhood and was stripped of the presidency and placed under house arrest. Nasser was absolute master of Egypt and would remain so until his death.

FORMALISING CONTROL

The June 1956 Constitution formalised Nasser's supreme position in Egypt and laid out the principles for a new governmental system. The first president was to be chosen by national plebiscite (women were granted suffrage for the first time) and Nasser was duly elected on 23 July with 99.9 per cent of the vote against no opponents. Thereafter the newly created unicameral National Assembly would choose future presidents to be confirmed by public referendum. The constitution granted the president 'the right to initiate, to promulgate, or to veto legislation' ensuring his primacy above the assembly, and put him in control of the executive of the National Union, a new political organisation open to all Egyptians to replace the Liberation Rally. From its membership a list of candidates, closely screened by Nasser, would be drawn up for election to the 350-seat National Assembly. The constitution placed the entire political system under Nasser's control.

Nasser: National Hero, World Leader

BRITISH WITHDRAWAL

The settlement of the two thorniest issues in Egyptian politics – the continuing presence of British troops and the status of Sudan – gave Nasser greater freedom than any Egyptian politician had enjoyed since independence. Talks with the British over both matters began shortly after the revolution. In February 1953 it was decided that the Sudanese people should choose, after a three-year transitional period, between a union with Egypt and complete independence. Either way, the problematic Anglo-Egyptian Condominium arrangement was to be terminated. To the surprise and dismay of the Egyptians, Sudan declared its full independence on 1 January 1956.

After almost two years of difficult negotiation, a treaty for British evacuation was signed on 19 October 1954, providing for the complete withdrawal of British troops from Egypt within twenty months. Military installations in the Canal Zone were to be kept serviceable for seven years, so that the British army could reoccupy them in the event of an attack by an outside power on any member of the Arab League or Turkey – a safeguard against the communist threat on a strategic area. This proviso angered some, but Nasser, who had led the negotiations, believed the evacuation itself was paramount. As the treaty was signed, he said, 'The ugly page in Anglo–Egyptian relations has been turned and another page is being written…There is now no reason why Britain and Egypt should not work constructively together.'

The last British soldier left Port Said on 13 June 1956, ending seventy-four years of continuous occupation. Unfortunately, less than five months later, British troops would be back as an invading force.

FOREIGN POLICY AND ARAB NATIONALISM

The removal of the British from Egypt was just one victory in what the Free Officers perceived as the global struggle against Western imperialism. Nasser pictured Egypt as the natural leader in this movement of resistance because of its key position in the Arab world, a region he believed to have 'the same conditions, the same problems, the same future and the same enemy, no matter how different the masks he might wear to conceal his identity'. But not all Arab countries shared Nasser's views. The monarchies of Saudi Arabia and Jordan eyed Egypt's young republican revolutionaries with deep suspicion and Iraq's prime minister, Nuri al-Said, head of the next most powerful independent Arab state after Egypt, was regarded by Nasser as the West's loudest cheerleader.

International relations were further complicated by the impact of the Cold War. In an attempt to contain Soviet expansion, the United States had engineered a series of defensive alliances encircling the USSR. The 1955 Baghdad Pact between Iraq and Turkey was a central link between NATO and SEATO (NATO's Southeast Asian counterpart). Nasser berated Nuri for joining, claiming he was betraying the Arab cause and playing into the hands of the 'imperialist West', a charge that seemed to be confirmed when Britain entered the Pact later that year (with Iran and Pakistan) to buttress its regional influence.

It was easy for Nasser to whip up popular opposition across the Arab world against both Nuri and the Pact in fiery broadcasts from his Cairo radio station *Voice of the Arabs*, a propaganda tool that he used to undermine his opponents throughout his presidency. His vitriolic attacks impressed ordinary Arabs but quickly made him the bugbear of the West.

After the Bandung Conference of April 1955, Nasser found that his reputation had extended far beyond the Arab-speaking world. The conference in Indonesia was between 'non-aligned' African and Asian leaders, the first meeting between young and newly decolonised nations seeking to find their place in a world polarised between two superpowers. Nasser was welcomed as a hero by such dignitaries as Jawaharlal Nehru of India and Chou En-lai of China for skilfully dealing with Britain and deposing a corrupt monarchy. In Bandung he became convinced that his brand of anti-imperialist Arab nationalism was an important part of a broader struggle between the developing world and the domination of global powers.

RELATIONS WITH ISRAEL

Since the Palestine War, a *détente* of sorts existed between Egypt and Israel. It was upset by Britain's agreement to evacuate the Canal Zone in 1954, which alarmed Israel and prompted it to send secret service agents to bomb Western targets in Alexandria and Cairo, simulating atrocities by Arab extremists in order to derail the newly convened treaty. However, the plot was foiled and the perpetrators caught and hanged. The Lavon Affair, as it became known (after the Israeli defence minister who resigned over the incident), ended the period of relative calm between Egypt and Israel and encouraged the return to politics of hardliner David Ben-Gurion from his retirement. As the new minister of defence, he initiated a policy of punitive reprisal against border incursions by Palestinian refugees and *fedayeen* (guerrillas). On 28 February 1955, an Israeli raid against Egyptian headquarters in Gaza inflicted many casualties and exposed the weakness of the Egyptian army.

For Nasser, leader of a military government and the defender of Arab nationalism, a penetration of this sort was deeply embarrassing. Yet Nasser had no arms to counterattack and the West had blocked weapons sales in response to his hostility to the Baghdad Pact. All he could do was provide more intensive training for the *fedayeen*, who were soon able to step up their sorties to destroy installations deep inside Israeli territory.

ARMS FROM CZECHOSLOVAKIA, A SUITCASE FROM AMERICA

At the Bandung Conference, delegates suggested that Nasser looked to buy arms from the communist regimes, who proved only too willing to provide assistance and agreed the sale of $200 million – a colossal sum at the time – of advanced Soviet weaponry, tanks, jet fighters and bombers from Czechoslovakia, to be paid for with rice and cotton. Arabs were overjoyed at the Egyptian army's much-needed upgrade. The West, on the other hand, was horrified at Nasser's very perceptible lean towards the communist East.

It may have been in reaction to this that the CIA allegedly sent Nasser a suitcase stuffed full of dollar bills totalling as much as $3 million according to some sources. Furious at the implication that he could be bribed, Nasser spent the money on the 614ft (187m) Cairo Tower, a soaring lotus flower in latticed concrete topped off by a revolving restaurant which still dominates the skyline. The tower was both a monument to the new technological age and a gigantic finger raised to the meddlesome West.

ASWAN HIGH DAM

The revival of Egypt's armed forces, the country's rising importance in world affairs, and international respect for Nasser had done much to rekindle national dignity and self-esteem as well as enhance the legitimacy of the revolutionary regime. But improvements in the country's social and economic condition were harder to discern. The population was approaching 25 million and was growing by more than half-a-million each year, placing enormous strain on the land, and negating the modest increases in productivity and exports.

The government's answer was to build a vast new dam at Aswan which would allow the irrigation of more than a million feddans of hitherto uncultivated land (increasing agricultural land by about a third), put an end to droughts and floods, and generate enough hydro-electric power to industrialise Egypt. As the cornerstone of Nasser's programme for national development, the high dam would be the proud symbol of a resurgent nation.

The cost of the immense project was far more than the cash-strapped government could afford, but the World Bank, the United States and Britain were keen to offer funds to stop the drift towards the Soviets. The terms were difficult for Nasser to accept as they involved a degree of Western control over the Egyptian economy and he hesitated, hoping that the USSR might come forward with a better deal. Meanwhile, US backers were beginning to get cold feet. Egypt's recognition of communist China in May 1956 did not help. Just as Nasser decided to accept, the US withdrew the offer, a move designed to cause maximum humiliation.

THE SUEZ CRISIS

If Nasser let himself be bullied by the West, he was nothing. His retort came eight days later on 26 July 1956, the fourth anniversary of Faruq's abdication. Talking to a huge and expectant crowd in Alexandria and the rest of the Arab world by radio, he announced the nationalisation of the Suez Canal. The revenues raised – only a tiny fraction of which had ever ended up in Egyptian pockets – would be used to pay for the Aswan High Dam.

The response was rapturous, not only amongst Arabs but across the developing world. Nasser had struck a blow against the old imperial powers by reclaiming the Canal, one of the world's most noxious symbols of colonial exploitation.

The gesture was as dangerous as it was provocative. The post-war break-up of the British Empire may have diminished the traditional importance of the Canal as a conduit to India and Southeast Asia, but by the 1950s the route had become the lifeline supplying two-thirds of Britain's oil needs, as well as a large proportion of those of France's. It was not only the threat to the economy that outraged the British prime minister, Sir Anthony Eden. As foreign secretary, he had negotiated terms for British withdrawal from the Canal Zone, and he believed that Nasser had betrayed him by the nationalisation, an act he considered comparable to Hitler's occupation of the Rhineland. Moreover, he maintained that Nasser had consistently undermined and thwarted Britain's influence in the Middle East, and if Nasser was a Hitler in the making, then appeasement was not enough; he had to be removed as quickly as possible.

France was equally angry, not only because of the obvious affront to the French-managed and Paris-based Suez Canal Company (even though Nasser promised to compensate the shareholders). Like the British, they considered Nasser the troublemaker of the region, and rightly or wrongly, saw him as the patron of Algerian rebels fighting for independence from France. Israeli anxieties had also been aroused by the Czech arms deal and Ben-Gurion wanted to strike before Egypt could absorb its new purchases. He hoped an attack would also knock out the *fedayeen* and break Egypt's blockade of the Tiran Straits which barred Israeli ships from the Red Sea.

At conferences at London and New York, efforts were made to put the waterway under international control, but contrary to Western predictions the new Egyptian authority was managing the Canal efficiently, and Nasser saw no reason to accept the proposals. Behind the scenes Britain and France made preparations for war, hatching secret plans with Ben-Gurion for an Israeli invasion, the pretext to their own intervention.

On 29 October 1956, Israeli soldiers poured over the border into Sinai while paratroopers landed at the strategic Mitla Pass further west. The following day, Britain and France issued an ultimatum requiring Egypt and Israel to evacuate an area ten miles from the Suez Canal. When Nasser refused, they bombed airfields and destroyed the Egyptian air force. On 5 November, French and British troops landed at Port Said and captured the town after naval bombardments and air strikes, before beginning an advance south along the canal.

The very next day, however, the offensive was halted when Britain and France agreed to a United Nations ceasefire. World opinion was utterly against them and the folly of their position could no longer be denied. The Egyptian people had not risen up against Nasser as they had hoped, but rallied behind him, more so because of Israel's involvement. Even the rival superpowers were united in their condemnation: the Soviet Union threatened to use 'every kind of modern destructive weapon' against the 'tripartite aggressors', and the United States applied heavy economic and political pressure that made it almost impossible for Britain to continue. United Nations peacekeeping forces arrived, and the British and French completed their departure by 22 December. The Israelis withdrew from Sinai in March 1957.

CONSEQUENCES OF SUEZ

Egypt had been crushed militarily, but had emerged from the Suez 'débâcle' as the political victor. It had survived the combined might of three greater powers and come through with total control of the Canal. Britain and France, on the other hand, had been humiliated and their influence in the Middle East badly damaged.

All French and British property in Egypt was sequestrated, their banks taken over, their schools seized and foreign professionals replaced by Egyptians, a process of nationalisation that would eventually be extended to nearly all foreign enterprises. The West retaliated with an economic blockade which only served to strengthen Egypt's trade links with the USSR.

Thousands of French and British citizens were expelled, or left voluntarily, soon followed by many other 'foreigners' – Greeks, Italians, Maltese, Levantines – whose families had lived in Egypt for decades but felt they no longer had a future there. It was also a watershed for many Jews in Egypt who found they were compelled to leave, despite many being anti-Zionist. Within a few years, there were very few Europeans and Jews left in Egypt and the celebrated cosmopolitanism infusing cities like Alexandria evaporated. On the other hand, Nasser had ended the dominant position of foreigners at a stroke and begun the swift process of 'Egyptianising' the economy and society, achievements that Urabi could only have dreamed of seventy-five years earlier.

Eden was a broken man and resigned due to ill health in January 1957. His nemesis, Nasser, on the other hand, scaled new heights of popularity among the Arab masses and was hailed as the new Saladin, the man that would lead a united Arab nation to victory against the Zionists, the crusaders of the modern era. But the expectations of a glorious Arab future did not tally with the economic and political realities of the time. Swept up in the fervour, Nasser learned this too late, only after he had driven the economy close to bankruptcy and taken his country into a disastrous war.

The Decline of Nasserism

Nasser's ability to speak directly to the people and his unbuckling defiance of the West had made him immensely popular among ordinary Arabs across the region. The enthusiasm was not shared by other Arab leaders, most of whom were, at bottom, conservatives who had much to lose by an Egyptian-style revolution. They were as unhappy as the US about Nasser's growing friendship with the Soviets, whose standing among the Arab people had risen sharply since Suez and further increased with their large offers of aid and technical help to build the Aswan High Dam. Nasser was no communist but the US contrived to isolate him and bolster pro-Western leaders through the 'Eisenhower Doctrine' of January 1957, a programme which promised financial and military aid to Middle Eastern countries that resisted 'international communism'.

THE UNITED ARAB REPUBLIC: EXPERIMENT IN ARAB UNITY

The Americans were particularly worried about Syria, which they were convinced was about to become a Soviet satellite after the socialist Baath Party came to power in early 1957. It was an unwarranted fear; the Baath advocated the union of all Arab-speaking nations and were no more inclined to side with the Soviets than with the West. On the contrary, they were struggling to contain communist agitators within their own regime.

On the verge of being caught up in the Cold War crossfire, the Baath sought Nasser's help, pleading for a political union with Egypt which they advertised as a vanguard to a union of all Arab states. Nasser foresaw many practical difficulties in the union of two non-contiguous and socially different countries, but Arab unity was a natural extension of his strident Arab nationalism and he could not resist. On 1 February 1958 Egypt and Syria merged under Nasser's leadership as the United Arab Republic (UAR). Yemen joined in March in a looser federation called the United Arab States.

When Nasser visited Syria as head of state a couple of weeks later, hundreds of thousands of well-wishers thronged the streets of Damascus in his honour. He was at the zenith of his power and the pan-Arab dream seemed close to reality, especially after the political convulsion of 1958, prompted in part by the formation of the UAR, which shook the Middle East. King Saud of Saudi Arabia fell from power to his half-brother Faisal after offering a Syrian politician a bribe to murder Nasser, and the Iraqi monarchy was deposed by a military coup inspired by that of Egypt. At first it looked as though both countries might join the UAR, but it soon became apparent that neither wanted to share their vast oil revenues. Their rejection effectively shattered the ideal of a pan-Arab state.

Meanwhile in Syria, the euphoria of the union was fast wearing off. Syrians struggled to reconcile their respect for Nasser with the authoritarian regime he tried to force onto them. In Egypt, people had become accustomed to Nasser's autocratic rule but Syrians balked when their political parties – even the Baath – were banned and their democratic institutions dissolved. They did not equate political liberalism with the incompetent rule of foreign elites and wealthy landowners as Egyptians did, and they did not cheer its demise as Egyptians had. Neither did Syrians welcome a government dominated by army officers and a cumbersome, inefficient bureaucracy imposed on them from Cairo, staffed by Egyptians who saw Syria as their 'northern province'. Resentment was palpable, particularly among the Syrian bourgeoisie and private business community which were far more prominent and developed than in Egypt.

Nasser's Socialist Laws of July 1961, which inaugurated the second phase of the revolution, were also not well received in Syria. The measures included the nationalisation or state supervision of most of the UAR's factories, public utilities, financial institutions and export firms; reduction of private landholdings to a hundred feddans; reduction of the hours of the working day; and limits to income and salary levels – all regarded by Syrians as deeply injurious to their economy. A day after a coup led by army officers in Damascus on 28 September,

Syria seceded from the union. Yemen left the fold in December. Nasser continued to use the name United Arab Republic in case either returned, but Egypt remained its sole member until 1971 when Anwar Sadat finally abandoned the name.

ARAB SOCIALISM

Nasser attributed the failure of the UAR to the infiltration of old-guard bourgeois 'reactionaries' into the National Union, prompting him to sequestrate the property of six hundred of Egypt's wealthiest families, most of whom were Jewish, Coptic or Greek. A period of soul-searching followed in which Nasser attempted to build a new programme for Egypt under the principles of 'Arab socialism', a loosely defined ideology that sought to overcome the economic and social burden of the colonial past while remaining true to Arab identity. Its socialism differed from Marxist ideology in its rejection of atheism, in favour of compatibility with Islam; of class struggle, seen as irrelevant and divisive in the Arab world; and of communal capital ownership, thought ill-suited to traditional Arab values of private property and inheritance.

Nasser set out the origins and direction of Arab socialism in the rambling 30,000-word National Charter of 1962. In it he endorsed state ownership for public services, industries and most of the import and export trade, and identified the need for family planning to avert a population explosion, which he believed was 'the most dangerous obstacle facing the Egyptian people in their drive to raise the standard of living in their country'.

The charter also devised a new political organisation to replace the discredited National Union. The Arab Socialist Union (ASU) was to be drawn from all sections of society with councils on village, district, provincial and national levels, half of the membership of which was to be filled by workers and peasants. In practice its pyramidal structure was little different in function from the old National Union with all the power concentrated in the twenty-five-member Supreme Executive Committee at the apex of the pyramid – and Nasser on top of that. The creation of the ASU reflected Nasser's modified approach towards Arab unity and the aims of the revolution. The ASU was designed to be adaptable to other Arab states, but Nasser accepted that political unity was unlikely to work with regimes not committed to socialist and republican principles, a view he summarised in the slogan 'unity of purpose, not unity of ranks'.

YEMENI CIVIL WAR

Guided by this notion, Nasser made the ill-advised decision in September 1962 to involve the Egyptian army in a protracted and debilitating war in Yemen. Republicans there claimed to have over-thrown the royalist government, but the deposed Imam had escaped and began a counter revolution which Nasser was committed to thwart. The five-year war, since described as 'the Egyptian Vietnam', tied up 70,000 Egyptian soldiers, brought Nasser into confrontation with Saudi Arabia (which simultaneously channelled arms to the royalists), harmed relations with Britain and the US, and was a terrible drain on scant public funds and resources.

INTERNAL DIFFICULTIES

That the country could ill afford to waste money and men in Yemen was becoming increasingly plain to ordinary Egyptians. In 1960, the government had issued the first of two ambitious five-year plans that aimed to double the national income in a decade. Nationalisation had till then been limited to foreign enterprises but that year it was extended to Egyptian businesses such as Bank Misr, the National Bank, and the press, a prologue to the wider-ranging Socialist Laws of July 1961. Work on the mainstay of Egypt's economic regeneration, the Aswan High Dam, had begun in 1960 but would not be complete for ten years. In the meantime, showcase industrial and land-reclama-tion projects, namely the huge steel works at Helwan and the 'Liberation Province' established in desert between Cairo and Alexandria, had cost a small fortune but produced little.

After 1963 the economy was beginning to falter. Waves of national-isations had put an increasing portion of the economy into the public sector and at the mercy of a creaking bureaucracy and an uncompetitive, centralised administration. Industry was troubled by surplus labour, low productivity and general mismanagement. By 1965, the second five-year plan was unofficially abandoned and austerity measures introduced. Lack of foreign currency had led to a scarcity of consumer goods, as well as raw materials and spare parts essential to keep industries running. And with the population increasing by 800,000 people a year the situation was steadily deteriorating. Egypt was heavily dependent on foreign loans and aid and a diplomatic upset with either the Soviets or Americans might mean the total collapse of the economy.

Most loans came from the USSR and the eastern bloc, which also rushed to provide technical expertise for new industrial and military facilities. Counterposing Soviet help, the US supplied vast amounts of food aid, almost $650 million of wheat between 1954 and 1966, unwittingly supporting a regime with which it was often at odds. It has been said that Nasser's commitment to non-alignment during the Cold War (or 'positive neutralism' as he called it), enabled him to get the USSR to underwrite the cost of industrialisation while the US fed the workforce.

Despite its evident shortcomings, Nasser would brook no opposition to Arab socialism. The press, radio and now television, introduced to Egypt in 1960, had all been incorporated into Nasser's propaganda machine and voices critical of the regime had few outlets. Rivals and enemies of the state were bugged, tapped and spied on; political arrests were widespread throughout the 1960s and the country's jails, notorious for torture and brutality, groaned with thousands of prisoners of conscience.

As ever, the Muslim Brothers were targeted and thousands were rounded up in 1965 after the authorities claimed to have uncovered a nationwide plot to depose the president. In a sense, this was an admission that there was public discontent in many quarters of society, calling into question the veracity of Nasser's triumphant re-election by national plebiscite earlier that year. The harsh treatment they received served to radicalise many Brothers, and the execution of Sayyid Qutb, the Brotherhood's leading ideologue, in 1966 shocked the Muslim world. Qutb's concept that Islam was in the grip of a modern–day *jahiliyya* (state of ignorance before Islam), had enormous influence on radicals for decades to come who used it to justify violence against all opponents, whether civilians, infidels, fellow Muslims or the state.

THE SIX-DAY (JUNE) WAR

The allure of the international stage was always a welcome distraction for Nasser away from the less than satisfactory situation at home. He hosted two Arab summits in 1964, in which the usually fractious Arab leaders found some common ground over the question of Israel and its plans to divert the River Jordan for irrigation schemes. They resolved to form the Palestine Liberation Organisation (PLO), with its own army, as an umbrella body to represent the Palestinian Arabs. The PLO duly began to gather a regular army, but the al-Fatah guerrilla movement, led by Yasser Arafat, was then the most effective Palestinian force. It was armed and supported by Syria but mainly launched its raids from Jordan, bringing the customary threats of overwhelming reprisal from Israel against both countries.

Nasser, self-styled scourge of Zionism and leader of the Arab world, could not refuse Syrian and then Jordanian requests for assistance and entered into defence pacts with them in 1966 and 1967 respectively. He well knew, however, that with much of his army entangled in Yemen, he was in no position to go to war with Israel – though this did not stop state media pumping out propaganda that a final victory over the Zionists was guaranteed.

Tensions rose in the spring of 1967 after a series of border clashes and dogfights between Syrian and Israeli warplanes; Israel's leaders issued increasingly severe threats of retaliation. In May, Soviet intelligence reported to Nasser, falsely as it later turned out, that Israel was amassing its troops for an imminent offensive against Syria.

Nasser raised the stakes by asking the UN to withdraw their forces in Sinai (stationed there since the Suez War) and swiftly replaced them with Egyptian army divisions. His second provocative decision was to close the Tiran Straits to Israeli shipping, a move regarded in itself as a *casus belli* by the Knesset. Bluffing or not, the almost total lack of

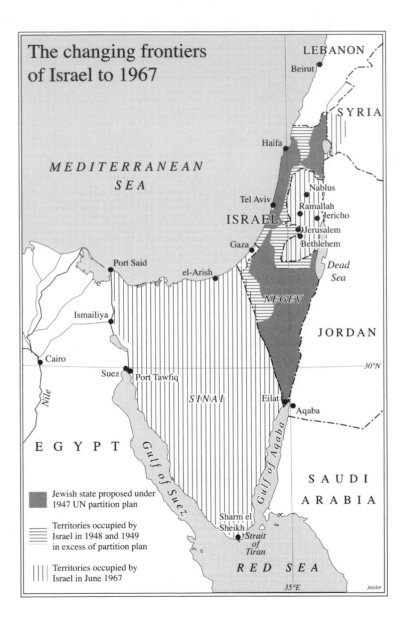

The changing frontiers
of Israel to 1967

LEBANON
Beirut

SYRIA

MEDITERRANEAN
SEA

Haifa

Nablus
Tel Aviv
Ramallah
Jericho
ISRAEL
Jerusalem
Gaza
Bethlehem

Dead
Sea

Port Said
el-Arish

NEGEV

Ismailiya

JORDAN

Cairo

30°N

Suez
Port Tawfiq

SINAI
Eilat
Aqaba

Nile

Gulf of Aqaba

E G Y P T

Gulf of Suez

SAUDI

ARABIA

Jewish state proposed under
1947 UN partition plan

Territories occupied by
Israel in 1948 and 1949
in excess of partition plan

Territories occupied by
Israel in June 1967

Sharm el
Sheikh
Strait
of
Tiran

RED SEA

35°E

jtaylor

·preparation for war suggests that Nasser was still expecting to avoid armed confrontation. Israel, on the other hand, had no such illusions and immediately mobilised for all-out war, calling up reserve units and making a coalition war cabinet.

On 5 June 1967, Israel launched pre-emptive air strikes against bases in Egypt, Jordan, Syria and Iraq, destroying most of the Arab air forces on the ground. Without air cover, there was little the various Arab armies – which still had no unified command structure – could do to resist Israeli advances. While Egypt's warplanes smouldered in ruins on the runway and some ten thousand Egyptian soldiers lay dead from battle or thirst in the Sinai desert, state-controlled media continued to celebrate spectacular fictitious victories. By the 10 June ceasefire, Israel had taken possession of Gaza, the West Bank with East Jerusalem, the Golan Heights and all of Sinai to the banks of the Suez Canal.

NASSER IN DEFEAT

When the truth emerged of the terrible Arab defeat, Egypt was stunned. On 9 June, Nasser appeared on television to take full responsibility and offer his resignation; there was no corrupt monarchy to take the blame for the disaster this time. But within minutes of his resignation speech, huge crowds filled the streets chanting, 'Nasser, do not leave us, we need you'; in this moment of deep national crisis, they would have no other leader. Nasser stayed on.

The full scale of the defeat came to light afterwards during trials of army commanders accused of dereliction of duty. The trials laid bare the emptiness of Nasser's claims to military strength, and the limitations of his social and political reforms. The lenient sentences provoked immediate riots from workers and students in February and November 1968, the first major protests since 1954. While Nasser deflected the blame on to corrupt 'centres of power' within the administration, students called for a return to political liberty, proper parliamentary representation and freedom of speech. At first Nasser made some small concessions but then resorted to mass arrests, justifying the crackdown in the name of maintaining internal stability against the Zionist threat.

The same threat was also cited to account for the sharp increase in defence expenditure, which now swallowed up a quarter of the national income, to make good the loss of around 80 per cent of the country's military hardware. Following the defeat, Egypt could hardly spare the money: half of its oilfields were in Sinai and now in Israeli hands; the Suez Canal had been blocked by scuttled ships at the outbreak of war, and its continued closure ended a source of much-needed foreign currency; tourism slumped; and the US halted its aid shipments of wheat. The economy was in dire trouble and austerity measures could not save the people from daily shortages, nor the country's infrastructure and public services from sore neglect.

Nasser had to look for new sources of aid and found unlikely donors in Saudi Arabia and Kuwait, the same 'reactionaries and feudalists' he used to fulminate against on Cairo Radio. In return, he agreed to withdraw Egyptian troops from Yemen and adopt more moderate international policies favoured by Arab conservatives. With respect to Israel this entailed toeing the line of 'no war, no peace, no negotiation'. Egypt's dependence on the Soviets also reached unprecedented levels. They agreed to rebuild Egypt's national defences, but in the process implanted thousands of advisers and technicians into the apparatus of state.

WAR OF ATTRITION

The failure of UN Resolution 242 to bring Israel's removal from recently occupied territories and to secure its formal recognition by Arab states encouraged Nasser to embark on his 'War of Attrition' in September 1968, formally declared in March 1969, an escalation of the sporadic artillery exchanges across the Suez Canal that had been ongoing since the 1967 ceasefire. Even the installation of a sophisticated new Soviet missile defence system, the arrival of Russian pilots and thousands more military advisers could not dislodge the Israelis from their defensive position along the Bar Lev line, nor stop them from executing devastating commando and air raids deep inside Egypt.

A provisional US-sponsored ceasefire was reached in August 1970.

However, the situation was so delicate that even a temporary peace between Israel and Egypt had violent repercussions. Palestinian extremists took it as a sign that their cause was being forgotten and consequently orchestrated a series of airline hijackings. Many Palestinian resistance groups were based in Jordan and when King Husayn tried to oust them from the country, a civil war broke out.

It took a man of Nasser's stature and energy to negotiate a peace between Husayn and Arafat, now head of the PLO. But Nasser's energy was running out. He was a very sick man and after treatments in the USSR for diabetes, heart problems and arteriosclerosis, he had been told to avoid stress. On 28 September, after exhausting but successful peace talks in Cairo, he saw his guests off at the airport, suddenly collapsed with a heart attack and died.

In a massive, immediate and spontaneous paroxysm of grief, more than two million mourners (some sources say five million) thronged the avenues of Cairo during Nasser's funeral procession. Few denied that his government had made mistakes, that the economy was in a mess and the regime uncomfortably repressive. But most respected that Nasser's intentions to modernise and industrialise Egypt, to unite the Arabs in peace, to create a more just and equal society were completely genuine. He had been incorruptible although he had allowed corruption to creep into the administration beneath him. Most importantly of all, Nasser had been the first Egyptian to rule his country for more than 2200 years. After this aeon of subjugation, the Egyptians had had at last a leader, the father of a new nation, who for good or ill, had been a colossus of Middle Eastern politics and had reawoken the dignity of the people and their pride for their country.

Sadat: undoing the legacy

Vice president Anwar Sadat (1918–1981) came to power as provided for by the constitution, but few expected him to survive at the top for long. He was one of the few original Free Officers to have lasted inside the Nasser administration, despite, or perhaps because of, being regarded as something of a political nonentity. He had never been assigned a ministerial post and his obedience and docility had earned

Anwar Sadat, the inventor of 'electric shock' politics,
who tried to seek peace with Israel

him the nickname *Bimbashi Sah-Sah*, 'Colonel Yes-Yes', among his
colleagues, but his longevity under Nasser alone should have alerted
them to a shrewd political mind within.

In May 1971, Sadat acted to consolidate his position by rooting out
the old Nasserite power centres from the administration, arresting and
removing the very people who were manoeuvring to oust him from
the presidency. This so-called 'Corrective Revolution' effectively
marked a break with the past and signalled Sadat's intention to redress
the errors of Nasser's administration while staying true to the 1952
revolution. Changing the official name of the country from the UAR
to the Arab Republic of Egypt was therefore more than just a cosmetic
adjustment.

Initially Sadat was careful to pay lip service to Nasser's legacy,
though it was soon clear that he had very different ideas. A naturally
more liberal and effusive character than his rather austere predecessor,
Sadat promised to curb the repressive activities of the security services,

open up the economy, respect the rule of law and introduce free parliamentary elections. He believed that the nation had been left politically fatigued and economically drained by Nasser's commitment to international issues, and the time had come to put 'Egypt first'.

This struck a chord with many, but it was widely felt that domestic issues could not be adequately tackled until a solution to the Arab-Israeli conflict was found and Egypt regained Sinai. Sadat had promised that 1971 would be a 'decisive year' in this respect but lack of progress had been demoralising and made him look foolish, doing little to help him emerge from Nasser's shadow and win the respect of the people.

His popularity surged considerably after his shock decision to expel around fifteen thousand Soviet advisers and military personnel from Egypt in July 1972. The Soviets had become an increasingly visible and unwelcome presence in Egypt and few mourned their departure. More importantly, the snub to the USSR heralded a completely fresh approach to international relations, making clear Sadat's desire for *rapprochement* with the United States, which he believed held '99 per cent of the cards' in the Arab–Israeli issue. Diplomatic ties had been cut in 1967, but it would take more than the Soviet expulsion to distract Washington from the unfolding horror of Vietnam and then win its sympathy. After all, the US was Israel's closest ally. Something far more dramatic was needed.

THE OCTOBER (YOM KIPPUR) WAR

Throughout 1973, Sadat made preparations with Syria for a concerted attack on the occupied territories of Sinai and the Golan Heights. The object was not the total destruction of the Israeli state, but a situation in which the superpowers and the world at large would reassess their Middle East policies to offer a way out of the current impasse. Another war was a risky strategy but the Arabs were in a sense helped by their previous dismal performances; no one thought they had the stomach nor resources to invade, let alone that they could defeat Israel.

Having orchestrated a series of bluffs in preceding months that caused Israel twice to go on a full war footing needlessly, the Arabs launched a surprise attack on 6 October 1973, the Jewish Day of Atonement (Yom Kippur). The early gains were spectacular. Egyptian troops and tanks surged across the canal and stormed through the Bar Lev line, pushing the Israelis back in terrified confusion; the Syrians scored similar successes in the Golan Heights.

Perhaps unnerved by the speed of their initial advances, the Arabs hesitated, giving Israeli forces an opportunity to regroup and counter-attack, aided in no small part by the urgent airlifting of state-of-the-art weaponry from the US (prompting the dispatch of similar shipments to the Arabs from the USSR). General Ariel Sharon located a weak point in the Arab lines, broke through on 18 October under ferocious fire, cut off the Egyptian Third Army in Sinai, built a bridge-head over the Suez Canal and came to within an hour's drive of Cairo. Another Arab defeat seemed all too possible, but the Arab world – or more specifically, the Arab members of OPEC (Organisation of Petroleum Exporting Countries) – had yet to deploy the 'oil weapon'. Their declaration of an oil boycott on countries supporting Israel sparked hurried negotiations for a ceasefire. An embargo was placed on the US and the Netherlands, and cutbacks in production were enforced until Israel withdrew from all the occupied territories and had recognised the rights of Palestinians for self-determination. With winter approaching and oil already in short supply, prices soared, quadrupling by the end of 1974. The European Economic Community and Japan were quick to issue a joint declaration on the Middle East problem, supporting the Arab viewpoint as never before. By 25 October, a ceasefire was successfully being observed by all sides, after a nerve-racking few days when the US and USSR seemed on the brink of being drawn into a direct confrontation. Henry Kissinger's frantic 'shuttle diplomacy' between Jersualem and Cairo in January 1974, resulted in an agreement over disengagement of forces and paved the way for further peace negotiations.

Sadat proclaimed the war a glorious triumph, despite narrowly escaping another military defeat and despite the heavy cost in Egyptian lives (about 5500 killed, roughly double Israel's casualties). Even so, this was not hollow rhetoric: the Arab achievements during the first days of fighting had exploded the myth of Israeli invincibility;

the deadlock on the Arab-Israeli issue had been broken; the oil states clamoured to supply Egypt with financial and military aid; and diplomatic relations were soon re-established with Washington. Moreover, in the eyes of Arab leaders and the Egyptian public, Sadat, the so-called 'Hero of the Crossing' into Sinai, had been transformed from a political lightweight into a president of substance. The new legitimacy enabled him to distance himself further from Nasser and follow his own economic and political agenda.

INFITAH: OPENING THE DOOR

Renewed relations with the West after the October War made it possible for Sadat to introduce *infitah*, the 'open door' policy. Its key legislation, Law 43, passed in June 1974, offered incentives, guarantees and privileges to attract foreign investment, Western technology and Arab oil money to revitalise the private sector. It was hoped this would liberalise the market, reverse the suffocating centralisation of the Nasserist economy and pare down the serpentine bureaucracy that supported it.

Initially there were some promising signs. Foreign banks opened new branches in Cairo and the oil-producing states injected large sums into the Egyptian economy through aid and in property purchases. A construction boom in the battle-damaged canal cities created jobs and regenerated a long-suffering area, while the Suez Canal itself was cleared with Western help and reopened in June 1975, after exactly eight years of closure. When the government lifted restrictions on labour migration in 1974, 500,000 peasants and labourers, not to mention a sizeable number of skilled workers and professionals, emigrated to Saudi Arabia, Libya and the oil-rich Gulf states in search of employment and a better life. In five years, foreign remittances totalled $2bn, a sum matching Egypt's combined earnings from cotton exports, Suez Canal transit fees and tourism.

However, it soon became apparent that *infitah* had not pulled in the level of investment that Egypt needed with only a few dozen foreign enterprises registering under the new law by the end of 1976. Most had been put off by the prospect of more fighting with Israel in the absence of a definitive peace settlement. The oil states had vast new funds to invest, but had spent it mostly on real estate rather than productive activities, which contributed to inflation instead of generating jobs. Money had failed to trickle down to the masses but accrued among a small number of entrepreneurs and members of the upper classes who had been restored to some of their old wealth. They tended to flaunt their riches with luxury villas and flashy imported cars, splashing out on the foreign goods and foods on offer in the pricey Western-style boutiques springing up in urban centres. The gap between rich and poor was widening, and while a lucky few creamed the profits of a liberalised economy, most ordinary Egyptians began to feel 'unwelcome in the new consumer society', dazzled by the new electronic gadgets and mod-cons filling shop windows which they were unable to buy. The days of land distribution were over, and the poor now found they had to bear the burden of deteriorating public services, rising prices and high unemployment. On the other hand, highly educated people – the doctors, teachers and engineers on whom the country depended – were emigrating in ever greater numbers to the wealthy oil states, the US and Europe, creating a serious skills shortage at home.

Neither did *infitah* solve the problem of mounting foreign debt nor provide food for a population fast approaching forty million people. Where Egypt had for centuries been the breadbasket of the world, it now had to import more than half of its grain. High inflation had forced the government to put subsidies on basic consumer goods at huge expense to the treasury, which resorted to short-term loans to cover the costs. The International Monetary Fund recommended reducing the subsidies, a measure cautiously adopted by the regime in January 1977 on a selection of 'luxury' goods: butane gas, granulated sugar, beer, fine flour, macaroni and so on. The instant and violent reaction from the people rocked the regime. Riots broke out in Cairo, Alexandria and other provincial towns, shops and nightclubs were looted and burnt, eighty people were killed and eight hundred injured. Such scenes had not been seen since the riots of 1952, which was also the last time that the army had to be called in to restore order. The government quickly backtracked, restoring subsidies and increasing salaries and pensions, and to this day bread subsidies have remained almost sacrosanct in Egyptian financial policy, no matter the cost. Sadat blamed leftist agitators for the riots, but most knew that the country's woeful economic condition was the underlying cause. Most also recognised that it would not be relieved, that proper foreign investment would not come, until Egypt had peace with Israel.

A SEPARATE PEACE

Radical action was needed to break the latest impasse with Israel. On 9 November 1977, Sadat, the inventor of 'electric shock' politics, announced to parliament that he was 'prepared to go to the end of the world...to the Knesset itself' to secure a lasting peace. Ten days later, he astounded the world by flying to Jerusalem to deliver an eloquent and dignified speech before the Knesset, welcoming Israel to the Middle East, but calling for its withdrawal from occupied lands and the recognition of a Palestinian state. The historic event, broadcast across the globe, won him respect and admiration, not least from the majority of Egyptians, who had made sacrifices and suffered in five wars against Israel and now wanted an end to it all. Most Arab leaders, however, felt that Sadat was betraying their cause by seeking a separate peace.

The momentum of the Jerusalem visit carried over to the Camp David accords, signed on 17 September 1978 by Sadat and the Israeli prime minister, Menachem Begin in the presence of US president Jimmy Carter. The accords provided two 'frameworks' for a Middle East peace treaty, one to deal with Egypt, Israel and the evacuation of the Sinai, the other with the Palestine question. The terms of the latter agreement were vague at best and it was obvious that the distinction of the two issues provided a formula for Egypt to obtain a separate peace. Other Arab states hurried to condemn the treaty and offered Sadat $2bn in aid for Egypt if he refused to put his name to it. But he could not be dissuaded and the Treaty of Washington was signed on the White House lawn on 26 March 1979 ending the state of war between the two countries that had persisted since Israel's inception. Ambassadors were swapped the following year, and Israel evacuated

Sinai according to the agreement in March 1982.

The peace had an immediate and beneficial effect on Egypt's economy, largely helped by a damburst of US aid. From 1979, Egypt received between $1bn and $1.5bn in civilian aid from the US, almost as much as Israel, as well as plentiful military credit and technical know-how to revive its threadbare infrastructure; transport, communications and energy systems had been surviving on a skeleton basis since the economic crises of the mid-1960s.

But the treaty also alienated Egypt from the rest of the Arab world, which, with the exception of Sudan and Oman, instantly broke off trade and diplomatic relations. Expelled from the Arab League, Egypt went from being regional leader to pariah. This hurt public opinion and many thought Sadat had sold the country – and the Palestinians – short, particularly as the future of the other occupied territories became increasingly bleak.

POLITICAL LIBERALISATION AND THE RISE OF ISLAMIST OPPOSITION

When Sadat introduced *infitah* at the height of his popularity after the October 1973 War, he also sought to overhaul and liberalise the stifling political apparatus set up by Nasser. Censorship was relaxed and 'platforms' representing right, left and centre were introduced into the Arab Socialist Union. These embryonic political parties received full status in May 1977 with the dissolution of the ASU.

Far from being a true multi-party democracy, however, the new set-up was tightly managed from above and a host of restrictions made it virtually impossible for real opposition to form. Sadat guaranteed his primacy by taking control of the majority centre party, which he restructured as the National Democratic Party (NDP); it has remained Egypt's dominant political party ever since. He was ever vigilant to prevent the changes from undermining his authority, as illustrated by his lighting move to disband the newly reformed Wafd Party in 1978. Parties could not be constituted on a religious basis, but from the early years Sadat, the self-proclaimed 'pious president', had encouraged the resuscitation of Islamic organisations. He hoped this would please his donors in the religiously conservative Arab world, and also counter the activities of the 'atheist' left at home, which he regarded as his most dangerous opponent. Students loyal to the Nasserite left had rioted in 1972 and 1973, leading Sadat to nurture Islamic interest in universities to attract young people to movements apparently less hostile to his regime. Within a couple of years, radical Islamic organisations including the Muslim Brotherhood were not only dominating student unions but also flourishing in society at large. The public seemed to be rediscovering religion since the passing of the Nasser years, and changing social attitudes became increasingly evident. Television programmes began to censor 'offensive' scenes featuring kissing, drinking or adultery, and punctuated their broadcasts with calls to prayer. Islamic dress codes became more popular, with women adopting the *hijab* (veil) and men cultivating fuller beards. The Coptic Church also enjoyed a spiritual reinvigoration from 1971 under the dynamic leadership of Pope Shenouda III.

In this more devout atmosphere, it was hardly surprising that a militant Islamist underground was also gathering strength. With hindsight there had been warnings of the trouble that was to come: one radical group had carried out an armed attack on a military academy in 1974 with many casualties, and another had kidnapped and executed a government minister following the 'bread riots' of 1977. But Sadat felt allied to the general Islamic trend, and wrote these off as marginal and sporadic incidents.

The situation changed markedly after the Islamist rejection of the 1978 Camp David accords. Suddenly Sadat found that a resurgent Muslim Brotherhood and dozens of other radical splinter groups vehemently opposed him and his regime. The small-scale Islamic press that the president had encouraged went into overdrive in their attacks on the government, calling for a new state based solely on Islamic law and values. The 1979 Islamic revolution in Iran was held up by radicals as a model of what was possible; no wonder then that Sadat's generous welcome to the deposed shah was interpreted by them as deliberate provocation.

Amending the constitution to make sharia law the principal source of legislation was an attempt to assuage fundamentalist anger, but this in turn upset the increasingly vociferous Coptic community. Recurring clashes between Muslims and Copts culminated in bitter sectarian riots in Cairo in June 1981 that left at least ten dead and dozens injured.

The rising militancy was not only fuelled by Sadat's separate peace with Israel – though it hardly helped that Begin had started to pursue aggressive policies against Lebanon, Iraq and local Palestinians in full knowledge that Egypt would not react. It was fired also by deepening social inequalities and the broken promise that *infitah* represented; wealth had come to Egypt but it had stayed in the pockets of the few while millions still languished in abject poverty. And all the while it seemed that Sadat was more interested in the adulation of the West than caring for his own people. His rambling and increasingly erratic speeches revealed an isolated leader completely out of touch with the Egyptian people in whose name he claimed to speak and act.

As criticism of Sadat's regime mounted, the president became more intolerant and autocratic. Using his notorious new 'Law of Shame' to muzzle his detractors, he ordered the arrest of 1536 people in September 1981, including Muslim extremists, journalists, intellectuals, university professors, even feminists and the Coptic Pope Shenouda, who was banished to a monastery in the Wadi Natrun. The crackdown recalled the worst repressions of the past, destroying the remains of Sadat's liberal credentials and doing further damage to his fast-crumbling legitimacy. For one young army officer, Lieutenant Khalid Islambuli, the news of his brother's arrest was the last straw; there and then, he vowed to kill the president.

ASSASSINATION

For months Sadat had feared an attempt on his life, but when it came on 6 October 1981 during a military parade to commemorate the eighth anniversary of the October War, he, his guards and the country were taken completely by surprise. As dignitaries craned their necks to enjoy the colourful flypast, four soldiers jumped down from one of a file of processional trucks and rushed towards the grandstand spraying it with submachine-gun fire. Amid the screams and mayhem, Sadat slumped to the ground and the man leading the attack shouted, 'I am Khalid Islambuli, I have killed Pharaoh, and I do not fear death!' Sadat was dead before he reached hospital. Seven others were also killed.

Sadat's funeral took place on the bullet-marked parade ground where he had been assassinated. Three American presidents and the Israeli prime minister attended, but in Cairo the streets were empty. The contrast could not have been greater to the grief-stricken scenes at Nasser's funeral. The people were shocked and dismayed by the manner of Sadat's death, but largely indifferent to his departure. Militants hated him for making peace with Israel, but most Egyptians had a quite different grievance; they believed he had forgotten their plight and abandoned them.

Mubarak and contemporary Egypt

STRIKING A BALANCE

Sadat's vice president, Hosni Mubarak (b.1928), who was himself injured in the attack, assumed control and was officially sworn in as president on 14 October 1981 after a national referendum. Even before the formalities were complete, Mubarak had to face off a second challenge to the regime by the militant fundamentalist group, al-Jihad (also known as Egyptian Islamic Jihad), responsible for Sadat's murder. They believed the assassination would touch off an Islamic revolution and staged an armed uprising in Asyut as a catalyst to countrywide rebellion. The new president moved decisively to restore calm, imposing a state of emergency and sending in special forces to crush the revolt. In Asyut, eighty-seven were killed and hundreds were arrested, while in Cairo other members of al-Jihad were rounded up and thrown into prison.

It had the hallmarks of a savagely repressive new chapter in Egypt's history, but appearances were deceptive. The execution of Khalid Islambuli and four accomplices in April 1982 turned out to be exceptional. Mubarak sought conciliation in the name of stability. The rising tide of Islamism had engulfed his predecessor, and Mubarak saw the best defence against a similar fate was to extend a placatory hand not

Hosni Mubarak, Egypt's president since 1981

only to the Islamists but to the opposition in general. Many of Sadat's more prominent political prisoners were released and some were even received as guests at the presidential palace. Censorship was relaxed and 1984 saw the freest parliamentary elections since the revolution, though they were still some degree short of being fully fair and open by international standards. Even the Muslim Brotherhood was allowed to field candidates on the lists of the New Wafd Party, an attempt to divide the Islamist movement between 'moderates' content to work peaceably within the formal political system, and 'radicals' who considered violence the necessary means to the same end. Mubarak hoped that politically empowered moderates might be able to persuade militant groups to reject violence and operate within the law.

The more permissive climate was welcomed in light of the last confused and frenetic years of Sadat's rule, and Mubarak's businesslike, no-nonsense style contrasted favourably with the flamboyant excesses of his predecessor. Quiet dependability and hard work had propelled him through the ranks of the Egyptian Air Force until he had become its commander-in-chief in 1972. Three years later he was promoted to vice president, performing loyally, if somewhat unmemorably, at Sadat's side. Constitutional machinery rather than personal charisma carried him over the last hurdle to the presidency.

For a time, his low-key leadership was a balm to the population, a restorative after the high-adrenaline 'electric shock' politics of Sadat and the relentless bravura of Nasser. He gradually expanded the political freedoms of the opposition. He continued the economic liberalisation of *infitah* without slashing the subsidies on basic goods relied on by the poor. On the international stage he quietly mended relations with the Soviet Union and the Arab world, winning back the confidence of his neighbours one by one until Egypt regained full membership of the Arab League in 1989. This he managed to achieve while reaffirming peace with Israel, which ensured good relations with the US and large amounts of American aid.

He deliberately avoided the kind of grand gestures that had brought triumph and calamity to the country in the past. But while Nasser had his Suez and Sadat the October War, Mubarak missed – and as yet, still misses – the great accomplishment to inspire his people and win true legitimacy. As a result, he has had to tread a fine line between the military, Islamists, secularists, vested interests within his own party and public opinion at large, using a combination of compromise, consensus and a heavy hand to keep his authority. Only once, briefly, has there been speculation that Mubarak had a serious rival to the leadership, after 17,000 conscripts of the Central Security Forces rioted in February 1986 over poor wages and living conditions, setting fire to hotels, cars and nightclubs in the tourist areas around the pyramids at Giza. The ease with which Abu Ghazala, field marshal and defence minister, quelled the revolt with the army and delivered the government from a sticky situation fed rumours that he was strong enough to take over the presidency, though he was at pains not to undercut Mubarak's authority. Abu Ghazala was removed from office in 1989.

By such means, Mubarak has defied those who regarded him as a 'caretaker president', to emerge as Egypt's longest-serving ruler since Muhammad Ali and one of the longest-serving leaders in the contemporary Arab world. However, the passing of the years has not seen the kind of political and economic reform that was once expected. In fact, critics claim the regime is as entrenched, repressive and isolated as it ever has been since 1952.

SOCIETY UNDER PRESSURE

After his early emphasis on stability and continuity, Mubarak has been reluctant to make radical changes to Sadat's policies. Reform has been slow, infuriatingly so for many Egyptians, despite the country's considerable economic and social problems.

The 1980s continued to be a period of serious economic difficulty characterised by enormous budget deficits, a bloated and inefficient public sector, rampant corruption and rapidly growing foreign debt. The International Monetary Fund demanded reforms in return for its financial aid, such as reducing imports and subsidies, and making devaluations to the currency. For the most part, Mubarak found such measures difficult to implement because of the hardship and resentment they would cause. By the end of the decade, foreign debt had topped $53bn and Egypt was in serious danger of defaulting on its interest repayments and suffering the kind of indignities Khedive Ismail underwent at the hands of his creditors more than a century before.

However, Mubarak's response to Iraq's invasion of Kuwait in August 1990 was well rewarded by the West. He quickly persuaded several Arab states to join the US-led coalition to liberate Kuwait, provided military bases and airspace rights and sent 36,000 Egyptian soldiers into battle, acts above anything else that gave the operation legitimacy in the Arab world. Consequently a substantial amount of Egypt's existing debt was cancelled, while US foreign aid was upped to around $2bn a year. The implementation of IMF reforms in 1991 and 1993, which included initiating privatisation schemes for public firms, led to further debt reductions.

Egypt enjoyed a minor economic recovery in the late 1990s, though the flow of privatisations and reforms dried up after 2000 and national income still depends heavily on tourism, oil and gas production, revenues from the Suez Canal (also closely linked to the oil industry) and remittances from workers abroad, all areas which are vulnerable to events outside the government's control. In addition, economic growth has to be set against Egypt's population of well over seventy

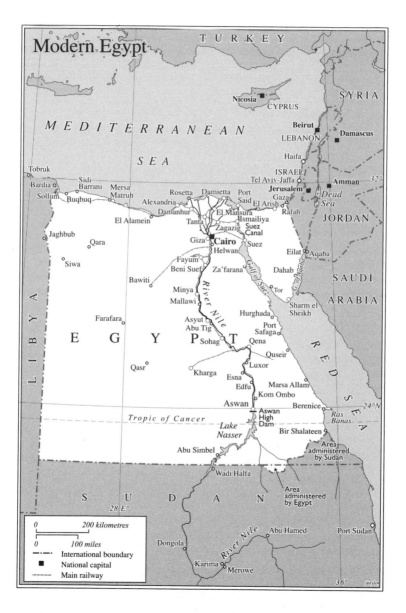

Modern Egypt

TURKEY

SYRIA

Nicosia
CYPRUS

MEDITERRANEAN

Beirut
LEBANON   Damascus

SEA   Haifa

Tobruk   ISRAEL
                                          Tel Aviv-Jaffa   32°
Sidi   Jerusalem   Amman
Bardia   Barrani   Mersa   Rosetta Damietta Port   Gaza   Dead
Sollum   Buqbuq   Matruh   Alexandria   Said El Arish   Sea
                          Damanhur   El Mansura Rafah   JORDAN
El Alamein   Tanta   Zagazig Ismailiya
                          Giza Cairo Suez Canal
Jaghbub   Helwan   Suez   Eilat Aqaba
        Qara   Fayum   Za'farana   Dahab
                  Beni Suef
Siwa   Bawiti   Minya   Tor   SAUDI
                          Mallawi   Sharm el   ARABIA
        Farafara   Hurghada   Sheikh
                          Asyut
        E   G   Y   P   T   Abu Tig   Port
                          Sohag   Safaga
                                          Qena
                  Qasr   Quseir
                          Kharga   Esna   Luxor
                                   Edfu   Marsa Allam
                                   Kom Ombo
                          Aswan   Berenice   24°N
Tropic of Cancer   Aswan   Ras
                  Lake   High   Banas
                  Nasser Dam   Bir Shalateen
                          Abu Simbel   Area
                                          administered
                                          by Sudan
                          Wadi Halfa
                                          Area
        S   U   D   A   N   administered
              28°E   by Egypt

0   200 kilometres   Abu Hamed   Port Sudan
0   100 miles   Dongola   River Nile
—·—· International boundary
■   National capital   Karima Merowe
—+— Main railway   36°

million people, a quarter of the Arab world, which is growing by a million people every eight months. While Egypt's GDP is second only to Saudi Arabia's among Arab countries, per capita GNP has stuck at around $1500 a year, and thirteen million Egyptians live below the poverty line. A third of Egyptians are under the age of fifteen, and of the rest, 40 per cent are illiterate. At the other end of the spectrum, 800,000 new graduates enter the job market every year, but most fail to find work and end up comprising 90 per cent of the country's 10 per cent unemployed.

Most analysts agree that a thorough overhaul of the economy cannot be carried out without deep and lasting political reform. Given the choice of opening up the system and facing the consequences, the regime has tended to tread the road of political stasis and financial stagnation. In the meantime, it has groped around for a miracle cure to the economic malaise – like Nasser's high dam at Aswan – and came up in 1997 with the immense 'New Valley scheme', a twenty-year project to create a second Nile Valley in the Western Desert. By siphoning off water from Lake Nasser along a new canal, it is hoped that forty-nine million feddans of desert land will be made good for industry, mining and agriculture, and relieve the pressures on the Nile Valley and Delta, one of the most densely populated areas in the world. Whether the dream will be realised remains to be seen.

Mubarak's other landmark project was the Bibliotheca Alexandrina, a new library to rival and replace its famous Ptolemaic forbear as a world-class centre of scholarship and learning in contemporary Egypt. The $220 million building, designed as a tilting disc rising from the Alexandria seashore, was opened by the president's half-Welsh wife, Suzanne, in October 2002. No mere book depository, it includes three museums, exhibition galleries, a planetarium, research centre, six specialist libraries in addition to the main library, an enormous seven-tiered main reading hall seating two-thousand readers, and storage space for at least eight million volumes. If it is to achieve its aims of compiling the largest collection of ancient manuscripts in the world as well as to form 'a collection of all achievements of the human mind from all civilisation at all times', it will require major new investment to meet its mammoth acquisitions programme. It will also need to reconcile the needs of its collection with Egypt's censorship laws, which under normal circumstances would mean that thousands of titles would be missing from its shelves.

The fact that Mubarak has done little to curtail the powers of the censors, promote freedom of expression and embrace fully political liberalisation, has been a source of continuing disappointment and frustration to his people. The current skewed electoral system precludes genuine democracy, while emergency measures and censorship laws are routinely invoked to smother the opposition. In 1995, Amnesty International described Egyptian parliamentary elections as 'fraudulent, undemocratic, and grossly unfair'. Though some improvements have since been made, it is never in doubt that the ruling National Democratic Party will win a huge majority and never in doubt that Mubarak will prevail as president with a suspiciously high share of the vote. Almost as certain is the prolongation of the state of emergency which has been regularly extended since Sadat's death, conferring sweeping powers such as arbitrary arrest, detention without trial, and use of military courts for civilian defendants. Human rights organisations, whose activities are severely restricted in Egypt, have reported the criminalisation of political dissent, systematic discrimination against women, suppression of non-violent demonstrations and routine torture of detainees.

The Battle with Islamism

No one has exploited public discontent better than the Islamist groups, and chief among them is the Muslim Brotherhood, now the most powerful and effective opposition to the government despite being officially banned.

Following Sadat's murder in 1981, the Muslim Brotherhood was forced to distance itself from militants and adopt a more moderate line. It renounced violence and in return was offered new opportunities to extend its political influence and religious infrastructure. By this strategy, the government hoped not only to bring the entire Islamist movement inside the political system which it dominated, but also to boost its own Islamic credentials. The Brothers made quick progress, capturing the high-ground in moral and cultural debates and winning support in areas whose elections were outside direct government control – student unions and professional guilds, including those for doctors, dentists, engineers, pharmacists and finally lawyers too. In the 1987 parliamentary elections they took sixty seats in coalition with the Socialist Labour Party, a measure of their enormous informal power and backing by the devout and educated middle classes.

For a while, the militants kept a low profile. Some that had been arrested in the 1981 clampdown and released in 1984 began to reform secretly as Jamaa Islamiya ('Islamic Group'), under the tutelage of the blind Sheik Umar Abd al-Rahman, the mufti of Sadat's assassins. Others, like the physician Ayman al-Zawahiri, leader of al-Jihad, were hustled out of the country and urged to join the jihad in Afghanistan against the Soviets. Of course, the government hoped that they would never be seen again. Instead, the USSR collapsed and the militants returned battle-hardened and fanatical, as convinced of their invincibility as of the justness of their cause.

The two extremist groups, Jamaa Islamiya and al-Jihad, unleashed a brutal terror offensive against the Mubarak regime between 1992 and 1997. Jamaa Islamiya had been fomenting unrest and provoking attacks against Copts in Upper Egypt since the late 1980s, but the return of the Afghanistan veterans in 1992 encouraged them to magnify their campaign. The new era of violence – characterised by assassinations of prominent personalities, massacres of tourists and the creation of no-go city areas under Islamist control – began with the murder of the liberal writer Faraq Fuda by Jamaa Islamiya on 8 June 1992. He had been a tireless and outspoken critic of Islamic fundamentalism and had ridiculed such fanatical decrees as this: 'The Cairo Tower is against religion and Islamic sharia law. It must be destroyed as its shape and construction amid the greenery could excite Egyptian women.' His death was designed to inculcate terror in anyone tempted to speak out. The attack on secularism continued with an attempt on the great novelist Naguib Mahfuz, the 'Egyptian Dickens' and the first Arab to win the Nobel Prize for Literature (1988), who narrowly escaped death after he was stabbed in the neck by a Jamaa member. Then an eminent university professor, Dr Nasr Abu Zaid, was declared an apostate by Islamist judges for his literary analyses of the Koran and forced to divorce his wife, on the grounds that an apostate could not remain married to a Muslim woman. The couple fled to the Netherlands after repeated death threats.

Mubarak's early distinction between Islamist moderates and radicals had not weakened the Islamist movement. On the contrary, some 'moderates' within the legal system worked in tandem with extremists, identifying potential enemies for them to attack and then defending them in the courts if charged, although in public they claimed to deplore such violence. Islamists also had recall to extensive charitable projects and welfare institutions which acted as a popular counterweight to the increasingly outrageous atrocities. After the Cairo earthquake of October 1992, for example, the Muslim Brotherhood were immediately on the scene to provide tents to the fifty thousand people left homeless by the disaster, a conspicuous act which contrasted favourably with the incompetence of the state's rescue effort. But charitable schemes in Imbaba, an impoverished district of Cairo, were gradually taken over by Jamaa Islamiya until it had complete control of the local infrastructure. It brazenly declared the area an independent Islamic Republic in November 1992; the following month fourteen thousand soldiers stormed the area and removed five thousand 'troublemakers'. Vast sums of public money were injected into the community, effectively winning it back to the state.

The struggle continued to claim hundreds of lives, with daring attacks against state security targets and personnel, including at least six assassination attempts on Mubarak himself, the most dramatic being in Addis Ababa in June 1995. Jamaa Islamiya launched a simultaneous offensive against tourists during the summer of 1992, justified in a manner by Sheik Umar Abd al-Rahman's assertion that the industry was underpinned by alcohol and debauchery and was therefore forbidden by religion. Sporadic attacks on trains, cruise boats, tour buses, hotels and other targets continued for several years and culminated in the devastating Luxor massacre of 17 November 1997 in which fifty-eight foreign tourists and four Egyptians were gunned down on the steps of Queen Hatshepsut's temple. The atrocity did enormous damage to Egypt's image abroad and the tourism industry on which at least one in five Egyptians depended.

Thankfully, the massacre was also the dying gasp of Jamaa, which by 1996 had been left broken and exhausted by the government's ruthless zero-tolerance policy against extremism. Its best fighters had been killed or executed, its leader Sheik Abd al-Rahman was serving multiple life-sentences in the US for his part in the 1993 World Trade Center bombing, and the group's increasingly desperate savagery had lost them the sympathy of the Arab street. Jamaa called a formal cease-fire in 1999, but the massacre itself was its last major violent act in Egypt.

AL-QAEDA AND SEPTEMBER 11: THE EGYPTIAN ANGLE

Having been defeated at home, some of the surviving Egyptian militant Islamists took the battle to a new, global dimension. Many Egyptians were respected in fundamentalist circles as the 'thinkers and the brains' behind Islamism, none more so than the leader of al-Jihad, Ayman al-Zawahiri, who had become radicalised after being tortured in Mubarak's prisons. Once back in Afghanistan, Zawahiri joined forces with the Saudi millionaire Osama bin Laden, soon becoming his right-hand man and the principal strategist and ideologue of bin Laden's organisation, al-Qaeda, ('the Base'), a loose affiliation of militant groups and cells that included many Egyptian al-Jihad members.

In February 1998, Zawahiri and bin Laden jointly announced the foundation of the International Islamic Front against Jews and Crusaders, the charter of which claimed that 'every Muslim who is capable of doing so has the personal duty to kill Americans and their allies, whether civilians or military personnel, in every country where this is possible'. The bombing of US embassies in Kenya and Tanzania later that year heralded a new type of media-conscious and 'spectacular' global terrorism which gave bin Laden instant worldwide exposure.

The attacks of 11 September 2001 brought the flaws of Egypt's problematic relationship with the US into the harsh light. Public sentiment was caught between genuine shock, grief and sympathy, and the nagging belief that the attacks were retribution for unpopular American foreign policy in the Middle East. Passions were already running high since the outbreak of the second Palestinian 'al-Aqsa' *intifada* a year earlier, especially in light of Israel's extreme tactics to contain it. In the moral and emotional confusion following the September 11 attacks, rumours quickly took root that it was a Jewish conspiracy orchestrated by Mossad, the Israeli secret service, to boost sympathy for Israel and turn world opinion against Arabs and Muslims. Even as evidence emerged of al-Qaeda's involvement, it was difficult for many Egyptians to accept the part played by their compatriots — men like Zawahiri, as well as the Egyptian ex-policeman Muhammad Atef, thought to be al-Qaeda's chief of military operations, and Muhammad Atta, the son of a Cairo lawyer who flew the first plane into the World Trade Center.

A straw poll conducted by a Cairo newspaper a year after the attacks found that more than half of respondents felt that the US 'deserved it' and 39 per cent believed Mossad to be responsible, presumably not the same people as the 28 per cent who expressed admiration for the perpetrators. In part, these attitudes are the latest expression of the old tension between westernisation and Islamic tradition that has existed in Egypt since Napoleon — a tension which has become more acute in recent years as contemporary Egyptians wrestle with the desire to participate in globalised culture and the free market while remaining 'true' to the values of Islam.

WAR ON TERROR

Egypt's position as a key ally of the US in the Arab world has continued to be tested by President George W. Bush's 'War on Terror' and further complicated by Israel's attempts to link this global war to its own struggle with the Palestinians. As violence reached gruesome new heights in the occupied territories in April 2002, tens of thousands of Egyptians took to the streets in countrywide protests against Israel, the US, and Mubarak's passive leadership, defying Egyptian emergency laws that prohibit demonstrations. A rattled government, fearing that the restive crowds could easily turn on it, tried to ride the wave of anger in a show of solidarity, filling state television output with images of Palestinian carnage and allowing religious leaders airtime to extol the sanctity and martyrdom of suicide bombers. Many have questioned the wisdom of rekindling the militancy most of the 1990s were spent trying to subdue.

Little wonder then that, when faced with the invasion of Iraq in 2003, Mubarak could not risk inflaming public opinion further. Despite heavy pressure from the US to repeat his 1991 Gulf War performance when he contributed the third largest force to the US-led coalition, Mubarak resolutely refused to provide assistance and openly criticised the whole operation, warning the White House that the invasion and occupation would only create 'a hundred bin Ladens'. In retaliation, Bush's call to 'expand democracy' in the 2005 inaugural speech for his second term was not just aimed at the so-called 'axis of evil', but also served as a reminder to ageing authoritarian regimes such as Mubarak's that US support is not unconditional. Such comments, compounded with mounting domestic pressure for electoral reform, have more or less forced Mubarak to make concessions, most notably a change in the constitution which allowed for the country's first ever multiple-candidate presidential elections in September 2005, albeit with the kind of restrictions that made – and will make – it extremely difficult for him to lose. The parliamentary elections contested a month later also saw unprecedented freedoms extended to opposition groups during campaigning and new levels of transparency during the vote. Of course, there were no surprises that the NDP won comfortably, but significant gains were made by the Muslim Brotherhood (its members standing as independents rather than for the outlawed party by name), revealing another complication – that 'expanding democracy' in Egypt would probably give an election victory to Islamists.

On the other hand, the War on Terror has allowed the Egyptian government to renew its crackdown against political opponents in the name of its own fight against militant Islamist terrorists. To the dismay of human rights organisations, the kind of oppressive measures that Egypt has long used and long been upbraided for by the West (for example, summary trials, indefinite internment and guilt by association) have become the very model of how to combat terrorism in the wake of September 11. Torture is apparently beyond the pale for most Western governments – within their own borders at least. Reports have emerged of a practice known as 'extraordinary rendition' whereby Western secret services, especially the CIA, forcibly deliver terror suspects without extradition proceedings to countries such as Egypt, in full knowledge that they are likely to be tortured there for information or confessions.

For the time being therefore, Bush and Mubarak have a common enemy in the Islamist terrorist, and the US aid that props up the regime will continue to pour in. They also have a joint interest in finding a solution to the Arab-Israeli conflict, the kernel of hate at the heart of so much extremist militancy, and, in his favour, Mubarak has been a constant force for peace in the Middle East, personally intervening on many occasions to host negotiations between Palestinians and Israelis. However, the bombings of tourist resorts in Sinai, at Taba and Ras Shitan in October 2004, Sharm el-Sheikh in July 2005 (where Mahmud Abbas, the new president of the Palestinian Authority following the death of Yasser Arafat, shook hands with Ariel Sharon to declare a truce the February before), and Dahab in April 2006 seem to have been primarily aimed at national holidaymakers and the economically crucial tourism industry, attacks on the Egyptian state rather than the blind anti-Western rage that al-Qaeda has made its hallmark. It is precisely Mubarak's willingness to compromise, and his alliance with the US in the War on Terror, however complex and conditioned, that may have contributed to this wave of domestic terrorist atrocities.

The Successor

Having won 88.6 per cent of the vote in the 2005 presidential elections, Mubarak began his fifth successive six-year term aged seventy-seven, nine years older than the life expectancy for the average Egyptian male. A sense of his mortality was never more apparent than after his collapse while addressing parliament two years earlier, which at the time sparked a frenzy of rumours about his health and what would happen if it deteriorated. He made a full recovery, but speculation surrounding the identity of his successor has only grown more clamorous, in no small part encouraged by Mubarak's persistent refusal to appoint a vice president.

Much comment has been made about the meteoric rise of the president's younger son, Gamal, who came to sudden political prominence in 2002 when he was made head of the ruling party's policy-making committee at his father's behest. Gamal, a former investment banker in his early forties, comes with a reputation as a playboy, but moves among Egypt's small and hugely wealthy financial community, which, like him, understands the need for economic reform – in contrast to the older generation of military retainers and party officials clustered around his father. A cabinet reshuffle in the summer of 2004, which saw a number of young modernisers, basically Gamal's friends and associates, replace old figures of the ruling class was interpreted as another sign that Mubarak was preparing the ground for his son's succession.

There is another player in the picture. Lieutenant General Umar Sulayman, the powerful chief of intelligence, emerged from the inscrutable shadows of his ministry into clear public view at roughly the same time as Gamal's ascent. A military man of the old school, and thus a member of Egypt's highest caste, he represents order and stability, cautious reform but in the main, the continuation of the regime.

The two men embody two different futures for Egypt, neither of which threatens to overturn the existing political order. In the absence of a bold pronouncement from Mubarak about a successor, the constitution dictates that parliament must choose a president when there is no vice president. The circumstances surrounding Mubarak's demise may hold the key: a sudden death or a flare-up in the region will doubtless favour the accession of a strong army man. In less stressful situations, Gamal may prevail.

Taking the broad view, however, the minutiae of twenty-first century politics is swallowed up by the vastness of the Egyptian experience. Cairo is today the cultural, intellectual and political capital of the Arab world, just as Memphis, Thebes and Alexandria were the centres of their worlds before. In the course of five thousand years of statehood, dynasties and rulers have come and gone, but Egypt has always stood at the crossroads of three continents and the centre of the world, casting its shadow far beyond the green curves of the Nile.

Notes

Rulers of Egypt

PREDYNASTIC PERIOD	*c.5500–3000* BC
Badarian	*c.5500–4000* BC
Naqada I (Amratian)	*c.4000–3500* BC
Naqada II (Gerzean)	*c.3500–3200* BC

Naqada III ('Dynasty 0')	*c.3200–3000* BC
Iry-Hor	
Ka	
'King Scorpion'	

EARLY DYNASTIC PERIOD	*c.3000–2686* BC
1st Dynasty	*c.3000–2890* BC
(Narmer)	
Aha	
Djer	
Djet	
Den	
Mereneith	
Anedjib	
Semerkhet	
Qaa	

2nd Dynasty	*c.2890–2686* BC
Hetepsekhemwy	
Raneb	
Nynetjer	
Weneg	
Sened	
Peribsen	
Khasekhemwy	

OLD KINGDOM	c.2686–2160 BC
3rd Dynasty	**c.2686–2613 BC**
Nebka	c.2686–2667 BC
Djoser	c.2667–2648 BC
Sekhemkhet	c.2648–2640 BC
Khaba	c.2640–2637 BC
Huni	c.2637–2613 BC
4th Dynasty	**c.2613–2494 BC**
Sneferu	c.2613–2589 BC
Khufu (Cheops)	c.2589–2566 BC
Djedefra	c.2566–2558 BC
Khafra (Chephren)	c.2558–2532 BC
Menkaura (Mycerinus)	c.2532–2503 BC
Shepseskaf	c.2503–2498 BC
5th Dynasty	**c.2494–2345 BC**
Userkaf	c.2494–2487 BC
Sahura	c.2487–2475 BC
Neferirkara	c.2475–2455 BC
Shepseskara	c.2455–2448 BC
Raneferef	c.2448–2445 BC
Nyuserra	c.2445–2421 BC
Menkauhor	c.2421–2414 BC
Djedkara	c.2414–2375 BC
Unas	c.2375–2345 BC
6th Dynasty	**c.2345–2181 BC**
Teti	c.2345–2181 BC
Userkara	c.2323–2321 BC
Pepy I	c.2321–2287 BC
Merenra	c.2287–2278 BC
Pepy II	c.2278–2184 BC
Merenra II	c.2184 BC
Nitiqret	c.2184–2181 BC

7th Dynasty
According to tradition, 70 kings in 70 days, but there is no archaeological evidence for these kings.

8th Dynasty   **c.2181–2160 BC**
At least 25 ephemeral kings.

FIRST INTERMEDIATE PERIOD c.2160–2055 BC
9th & 10th Dynasties c.2160–2025 BC
(Herakleopolis) included:
Khety I
Khety II
Khety III
Merykara

11th Dynasty (Thebes) c.2125–2055 BC
(Mentuhotep I)
Intef I c.2125–2112 BC
Intef II c.2112–2063 BC
Intef III c.2063–2055 BC

MIDDLE KINGDOM c.2055–1650 BC
11th Dynasty c.2055–1985 BC
(Egypt reunified)
Mentuhotep II c.2055–2004 BC
Mentuhotep III c.2004–1992 BC
Mentuhotep IV c.1992–1985 BC

12th Dynasty c.1985–1773 BC
Amenemhat I c.1985–1956 BC
Senusret I c.1956–1911 BC
Amenemhat II c.1911–1877 BC
Senusret II c.1877–1870 BC
Senusret III c.1870–1831 BC
Amenemhat III c.1831–1786 BC
Amenemhat IV c.1786–1777 BC
Sobeknefru c.1777–1773 BC

13th Dynasty c.1773–after 1650 BC
At least 70 kings, of whom probably only the earlier ones ruled the whole country. Some may have ruled contemporaneously.

14th Dynasty c.1773–1650 BC
Minor rulers based in the Delta, probably ruling at the same time as the 13th or 15th Dynasties.

SECOND INTERMEDIATE PERIOD	*c.*1650–1550 BC
15th Dynasty (Hyksos)	***c.1650–1550 BC***

included:
Sekerher (Salitis)
Khyan
Apepi   *c.*1555 BC
Khamudi

16th Dynasty	***c.1650–1580 BC***

Minor kings ruling at the same time as the 15th Dynasty.

17th Dynasty (Thebes)	***c.1580–1550 BC***

included:
Seqenenra Tao II   *c.*1560 BC
Kamose   *c.*1555–1550 BC

NEW KINGDOM	*c.*1550–1069 BC
18th Dynasty	***c.1550–1295 BC***
Ahmose	*c.*1550–1525 BC
Amenhotep I	*c.*1525–1504 BC
Thutmose I	*c.*1504–1492 BC
Thutmose II	*c.*1492–1479 BC
Thutmose III	*c.*1479–1425 BC
Hatshepsut	*c.*1473–1458 BC
Amenhotep II	*c.*1427–1400 BC
Thutmose IV	*c.*1400–1390 BC
Amenhotep III	*c.*1390–1352 BC
Amenhotep IV/Akhenaten	*c.*1352–1336 BC
Smenkhkara	*c.*1338–1336 BC
Tutankhamun	*c.*1336–1327 BC
Ay	*c.*1327–1323 BC
Horemheb	*c.*1323–1295 BC

19th Dynasty	***c.1295–1186 BC***
Rameses I	*c.*1295–1294 BC
Sety I	*c.*1294–1279 BC
Rameses II	*c.*1279–1213 BC
Merenptah	*c.*1213–1203 BC
Amenmessu	*c.*1203–1200 BC
Sety II	*c.*1200–1194 BC
Saptah	*c.*1194–1188 BC
Tausret	*c.*1188–1186 BC

20th Dynasty	***c.1186–1069 BC***

Sethnakht	*c.*1186–1184 BC
Rameses III	*c.*1184–1153 BC
Rameses IV	*c.*1153–1147 BC
Rameses V	*c.*1147–1143 BC
Rameses VI	*c.*1143–1136 BC
Rameses VII	*c.*1136–1129 BC
Rameses VIII	*c.*1129–1126 BC
Rameses IX	*c.*1126–1108 BC
Rameses X	*c.*1108–1099 BC
Rameses XI	*c.*1099–1069 BC

THIRD INTERMEDIATE PERIOD	*c.*1069–664 BC
21st Dynasty (Tanis)	**c.1069–945 BC**
Smendes	*c.*1069–1043 BC
Amenemnisu	*c.*1043–1039 BC
Psusennes I	*c.*1039–991 BC
Amenemope	*c.*993–984 BC
Osorkon the Elder	*c.*984–978 BC
Siamun	*c.*978–959 BC
Psusennes II	*c.*959–945 BC

22nd Dynasty (Bubastis/Libyan)	**c.945–715 BC**
Sheshonq I	*c.*945–924 BC
Osorkon I	*c.*924–889 BC
Sheshonq II	*c.*890 BC
Takelot I	*c.*889–874 BC
Osorkon II	*c.*874–850 BC
Takelot II	*c.*850–825 BC
Sheshonq III	*c.*825–773 BC
Pimay	*c.*773–767 BC
Sheshonq V	*c.*767–730 BC
Osorkon IV	*c.*730–715 BC

23rd Dynasty	**c.818–715 BC**

Rulers based at various regional centres such as Leontopolis, Herakleopolis Magna, Hermopolis Magna and Tanis including:

Pedubastis I	*c.*818–793 BC
Sheshonq IV	*c.*780 BC
Osorkon III	*c.*777–749 BC
Takelot III	

24th Dyansty	**c.727–715 BC**
Tefnakht	*c.*727–720 BC
Bakenrenef (Bocchoris)	*c.*720–715 BC

25th Dynasty (Nubian/Kushite)	***c.747–656*** BC
Piy	*c.*747–716 BC
Shabaqo	*c.*716–702 BC
Shabitqo	*c.*702–690 BC
Taharqo	*c.*690–664 BC
Tanutamani	664–656 BC

LATE PERIOD	664–332 BC
26th Dynasty (Sais)	***664–525*** BC
[Nekau I (Necho)	672–664 BC]
Psamtek I	664–610 BC
Nekau II	610–595 BC
Psamtek II	595–589 BC
Apries (Wahibre)	589–570 BC
Ahmose II	570–526 BC
Psamtek III	526–525 BC

27th Dynasty (1st Persian Period)	***525–404*** BC
Cambyses	525–522 BC
Darius I	522–486 BC
Xerxes I	486–465 BC
Artaxerxes I	465–424 BC
Darius II	424–405 BC
Artaxerxes II	405–359 BC

28th Dynasty	***404–399*** BC
Amyrtaios (Amenirdis)	404–399 BC

29th Dynasty	***399–380*** BC
Nepherites I (Nefaarud)	399–393 BC
Psammuthis	393 BC
Hakor	393–380 BC
Nepherites II	*c.*380 BC

30th Dynasty	***380–343*** BC
Nectanebo I (Nakhtnebef)	380–362 BC
Teos (Djedher)	362–360 BC
Nectanebo II (Nakhthorhebyt)	360–343 BC

31st Dynasty (2nd Persian Period)	***343–332*** BC
Artaxerxes III Ochus	343–338 BC
Arses	338–336 BC
Darius III Codoman	336–332 BC

PTOLEMAIC PERIOD	332–30 BC
Macedonian Dynasty	*332–305 BC*
Alexander the Great	332–323 BC
Philip Arrhidaeus	323–317 BC
Alexander IV (nominally 310–305 BC)	317–305 BC
Ptolemaic Dynasty	*305–30 BC*
Ptolemy I Soter I	305–285 BC
Ptolemy II Philadelphus	285–246 BC
Ptolemy III Euergetes I	246–221 BC
Ptolemy IV Philopator	221–205 BC
Ptolemy V Epiphanes	205–180 BC
Ptolemy VI Philometor	180–145 BC
Ptolemy VII Neos Philopator	145 BC
Ptolemy VIII Euergetes II	170–116 BC
Ptolemy IX Soter II	116–107 BC
Ptolemy X Alexander I	107–88 BC
Ptolemy IX Soter II (2nd reign)	88–80 BC
Ptolemy XI Alexander II	80 BC
Ptolemy XII Neos Dionysos (Auletes)	80–51 BC
Cleopatra VII Philopator	51–30 BC
Ptolemy XIII	51–47 BC
Ptolemy XIV	47–44 BC
Ptolemy XV Caesarion	44–30 BC

ROMAN PERIOD	30 BC – 395 AD
Augustus (formerly Octavian)	30 BC – 14 AD
Tiberius	AD 14–37
Gaius (Caligula)	37–41
Claudius	41–54
Nero	54–68
Galba	68–69
Otho	69
Vespasian	69–79
Titus	79–81
Domitian	81–96
Nerva	96–98
Trajan	98–117
Hadrian	117–138
Antoninus Pius	138–161
Marcus Aurelius	161–180
Lucius Verus	161–169
Commodus	180–192

Zeno	474–491
Anastasius	491–518
Justin I	518–527
Justinian I	527–565
Justin II	565–578
Tiberius II Constantine	578–582
Maurice	582–602
Phocas	602–610
Heraclius	610–641
Heraclius Constantine	641
Heraclonas	641
Constans II	641–642

ARAB PERIOD	642–1250
Orthodox Caliphs	***642–661***
Umar	642–644
Uthman	644–656
Ali	656–661

Umayyad Caliphs	***661–750***
Muawiya I	661–680
Yazid I	680–683
Muawiya II	683–684
Marwan I	684–685
Abd al-Malik	685–705
Al-Walid	705–715
Sulayman	715–717
Umar (II)	717–720
Yazid II	720–724
Hisham	724–743
Al-Walid II	743–744
Yazid III	744
Ibrahim	744
Marwan II	744–750

Abbasid Caliphs	***750–868***
Al-Saffah	750–754
Al-Mansur	754–775
Al-Mahdi	775–785
Al-Hadi	785–786
Harun al-Rashid	786–809
Al-Amin	809–813
Al-Mamun	813–833
Al-Mutasim	833–842

Al-Wathiq	842–847
Al-Mutawakkil	847–861
Al-Muntasir	861–862
Al-Mustain	862–866
Al-Mutazz	866–868
Tulunids	***868–905***
Ahmad Ibn Tulun	868–884
Khumarawayh	884–896
Jaysh	896
Harun	896–904
Shayban	904–905
Abbasid Caliphs (2nd Period)	***905–935***
Al-Muktafi	905–908
Al-Muktadir	908–932
Al-Qahir	932–934
Al-Radi	934–935
Ikhshidids	***935–969***
Muhammad Ibn Tughj	935–946
Unujur	946–961
Ali	961–966
Abul Misk Kafur	966–968
Ahmad	968–969
Fatimid Caliphs	***969–1171***
Al-Muizz	969–975
Al-Aziz	975–996
Al-Hakim	996–1021
Al-Zahir	1021–1036
Al-Mustansir	1036–1094
Al-Mustali	1094–1101
Al-Amir	1101–1130
Al-Hafiz (proclaimed caliph 1131)	1130–1149
Al-Zafir	1149–1154
Al-Faiz	1154–1160
Al-Adid	1160–1171
Ayyubids	***1171–1250***
Salah al-Din (Saladin)	1171–1193
Al-Aziz	1193–1198
Al-Mansur	1198–1200
Al-Adil (Safadin)	1200–1218

Al-Kamil	1218–1238
Al-Adil II	1238–1240
Al-Salih Ayyub	1240–1249
Turan Shah	1249–1250

MAMLUK PERIOD	1250–1517
Bahri line	***1250–1382***
Shajar al-Durr	1250
Aybak	1250
Al-Ashraf (nominal Ayyubid sultan)	1250–1254
Aybak (2nd reign)	1254–1257
Ali I	1257–1259
Qutuz	1259–1260
Baybars I	1260–1277
Berke Khan	1277–1279
Salamish	1279
Qalawun	1279–1290
Khalil	1290–1293
Baydara	1293
Al-Nasir Muhammad I	1293–1294
Kitbugha	1294–1296
Lajin	1296–1299
Al-Nasir Muhammad I (2nd reign)	1299–1309
Baybars II (Burji)	1309–1310
Al-Nasir Muhammad I (3rd reign)	1310–1341
Abu Bakr	1341
Kujuk	1341–1342
Ahmad I	1342
Ismail	1342–1345
Shaban I	1345–1346
Hajji I	1346–1347
Hasan	1347–1351
Salih	1351–1354
Hasan (2nd reign)	1354–1361
Muhammad II	1361–1363
Shaban II	1363–1377
Ali II	1377–1382

Burji / Circassian line	***1382–1517***
Barquq	1382–1389
Hajji II (Bahri; 2nd reign)	1389–1390
Barquq (2nd reign)	1390–1399
Faraj	1399–1405
Abd al-Aziz	1405

Faraj (2nd reign)	1405–1412
Al-Mustain (Abbasid caliph)	1412
Shaykh	1412–1421
Ahmad II	1421
Tatar	1421
Muhammad III	1421–1422
Barsbay	1422–1438
Yusuf	1438
Chaqmaq	1438–1453
Uthman	1453
Inal	1453–1461
Ahmad III	1461
Khushqadam	1461–1467
Yalbay	1467
Timurbugha	1467–1468
Qaytbay	1468–1496
Muhammad IV	1496–1498
Qansawh I	1498–1500
Janbulat	1500–1501
Tumanbay I	1501
Qansawh II al-Ghawri	1501–1516
Tumanbay II	1516–1517
OTTOMAN PERIOD	1517–1914
Selim I the Grim	1517–1520
Sulayman II the Magnificent	1520–1566
Selim II	1566–1574
Murad III	1574–1595
Muhammad III	1595–1603
Ahmed I	1603–1617
Mustafa I	1617–1618
Uthman II	1618–1622
Mustafa I (2nd reign)	1622–1623
Murad IV	1623–1640
Ibrahim I	1640–1648
Muhammad IV	1648–1687
Sulayman III	1687–1691
Ahmed II	1691–1695
Mustafa II	1695–1703
Ahmed III	1703–1730
Mahmud I	1730–1754
Uthman III	1754–1757
Mustafa III	1757–1774
Abd al-Hamid I	1774–1789

Selim III	1789–1807
Mustafa IV	1807–1808
Mahmud II	1808–1839
Abd al-Majid	1839–1861
Abd al-Aziz	1861–1876
Murad V	1876
Abd al-Hamid II	1876–1909
Muhammad V	1909–1914

FRENCH OCCUPATION	1798–1801
Napoleon Bonaparte	1798–1799
General Jean-Baptiste Kléber	1799–1800
General Jacques-François Menou	1800–1801

DYNASTY OF MUHAMMAD ALI	1805–1953
Governors (Pashas/Walis)	*1805–1867*
Muhammad Ali	1805–1848
Ibrahim	1848
Abbas Hilmi I	1848–1854
Said	1854–1863
Ismail	1863–1867

Khedives	*1867–1914*
Ismail	1867–1879
Tawfiq	1879–1892
Abbas Hilmi II	1892–1914

Sultans	*1914–1922*
Husayn Kamil	1914–1917
Fuad I	1917–1922

Kings	*1922–1953*
Fuad I	1922–1936
Faruq	1936–1952
Fuad II	1952–1953

BRITISH OCCUPATION	1883–1936
Consuls General	*1883–1914*
Sir Evelyn Baring (Lord Cromer)	1883–1907
Sir John Eldon Gorst	1907–1911
Herbert Horatio Kitchener	1911–1914

High Commissioners	*1914–1936*
Sir Milne Cheetham	1914–1915

Sir Henry McMahon	1915–1917
Sir Reginald Wingate	1917–1919
Sir Edmund Allenby	1919–1925
Sir George Lloyd (Lord Lloyd)	1925–1929
Sir Percy Loraine	1929–1933
Sir Miles Lampson	1933–1936

PRESIDENTS OF THE REPUBLIC	1953–
Muhammad Naguib	1953–1954
Gamal Abdel Nasser	1954–1970
Anwar Sadat	1970–1981
Hosni Mubarak	1981–

Chronology of Major Events

c.600,000 BC	Earliest human tools in Egypt
c.50,000 BC	Earliest known anatomically 'modern' human remains in Egypt
c.12,000 BC	Experiments with agriculture on the Nile
c.8800 BC	First pottery, possible cattle rearing in the Western Desert
c.5900 BC	Goats domesticated in Western and Eastern Deserts
c.5500 BC	Animal husbandry, agriculture on the Nile
c.5000 BC	Copper smelting
c.4800 BC	World's first known astronomical calendar in Western Desert
c.4600 BC	Earliest known figurines in Egyptian art
c.3500 BC	Expansion of Upper Egyptian culture, formation of urban centres
c.3200 BC	Emergence of hieroglyphic script
c.3000 BC	Creation of the Egyptian state, beginning of the First Dynasty and foundation of Memphis
c.2650 BC	Djoser's Step Pyramid, the first pyramid
c.2560 BC	The Great Pyramid of Khufu (Cheops)
c.2350 BC	First appearance of the Pyramid Texts
c.2160 BC	Collapse of the Old Kingdom
c.2025 BC	Egypt reunited under Mentuhotep II; the beginning of the Middle Kingdom
c.1980 BC	New capital founded at Itjtawy
c.1920 BC	Fiction appears as a literary form
c.1650 BC	Collapse of the Middle Kingdom
c.1650 BC	The Hyksos introduce the horse and chariot, as well as new crops, animals and alloys of bronze
c.1550 BC	Expulsion of the Hyksos and reunification of Egypt; beginning of the New Kingdom; capital at Thebes
c.1500 BC	Thutmose I leads the first major military campaign into Syria
c.1473 BC	Hatshepsut proclaims herself king

*c.*1457 BC	Thutmose III wins the Battle of Megiddo for control of Syria–Palestine
*c.*1347 BC	Akhenaten founds a new capital at Amarna and begins to promote the cult of Aten to the exclusion of all others
*c.*1336 BC	Tutankhamun leaves Armana and restores the old cults
*c.*1275 BC	Rameses II fights heroically at the Battle of Kadesh
*c.*1208 BC	First invasion of the Sea Peoples repelled by Merenptah
*c.*1178 BC	Second invasion of the Sea Peoples seen off by Rameses III
*c.*1069 BC	Collapse of the New Kingdom
*c.*945 BC	Sheshonq I ushers in a period of Libyan dominance
*c.*716 BC	Shabaqo brings Egypt under the sway of Nubian kings
663 BC	The sack of Thebes by the Assyrians
658 BC	Psamtek wrests Egypt from the Assyrians
612 BC	The Babylonians sack Nineveh, capital of Assyria
605 BC	Nekau II clashes with the Babylonians at Carchemish
539 BC	Cyrus the Great of Persia sacks Babylon
525 BC	The Persians under Cambyses conquer Egypt
486 BC	Rebellion in the Delta is crushed by Xerxes
404 BC	Egypt under Amyrtaios of Sais throws off the Persians
373 BC	Nectanebo I successfully defends Egypt from a combined Persian–Greek attack
343 BC	Nectanebo II, the last native pharaoh, abandons Egypt to the Persians
332 BC	Alexander the Great chases the Persians out of Egypt
331 BC	Alexander founds a new capital on the coast called Alexandria
323 BC	Alexander dies, triggering the 'Wars of the Successors'
305 BC	Ptolemy declares himself king of Egypt
280 BC	The Lighthouse of Alexandria is completed
217 BC	Ptolemy IV Philopator defeats the Seleucids at Raphia
200 BC	The Seleucids take Syria from Egypt after the Battle of Panion
196 BC	The Seleucids take Asia Minor from Egypt; Rosetta stone carved
168 BC	The Seleucids invade Egypt, which is saved by an intervention from Rome
75 BC	Rome annexes Cyrenaica from Egypt
65 BC	Rome annexes Crete from Egypt
60 BC	First triumvirate of Rome between Julius Caesar, Pompey and Crassus
58 BC	Rome annexes Cyprus from Egypt
48 BC	Caesar defeats Pompey at Pharsalus; Pompey flees to Egypt and is murdered by Ptolemy XIII

47 BC	Caesar defeats Ptolemy XIII and proclaims his sister Cleopatra queen
44 BC	Caesar assassinated in Rome
43 BC	Second triumvirate between Mark Antony, Octavian and Lepidus
42 BC	Antony takes control of the eastern half of the Roman Empire
40 BC	Antony has twins by Cleopatra
31 BC	Antony and Cleopatra defeated by Octavian at the Battle of Actium
30 BC	Suicides of Antony and Cleopatra; Octavian annexes Egypt
27 BC	Octavian becomes Augustus Caesar
c.4 BC	Birth of Jesus Christ; the Holy Family takes refuge in Egypt
c.30 AD	Jesus Christ is crucified in Jerusalem
38	Greeks massacre Jews in Alexandria
c.42	St Mark founds the Church in Egypt
c.68	St Mark is martyred in Alexandria
115	Jewish revolt across the eastern Mediterranean, brutally suppressed in Egypt
171	Peasants' revolt breaks out in the Delta
202	Septimius Severus bans Christians from preaching
215	Caracalla ransacks Alexandria after the mob insults him
c.220	Emergence of Coptic script
249	Systematic persecution of Christians begins under Decius
c.250	The first Christian hermits retreat into the desert
270–272	Queen Zenobia of Palmyra seizes control of Egypt; Emperor Aurelian regains power but possibly destroys the Great Library and the Soma in the process
293	Diocletian splits the Roman empire into two and introduces the four-man government known as the Tetrarchy
297	Diocletian erects 'Pompey's Pillar' in commemoration of his victory over an Alexandrian usurper
303	Diocletian initiates the Great Persecution against Christians
313	Constantine the Great issues the Edict of Milan, granting to all the freedom to worship
324	Constantine unites the Roman Empire and founds Constantinople
325	Council of Nicaea
c.350	First monasteries
391	Theodosius outlaws paganism; the Serapeum and its library are destroyed by Christians
394	Last hieroglyphic inscription

868	Ibn Tulun breaks away from the Abbasid caliphate and establishes his own dynastic line in Egypt
880	Ibn Tulun Mosque completed
905	Abbasids regain control of Egypt
935	Ibn Tughj made *al-Ikhshid*, prince, of an autonomous Egypt by the Abbasids
944	The Ikhshidids seize Mecca and Medina
969	The Fatimids successfully invade Egypt; found royal city al-Qahira (Cairo)
972	Azhar Mosque completed
1009	Al-Hakim orders the destruction of the Church of the Holy Sepulchre in Jerusalem
1065–1072	Terrible famine
1095–1099	The First Crusade
1099	The crusaders sack Jerusalem
1147–1149	The Second Crusade
1167	Nur al-Din invades Egypt
1168	Fustat deliberately torched to foil the crusaders
1171	Saladin deposes the Fatimids, and founds a new dynasty, the Ayyubids
1176	Saladin begins building Cairo's Citadel
1187	Saladin wins the Battle of Hattin in July and captures Jerusalem in October
1189–1192	The Third Crusade
1193	Saladin dies
1217–1229	The Fifth Crusade; the Latins capture Damietta in 1219 but are driven from Egypt in 1221
1229	Al-Kamil cedes Jerusalem to Frederick II in return for military aid
1248–1254	The Seventh Crusade; Latins repelled from Egypt in 1250 by the Mamluks
1250	Mamluk period begins with the murder of the Ayyubid Turan Shah; Shajar al-Durr becomes the first and only Muslim queen of Egypt
1258	The Mongols sack Baghdad and execute the Abbasid caliph
1260	The Mamluks defeat the Mongols at Ayn Jalut; the Bahri Mamluks take control of Egypt
1291	The Mamluks chase the last crusaders from the Holy Land
1347	Black Death reaches Egypt and wipes out a third of the population
1361	Sultan Hasan Mosque completed
1382	The Circassian or Burji Mamluks come to power
1399	Tamerlane attacks Mamluk territory in Syria; Aleppo is sacked

1453	Ottomans capture Constantinople and bring the Byzantine Empire to an end
1491	Mamluks advance to Kayseri in Anatolia and secure peace with the Ottomans
1498	Vasco da Gama circumnavigates Africa, creating new sea routes to the East that bypass Egypt
1511	The Mamluks, slow to incorporate firearms into their armies, create their first dedicated arquebusier unit
1516	The Ottomans defeat the Mamluks at Marj Dabiq
1517	The last Mamluk sultan, Tumanbay, is defeated by the Ottomans; Egypt becomes a province of the Ottoman Empire
1604	Rebels assassinate the Ottoman pasha
1631	The beys depose the pasha with the official backing of the sultan, starting a precedent that the pasha should have their approval
1711	Factionalism between military households erupts into civil war
1736	Ten leading beys are assassinated by the pasha, allowing the Qazdagli household to come to the fore
1771	Ali Bey attempts to take Egypt and Syria out of the Ottoman Empire; he fails
1786	The sultan sends a taskforce to unseat Ibrahim and Murad Bey
1791	Ibrahim and Murad Bey return to power
1798	Napoleon invades Egypt, defeating the Mamluk army and capturing Alexandria and Cairo in July; on 1 August Nelson destroys the French fleet at the Battle of the Nile, effectively ending Napoleon's dream of an eastern empire
1799	Napoleon is defeated at Acre, but beats off the Ottomans at Abu Qir, before slipping out of the country; Rosetta stone discovered
1801	The French are driven from Egypt after being defeated by the British at the Battle of Alexandria
1805	Muhammad Ali becomes governor of Egypt
1811	The massacre of the Mamluks in the Citadel
1813	John Lewis Buckhardt is the first modern European to encounter the temple of Rameses II at Abu Simbel
1815	*Jizya* paid by non-Muslims since the Arab conquest is abolished
1818	Muhammad Ali wins the Hijaz for the Ottomans
1820	A new strain of cotton proves to be highly successful and highly lucrative
1822	Jean-François Champollion deciphers hieroglyphs;

	Muhammad Ali conquers Sudan; Arabic printing press established in Bulaq; Belzoni puts on a grand exhibition of Egyptian finds in London
1827	The Egyptian-Ottoman fleet is destroyed in Navarino Bay by the European powers
1828	The first Arabic newspaper is published by the state printing press
1830	The first guidebook to Egypt is published
1831–1833	Egypt invades Syria and Turkey
1833	Peace of Kutahia with the Ottomans recognises Muhammad Ali's claim to territories as far as the Taurus mountains
1835	The Egyptian Antiquities Service is founded
1839	Ottomans defeated by the Egyptian army at the Battle of Nezib
1841	Muhammad Ali is forced to give up most of his empire and army; in return he and his heirs are granted the Viceroyalty of Egypt
1844	The Muhammad Ali Mosque on the Citadel is completed after 20 years of construction
1847	Muhammad Ali falls ill and abandons Egypt to convalesce in Naples
1850	Auguste Mariette discovers the Serapeum at Saqqara
1855	The railway between Alexandria and Cairo opens
1858	Egyptian Antiquities Service re-founded under Auguste Mariette
1859	Work begins on the Suez Canal
1861–1865	The American Civil War sparks a global cotton shortage and fortunes are made in Egypt as prices soar
1866	A chamber of delegates is set up consisting of 75 village headmen
1867	Ismail receives the title 'khedive' from the Ottoman sultan
1868	Thomas Cook is granted permission to conduct tours of the Nile
1869	Opening of the Suez Canal
1875	Foundation of *Al-Ahram* newspaper; foundation of the Mixed Courts
1876	British and French creditors take joint control over key areas of the Egyptian economy
1878	'European Ministry' set up, giving Europeans greater governmental powers, and sparking widespread national resentment; Cleopatra's Needle is erected on London's Embankment
1879	Ismail is deposed by royal decree and leaves Egypt for Naples
1881	Opposition leader, Ahmad Urabi, forces Khedive Tawfiq to

	give more power to indigenous institutions; Sir Gaston Maspero transports royal mummies from their cache in the cliffs at Deir el-Bahri to Cairo; the Mahdi's revolt in Sudan begins; Cleopatra's Needle erected in New York's Central Park
1882	June riots in Alexandria; the British bombard the city from the sea in July; Urabi is defeated at Tell el-Kebir in September; Tawfiq is restored under British protection
1883–1907	Lord Cromer is effectively the ruler of Egypt
1883	Egyptian expedition to subdue the Mahdi is annihilated
1884	General Gordon arrives in Khartoum and is soon besieged
1885	Gordon killed by the Mahdists
1887	Economic recovery in Egypt
1889	The British government abandons plans to withdraw from Egypt
1895	Ismail dies in Constantinople
1898	Kitchener defeats the Mahdists at the Battle of Omdurman
1899	Anglo-Egyptian Condominium established over Sudan; the population of Egypt reaches 10 million
1902	The Egyptian Museum opens in its current building in Cairo; first Aswan Dam completed
1904	Entente Cordiale between Britain and France
1906	The Dinshawai incident
1907	Egypt's first political parties are founded
1908	First private secular national university is founded, which later becomes Cairo University
1910	Assassination of Butrus Ghali, the Egyptian prime minister, by a Muslim extremist
1911–1914	Kitchener consul general
1914	First World War breaks out; Ottoman Empire sides with the Germans in November; Britain declares Egypt a Protectorate in December, taking it out of the Ottoman Empire; Khedive Abbas Hilmi II is deposed for his uncle Husayn Kamil, who is given the new title 'sultan'
1916	The Ottoman threat against Egypt is neutralised; counter-offensive launched from Egypt into Palestine with Arab help
1917	The Balfour Declaration
1918	Armistice; Saad Zaghlul heads a delegation (*wafd*) to demand independence from Britain
1919	Widespread civil unrest breaks out after Zaghlul is arrested and exiled; foundation of the American University in Cairo
1920	Talaat Harb founds Bank Misr
1922	Britain unilaterally declares Egyptian independence with four 'Reserved Points'; Sultan Fuad becomes King Fuad;

	Howard Carter discovers Tutankhamun's tomb
1923	A national constitution is passed making Egypt a parliamentary democracy
1924	The Wafd triumphs at the first general election and Zaghlul becomes prime minister; Sir Lee Stack is assassinated by nationalists
1925	The private university is reorganised and inaugurated as a state university, later becoming Cairo University
1927	Saad Zaghlul dies; Mustafa Nahhas takes over as leader of the Wafd
1928	The Muslim Brotherhood is founded by Hasan al-Banna
1935	The first collection of the works of the Greek-Alexandrian poet, Constantine Cavafy (1863–1933), is published, two years after his death
1936	The Anglo-Egyptian Treaty is agreed; Faruq becomes king
1937	Egypt becomes a member of the League of Nations; the Capitulations are abolished
1938	The Muslim Brotherhood institutes a terrorist wing; Naguib Mahfouz publishes his first novel *Whisper of Madness*
1939	World War II breaks out, Egypt remains neutral, but under the terms of the 1936 Treaty is re-occupied by British and Allied forces; the foundation of the Free Officers movement
1941	Rommel begins his offensive in the North African desert
1942	The British win the Battle of El Alamein
1945	Egypt declares war on Germany; the prime minister Ahmad Mahir is assassinated by a member of the Muslim Brotherhood; the Arab League is formed in Cairo; Naguib Mahfouz begins writing the *Cairo Trilogy*
1947	British forces evacuate to the Canal Zone
1948	Israel comes into being and combined Arab armies invade and are defeated; prime minister Nuqrashi is assassinated by the Muslim Brotherhood
1949	Armistice agreed between Egypt and Israel; assassination of Hasan al-Bana, supreme guide of the Muslim Brotherhood; abolition of the Mixed Courts
1950	Egypt's population reaches 20 million people
1951	Nahhas declares the 1936 Treaty void and proclaims Faruq king of Egypt and Sudan; guerrilla attacks on British installations
1952	'Black Saturday' riots in Cairo in January; the Free Officers conduct a successful *coup d'état* on 22-23 July and force the abdication and exile of King Faruq; the Revolutionary Command Council passes the Agrarian Reform Law
1953	Dissolution of political parties, monarchy abolished and

	Egypt proclaimed a republic (June 18)
1954	The Muslim Brotherhood is outlawed, its leaders executed or imprisoned; Nasser ousts General Naguib; treaty for British evacuation agreed
1955	Nasser feted at the Bandung Conference for non-aligned states
1956	New constitution is promulgated, National Assembly established and Nasser elected president against no opponents; Sudan declares its independence; full evacuation of British forces from Egypt completed on 13 June; Nasser nationalises the Suez Canal on 26 July; Israel invades Sinai on 29 October, and France and Britain join the fray two days later only to call a ceasefire on 6 November in the face of global outrage; sequestration of French and British property and expulsion of their citizens
1958	Egypt and Syria form the United Arab Republic (UAR)
1960	Work begins on the Aswan High Dam
1961	Nasser passes the Socialist Laws; Syria secedes from the UAR
1962–1967	Egypt is embroiled in the Yemeni Civil War
1964	The Palestine Liberation Organisation (PLO) is founded
1965	Faruk dies in Rome, apparently after gorging on oysters, and is buried in Cairo
1966	Sayyid Qutb is executed; the population reaches 30 million;
1967	The Six-Day or June War with Israel
1968–1970	The 'War of Attrition' with Israel
1970	Nasser dies and Anwar Sadat takes over; Aswan High Dam completed
1971	Sadat's 'Corrective Revolution'
1972	Sadat expels 15,000 Soviet advisers and technicians
1973	The October (Yom Kippur) War with Israel
1974	Sadat introduces *infitah* economic policies
1975	Suez Canal reopens, having been shut since the Six-Day War
1977	'Bread riots' break out after subsidies on certain basics are cut; Sadat makes a speech for peace in the Knesset
1978	The Camp David accords
1979	Egypt and Israel sign the Treaty of Washington and most of the Arab world breaks diplomatic relations; Egypt is expelled from the Arab League; the population reaches 40 million
1981	Sectarian riots between Copts and Muslims; political arrests and the banishment of the Coptic Pope Shenouda III; Sadat assassinated on 6 October; Hosni Mubarak becomes president
1982	Israel evacuates Sinai

1988	Naguib Mahfouz becomes the first Arab to win the Nobel Prize for literature
1989	Egypt readmitted into the Arab League, the headquarters of which returns to Cairo
1991	The Gulf War: Egypt joins the US-led coalition to liberate Kuwait after the Iraqi invasion
1992	Assassination of the writer Faraq Fuda by Jamaa Islamiya, taken as the start of a five-year terror offensive against the state; Cairo earthquake
1995	Assassination attempt on Mubarak in Addis Ababa
1997	The Luxor massacre
2001	Attacks of September 11 against US targets
2002	The Bibliotheca Alexandrina is opened
2003	A US-led coalition invades Iraq, but Egypt does not join it
2004	First in a wave of Sinai terrorist bombs; funeral of Yasser Arafat in Cairo
2005	Sharm el-Sheikh bomb; constitution amended to allow multiple candidates in presidential elections; Mubarak elected for his fifth consecutive term; Muslim Brotherhood makes gains in parliamentary elections
2006	Intact 18th Dynasty tomb discovered in the Valley of the Kings, the first since Tutankhamun's; three simultaneous bombs in Dahab

Further Reading

GENERAL REFERENCE FOR ANCIENT EGYPT

BAINES, JOHN & JAROMIR MALEK *Atlas of Ancient Egypt* (Oxford, 1980)

BARD, KATHRYN A., ed. *Encylopedia of the Archaeology of Ancient Egypt* (London, 1999)

CLAYTON, PETER A. *Chronicle of the Pharaohs: The Reign-by-Reign Record of the Rulers and Dynasties of Ancient Egypt* (London, 1994)

GRIMAL, NICOLAS *A History of Ancient Egypt*, tr. IAN SHAW (Oxford, 1992)

REDFORD, DONALD, ed. *The Oxford Encyclopedia of Ancient Egypt* (Oxford, 2001)

SHAW, IAN *The Oxford History of Ancient Egypt* (Oxford, 2000)

SHAW, IAN & PAUL NICHOLSON *The British Museum Dictionary of Ancient Egypt* (London, 1995)

TRIGGER, B. G. et al. *Ancient Egypt: A Social History* (Cambridge, 1983)

GENERAL MODERN HISTORIES

AHMED, MOUSTAFA *Egypt in the 20th Century: Chronology of Major Events* (London, 2003)

GOLDSCHMIDT JR., ARTHUR *A Concise History of the Middle East* (Boulder, 2001)

GOLDSCHMIDT JR., ARTHUR *Historical Dictionary of Egypt* (London, 2004)

MANSFIELD, PETER *The History of the Middle East* (London, 2003)

SAYYID MARSOT, AFAF LUTFI AL- *A Short History of Modern Egypt* (Cambridge, 1985)

VATIKIOTIS, P. J. *The History of Modern Egypt: From Muhammad Ali to Mubarak* (London, 1991)

PREHISTORY

HAYES, WILLIAM C. *Most Ancient Egypt* (London, 1965)

HOFFMAN, MICHAEL *Before the Pharaohs: The Prehistoric Foundations of Egyptian Civilization* (London, 1991)

KEMP, BARRY J. *Ancient Egypt: Anatomy of a Civilization* (London, 1989)

MIDANT-REYNES, BEATRIX   *The Prehistory of Egypt: From the First Egyptians to the First Pharaohs* (Oxford, 2001)

RICE, MICHAEL   *Egypt's Making: The Origins of Ancient Egypt, 5000-2000 BC* (London, 2003)

SPENCER, A. J.   *Early Egypt: The Rise of Civilisation in the Nile Valley* (London, 1993)

WENDORF, FRED   *Prehistory of the Nile Valley* (London, 1976)

PHARAONIC EGYPT 3000 BC – 332 BC

ALDRED, CYRIL   *Akhenaten: King of Egypt* (London, 1988)

ALDRED, CYRIL   *Egyptian Art in the Days of the Pharaohs* (London, 1980)

ALDRED, CYRIL   *The Egyptians* (London, 1998)

BRIER, BOB & HOYT HOBBS   *Daily Life of the Ancient Egyptians* (Westport, 1999)

CARTER, HOWARD   *The Tomb of Tutankhamun* (London, 1983)

DAVID, A. ROSALIE   *The Ancient Egyptians: Religious Beliefs and Practices* (London, 1982)

EDWARDS, I. E. S.   *The Pyramids of Egypt* (Harmondsworth, 1991)

EMERY, W. B.   *Archaic Egypt* (Harmondsworth, 1972)

FLETCHER, JOANN   *Egypt's Sun King: Amenhotep III* (London, 2000)

GARDINER, ALAN   *Egypt of the Pharaohs* (London, 1961)

HART, GEORGE   *Pharaohs and Pyramids: A Guide through Old Kingdom Egypt* (London, 1991)

HERODOTUS   *The Histories*, tr. AUBREY DE SÉLINCOURT (London, 1996)

HODGES, PETER   *How the Pyramids Were Built* (Warminster, 1993)

KITCHEN, KENNETH   *Pharaoh Triumphant: The Life and Times of Ramesses II* (Warminster, 1982)

KITCHEN, KENNETH   *The Third Intermediate Period in Egypt* (Warminster, 1986)

LEHNER, MARK   *The Complete Pyramids* (London, 1997)

MALEK, JAROMIR   *In the Shadow of the Pyramids: Egypt during the Old Kingdom* (London, 1986)

MORENZ, SIEGFRIED   *Egyptian Religion*, tr. ANN E. KEEP (Ithaca, 1992)

MYSLIWIEC, KAROL   *The Twilight of Ancient Egypt: First Millennium BCE* tr. DAVID LORTON (Ithaca, 2000)

PARKINSON, R. B.   *Poetry and Culture in Middle Kingdom Egypt* (London, 2002)

PARKINSON, R. B.   *Voices from Ancient Egypt* (London, 1991)

REDFORD, DONALD   *Akhenaten: The Heretic King* (Princeton, 1984)

ROBINS, GAY   *Women in Ancient Egypt* (London, 1993)

ROBINS, GAY   *The Art of Ancient Egypt* (London, 1997)

STRUDWICK, NIGEL *The Administration of Egypt in the Old Kingdom* (London, 1985)

TYLDESLEY, JOYCE A. *Daughters of Isis* (London, 1984)

TYLDESLEY, JOYCE A. *Egypt's Golden Empire: The Age of the New Kingdom* (London, 2001)

TYLDESLEY, JOYCE A. *The Private Lives of the Pharaohs* (London, 2000)

VERNER, MIROSLAV *The Pyramids: The Mystery, Culture, and Science of Egypt's Great Monuments*, tr. STEVEN RENDALL (Cairo, 2002)

WATSON, PHILIP J. *Egyptian Pyramids and Mastaba Tombs of the Old and Middle Kingdoms* (Princes Risborough, 1987)

WILKINSON, TOBY *Early Dynastic Egypt* (London, 1999)

PTOLEMAIC EGYPT 332 BC – 30 BC

ANSSI, LAMPELA *Rome and the Ptolemies of Egypt* (Helsinki, 1998)

ASHTON, SALLY-ANN *The Last Queens of Egypt* (Harlow, 2003)

BOWMAN, ALAN K. *Egypt after the Pharaohs: 332 BC-AD 642: From Alexander to the Arab Conquest* (Oxford, 1990)

FORSTER, E. M. *Pharos and Pharillon: An Evocation of Alexandria* (London, 1983)

FORSTER, E. M. *Alexandria: A History and a Guide* (London, 1982)

FRASER, P. M. *Ptolemaic Alexandria* (Oxford, 1972)

GRANT, MICHAEL *Cleopatra* (London, 1972)

GRANT, MICHAEL *The Hellenistic Greeks: From Alexander to Cleopatra* (London, 1990)

HÖLBL, GÜNTHER *History of the Ptolemaic Empire* (London, 2001)

LEWIS, NAPHTALI *Greeks in Ptolemaic Egypt* (Oakville, Connecticut, 2001)

LOVRIC, MICHELLE *Cleopatra's Face: Fatal Beauty* (London, 2001)

PLUTARCH *The Age of Alexander: Nine Greek Lives*, tr. IAN SCOTT-KILVERT (Harmondworth, 1977)

POLYBIUS *The Rise of the Roman Empire*, tr. IAN SCOTT-KILVERT (Harmondsworth, 1979)

WALKER, SUSAN & PETER HIGGS *Cleopatra of Egypt: From History to Myth* (London, 2001)

ROMAN AND CHRISTIAN EGYPT 30 BC – 642 AD

BAGNALL, ROGER S. *Egypt in Late Antiquity* (Princeton, 1993)

BUTCHER, E. L. *The Story of the Church of Egypt* (London, 1897)

CANNUYER, CHRISTIAN *Coptic Egypt: The Christians of the Nile* (London, 2001)

DIODORUS SICULUS *Diodorus on Egypt*, tr. EDWIN MURPHY (London, 1985)

FRIEDMAN, FLORENCE D. *Beyond the Pharaohs, Egypt and the Copts in the 2nd to 7th Centuries AD* (Baltimore, 1989)

LEWIS, NAPHTALI *Life in Egypt under Roman Rule* (Oxford, 1983)

MEINARDUS, OTTO F. A. *Two Thousand Years of Coptic Christianity* (Cairo, 1999)

MILNE, J. GRAFTON *A History of Egypt under Roman Rule* (Chicago, 1924)

PATRICK, T. H. *Traditional Egyptian Christianity* (Greensboro, 1996)

PEARSON, BIRGER & JAMES GOEHRING eds. *The Roots of Egyptian Christianity* (Philadelphia, 1986)

PLUTARCH *Roman Lives*, tr. ROBIN WATERFIELD (Oxford, 1999)

WATTERSON, BARBARA *Coptic Egypt* (Scottish Academic, 1988)

THE ARABS, MAMLUKS AND OTTOMANS 642–1798

AYALON, DAVID *Islam and the Abode of War* (London, 1994)

BEATTIE, ANDREW *Cairo: A Cultural and Literary History* (Oxford, 2005)

BUTLER, ALFRED J. *The Arab Conquest of Egypt and the Last Thirty Years of the Roman Dominion* (Oxford, 1978)

DALY, M. W. *The Cambridge History of Egypt: Volume II Modern Egypt, from 1517 to the End of the Twentieth Century* (Cambridge, 1998)

HITTI, PHILIP K. *The History of the Arabs* (Basingstoke, 2002)

HOLT, P. M. *Egypt and the Fertile Crescent 1516–1922* (London, 1966)

IRWIN, ROBERT *The Middle East in the Middle Ages: The Early Mamluk Sultanate 1250-1382* (London, 1986)

LEWIS, BERNARD *The Arabs in History* (Oxford, 1993)

NASIR-I KHUSRAW *Naser-e Khosraw's Book of Travels (Safarnama)*, tr. W. M. THACKSTON, JR. (Albany, 1986)

PETRY, CARL F., ed. *The Cambridge History of Egypt: Volume I Islamic Egypt, 640-1517* (Cambridge, 1998)

RAYMOND, ANDRÉ *Cairo*, tr. WILLARD WOOD (London, 2000)

RILEY-SMITH, JONATHAN *The Oxford History of the Crusades* (Oxford, 1999)

RODENBECK, MAX *Cairo: The City Victorious* (London, 1998)

STEWART, DESMOND *Great Cairo: Mother of the World* (London, 1969)

WATERFIELD, GORDON *Egypt* (London, 1967)

WINTER, MICHAEL *Egyptian Society under Ottoman Rule 1517–1798* (London, 1992)

EGYPT BETWEEN 1798 AND 1882

BELZONI, GIOVANNI *Belzoni's Travels: Narrative of the Operations and Recent Discoveries in Egypt and Nubia* (London, 2001)

FAHMY, KHALED *All the Pasha's Men: Mehmed Ali, His Army and the Making of Modern Egypt* (Cambridge, 1997)

FLOWER, RAYMOND *Napoleon to Nasser: The Story of Modern Egypt* (London, 1972)

HEROLD, J. CHRISTOPHER *Bonaparte in Egypt* (London, 1962)

JABARTI, ABD AL-RAHMAN AL- *Napoleon in Egypt: Al-Jabarti's Chronicle of the First Seven Months of the French Occupation, 1798*, tr. SMUEL MOREH (Princeton, 1993)

LANE, EDWARD WILLIAM *An Account of the Manners and Customs of Modern Egyptians* (Cairo, 2003)

MOIRET, CAPTAIN JOSEPH-MARIE *Memoirs of Napoleon's Egyptian Expedition, 1798–1801*, tr. ROSEMARY BRINDLE (London, 2001)

MOOREHEAD, ALAN *The Blue Nile* (London, 2001)

POCOCK, TOM *The Thirst for Glory: The Life of Admiral Sir Sidney Smith* (London, 1996)

PUDNEY, JOHN *Suez: De Lessep's Canal* (London, 1969)

REID, DONALD MALCOLM *Whose Pharaohs? Archaeology, Museums, and Egyptian National Identity from Napoleon to World War I* (London, 2002)

RICHMOND, J. C. B. *Egypt 1798–1952: Her Advance Towards a Modern Identity* (London, 1977)

SAID, EDWARD W. *Orientalism* (Harmondsworth, 1978)

SAYYID MARSOT, AFAF LUTFI AL- *Egypt in the Reign of Muhammad Ali* (Cambridge, 1984)

STARKEY, PAUL & JANET STARKEY, eds. *Travellers in Egypt* (New York, 2001)

STORRS, RONALD *Orientations* (London, 1937)

VERCOUTTER, JEAN *The Search for Ancient Egypt* (London, 1986)

THE BRITISH OCCUPATION 1882–1952

ANNESLEY, GEORGE *The Rise of Modern Egypt: A Century and a Half of Egyptian History 1798-1957* (Edinburgh, 1994)

BARNETT, CORRELLI *The Desert Generals* (London, 1983)

COOPER, ARTEMIS *Cairo in the War 1939–1945* (London, 1989)

CROMER, EARL OF *Modern Egypt* (London, 1908)

GERSHONI, ISRAEL & JAMES P. JANKOWSKI *Egypt, Islam and the Arabs: The Search for Nationhood, 1900–1930* (Cambridge, 1995)

MAGNUS, PHILIP *Kitchener: Portrait of an Imperialist* (London, 1958)

MARLOWE, JOHN *Cromer in Egypt* (London, 1970)

MOOREHEAD, ALAN *The White Nile* (Harmondsworth, 1973)

SATTIN, ANTHONY *Lifting the Veil: British Society in Egypt 1768–1956* (London, 1988)

SAYYID MARSOT, AFAF LUTFI AL- *Egypt's Liberal Experiment: 1922–1936* (Berkeley, 1977)

SMITH, CHARLES D. *Palestine and the Arab-Israel Conflict: A History with Documents* (Boston, 2004)

TERRY, JANICE J. *The Wafd: 1919–1952* (London, 1982)

REPUBLICAN EGYPT FROM 1952

AMIN, GALAL   *Whatever Happened to the Egyptians: Changes in Egyptian Society from 1950 to the Present* (Cairo, 2000)

GOLDSCHMIDT JR., ARTHUR   *Modern Egypt: The Formation of the Nation State* (Boulder, 2004)

HEIKAL, MOHAMED   *Cutting the Lion's Tail: Suez through Egyptian Eyes* (London, 1986)

KEPEL, GILLES   *Bad Moon Rising: A Chronicle of the Middle East Today* (London, 2003)

KEPEL, GILLES   *Jihad: The Trail of Political Islam* (London, 2002)

MANSFIELD, PETER   *Nasser* (London, 1969)

MCDERMOTT, ANTHONY   *Egypt from Nasser to Mubarak: A Flawed Revolution* (London, 1987)

NEGUIB, MUHAMMAD   *Egypt's Destiny* (London, 1955)

SADAT, ANWAR EL-   *Revolt on the Nile* (London, 1957)

SPRINGBORG, ROBERT   *Mubarak's Egypt: Fragmentation of the Political Order* (London, 1989)

THOMAS, HUGH   *The Suez Affair* (London, 1986)

WATERBURY, JOHN   *The Egypt of Nasser and Sadat: The Political Economy of Two Regimes* (Princeton, 1983)

WEAVER, MARY ANNE   *Portrait of Egypt: A Journey through the World of Militant Islam* (New York, 2000)

ZAYYAT, MUNTASIR   *The Road to al-Qaeda: The Story of Bin Laden's Right-Hand Man* (London, 2004)

REFERENCES FOR TRANSLATIONS IN TEXT

p.151-2 Herodas, *Mimiambs*, 1.23–34 translated by TIMOTHY ADÈS.

p.152, *Didorus of Sicily in Twelve Volumes* translated by C. BRADFORD WELLES (London, 1963).

p.158, adapted from *Demotic Grammar in the Ptolemaic Sacerdotal Decrees* translated by R. S. SIMPSON (Oxford, 1996).

p.182, *The Chronicle of John Malalas* translated by ELIZABETH JEFFREYS et al.(Melbourne, 1986)

p.187, *The History of the Church* by Eusebius, translated by G. A. WILLIAMSON (Harmondsworth, 1989)

p.199, The Koran, translated by N. J. DAWOOD (London, 2003)

p.204, *The Chronicle of John, Bishop of Nikiu* translated by R. H. CHARLES (London, 1916).

Historical Gazetteer

Numbers in bold refer to main text
Abbreviations – A: Arabic; E: Ancient Egyptian; G: Ancient Greek.

Abu Simbel Rock-cut temples built by Rameses II about 155 miles (250km) southeast of Aswan, rediscovered in 1813 by J. L. Burckhardt and cleared in 1817 by Belzoni. The temples were moved to higher ground by UNESCO during the 1960s to save them from being submerged under Lake Nasser, created by the construction of the Aswan High Dam. **118, 139, 272**

Abuqir Sweeping bay to the northeast of Alexandria, where Nelson sank Napoleon's fleet at the Battle of the Nile in 1798, and where the French defeated an Ottoman task force that was landed there by the Royal Navy the following year. **259, 262, 263, 267**

Abusir A necropolis belonging to ancient Memphis, north of Saqqara, mainly containing Old Kingdom pyramids and mastaba tombs. Just to the north is Abu Gurab the site of a sun temple built by the 5th-Dynasty king Nyuserra, while to the south on the way to Giza is Abu Roash, where there are ruins of Old Kingdom pyramid complexes, principally of the 4th-Dynasty king Djedefra. **56**

Abydos (E: Abdju) Ancient necropolis dating from Predynastic times, which became the principal cult centre for Osiris and one of the most important religious sites in the country. It lies 30 miles (50km) south of modern Sohag and is mainly visited for Sety I's temple and its associated Cenotaph, the Osireion, but also features a temple of Rameses II and the Early Dynastic cemeteries at Umm el-Qaab. **20, 23, 24, 42, 43, 45, 71, 115**,

Akhmim (G: Panopolis, E: Ipu, Khent-Mim) The capital of the ninth Upper Egyptian nome, named after the ithyphallic fertility god Min, and the site of some rock tombs and a colossal statue of Meritatum, probable daughter of Rameses II. Queen Tiye's family is thought to have come from Akhmim. **104**

Alexandria (A: el-Iskandariya) Founded by Alexander the Great on the site of an old fishing village, Alexandria became not only the Egyptian capital until the Arab conquest, but also the 'Queen' or 'Pearl of the Mediterranean', a bustling commercial hub and the greatest centre of learning and scholarship in the Ancient World. Its most famous monuments and institutions were founded and built by the first two Ptolemies, and included the Mouseion, which boasted by far the best-stocked library in the world, the Great Lighthouse (a wonder of the world), the Serapeum and the grand Sema, the tomb of Alexander. Its decline began during the Roman period when Egypt became a province of the empire. A combination of riots, brutal suppressions, neglect and natural disasters did for most of its fine landmarks even before the Arabs arrived, though the lighthouse survived until toppled by an earthquake in the 14th century. The city enjoyed a resurgence under Muhammad Ali when Egypt became an important cotton exporter after 1820, and with the steady influx of Europeans and Levantines over the century much of its old cosmopolitanism returned. So did its literary clout under figures such as Constantine Cavafy, E. M. Forster and Lawrence Durrell. After the Suez Crisis of 1956, many of its 'foreigners' emigrated or were expelled. Among its main attractions today are Pompey's Pillar, actually erected by Diocletian, the Catacombs of Kom el-Shugafa, the Roman theatre, Qaytbay's Fort and the Bibliotheca Alexandrina, a grand library opened in 2002 to recapture some of the city's Ptolemaic glory. **151–155, 157, 168, 170, 178–179, 185, 188, 192–193, 195, 201, 203, 206–207, 257, 266, 337, 362**

Amarna (A: Tell el-Amarna, E: Akhetaten) The capital city founded in *c.*1347 BC by the 'heretic' Akhenaten, but abandoned about 20 years later after the collapse of his religious revolution. **106, 110–112**

Aswan (E: Swenet, G: Syene) Just north of the First Cataract, an historic border town, mining base and trading centre with Nubia. The town itself and the ancient granite quarries lie on the east bank of the Nile, while a series of rock tombs were hewn from the cliffs on the west bank, and between them sits the island of Elephantine, with its ancient temples and Nilometer. To the south are the First Aswan Dam (1899–1902), the High Dam (1960–1970) and Lake Nasser. **9, 10, 93, 207, 408**

Asyut (E: Djawty, G: Lycopolis) Since the 1970s, one of the centres of militant Islamism in Egypt, despite its sizeable Coptic community. The modern city stands on the ancient capital of the 13th Upper Egyptian nome, the cult centre of the jackal-god Wepwawet, whence its Greek name. **18, 62, 104, 357**

Athribis (A: Tell el-Atrib, E: Hwt-Heryib) Ancient town near modern Behna where there was once an important temple to Amenhotep III, nothing of which remains. A few ruins have survived, however, of a temple to Ahmose II and a cemetery from the Ptolemaic and Roman periods. **131, 134**

Avaris (A: Tell el-Daba) Ruined eastern Delta settlement dating from the First Intermediate Period. During the Second Intermediate it became a capital for the 14th and 15th (Hyksos) Dynasties, and was then partly incorporated into Rameses II's capital Piramesse. **77–79, 81–83, 117, 126**

Badari, el- Site of several large Predynastic cemeteries to the south of Asyut, particularly rich in finds from the Badarian period. **18-19**

Bahariya Oasis Small desert oasis 124 miles (200km) west of the Nile. Although it probably came under the control of the pharaohs during the Middle Kingdom, most of the archaeological remains here date to the Roman period, not least the enormous Roman cemetery uncovered in 1999, which is thought to contain thousands of gilded mummies. **7, 8**

Battles

ABUQIR (*Lower Egypt*), 1799: The French repelled an Ottoman task force that was landed by the British Royal Navy; the Battle of Alexandria (qv) is also known as the Second Battle of Abuqir. **262, 263**

ACRE (*Palestine*): The Mamluks chased the last crusaders from the Holy Land, taking this, their last stronghold, in 1291. Sir Sidney Smith and Ottoman irregulars also held Napoleon at bay here in 1799, dimming the lights on his eastern campaign. **233, 261**

ACTIUM (*Greece*), 31 BC: Octavian won decisively against Antony and Cleopatra. The following year the pair committed suicide, Egypt fell under Roman control, and Octavian became Emperor Augustus. **171**

ALEXANDRIA (*Lower Egypt*): Amr captured the city twice, the first time in 641 through negotiation, the second in 645 by force; Napoleon took a much diminished Alexandria from the Mamluks in 1798; and the British ended the French Occupation at the Battle of Alexandria in 1801. **201, 207, 257, 263**

AL-RAYDANIYYA (*Lower Egypt*), 1517: A swift victory for the Ottomans on the outskirts of Cairo against severely weakened Egyptian forces, marking the end of the Mamluk and beginning of the Ottoman periods. **245**

AYN JALUT (*Palestine*), 1260: The Mamluks under sultan Baybars prevented the Mongols from invading Egypt. It was the Mongols' first serious defeat. **231**

BEYLAN (*Syria*), 1831: A victory for Muhammad Ali in his campaign to win Syria. **270**

BILBEIS (*Lower Egypt*): Delta fortress which featured in the struggle between the Fatimids, Nur al-Din and Amalric of Jerusalem in 1167–1168; also the site of al-Adil's victory over his nephews to become the Ayyubid sultan of Egypt in 1200. **223, 226**

CARCHEMISH (*northern Syria*): Thutmose I & III won battles here against the Mitannians in the 15th century BC, but Nekau II suffered a serious setback at this imperial outpost in 605 BC. **89, 97, 138**

DAMIETTA (*Lower Egypt*): Captured by the Latins in 1219 during the Fifth Crusade and again in 1249 during the Seventh. On both occasions the crusaders were forced to give the port up shortly afterwards. **226, 227**

EL ALAMEIN (*Western Desert*), 1942: Two battles were fought. In the first General Auchinleck stabilised the Allied retreat and prevented Rommel from breaking through. In the second, Montgomery pushed the

Germans back, eventually to drive them from North Africa altogether. It was a turning point in the war. **315**

EL OBEID (*Sudan*), 1883: Egyptian force under the command of the British general William Hicks was annihilated by the Mahdi. The temptation was presented to the British to expand their influence out of Egypt in order to make amends. **295**

FALUJA (*Palestine*), 1948: Focus of ferocious fighting in the Palestine War, where Nasser and many of the Free Officers were trapped. **320**

GAZA (*Palestine*), 312 BC: Ptolemy I and Seleucus defeated the Antigonids in the Third War of the Successors. **149**

HATTIN (*Palestine*), 1187: Saladin routed the Latin army, sparking the Third Crusade. **225**

HELIOPOLIS (*Lower Egypt*): Amr defeated the Byzantines in 640; the French defeated the Ottomans in 1800. **200**

KADESH (*Syria*), c.1274 BC: Earliest well-documented battle in the Ancient World. The clash between Rameses II and the Hittite king Muwatallis was not decisive, but Rameses declared victory in temple reliefs across Egypt and Nubia. **116**

KHARTOUM (*Sudan*), 1885: General Gordon and his garrison, who had been under siege for almost a year, were killed by the Mahdi just before relief came. The British public was appalled and clamoured for revenge. **296**

KONYA (*Anatolia*), 1833: Stunning victory for Muhammad Ali against the Ottomans, which gave him control of Syria-Palestine as far as the Taurus mountains. **270**

MANSURA (*Lower Egypt*), 1250: The Mamluks defeated the crusaders and drove them from Egypt during the Seventh Crusade. **227**

MARJ DABIQ (*Syria*), 1516: An overwhelmingly powerful Ottoman army under Selim the Grim demolished the Mamluks, paving the way for a rapid conquest of Egypt. **245**

MEGIDDO (*Palestine*), c.1457 BC: Thutmose III executed a successful surprise attack and siege over the king of Kadesh. **96–97**

MOMEMPHIS (*Lower Egypt*), 570 BC: Ahmose usurped the throne after defeating the mercenaries of Apries. **139**

NAVARINO (*Greece*), 1827: Muhammad Ali's navy was destroyed by an allied force of British, French and Russian warships. **269**

NEZIB (*Palestine*), 1839: The Ottoman sultan failed to remove Muhammad Ali from Syria, and suffered a bad defeat. The Ottoman Empire was only saved by the intervention of European powers. **270**

THE NILE (*Lower Egypt*), 1798: Nelson sank the French fleet in Abuqir Bay. **259**

OMDURMAN (*Sudan*), 1898: Kitchener avenged the deaths of Gordon and Hicks, and destroyed the Mahdists with far superior firepower. Sudan became part of the Anglo-Egyptian Condominium. **410**

PANION (*Palestine*), 200 BC: Ptolemy V was defeated by the Seleucids and had to concede Syria-Palestine. **149**

PELUSIUM (A: Tell el-Farama, *Lower Egypt*): The 'Gateway to Egypt' at the edge of the Delta was the site of numerous ancient battles against armies invading from the east. In the 7th century BC it was a key point of resistance against the Assyrians; in 605 BC the Babylonians were held at bay, but in 525 BC the Persian Cambyses won a crushing victory here; Ptolemy VI was captured by Antiochus IV in 170 BC ; the Persians took the town in 616, a feat repeated by Amr in 639 at the start of the Arab conquest; in 1117 Baldwin of Boulogne inflicted severe damage on the fort, but died shortly afterwards. **133, 138, 140, 163, 197, 199**

THE PYRAMIDS (*Lower Egypt*), 1798: Napoleon crushed the Mamluks at Imbaba near the pyramids, completing his conquest of Egypt. **258**

RAPHIA (*Palestine*), 217 BC : Ptolemy IV triumphed over the Seleucids, regaining most of his Syrian possessions. **161**

ROSETTA (*Lower Egypt*), 1807: Muhammad Ali made light work of a bungled invasion by the British. **264**

TELL EL-KEBIR (*Lower Egypt*), 1882: The British intervened in the Urabi uprising, defeating the rebels to prop up the reign of Khedive Tawfiq. Initially conceived as a temporary emergency measure, this was the beginning of the British occupation. **287**

Behbeit el-Hagar (E: Per-Hebyt, G: Iseum) In the central Delta, once the site of a great temple to Isis, begun by the last Egyptian pharaoh, Nectanebo II and finished by Ptolemy III.

Beni Hasan Middle Kingdom necropolis on the east bank of the Nile, about 14 miles (23km) south of Minya, consisting of 39 rock-cut tombs decorated with fine wall-paintings.

Berenice A Red Sea trading port founded by Ptolemy II and named after his wife. It was abandoned during the 5th century AD and rediscovered by Belzoni in 1818. **273**

Bubastis (A: Tell Basta, E: Per-Bastet) From at least the 4th Dynasty, the ceremonial centre for the cat-goddess Bastet, for whom a sizeable red granite temple was built. The eastern Delta city reached the pinnacle of its importance during the Third Intermediate Period when its Libyan-descended rulers established the 22nd Dynasty and resided here. **127, 129, 131**

Buhen Ancient outpost about 155 miles (250km) south of Aswan in Lower Nubia, originally used during the Old Kingdom as a base for mining expeditions, which became a frontier fortress during the Middle Kingdom. **66, 81, 83**

Busiris (E: Djedu) Ancient Delta town and cult centre for the god Osiris. **71, 210**

Buto (A: Tell el-Farain, E: Pe) Major Predynastic centre in the northwest Delta, and cult centre for the cobra-goddess Wadjet, which was associated with Lower Egypt throughout the pharaonic period. **21, 24**

Cairo (A: al-Qahira) The capital of Egypt is actually an agglomeration of older cities – but not Memphis, which lies across on the west bank of the Nile about 15 miles (25km) to the south. The first Arab capital was Fustat, founded in 643 by Amr at his encampment near the walls of the stronghold Babylon-in-Egypt, the origins of which probably date back to in the 6th century BC and which now forms part of 'Old Cairo'. The Abbasids built an exclusive royal city to the north of Fustat in 750 called al-Askar, and the Tulunids followed suit with al-Qatai in 868, but both were superseded by the expansion and growing prosperity of Fustat. In 969, the Fatimids founded a third royal city, al-Qahira (Cairo), which reversed the trend and came to be more powerful and influential than Fustat. Eventually Fustat was swallowed up by its larger neighbour, but when Saladin built a single wall encircling both cities in the late 12th century, there was still clear ground between them. The Mamluks graced the city with some of its finest medieval architecture, but its great expansion began in earnest during the reigns of Muhammad Ali and his successors, when Cairo was modernised and spread in all directions to incorporate the port of Bulaq and the suburbs to the north, including Heliopolis, as well as over the river via Gezira Island to Giza and the pyramids. Today Greater Cairo is home to more than 15 million people making it the most populated city in Africa; it's also the political and cultural capital of the Arab world.

ABDIN PALACE: Ismail moved his dynastic seat from the Citadel to this palace in 1872. After the revolution it was closed for twenty years until Sadat used its plush halls and salons for receiving heads of state. It now includes exhibition areas: a military museum, Mubarak's Hall displaying gifts he has received, and a collec-tion of luxury objects once owned by the royal family. **287, 315**

AL-HAKIM MOSQUE: Large congregational mosque from the early 11th century, which for much of its history was used for profane purposes, because its namesake heretically proclaimed himself divine. Most of its original features have disappeared under marble since its restoration by Ismaili Shiites in 1980. **220**

AMR MOSQUE: First mosque in Egypt, though it has been extensively remodelled and virtually none of its original fabric remains. **204**

AZHAR MOSQUE: One of the world's oldest universities, originally built by the Fatimids to propagate the Shiite faith. Saladin changed it into a font of Sunni knowledge, and it has remained the highest authority in Egypt on Islamic theology ever since. It has often been a hotbed of political agitation. **217, 260**

BAB ZUWAYLA: An imposing twin-towered gate built by the Fatimids at the southern entrance to the city. When Cairo spilled far beyond its walls during the Mamluk period, it became a focus of the city, seething with acrobats, snake charmers, conjurors and dancers; it also became the arena for public executions where thieves and lowly criminals were hanged, garrotted, impaled, beheaded or nailed to the doors. **246,249**

BULAQ: When the Fatimid port of al-Maks silted up, Bulaq took over and became the major hub in the spice and coffee trade during the Mamluk and Ottoman periods.

CAIRO TOWER: A 67ft (187m) tower resembling a lotus plant built on

Gezira Island by Nasser to give unrivalled views across Cairo. **334, 364**

CITADEL: The unmistakable hilltop fortress dominating the Cairo skyline, graced by the elegant minarets and imposing domes of the Muhammad Ali Mosque. Begun by Saladin in 1176, it remained the seat of national power for almost 700 years. **226, 230, 241, 249, 265**

CITIES OF THE DEAD: Two vast cemeteries extending from the Citadel. The older and larger southern cemetery (el-Khalifa) includes the tomb of the Muslim queen Shajar al-Durr, while the northern holds the mausoleums of the great Burji Mamluks, such as Qaytbay, Barquq and Barsbay, the finest funerary monuments in Cairo. **230, 243**

EGYPTIAN MUSEUM: The creation of a national collection began in 1835 when Muhammad Ali decided Cairo should have a museum like those in Europe that had already begun to acquire large numbers of Egyptian antiquities. The project foundered but was reinvigorated by Auguste Mariette in 1858, the new director of the Antiquities Service. The collection was moved in 1880 from its first home in Bulaq to a wing of Ismail's palace in Giza, and then in 1902 to its present location on Midan al-Tahrir in a grand neoclassical building designed by Frenchman Marcel Dourgnon. It makes a fine setting for the greatest collection of Egyptian antiquities in the world. **38, 52, 126, 274, 275**

EZBEKIYA GARDENS: In medieval times the Ezbekiya lake and its surrounding orchards became the favoured spot for the rich and powerful to build their residences. Over the years, they became the most luxurious private houses in Cairo, and were commandeered by Napoleon and his officers during the French Occupation. In the 1870s, Ismail converted the area into a pleasure garden, which eventually became infamous for debauchery; Allied soldiers filled the streets surrounding the gardens looking for entertainment in the brothels nearby. The gardens are now far less lively and have lost out to new roads. **252**

IBN TULUN MOSQUE: A vast congregational mosque, the city's largest, and the oldest one to retain its original features, featuring a spiral minaret based on the ziggurats of Babylon. **213**

ISLAMIC MUSEUM (Museum of Islamic Art): Khedive Tawfiq founded a museum to house priceless Islamic art salvaged from historic buildings and monuments. Initially the collection was held in the Sultan Hakim Mosque, but was moved to its present location in 1903. It is one of the finest collections of its type in the world.

KHAN EL-KHALILI: The most famous market area, a maze of narrow streets and bazaars, each of which is dedicated to a particular trade, such as spices, perfumes, cloth, carpets, copper, leather, alabaster, jewels, silver or gold. It was named after el-Khalil, the Master of the Horse for the Circassian Mamluk sultan Barquq, who built a caravanserai here in 1382. It was favoured by foreign merchants and soon became a hive of commerce.

MIDAN AL-TAHRIR (Liberation

Square): A grand square in the heart of Cairo created after the 1952 revolution by the demolition of the British Qasr al-Nil barracks. **274**

OLD CAIRO: Twin circular towers, the remains of the Roman fortress Babylon-in-Egypt, are still visible, but the area is best known as the nucleus of the Coptic community, and is home to some of its finest churches as well as the Coptic Museum. It used also to be a centre for Egypt's Jews (the Ben Ezra synagogue is here), now much diminished in number. **182, 200**

Old Cairo

RODA ISLAND: Opposite the oldest parts of Cairo at Babylon and Fustat, the island made a natural crossing place over the river, and was the site of an ancient Nilometer (though the current one dates to the 9th century). The Bahri Mamluks were barracked here, but nothing remains of their quarters, whereas the Manial Palace, built by Faruq's uncle Muhammad Ali in 1903, is all too prominent, an exuberant concoction of Middle Eastern, Moroccan and Rococo styles. 000 **227**

SHARIA TALAAT HARB: As Sulayman Pasha Street, this was one of the finest boulevards in Ismail's Parisianised Cairo. It lost much of its charm and grandeur after the revolution, but renamed after the founder of Bank Misr, it is now a teeming shopping street and the commercial heart of downtown Cairo. **282**

SULTAN HASAN MOSQUE: Impressive Mamluk mosque built of stone in a cruciform plan to house four *madrasas*, one for each of the four Sunni rites. **240**

Crocodilopolis (A: Medinet el-Fayum, E: Shedyet) Cult centre of the crocodile god Sobek located in the heart of the Fayum region. It flourished during the Middle Kingdom. Medinet el-Fayum is still the capital of the region, a busy city that has been described as 'Cairo in miniature'. **76**

Dahshur The southernmost part of the necropolis associated with Memphis and the location of the Sneferu's two pyramids, the first ever 'true' pyramids. Nearby are the three pyramid complexes of Middle Kingdom rulers

Amenemhat II, Senusret III and Amenemhat III. **49, 67**

Dakhla Oasis Desert oasis about 185 miles/300km west of Luxor, which was under pharaonic control even in the Old Kingdom. Its modern capital is Mut. **7**

Damietta (A: Dumyat) Port in the northeast Delta, close to where the eastern branch of the Nile debouches into the Mediterranean. It was captured twice by the crusaders, so the Mamluks razed it in 1250 and rebuilt it, better fortified, further from the river. It enjoyed a resurgence during the Ottoman period, but it lost out as a trading centre to Port Said after the opening of the Suez Canal. **218, 224, 226, 227**

Dendera (E: Iunet, G: Tentyris) Ancient capital of the 9th Upper Egyptian nome, near the entrance to the Wadi Hammamat, and cult centre to the goddess Hathor. The beautiful temple dedicated to her includes a hypostyle hall built by Tiberius and a colossal carving of Cleopatra and Caesarion. **6, 12, 19, 58, 131, 158, 166**

Edfu (E: Djeb, G: Apollonopolis Magna) Once the capital of the 2nd Upper Egyptian nome, and now famous for its beautifully preserved Ptolemaic temple to the falcon-god Horus. It was a cult centre throughout the pharaonic period, and a rock carving nearby bears the name of the 1st-Dynasty king Djet. **6, 18, 131, 158**

ElKab (E: Nekheb) An Upper Egyptian settlement since prehistoric times and one of the first urban centres in the Early Dynastic period, which reached its apogee during the New Kingdom. It was also a cult

centre to the god Thoth and the vulture goddess Nekhbet. **15, 45**

Esna (E: Iunyt, Ta-senet, G: Latopolis) About 30 miles (50km) south of Luxor, best known now for the temple of the ram god Khnum, the hypostyle hall of which, built in the Roman period, is visible in the midst of the modern town. **6, 14, 131, 158**

Farafra Oasis (E: Ta-iht) Most isolated and least populated oasis, about 185 miles (300km) west of Asyut. It was mentioned in Old Kingdom texts, but has no remains from the pharaonic period. **7**

Fayum Depression (E: Ta-she, She-resy, G: Moeris) An oasis of palm groves, cotton fields and orchards some 55 miles (90km) southwest of Cairo, irrigated by a network of waterways fed by the Bahr Yussef channel. Archaeological remains date back to prehistoric times, when the depression was dominated by the salt-water Lake Moeris (now Lake Qarun). The area was favoured by the pharaohs of the Middle Kingdom, when the capital was nearby at Itjtawy, and they inaugurated the huge land reclamation and irrigation projects that made the region so fertile. It also flourished during the Graeco-Roman period and hundreds of beautiful mummy portraits dating to this time have been recovered here. The region is now dominated by the capital Medinet el-Fayum (ancient Crocodilopolis), but other sites such as Hawara and Lahun used to be important. **9, 15, 17, 61, 68, 76, 156, 180**

Gebel Barkal Religious centre in

Kush near Napata, where there was an important temple to Amun, established by Thutmose III as the god's residence in Nubia. **131**

Giza The site of probably the most famous landmarks in the world, the Great Pyramids. The plateau, now encroached upon by the sprawl of modern Cairo, was primarily used as the necropolis of the 4th Dynasty kings. Khufu built the largest pyramid; Khafra, the next largest but on higher ground and with the uppermost part of its limestone casing still intact; and Menkaura, the smallest of the three. Each pyramid was part of a larger funerary complex: Khafra's has survived best and features a causeway running from his mortuary temple down to a well-preserved valley temple, lying under the gaze of the Great Sphinx. Subsidiary pyramids (so-called queens' pyramids) and mastaba tombs, presumably belonging to favoured courtiers, officials and relatives, lie nearby. **50, 100, 226**

Hawara Royal necropolis in the southeastern Fayum area and location of Amenemhat III's pyramid complex (12th Dynasty). The mortuary temple was known as 'the Labyrinth' for its astounding complexity and was a major tourist attraction during the Graeco-Roman period. Unfortunately, it has not survived. **67**

Heliopolis (A: Tell Hisn, E: Iunu, On) The centre of the solar cult and site of the first sun temple, dedicated to the god Ra. It became the pre-eminent religious centre during the Old Kingdom, and continued to be important throughout the pharaonic period. Save for an obelisk of Senusret I, most of the site is now buried beneath the northern suburbs of Cairo. **46–47, 57, 170, 182, 199**

Herakleopolis Magna (A: Ihnasya el-Medina, E: Henen-nesw) Capital of the 20th Upper Egyptian nome, and cult centre for the ram god Herishef, (identified by the Greeks with Heracles) located about 10 miles (15km) west of Beni Suef. It was also the administrative capital of the 9th and 10th Dynasties during the First Intermediate Period, and came to prominence again during the 23rd Dynasty in the Third Intermediate Period. **59, 61, 130**

Hermopolis Magna (A: el-Ashmunein. E: Khmum) The cult centre of the god Thoth and capital of the 15th Upper Egyptian nome. Its remains are near the modern town of Mallawi. **130**

Hierakonpolis (A: Kom el-Ahmar, E: Nekhen) An ancient capital of Upper Egypt (about 50 miles (80km) south of Luxor), which thrived during the Predynastic and Early Dynastic periods. It became the cult centre of the god Horus, the falcon god, whence its Greek name. **18, 20, 23–24, 38, 45, 58**

Ismailiya Named after Khedive Ismail and built by the Suez Canal Company as a depot in 1861 on the shores of Lake Timsah, about halfway down the Suez Canal. The town was the birthplace of Hasan al-Banna, the founder of the Muslim Brotherhood, and the site of a bloody Anglo-Egyptian conflict which triggered the 'Black Saturday' riots in Cairo. **323**

Kharga Oasis About 105 miles (175km) west of Luxor, the closest oasis to the Nile. Now It has been occupied in one form or another since prehistory, but most of the surviving archaeological remains date to the Ptolemaic and Christian periods. **7, 127, 141**

Kom Ombo (G: Ombos) Elegant double temple 25 miles (40km) north of Aswan, dedicated to Sobek and Haroeris (Horus). Most of it dates to the Ptolemaic and Roman periods, but other remains in the area are far older. **6, 12, 158**

Koptos (A: Qift, E: Kebet) Settlement (now existing as Qift) at the mouth of the of the Wadi Hammamat, which was mined for gold and stone, and was the main trade route to the Red Sea coast. **181**

Lahun Ancient site at the mouth of the Fayum Depression best known for the pyramid complex of 12th Dynasty king Senusret II, and the remains of Kahun, a planned settlement housing the officials in charge of the king's mortuary cult. **67–69**

Leontopolis (A: Tell el-Muqdam, E: Taremu) Ancient town in the central Delta which came to prominence as a regional power centre during the Third Intermediate Period. **130**

Lisht (E: It-towe) Royal necropolis about 30 miles (50km) south of Cairo associated with the 12th-Dynasty capital at Itjtawy. It features the pyramid complexes of Amenemhat I and Senusret I, and scores of mastaba tombs of nobles and courtiers nearby. **65, 67**

Luxor (*Thebes*, E: Waset, G: Thebai) The modern city of Luxor is surrounded by the ruins of ancient Thebes, the great capital of the New Kingdom pharaohs. On the east bank are the splendid temples of Luxor and Karnak; on the west bank are the tombs and funerary monuments. Luxor is today a major centre for tourism and archaeological research. **4, 19, 62, 85–87, 112, 125, 135, 137, 365**

DEIR EL-BAHRI: At the foot of an arc of dramatic cliffs, a site of monuments and tombs, including the temples of Mentuhotep II, Thutmose III, and Hatshepsut, the best preserved and most famous of the three. **63, 89, 92, 93–94, 124, 275**

DEIR EL-MEDINA: Village for the workmen who built the royal tombs in the Valley of the Kings. **90, 122–124**

KARNAK (E: Ipet-isut): Enormous religious complex comprising three main precincts each containing various temples and shrines. The main temple was devoted to Amun-Ra, the principal state deity during the New Kingdom. Karnak was the spiritual centre of the country, as well as a major political and economic force. **68, 86–89, 94, 101, 105, 119, 122, 129, 131, 134, 144, 158, 273**

MEDINET HABU (E: Djamet, G: Djeme): New Kingdom temple complex dominated by the mortuary temple of Rameses III, who is shown victorious in battle on its walls. The workers of Deir el-Medina made the most of its fortifications and took refuge during the turmoil of the 20th Dynasty. The compound became a town in the Ptolemaic period. **122, 127, 131**

RAMESSEUM: Mortuary temple of Rameses II, which also included a palace, granaries and storerooms. It is famous for its toppled colossal statues, the inspiration for Shelley's *Ozymandias*. **119, 122, 123**

TEMPLE OF LUXOR (E: Ipet-resyt): Founded by Amenhotep III and extended many times since, as the main stage for the ceremonies of the Opet Festival. **87, 101, 131, 144**

VALLEY OF THE KINGS (A: Biban el-Muluk): Location of 63 royal tombs cut from the rock in a dry valley on the west bank belonging to New Kingdom pharaohs. **90, 104, 114, 115, 119, 124, 273, 399**

VALLEY OF THE QUEENS (A: Biban el-Harim): Cemetery for the queens (though many were buried with their husbands in the Valley of the Kings), royal wives, princes and high officials of the New Kingdom pharaohs. **119**

Maadi Predynastic site on the outskirts of modern Cairo. It was an entrepôt for goods from Palestine, and also a processing centre for copper ore imported from Sinai. **21**

Meidum A pyramid complex about 55 miles (90km) south of Cairo, usually ascribed to Huni, last king of the 3rd Dynasty, or Sneferu, his successor. It now resembles a terraced brick tower, but what remains is the actually the core of one of the earliest true pyramids. Near the complex are 4th Dynasty mastaba tombs, some painted with enthralling scenes of everyday life such as the famous 'Meidum geese'. **49**

Memphis (A: Mit Rahina, E: Ineb-hedj, Men-nefer) The first great capital of Egypt, said to have been founded by the mythical king Menes, who supposedly united Upper and Lower Egypt. Its strategic location at the 'balance of the two lands' ensured it retained its importance for the duration of the pharaonic period even when the capital was elsewhere. As well as being the seat of government, it was also an important religious centre and the home of the creator god Ptah. Its long decline began in the Ptolemaic period and its buildings were extensively plundered for masonry and fertiliser after the Arab conquest. Of the few surviving remains, the most notable are the colossus of Rameses II and an alabaster sphinx. **37–38, 55, 82, 112, 124, 131, 134, 140, 141, 147, 152, 164**

Merimde Predynastic site on the western edge of the Delta, where a sedentary agricultural community lived, among the first in the Nile Valley. **17–18**

Mersa Matruh (G: Paraetonium) A coastal resort 130 miles (209km) west of Alexandria, which was once an important Ptolemaic port.

Napata The political centre in Nubia of the kingdom of Kush. **100, 130, 131, 134**

Naqada (E: Nubt, G: Ombos) Huge Predynastic site about 15 miles (25km) north of Luxor, where Flinders Petrie excavated more than 2000 graves. **20, 23–24**

Naukratis (A: Kom Gieif) An ancient Greek settlement in the western Delta not far from Sais. In the 6th century BC the residents (mainly from Corinth and Milesia) were granted exclusive rights on seaborne trade. Before the rise of Alexandria, this was a wealthy trading city, and the only place in pharaonic Egypt known to have struck coins. **136, 140, 148, 176, 179**

Omari, el- Predynastic site near modern Helwan. **18**

Philae Island south of Aswan on which a beautiful temple to Isis was built (mainly dating to the Graeco-Roman period). The cult survived here long into the Christian period until it was closed *c.*535 during the reign of Justinian. The latest known hieroglyphic inscription and demotic graffito were also made here in 394 and 452 respectively. In the 1970s the temple was moved to the nearby island of Agilkia to save it from being submerged under Lake Nasser. **4, 6, 144, 158, 180, 196**

Piramesse (A: Qantir) Ancient port in the eastern Delta founded by Sety I and developed by Rameses II into the administrative capital and royal residence of Egypt. After the collapse of the New Kingdom, much of its material was used for building in Tanis and Bubastis. **117-118, 125-126, 129**

Port Said (A: Bur Said) Harbour town at the north end of the Suez Canal, founded in 1859 when work began on the canal and named after Said, who ordered its construction. It suffered damage at the hands of the British and French during the invasion of 1956, but is now the second port after Alexandria and the country's fourth largest city. **287, 332, 336**

Rosetta (A: Rashid) At the mouth of the western branch of the Nile, Rosetta was a major port during the Ottoman period, but its power waned with the recovery of Alexandria (40 miles (64km) to the west) in the 19th century. It is most famous for the discovery of the Rosetta Stone in 1799. **4, 158, 263, 264**

Sais (A: Sa el-Hagar) Ancient capital of the 5th Lower Egyptian nome, and the seat of the kings of the 24th and 26th Dynasties. It was also the cult centre of the early creator goddess Neith. **130, 131, 134-140, 142**

Saqqara The main necropolis of the capital Memphis containing tombs and funerary monuments from almost every period of Egypt's ancient history, from the 1st Dynasty to the Christian era. It was arguably most important during the Old Kingdom, when the power of the royal court at Memphis was at its height. This period saw the construction of the pyramid complexes of Djoser (the world's first pyramid), Unas (the first inscription of the Pyramid Texts), Userkaf, Sekhemkhet and Teti among many others, as well as countless mastaba tombs for the elite. Tombs of high administrators and viziers were cut here in the New Kingdom, when the practice of burying the Apis bull in the subterranean galleries of the Serapeum also took root, continuing into Roman times. The interment of animals became increasing popular during the Late period (25th to 31st Dynasties), when thousands of mummified baboons, hawks and ibises were entombed in huge catacombs. The entire necropolis stretches along a limestone scarp for more than 4 miles (6km), not including associated sites such as Abusir at its northern end. **43, 47-49, 54, 57, 136, 274**

Sharm el-Sheik Resort town near the southern tip of the Sinai peninsula. It has strategic importance for its proximity to the Tiran Straits and was developed by the Israelis after they captured it in 1967. More recently it has been the location for peace summits hosted by President Mubarak. **369**

Sinai The gateway between the African and Asian continents, and since antiquity a strategic battlefront as well as a source of mineral wealth, (especially turquoise and copper). The Hyksos, Assyrians, Babylonians, Persians, Greeks, Arabs, crusaders and Ottomans all invaded Egypt via Sinai. In modern times too it has been the site of the bloodiest Arab-Israeli confrontations. **1, 8, 21, 58, 63, 66, 77, 115, 196, 298, 302, 320, 336-337, 343, 345-346, 349-350, 353, 354**

Siwa Oasis (A: Sekhet-imit, G: Ammonium) Isolated desert oasis just 30 miles (50km) from the Libyan border but 185 miles (300km) south of Mersa Matruh. In ancient times Siwa had two temples to Amun, built by Ahmose II (26th Dynasty) and Nectanebo II (30th Dynasty), and it was here in 332 BC that Alexander the Great consulted the famous oracle of Amun, who proclaimed him the son of god. Siwans are fiercely independent and after Muhammad Ali compelled them to recognise Egyptian sovereignty in 1820, revolts were frequent. **7, 141, 147**

Sohag Town in Middle Egypt with a large Christian community. It is close to the Red and White Monasteries, founded in the 5th century. **42, 90**

Suez Canal Opened in 1869, dramatically cutting travel times by sea between the Mediterranean and Indian Oceans. As a result it was of central importance to imperial communications to India by the British and became a sticking point in Anglo-Egyptian negotiations over their withdrawal. **1, 8, 248, 279-282, 284, 288, 302, 314, 335, 345-347, 350-351, 360**

Tanis (A: San el-Hagar, E: Djanet) A power base in the northeastern Delta for rulers of the 21st and 23rd Dynasties, and the capital of the 19th Lower Egyptian nome. Several royal tombs were discovered here in 1939 of 21st and 22nd Dynasty kings, including the stunning silver coffins of Psusennes I and Sheshonq II now held in the Egyptian Museum. **68, 125-130, 219**

Wadi Hammamat Part of the oldest route across the Eastern Desert to the Red Sea coast between Koptos (modern Qift) and Quseir. It was also an important source of breccia, siltstone and gold, and is best known now for its pharaonic graffiti adorning the ancient quarry sites. **20, 64**

Wadi Natrun In the Western Desert, off the desert road between Cairo and Alexandria. In ancient times it was the main source of natron (whence its name), salty deposits that were used for everything from mummification to glazing to toothpaste. In the 3rd and 4th centuries, hermits and persecuted Christians took refuge in the Wadi and it eventually became the focus of several monastic communities. Four monasteries survive, and the Wadi remains one of the most important centres of Coptic spiritualism; the current Pope Shenouda III was confined here by Sadat. **190, 356**

Glossary

Abbasids	Islamic dynasty descended from Abbas, the uncle of the Prophet Muhammad, which ruled Egypt from 750–868 and 905–935
ablaq	striped masonry, typical of the Mamluk era
Acheulean	first tradition of standardised stone tool making, linked to *Homo erectus* and early *Homo sapiens*
akh	in ancient belief, a component of the person in which the dead occupied the underworld in afterlife, following the successful union of the *ba* and *ka*
arquebusier	infantryman with an arquebus, a primitive long-barrelled gun
Asiatics	used by Egyptologists for the Egyptian *aamu*, a catch-all word for foreigners from the Near East
Ayyubids	Islamic dynasty of Kurdish origin founded by Saladin that ruled Egypt from 1171–1250
ba	in ancient belief, non-physical components of an individual roughly corresponding to our notion of 'character'; depicted as a bird with a human head
Bahri Mamluks	Mamluk rulers from 1260–1382, so named because of their riverside barracks (*bahr* meaning river); they were Kipchak Turks from the Crimea region
Bedouin	nomadic Arab tribes of the desert
bey	Ottoman title meaning 'chieftain' accorded to Mamluk emirs and other officers outside the conventional garrisoned army; by the 19th century it was a widely used courtesy title to show respect
Burji Mamluks	Mamluk rulers from 1382–1517, so named because their barracks were in the *burj*, the towers of the Citadel; they were from Circassia in the Caucasus
caliph	the 'successor' to the Prophet Muhammad and spiritual leader of Islam
canopic jars	funerary jars containing the viscera removed from the deceased's body during mummification; the jar stoppers

	were made in the image of the four sons of Horus, each of which was responsible for a different organ, lungs, stomach, liver and intestines
caravanserai	an inn for caravans and travelling merchants set around a courtyard
cartouche	an oval ring inscribed around the nomen and prenomen (two of the five royal names) of a pharaoh, from the French word for 'cartridge' which Napoleonic officers thought it resembled
cataract	a series of rocky rapids; there are six cataracts between Aswan and Khartoum, the area corresponding to Ancient Nubia
Chalcolithic	society in which both metal and stone artefacts are made
Circassians	Mamluk rulers from 1382–1517 who originated from Circassia in the Caucasus, southwest Russia; also known as the Burji Mamluks
cleruch	holder of an allotment in the Ptolemaic period
cloisonné	decorative enamelwork using metal filaments, often gold, to create intricate designs
Copt	originally derived from the Greek word for native Egyptian, *Aiguptious* and coming to mean an Egyptian Christian in later centuries
corvée	conscripted or enforced labour, often taken in place of taxes
cuneiform	ancient script from Mesopotamia composed of small wedge-shaped characters
Cyrenaica	territory surrounding the ancient town of Cyrene on the Libyan coast
demotic	from the Greek, 'popular [script]'. A cursive script that developed out of hieratic in the 26th Dynasty. It appears on the Rosetta stone alongside Greek and hieroglyphic script
Deshret	'red land', the sterile land of the deserts surrounding the fertile 'black land' *Kemet*
deshret	the red crown of Lower Egypt
dhimmi	a tolerated but non-Muslim 'person of the book', subordinate to Muslims but offered protection in return for payment of the *jizya* poll tax
diophysitism	belief that Christ has divine and human natures
diwan	register of Arab Muslims entitled to receive a share of tax revenues
emir	in the Mamluk era, a military commander; the most powerful emirs had the best chances of becoming sultan
epistrategos	one of four regional administrators overseeing

governorships of the nomes during the Greek and Roman periods

faience ceramic made of quartz sand decorated with opaque coloured glazes, usually bright blue or green

Fatimids Shia dynasty originating from Syria which traced its descent from Fatima, the daughter of the Prophet Muhammad; ruled Egypt 969–1171

fatwa a legal ruling issued by an Islamic legal scholar

fedayeen people willing to martyr themselves; often applied to guerrillas, particularly to Palestinians fighting against Israel

feddan unit of area equivalent to 1.038 acres

fellah (pl. fellahin) peasant farmer or agricultural labourer

firman royal decree or grant issued by the Ottoman sultan

glyptics the art of seal making

granulation cumulative application of minute grains of metal, often gold, to decorate jewellery

hajj the pilgrimage made by Muslims to Mecca

hedjet the white crown of Upper Egypt

henotheism belief in a single god without denying the existence of other gods

hieratic cursive, shorthand form of writing used mainly for administration and education of scribes from the Early Dynastic period

hieroglyphs from the Greek 'sacred carved [letters]', Ancient Egyptian script primarily used on reliefs decorating temples and monuments

hijra the 'flight' of the Prophet Muhammad from Mecca to Medina in 622, marking the beginning of the Islamic calendar

Ikhshidids Islamic dynasty of Turkish origin named after the Persian princely title al-Ikhshid accorded to its founder Muhammad Ibn Tughj by the caliph; ruled Egypt 935–969

infitah Anwar Sadat's 'open-door' policy, aimed at economic liberalisation to stimulate the private sector and encourage foreign investment

intifada uprising by Palestinians against Israel. The first intifada was from 1987–1993. The second 'al-Aqsa' intifada began in 2000

Islamism a morally conservative movement concerned with implementing orthodox Islamic values in all areas of life

ithyphallic referring to deities that are depicted with an erect penis, such as Min

janissary	Ottoman infantryman, originally recruited from tributary Christian children from the Balkans
jizya	poll tax paid by *dhimmis* under Islamic rule for protection; abolished in 1815
jund	the Arab army in Egypt
ka	in ancient belief, the life-force of an individual, which it was believed continued to live after the body died and had to be sustained through offerings of food and drink
Kemet	'black land', referring to the fertile soil of the Nile, and the name that the ancient Egyptians gave to their country
kharaj	land tax paid under Islamic law
khedive	title of the ruler of Egypt first given by the Ottoman sultan to Ismail in 1867 and held by his dynastic line until 1914 when Egypt seceded from the Ottoman Empire
khepresh	the blue crown worn from the Eighteenth Dynasty onwards
kleroi	lots of land typically allocated to soldiers in the Ptolemaic period
kurbash	rawhide whip used on corvée labourers
Kush	a kingdom of Upper Nubia centred around Kerma, near the Third Cataract
maat	in ancient Egyptian belief, the divine harmony and order of the universe which had to be upheld to prevent the spread of chaos; personified by the goddess Maat
machimoi	Greek term for Egyptian army regulars as opposed to foreign mercenaries
madrasa	a mosque where Islamic theology and law is taught
Mahdi	in Islamic tradition, the 'divinely guided one' sent by God near the end of time to fight evil and uphold justice
mamluks	from Arabic for 'one who is owned', slave-soldiers imported to Egypt from Turkish central Asia and Circassia. Mamluks originally served the sultans and caliphs, but came to power and ruled Egypt 1250–1517
mastaba **tomb**	style of rectangular tomb in the pharaonic period resembling a mud-brick bench, or in Arabic '*mastaba*', common outside modern Egyptian houses
mawali	non-Arab Muslims
Melkite	An Eastern Orthodox Christian of Egypt or Syria upholding the designation of the Council of Chalcedon in 451 accepted by the Byzantine emperor
microliths	small stone blade less than 5mm long, 4mm thick used as weapon points or in combination for cutting tools
Misr	Arabic name for Egypt
monophysite	one that believes in a single nature of Christ

monophysitism	belief in the single divine nature of Christ
mufti	a Muslim legal scholar and interpreter of the sharia
natron	a mineral of sodium carbonate and sodium bicarbonate used by ancient Egyptians for embalming, daily cleansing and the making of glass
nebty	the 'Two Ladies name', one of the royal names in the 'fivefold titulary' after the goddesses Nekhbet and Wadjet
nemes	a style of royal head dress worn only by Egyptian kings, as seen on the Great Sphinx
nesu-bit	the prenomen or throne name of the king; 'He of the sedge and bee', representing Upper and Lower Egypt respectively
nomarch	governor of a nome
nome	administrative province, of which there were traditionally 22 in Upper Egypt, 20 in Lower Egypt; known as *sepat* by Ancient Egyptians but called nomes from the Ptolemaic period onwards
nomen	the birth name of a king
Nubia	ancient region to the south of Egypt covering the area between the first and sixth Nile cataracts; Lower Nubia lay between the first and second cataracts, Upper Nubia from second to sixth
palace-façade	an architectural style of niched and buttressed walls thought to have been derived from Mesopotamia, which was used mainly in the Early Dynastic period at the necropolises of Abydos and Saqqara
Palaeolithic	period of the Stone Age characterised by tools of chipped stone
pasha	Ottoman military or civil title of high rank; in Egypt it was initially the title given to the governor or viceroy
patriarch	highest ranking bishop in a holy see; in the Coptic Orthodox Church the patriarch is the pope; the Coptic patriarchs trace an apostolic line of succession from St Mark as Roman Catholic popes do from St Peter
pharaoh	derived from *per-aa* ('great house'), the royal palace, a term which from the New Kingdom onwards was applied to the king himself; modern historians use the term to refer to any ancient Egyptian king
pharaonic	of or relating to the pharaohs; the pharaonic period begins with the First Dynasty c.3000 BC and finishes at the end of the Thirty-first with Alexander the Great's conquest in 332 BC
pharaonism	a movement popular between the two World Wars which stressed the continuity of Egyptian civilisation before the

Islamic conquest, as well as the country's long-standing links with the Mediterranean world rather than the East

prenomen the throne name of the king

pschent the double crown of Upper and Lower Egypt

Punt ancient region of East Africa to which expeditions were sent for exotic goods; thought once to have been modern Somalia, but now considered more likely to be around modern Eritrea

pylon monumental gateway of an Egyptian temple, flanked by two connected towers in tapering trapezoidal form

pyramid stone funerary monument with a square base and four triangular sides tapering to a point. The term derives from the Greek *pyramis* for a 'wheat cake' which probably resembled it in shape. The ancient Egyptian term was *mer*

repoussé hammering or pressing raised decoration on metal from its reverse side

saff deriving from the Arabic word for 'row', a type of tomb characterised by a court and a portico cut into rock, from where a small corridor led to a tomb chapel and burial shaft. Used in 11th Dynasty Theban tombs

sarcophagus from Greek 'flesh eating', the stone container for one or more coffins

satrap governor of a satrapy

satrapy province of the Persian Empire

sed **festival** rejuvenation ritual traditionally held during the thirtieth year of a king's reign

serekh inscribed rectangular frame representing the royal palace surmounted by the falcon Horus, within which a king's Horus name was written

shabti a figurine usually in the shape of a mummy used in burials from the Middle Kingdom onwards, to serve and work for the grave owner in the afterlife

sharia the law of Islam based on the Koran and the teachings of the Prophet Muhammad

Shia minority sect in Islam which maintains that Ali, the son-in-law of the Prophet Muhammad, was appointed by God to succeed Muhammad as leader of the Muslim community; they believe that the first three caliphs were illegitimate

sirdar commander-in-chief of the Egyptian army in Sudan

steatite soapstone, having a greyish green or brown colour

stela (pl. stelae) commemorative inscribed stone (or less commonly, wood) marker, often of a rectangular shape with a

	rounded top
strategos	governor of a nome during the Greek and Roman periods
sultan	an Islamic monarch
Sunni	largest Islamic denomination who believe that the first caliphs were the rightful successors to the Prophet Muhammad
triad	a grouping of three gods, a holy family of father, mother and child, which became a prominent feature of religion during the New Kingdom
Tulunids	Islamic dynasty of Turkish origin founded by Ahmad Ibn Tulun that ruled Egypt 868–905
Umayyads	the first Islamic dynasty of caliphs that ruled Egypt 661–750
uraeus	the sacred cobra, an emblem of royalty, often depicted on the headdress of pharaohs
vizier	the chief minister in the Ottoman Empire, also used to refer to those holding the title *tjaty* in Ancient Egypt, the highest administrative post below the king
wadi	dry desert gully or valley that can fill with water after rain
Wafd	originally the delegation (*wafd*), under the leadership of Saad Zaghlul, demanding Egyptian independence after the First World War, it was reorganised as a political party in 1923 and was the most popular party until its dissolution in 1953
wujuh	Arab ruling classes in Egypt during the Arab period
Zionism	a movement originating in the late nineteenth century, initially seeking to establish a Jewish national home in Palestine

Index